# LATIN AMERICA:
# UNDERDEVELOPMENT OR REVOLUTION

# LATIN AMERICA: UNDERDEVELOPMENT OR REVOLUTION

*Essays on the Development*
*of Underdevelopment and*
*the Immediate Enemy*
by Andre Gunder Frank

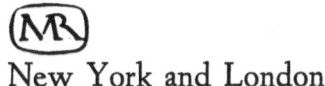

New York and London

ISBN 978-0-85345-165-5 (pbk.)

Monthly Review Press
146 W. 29th Street, Suite 6W
New York, NY 10001

*In dedication to*
*Marta and all other Latin American comrades*
*whose own dedication is to the Revolution*

# CONTENTS

### IV
### INTERNAL COLONIALIST AND CLASS POLITICS

### V
### WHO IS THE IMMEDIATE ENEMY?

# PREFACE

These essays were written to contribute to the Revolution in Latin America and the world, and they are collected here in the hope that they may help others to contribute more to the Revolution than the author has been able to. The essays arise out of the author's attempt, like that of millions of others, to assimilate the Latin American Revolution and the inspiration it finds in the Cuban Revolution, whose tenth glorious anniversary we celebrate while writing these lines. As such, the essays are the expression of the changing times and problems that gave them birth, filtered through the also-changing prism of the author's and others' concientization and understanding. In writing, the author directed himself almost entirely to the practice and theory of Latin American revolutionaries, or those striving to become revolutionaries at the time—and often the place—of writing.

The collection of these essays in a single volume in Spanish and Portuguese, and the composite picture that emerges from their topical arrangement, are intended to make this picture more available to the Latin American revolutionaries to whom this book is dedicated—or at least to those among them who read to formulate revolutionary theory to serve their revolutionary practice. To the extent to which the Revolution is worldwide, and all its parts form a single whole, perhaps the English, French, Italian, and German editions can be of some use to revolutionaries elsewhere as well. As for those who do not intend to dedicate themselves to the Revolution and the construction of a society for human beings, the author has no words for them.

Latin America suffers from a *colonial* underdevelopment, which makes its people economically, politically, and culturally dependent, not so much on themselves or on each other as on a foreign metropolitan power. As a result, in order to circulate at all, most of these essays, like the writings of most of the author's Latin American comrades, have often of necessity been published and republished (frequently without the author's knowledge) in innumerable journals, magazines, and newspapers of international (that is, metropolitan), national or often only local circulation, some still available but many long since defunct—if not by military coup then through the natural process of birth and death of political movements and their journals. Many of the essays were not published where or when intended, but were instead translated back and forth among English, Spanish, Portuguese, and French, and circulated, ·often clandestinely, in mimeographed form. (Chapter 8 has been published at least ten times in various languages, and Chapter 9 enjoys or suffers from three different translations into Spanish in as many Latin American countries—a symptom of the barriers to communication on the continent.) Though this collection cannot remove these barriers, perhaps it can overcome a few of them.

The essays are arranged topically and ordered so as to develop the central argument that emerges from the author's studies as a whole: Underdevelopment in Latin America (and elsewhere) developed as the result of the colonial structure of world capitalist development. This structure has penetrated all of Latin America, thereby forming and transforming the colonial and class structure of underdevelopment throughout the continent on the national and local levels. As a result, the development of underdevelopment will continue in Latin America until its people free themselves from this structure the only way possible, by violent revolutionary victory over their own bourgeoisie and over imperialism. The question is, Under the circumstances in Latin America and the world today, what is to be done? These essays were written to explore some of these circumstances and to inquire what is to be done—or at least what is not to be done.

The first essay introduces the thesis of the development of underdevelopment, and presents the context and general direction of the argument that is developed in the rest of the collection. This thesis, which was spelled out for two countries in the author's earlier book, *Capitalism and Underdevelopment in Latin America:*

*Historical Studies of Chile and Brazil*,[1] is here extended to Latin America as a whole. In reality, this essay is a series of related research hypotheses that serve as a guide for further study, leading to their confirmation, disconfirmation, or modification. Many of the other essays may suitably be read as bringing further study to bear on these hypotheses, though they do not constitute an organized attempt to test them for all Latin America. This task remains, and perhaps the writer and/or some readers of these lines will undertake it in the future. In the meantime, in collaboration with S. A. Shah, the author is extending this same approach to the problem and elimination of underdevelopment through the preparation of a two-volume anthology of analyses of the causes of underdevelopment—and of capitalist and socialist development policy—on a tricontinental scale in Asia, Africa, and Latin America taken as a whole. (This work, entitled *Underdevelopment*, should be ready for publication in about a year.)

Part II (Chapters 2–7) examines the North American emperor's social scientific clothes and exposes the scientific nakedness behind his ideological sham. This pseudo-science and ideology is increasingly being exported through innumerable channels to culturally colonial Latin America, where it is diffused not only to students but in various forms to the people as well. If the peoples of Latin America and other underdeveloped countries want to achieve development, they must avoid falling prey to this pseudo-science and its ideological diffusion. Most of the examination herein is devoted not to the most orthodox or reactionary North American thought and policy about development, but rather is expressly aimed at the most progressive and *liberal* expression of the same develop-ology. This examination shows that subjective intentions notwithstanding, the objective consequences of this liberal develop-apology are no less reactionary than its orthodox conservative counterpart. Instead, as is pointed out by my wife, Marta Fuentes —who claims no social scientific pretensions but only aspires to revolutionary dedication—those who espouse and accept these liberal positions are only stupid reactionaries rather than ordinary ones. But rejection of this reactionary *political* pseudo-science is of course not enough. Nor is weaving the emperor a new synthetic suit an adequate alternative for revolutionaries. Instead they must dethrone him and his colonial or neo-colonial collaborators through revolutionary practice—which also requires truly revolutionary theory. The remainder of the essays, most of which were written in contact with various forms of revolutionary practice in Latin America, represent attempts to contribute to the revolutionary theory required by the necessary revolutionary practice.

Part III examines some of the economic aspects and political manifestations of imperialism as they determine and generate underdevelopment in Latin America. This relationship cannot be understood outside of the historical context of the development of imperialism in the world and of the dependency of Latin America. Yet, since this context forms much of the content of my earlier book, this historical development is not treated in this section, though it is briefly reviewed in parts of Chapters 1, 2, and 25. The essays in Part III can do no more than call attention to some contemporary reflections, new developments, and consequences of North American overseas economic and political policy, themselves essentially the product and continuation of several centuries of world capitalist development. And while many intimately related political and military aspects of contemporary imperialist policy do not receive all the attention they deserve, the equally intimately related ideological and cultural attributes of imperialist policy and its consequences for Latin America are omitted altogether, although some of them may be inferred from the examination of the emperor's clothes in Part II.

Part IV, concerned with internal and class politics, brings the discussion onto the domestic scene in Latin America, where a debate rages among Latin American revolutionaries. Much of this debate about class policies and alliances is related to differing perceptions—or conceptions—of the structure of society in Latin America. Until recently the most widely sustained thesis, explicit or implicit, has been that Latin America has a "dual" society or economy in which the national bourgeoisie (or "middle-class entrepreneurship," to use the term that is often erroneously substituted) in the advanced capitalist sector can and must pursue a class policy of extending capitalism and development to the archaic "feudal" sector in the "other" Latin America. By contrast, the principal thesis sustained in Part IV, which is confirmed by the evidence presented in many of its chapters, is that Latin America has a dialectically integrated society and economy which today obliges the bourgeoisie—including its most nationalist sectors—to pursue policies which, however much development they may generate for the minority, condemn the majority of Latin Americans to ever-deeper underdevelopment, and the bourgeoisie itself to increasing dependence on and absorption into the metropolitan bourgeoisie of the neo-imperialist system. Chapters 15–17 present part of the argument and evidence with respect to the rural sector in general and the latifundium in particular (thereby also helping to confirm the last two hypotheses of Chapter 1); Chapter 18 extends the argument to the miscalled "marginal" population of the urban areas; and Chapters 19–22 go on to examine the objectively determined contemporary limitations of bourgeois capacity and policy, as demonstrated particularly by the experiences of Brazil and Mexico. The last two chapters of Part IV (23 and 24) explicitly extend the argument to revolutionary policy, which aims to combat the bourgeoisie and capitalism in Latin America itself.

The concluding chapter returns to the starting point of the collection and reviews much of the argument of the intervening essays while attempting to carry it a step further: in scientific terms, by explicating the relationship between the "external" colonial or neo-colonial structure and the "internal" class structure of Latin America; and in political terms, by arguing that because of this relationship, tactically the immediate enemy of all revolutionaries in Latin America is their own bourgeoisie, notwithstanding that strategically their principal enemy remains imperialism. At the same time, this concluding essay also complements Parts I and II by posing still further research problems, albeit at a greater level of specificity and hopefully at a level of higher theoretical sophistication.

Since these essays are not presented in chronological order, the year in which the essay was written (e.g., 1965 or 1965–66) or originally written and subsequently revised (e.g., 1964/65) is indicated in each case. The reader should take the time of writing into consideration, because almost all of the essays are products and expressions of a particular historical moment. This is so in

two senses. Since the writing of these essays was politically motivated (which rather than precluding—as liberals would argue—
enhances the probability of their scientific adequacy) each intentionally—and perhaps to some extent unintentionally as well
—expresses part of the moment of world history at which it was
written. (And since the victory of the Cuban Revolution, Latin
America and the world have witnessed important economic and
political changes and crises.) Secondly, each essay reflects a stage
of scientific and political development in the author's personal
history. The latter, like everybody's, was of course influenced in
part by the former; but since the author arrived in Latin America
in 1962 with no knowledge of the area and no political training,
his personal development also followed a course of its own. (The
formulation of some of the essays was also partially influenced
by the particular audience or publication to which they were directed, but because of the multiplicity of reprintings it would
be cumbersome to try to indicate these here.)

Thus, the earliest piece (Chapter 19 on Mexico) was written
in early 1962. It reveals a total failure to comprehend the significance—or even the existence—of imperialism, without which
any minimally adequate understanding of Latin American affairs
is, by the objective nature of things, necessarily precluded. The
same piece (and Chapter 17, on land reform, written later in
1962) also reveals the author's acceptance at that time of the
orthodox thesis that Latin America suffers from feudalism or
feudal survivals and that the Mexican Revolution was anti-feudal.
(That the latter is false is admirably demonstrated in a recent
book by James Cockcroft.[2]) Nonetheless, the essay on Mexico is
included because it displays incipient dissatisfaction with the
general "dual" society thesis, of which the feudalism thesis is only
a particular version. The author's later total rejection of the
thesis that there are two Latin Americas and his recognition—
intimated in this essay—that there is only one dialectically
integrated, but exploitative, capitalist society which is in turn an
integral part of the world capitalist—that is, imperialist—system
led the author in Chapter 23, written in December 1963, to reject
the feudalism thesis in a review article about the book *Whither
Latin America?*, in which the author's two aforementioned essays

constituted two of the twelve chapters. (The thesis is rejected and an alternative one proposed in much greater detail in the section "Capitalism and the Myth of Feudalism in Brazilian Agriculture," also written in 1963, in *Capitalism and Underdevelopment in Latin America*.) At the same time, to be frank, this essay (and section) also reflects the optimism of the year in which the Sino/Soviet debate had clarified much of the revisionism and reformism of orthodox Communist theory and policy and in which the guerrilla movements in Venezuela and elsewhere in Latin America were on the rise.

In the meantime, the author also initiated his study of imperialism, beginning, however, with its more visible and superficial mechanisms rather than with its more important internal structure and dynamic. The two major propositions of Chapter 10 on Latin American economic integration, also written in 1962, have unfortunately been amply confirmed by subsequent history. The major American monopolies have, as predicted, become the principal beneficiaries of the "wider" market; and "external" integration—as was so authoritatively confirmed by the 1967 American Presidents' Conference at Punta del Este, which totally reversed the priorities established at Punta del Este in 1961 by the Alliance for Progress—has become, as predicted in 1962, a vain attempt to replace internal changes, principally land reform, as solutions for Latin America's increasingly acute economic and political problems. (The failure of bourgeois governments' "land reform" policies was predicted in Chapter 17 long before such presidents as Frei and Belaunde were elected and had tried and failed to impose them in Chile, Peru, and elsewhere.) The essays on the mechanisms of imperialism (Chapters 8–12) were written while these new forms of operation by foreign monopoly capital were still being introduced in Latin America. It then seemed as important to expose them and their under-development-generating consequences as it now is to analyze the latter more deeply. (Chapter 8 was first published in the Sunday supplement of a major Brazilian newspaper and became the subject of debate in parliament and the press.)

Several of the essays of Part IV, especially Chapters 20, 21, and 22, were written to expose the congenital—or perhaps

better, structurally determined—weakness of the "national" bourgeoisie in Latin America in the face of the advance of neo-imperialism or neo-colonialism after the Korean War; all the more
so because of the need of the bourgeoisie (both its more "comprador" and its more "national" wing) to rely upon an internal
colonialism and an increase in the degree of exploitation—which
has spelled the abandonment of the populism of the 1930's and
1940's—at home. The political objective of all of these essays
was to intervene in the growing debate on the Left—especially
between those still captive of the theories and policies of the
orthodox Communist parties on the one hand, and the widely
dispersed elements of the "new Left" in Latin America on the
other. (The author has long since given up debating with
liberals, considering it a waste of time.) This debate was primarily about the kinds of political alliances that the Left should
or should not make with sectors of the bourgeoisie, and about
the political policies the forces of the Left itself should pursue.
Although, due to particular circumstances, some chapters were
more "nationalist" or "reformist" than revolutionary in tone
(for instance, Chapter 11, which was written for publication in
the Mexican government's foreign trade journal, and Chapters
16 and 18, which were written under contract to the United
Nations Economic Commission for Latin America), the author's
purpose has always been to lend support to the more revolutionary
elements and policies in Latin America.

But this political intention and the increasing scientific realization that orthodox political policy on the Left was built on (or
more accurately, was said to be supported by) what turned out
upon examination to be empirically shabby and theoretically
weak foundations, led the author to inquire into the historical
roots of contemporary underdevelopment and to seek formulations, empirically more accurate and theoretically more cogent,
that might contribute to the development of the revolutionary
theory necessary for revolutionary practice. This led to the
studies published in *Capitalism and Underdevelopment* and to
Chapters 1, 15, 20, and 25 of this book (which are really research projects for studies that are still in preparation), in which
the author has been trying to subject the imperialist system's

historical dimension, structural contradictions, and the contemporary developments emerging therefrom to scientific analysis. A by-product of this effort is the critical analysis of received bourgeois theory collected in Part II. It was during these years, beginning in 1964, that the author began to show, for instance, that Latin America (or part of its agriculture) cannot be feudal today because the Iberian conquerors and settlers, far from implanting feudal institutions, immediately incorporated the continent into the then expanding mercantile capitalist system. At the same time, increasingly in the company and mutual influence of such Latin American friends as Alonso Aguilar in Mexico, Aníbal Quijano of Peru, Edelberto Torres of Guatemala, Enzo Falleto and Luis Vitale of Chile, Fernando Henrique Cardoso, Ruy Mauro Marini, and Theotonio dos Santos of Brazil, and others (though we are not always in entire agreement about immediate political policy), the author has sought to distill a new theoretical formulation of underdevelopment from this historical and contemporary experience, in which the still growing structural dependence and exploitation of capitalism in Latin America plays the central role in the continued development of underdevelopment. (It is this same approach which serves the author and his Indian friend S. A. Shah as their guide in analyzing the various and yet common causes of underdevelopment on a tricontinental scale in the aforementioned forthcoming book on *Underdevelopment*.) And the principal objective of this scientific effort, of course, remains frankly political and humane: the liberation of man from exploitation by man, and the construction of a society worthy of man's potential.

To answer the question of how to do what has to be done, it is necessary to advance beyond this work. The last chapter in Part IV was written in 1968 (five years after Chapter 23, which was inspired in part by the guerrillas in Venezuela, and a half year after the death of Che Guevara), and raises issues about the analysis of class structure, the mobilization of political forces, and the theses of Debray, which remain largely unanswered—and unanswerable—by this author's works and unfortunately by all but very exceptional ones of other writers and political activists in Latin America. The concluding chapter in this collection, prepared for the Cultural Congress in Havana in January 1968, represents an attempt to translate some of these issues into researchable questions and to offer a tentative approach to answering them by suggesting how the colonial and neo-colonial structure of Latin American economic, political, and cultural dependence continuously generates the changing class structure and the deepening political contradictions that only socialist revolution can resolve.

It is an honor to acknowledge the aid and encouragement of many friends, and especially those at *Monthly Review* in New York, Buenos Aires, and Santiago, as well as several comrades and organizations, who must remain unnamed, who did what they could to publish or otherwise circulate many of these essays. It is a pleasure to acknowledge the timely financial support received from Thacher Robinson in 1962 and from the Louis M. Rabinowitz Foundation in 1965–66, when many of these essays were written or revised. It is impossible to identify and acknowledge the political, intellectual, and moral debt incurred and aid received in the conception and realization of this work, for that is due to the Cuban and Latin American Revolution and to the revolutionary comrades—some of them known to me, like my wife Marta, and most unknown to me and the future—to whom this work is dedicated.

—A. G. F.

*Santiago de Chile*
*January 2, 1969*

## NOTES

1. Published by Monthly Review Press in 1967.
2. James Cockcroft, *Intellectual Precursors of the Mexican Revolution, 1900–1913* (Austin: University of Texas Press, 1968).

I

# 1

# THE DEVELOPMENT
# OF UNDERDEVELOPMENT

We cannot hope to formulate adequate development theory and
policy for the majority of the world's population who suffer from
underdevelopment without first learning how their past economic
and social history gave rise to their present underdevelopment. Yet
most historians study only the developed metropolitan countries
and pay scant attention to the colonial and underdeveloped lands.
For this reason most of our theoretical categories and guides to
development policy have been distilled exclusively from the historical experience of the European and North American advanced
capitalist nations.

Since the historical experience of the colonial and underdeveloped countries has demonstrably been quite different, available
theory therefore fails to reflect the past of the underdeveloped
part of the world entirely, and reflects the past of the world as a
whole only in part. More important, our ignorance of the underdeveloped countries' history leads us to assume that their past and
indeed their present resembles earlier stages of the history of the
now developed countries. This ignorance and this assumption
lead us into serious misconceptions about contemporary underdevelopment and development. Further, most studies of development and underdevelopment fail to take account of the economic
and other relations between the metropolis and its economic
colonies throughout the history of the worldwide expansion and
development of the mercantilist and capitalist system. Consequently, most of our theory fails to explain the structure and

1965–66. This essay originally appeared in the September 1966 issue of
*Monthly Review*.

development of the capitalist system as a whole and to account for its simultaneous generation of underdevelopment in some of its parts and of economic development in others.

It is generally held that economic development occurs in a succession of capitalist stages and that today's underdeveloped countries are still in a stage, sometimes depicted as an original stage, of history through which the now developed countries passed long ago. Yet even a modest acquaintance with history shows that underdevelopment is not original or traditional and that neither the past nor the present of the underdeveloped countries resembles in any important respect the past of the now developed countries. The now developed countries were never *under*developed, though they may have been *un*developed. It is also widely believed that the contemporary underdevelopment of a country can be understood as the product or reflection solely of its own economic, political, social, and cultural characteristics or structure. Yet historical research demonstrates that contemporary underdevelopment is in large part the historical product of past and continuing economic and other relations between the satellite underdeveloped and the now developed metropolitan countries. Furthermore, these relations are an essential part of the structure and development of the capitalist system on a world scale as a whole. A related and also largely erroneous view is that the development of these underdeveloped countries, and within them of their most underdeveloped domestic areas, must and will be generated or stimulated by diffusing capital, institutions, values, etc., to them from the international and national capitalist metropoles. Historical perspective based on the underdeveloped countries' past experience suggests that on the contrary, economic development in the underdeveloped countries can now occur only independently of most of these relations of diffusion.

Evident inequalities of income and differences in culture have led many observers to see "dual" societies and economies in the underdeveloped countries. Each of the two parts is supposed to have a history of its own, a structure, and a contemporary dynamic largely independent of the other. Supposedly only one part of the economy and society has been importantly affected by intimate economic relations with the "outside" capitalist world; and that part, it is held, became modern, capitalist, and relatively developed precisely because of this contact. The other part is widely regarded as variously isolated, subsistence-based, feudal, or pre-capitalist, and therefore more underdeveloped.

I believe on the contrary that the entire "dual" society thesis is false and that the policy recommendations to which it leads will, if acted upon, serve only to intensify and perpetuate the very conditions of underdevelopment they are supposedly designed to remedy.

A mounting body of evidence suggests, and I am confident that future historical research will confirm, that the expansion of the capitalist system over the past centuries effectively and entirely penetrated even the apparently most isolated sectors of the underdeveloped world. Therefore the economic, political, social, and cultural institutions and relations we now observe there are the products of the historical development of the capitalist system no less than are the seemingly more modern or capitalist features of the national metropoles of these underdeveloped countries. Analogous to the relations between development and underdevelopment on the international level, the contemporary underdeveloped institutions of the so-called backward or feudal domestic areas of an underdeveloped country are no less the product of the single historical process of capitalist development than are the so-called capitalist institutions of the supposedly more progressive areas. I should like to sketch the kinds of evidence which support this thesis and at the same time indicate lines along which further study and research could fruitfully proceed.

The Secretary General of the Latin American Center for Research in the Social Sciences writes in that Center's journal: "The privileged position of the city has its origin in the colonial period. It was founded by the Conqueror to serve the same ends that it still serves today; to incorporate the indigenous population into the economy brought and developed by that Conqueror and his descendants. The regional city was an instrument of conquest and is still today an instrument of domination." [1] The Instituto Nacional Indigenista (National Indian Institute) of Mexico confirms this observation when it notes that "the mestizo population, in fact, always lives in a city, a center of an intercultural region, which acts as the metropolis of a zone of indigenous population and which maintains with the underdeveloped communities an intimate relation which links the center with the satellite communities." [2] The Institute goes on to point out that "between the mestizos who live in the nuclear city of the region and the Indians who live in the peasant hinterland there is in reality a closer economic and social interdependence than might at first glance appear" and that the provincial metropoles "by being centers of intercourse are also centers of exploitation." [3]

Thus these metropolis-satellite relations are not limited to the imperial or international level but penetrate and structure the very economic, political, and social life of the Latin American colonies and countries. Just as the colonial and national capital and its export sector become the satellite of the Iberian (and later of other) metropoles of the world economic system, this satellite immediately becomes a colonial and then a national metropolis with respect to the productive sectors and population of the interior. Furthermore, the provincial capitals, which thus are themselves satellites of the national metropolis—and through the latter of the world metropolis—are in turn provincial centers around which their own local satellites orbit. Thus, a whole chain of constellations of metropoles and satellites relates all parts of the whole system from its metropolitan center in Europe or the United States to the farthest outpost in the Latin American countryside.

When we examine this metropolis-satellite structure, we find that each of the satellites, including now underdeveloped Spain and Portugal, serves as an instrument to suck capital or economic surplus out of its own satellites and to channel part of this surplus to the world metropolis of which all are satellites. Moreover, each national and local metropolis serves to impose and maintain the monopolistic structure and exploitative relationship of this system (as the Instituto Nacional Indigenista of Mexico calls it) as long as it serves the interests of the metropoles which take advantage of this global, national, and local structure to promote their own development and the enrichment of their ruling classes.

These are the principal and still surviving structural characteristics which were implanted in Latin America by the Conquest. Beyond examining the establishment of this colonial structure in its historical context, the proposed approach calls for study of the development—and underdevelopment—of these metropoles and satellites of Latin America throughout the following and still continuing historical process. In this way we can understand why there were aṇd still are tendencies in the Latin American and world capitalist structure which seem to lead to the development of the metropolis and the underdevelopment of the satellite and why, particularly, the satellized national, regional, and local metropoles in Latin America find that their economic development is at best a limited or underdeveloped development.

That present underdevelopment of Latin America is the result of its centuries-long participation in the process of world capitalist development, I believe I have shown in my case studies of the economic and social histories of Chile and Brazil.[4] My study of Chilean history suggests that the Conquest not only incorporated this country fully into the expansion and development of the world mercantile and later industrial capitalist system but that it also introduced the monopolistic metropolis-satellite structure and development of capitalism into the Chilean domestic economy and society itself. This structure then penetrated and permeated all of Chile very quickly. Since that time and in the course of world and Chilean history during the epochs of colonialism, free trade, imperialism, and the present, Chile has become increasingly marked by the economic, social, and political structure of satellite underdevelopment. This development of underdevelopment continues today, both in Chile's still increasing satellization by the world metropolis and through the ever more acute polarization of Chile's domestic economy.

The history of Brazil is perhaps the clearest case of both national and regional development of underdevelopment. The expansion of the world economy since the beginning of the sixteenth century successively converted the Northeast, the Minas

Gerais interior, the North, and the Center-South (Rio de Janeiro, São Paulo, and Paraná) into export economies and incorporated them into the structure and development of the world capitalist system. Each of these regions experienced what may have appeared as economic development during the period of its golden age. But it was a satellite development which was neither self-generating nor self-perpetuating. As the market or the productivity of the first three regions declined, foreign and domestic economic interest in them waned and they were left to develop the underdevelopment they live today. In the fourth region, the coffee economy experienced a similar though not yet quite as serious fate (though the development of a synthetic coffee substitute promises to deal it a mortal blow in the not too distant future). All of this historical evidence contradicts the generally accepted theses that Latin America suffers from a dual society or from the survival of feudal institutions and that these are important obstacles to its economic development.

During the First World War, however, and even more during the Great Depression and the Second World War, São Paulo began to build up an industrial establishment which is the largest in Latin America today. The question arises whether this industrial development did or can break Brazil out of the cycle of satellite development and underdevelopment which has characterized its other regions and national history within the capitalist system so far. I believe that the answer is no. Domestically the evidence so far is fairly clear. The development of industry in São Paulo has not brought greater riches to the other regions of Brazil. Instead, it has converted them into internal colonial satellites, de-capitalized them further, and consolidated or even deepened their underdevelopment. There is little evidence to suggest that this process is likely to be reversed in the foreseeable future except insofar as the provincial poor migrate and become the poor of the metropolitan cities. Externally, the evidence is that although the initial development of São Paulo's industry was relatively autonomous it is being increasingly satellized by the world capitalist metropolis and its future development possibilities are increasingly restricted.[5] This development, my studies lead me to believe, also appears destined to limited or underdeveloped development as long as it takes place in the present economic, political, and social framework.

We must conclude, in short, that underdevelopment is not due to the survival of archaic institutions and the existence of capital shortage in regions that have remained isolated from the stream of world history. On the contrary, underdevelopment was and still is generated by the very same historical process which also generated economic development: the development of capitalism itself. This view, I am glad to say, is gaining adherents among students of Latin America and is proving its worth in shedding new light on the problems of the area and in affording a better perspective for the formulation of theory and policy.[6]

The same historical and structural approach can also lead to better development theory and policy by generating a series of hypotheses about development and underdevelopment such as those I am testing in my current research. The hypotheses are derived from the empirical observation and theoretical assumption that within this world-embracing metropolis-satellite structure the metropoles tend to develop and the satellites to underdevelop. The first hypothesis has already been mentioned above: that in contrast to the development of the world metropolis which is no one's satellite, the development of the national and other subordinate metropoles is limited by their satellite status. It is perhaps more difficult to test this hypothesis than the following ones because part of its confirmation depends on the test of the other hypotheses. Nonetheless, this hypothesis appears to be generally confirmed by the non-autonomous and unsatisfactory economic and especially industrial development of Latin America's national metropoles, as documented in the studies already cited. The most important and at the same time most confirmatory examples are the metropolitan regions of Buenos Aires and São Paulo whose growth only began in the nineteenth century, was therefore largely untrammeled by any colonial heritage, but was and remains a satellite development largely dependent on the outside metropolis, first of Britain and then of the United States.

A second hypothesis is that the satellites experience their greatest economic development and especially their most classically capitalist industrial development if and when their ties to their metropolis are weakest. This hypothesis is almost diametrically opposed to the generally accepted thesis that development in the underdeveloped countries follows from the greatest degree of contact with and diffusion from the metropolitan developed countries. This hypothesis seems to be confirmed by two kinds of relative isolation that Latin America has experienced in the course of its history. One is the temporary isolation caused by the crises of war or depression in the world metropolis. Apart from minor ones, five periods of such major crises stand out and are seen to confirm the hypothesis. These are: the European (and especially Spanish) depression of the seventeenth century, the Napoleonic Wars, the First World War, the Depression of the 1930's, and the Second World War. It is clearly established and generally recognized that the most important recent industrial development—especially of Argentina, Brazil, and Mexico, but also of other countries such as Chile—has taken place precisely during the periods of the two world wars and the intervening Depression. Thanks to the consequent loosening of trade and investment ties during these periods, the satellites initiated marked autonomous industrialization and growth. Historical research demonstrates that the same thing happened in Latin America during Europe's seventeenth-century depression. Manufacturing grew in the Latin American countries, and several, such as Chile, became exporters of manufactured goods. The Napoleonic Wars gave rise to independence movements in Latin America, and these should perhaps also be interpreted as in part confirming the development hypothesis.

The other kind of isolation which tends to confirm the second hypothesis is the geographic and economic isolation of regions which at one time were relatively weakly tied to and poorly integrated into the mercantilist and capitalist system. My preliminary research suggests that in Latin America it was these regions which initiated and experienced the most promising self-generating economic development of the classical industrial capitalist type. The most important regional cases probably are Tucumán and Asunción, as well as other cities, such as Mendoza and Rosario, in the interior of Argentina and Paraguay during the end of the eighteenth and the beginning of the nineteenth centuries. Seventeenth- and eighteenth-century São Paulo, long before coffee was grown there, is another example. Perhaps Antioquia in Colombia and Puebla and Querétaro in Mexico are other examples. In its own way, Chile was also an example since before the sea route around the Horn was opened this country was relatively isolated at the end of a long voyage from Europe via Panama. All of these regions became manufacturing centers and even exporters, usually of textiles, during the periods preceding their effective incorporation as satellites into the colonial, national, and world capitalist system.

Internationally, of course, the classic case of industrialization through non-participation as a satellite in the capitalist world system is obviously that of Japan after the Meiji Restoration. Why, one may ask, was resource-poor but unsatellized Japan able to industrialize so quickly at the end of the century while resource-rich Latin American countries and Russia were not able to do so and the latter was easily beaten by Japan in the War of 1904 after the same forty years of development efforts? The second hypothesis suggests that the fundamental reason is that Japan was not satellized either during the Tokugawa or the Meiji period and therefore did not have its development structurally limited as did the countries which were so satellized.

A corollary of the second hypothesis is that when the metropolis recovers from its crisis and re-establishes the trade and investment ties which fully re-incorporate the satellites into the system, or when the metropolis expands to incorporate previously isolated regions into the worldwide system, the previous development and industrialization of these regions is choked off or channeled into directions which are not self-perpetuating and promising. This happened after each of the five crises cited above. The renewed expansion of trade and the spread of economic liberalism in the eighteenth and nineteenth centuries choked off and reversed the manufacturing development which Latin America had experienced during the seventeenth century, and in some places at the beginning of the nineteenth. After the First World War, the new national industry of Brazil suffered serious consequences from American economic invasion. The increase in the growth rate of

Gross National Product and particularly of industrialization throughout Latin America was again reversed and industry became increasingly satellized after the Second World War and especially after the post-Korean War recovery and expansion of the metropolis. Far from having become more developed since then, industrial sectors of Brazil and most conspicuously of Argentina have become structurally more and more underdeveloped and less and less able to generate continued industrialization and/or sustain development of the economy. This process, from which India also suffers, is reflected in a whole gamut of balance-of-payments, inflationary, and other economic and political difficulties, and promises to yield to no solution short of far-reaching structural change.

Our hypothesis suggests that fundamentally the same process occurred even more dramatically with the incorporation into the system of previously unsatellized regions. The expansion of Buenos Aires as a satellite of Great Britain and the introduction of free trade in the interest of the ruling groups of both metropoles destroyed the manufacturing and much of the remainder of the economic base of the previously relatively prosperous interior almost entirely. Manufacturing was destroyed by foreign competition, lands were taken and concentrated into latifundia by the rapaciously growing export economy, intra-regional distribution of income became much more unequal, and the previously developing regions became simple satellites of Buenos Aires and through it of London. The provincial centers did not yield to satellization without a struggle. This metropolis-satellite conflict was much of the cause of the long political and armed struggle between the Unitarists in Buenos Aires and the Federalists in the provinces, and it may be said to have been the sole important cause of the War of the Triple Alliance in which Buenos Aires, Montevideo, and Rio de Janeiro, encouraged and helped by London, destroyed not only the autonomously developing economy of Paraguay but killed off nearly all of its population unwilling to give in. Though this is no doubt the most spectacular example which tends to confirm the hypothesis, I believe that historical research on the satellization of previously relatively independent yeoman-farming and incipient manufacturing regions such as the Caribbean islands will confirm it further.[7] These regions did not have a chance against the forces of expanding and developing capitalism, and their own development had to be sacrificed to that of others. The economy and industry of Argentina, Brazil, and other countries which have experienced the effects of metropolitan recovery since the Second World War are today suffering much the same fate, if fortunately still in lesser degree.

A third major hypothesis derived from the metropolis-satellite structure is that the regions which are the most underdeveloped and feudal-seeming today are the ones which had the closest ties to the metropolis in the past. They are the regions which were the greatest exporters of primary products to and the biggest sources of capital for the world metropolis and were abandoned by the metropolis when for one reason or another business fell off. This hypothesis also contradicts the generally held thesis that the source of a region's underdevelopment is its isolation and its pre-capitalist institutions.

This hypothesis seems to be amply confirmed by the former super-satellite development and present ultra-underdevelopment of the once sugar-exporting West Indies, Northeastern Brazil, the ex-mining districts of Minas Gerais in Brazil, highland Peru, and Bolivia, and the central Mexican states of Guanajuato, Zacatecas, and others whose names were made world famous centuries ago by their silver. There surely are no major regions in Latin America which are today more cursed by underdevelopment and poverty; yet all of these regions, like Bengal in India, once provided the life blood of mercantile and industrial capitalist development— in the metropolis. These regions' participation in the development of the world capitalist system gave them, already in their golden age, the typical structure of underdevelopment of a capitalist export economy. When the market for their sugar or the wealth of their mines disappeared and the metropolis abandoned them to their own devices, the already existing economic, political, and social structure of these regions prohibited autonomous generation of economic development and left them no alternative but to turn in upon themselves and to degenerate into the ultra-underdevelopment we find there today.

These considerations suggest two further and related hypotheses. One is that the latifundium, irrespective of whether it appears today as a plantation or a hacienda, was typically born as a commercial enterprise which created for itself the institutions which permitted it to respond to increased demand in the world or national market by expanding the amount of its land, capital, and labor and to increase the supply of its products. The fifth hypothesis is that the latifundia which appear isolated, subsistence-based, and semi-feudal today saw the demand for their products or their productive capacity decline and that they are to be found principally in the above-named former agricultural and mining export regions whose economic activity declined in general. These two hypotheses run counter to the notions of most people, and even to the opinions of some historians and other students of the subject, according to whom the historical roots and socioeconomic causes of Latin American latifundia and agrarian institutions are to be found in the transfer of feudal institutions from Europe and/or in economic depression.

The evidence to test these hypotheses is not open to easy general inspection and requires detailed analyses of many cases. Nonetheless, some important confirming evidence is available. The growth of the latifundium in nineteenth-century Argentina and Cuba is a clear case in support of the fourth hypothesis and can in no way be attributed to the transfer of feudal institutions during colonial times. The same is evidently the case of the post-revolutionary and contemporary resurgence of latifundia, particularly in the north of Mexico, which produce for the American market, and of similar ones on the coast of Peru and the new coffee regions of Brazil. The conversion of previously yeoman-farming Caribbean islands, such as Barbados, into sugar-exporting economies at various times between the seventeenth and twentieth centuries and the resulting rise of the latifundia in these islands would seem to confirm the fourth hypothesis as well. In Chile, the rise of the latifundium and the creation of the institutions of servitude which later came to be called feudal occurred in the eighteenth century and have been conclusively shown to be the result of and response to the opening of a market for Chilean wheat in Lima.[8] Even the growth and consolidation of the latifundium in seventeenth-century Mexico—which most expert students have attributed to a depression of the economy caused by the decline of mining and a shortage of Indian labor and to a consequent turning in upon itself and ruralization of the economy —occurred at a time when urban population and demand were growing, food shortages were acute, food prices skyrocketing, and the profitability of other economic activities such as mining and foreign trade declining.[9] All of these and other factors rendered hacienda agriculture more profitable. Thus, even this case would seem to confirm the hypothesis that the growth of the latifundium and its feudal-seeming conditions of servitude in Latin America has always been and is still the commercial response to increased demand and that it does not represent the transfer or survival of alien institutions that have remained beyond the reach of capitalist development. The emergence of latifundia, which today really are more or less (though not entirely) isolated, might then be attributed to the causes advanced in the fifth hypothesis —i.e., the decline of previously profitable agricultural enterprises whose capital was, and whose currently produced economic surplus still is, transferred elsewhere by owners and merchants who frequently are the same persons or families. Testing this hypothesis requires still more detailed analysis, some of which I have undertaken in a study on Brazilian agriculture.[10]

All of these hypotheses and studies suggest that the global extension and unity of the capitalist system, its monopoly structure and uneven development throughout its history, and the resulting persistence of commercial rather than industrial capitalism in the underdeveloped world (including its most industrially advanced countries) deserve much more attention in the study of economic development and cultural change than they have hitherto received. Though science and truth know no national boundaries, it is probably new generations of scientists from the underdeveloped countries themselves who most need to, and best can, devote the necessary attention to these problems and clarify the process of underdevelopment and development. It is their people who in the last analysis face the task of changing this no longer acceptable process and eliminating this miserable reality.

They will not be able to accomplish these goals by importing sterile stereotypes from the metropolis which do not correspond to their satellite economic reality and do not respond to their liberating political needs. To change their reality they must understand it. For this reason, I hope that better confirmation of these hypotheses and further pursuit of the proposed historical, holistic, and structural approach may help the peoples of the underdeveloped countries to understand the causes and eliminate the reality of their development of underdevelopment and their underdevelopment of development.

## NOTES

1. *América Latina*, Año 6, No. 4 (October–December 1963), p. 8.
2. Instituto Nacional Indigenista, *Los centros coordinadores indigenistas* (Mexico, 1962), p. 34.
3. *Ibid.*, pp. 33–34, 88.
4. "Capitalist Development of Underdevelopment in Chile" and "Capitalist Development of Underdevelopment in Brazil" in *Capitalism and Underdevelopment in Latin America* (New York & London: Monthly Review Press, 1967 and 1969).
5. Also see, "The Growth and Decline of Import Substitution," *Economic Bulletin for Latin America*, IX, No. 1 (March 1964); and Celso Furtado, *Dialectica do Desenvolvimiento* (Rio de Janeiro: Fundo de Cultura, 1964).
6. Others who use a similar approach, though their ideologies do not permit them to derive the logically following conclusions, are Aníbal Pinto, *Chile: Un caso de desarrollo frustrado* (Santiago: Editorial Universitaria, 1957); Celso Furtado, *A formaçao económica do Brasil* (Rio de Janeiro: Fundo de Cultura, 1959) which was recently translated into English and published as *The Economic Growth of Brazil* by the University of California Press; and Caio Prado Junior, *Historia Económica do Brasil* (7th ed., São Paulo: Editora Brasiliense, 1962).
7. See for instance Ramiro Guerra y Sánchez, *Azúcar y Problación en las Antillas*, 2nd ed. (Havana, 1942), also published as *Sugar and Society in the Caribbean* (New Haven: Yale University Press, 1964).
8. Mario Góngora, *Origen de los "inquilinos" de Chile central* (Santiago: Editorial Universitaria, 1960); Jean Borde and Mario

Góngora, *Evolución de la propiedad rural en el Valle del Puango* (Santiago: Instituto de Sociología de la Universidad de Chile); Sergio Sepúlveda, *El trigo chileno en el mercado mundial* (Santiago: Editorial Universitaria, 1959).

9. Woodrow Borah makes depression the centerpiece of his explanation in "New Spain's Century of Depression," *Ibero-Americana*, No. 35 (Berkeley, 1951). François Chevalier speaks of turning in upon itself in the most authoritative study of the subject, "La formación de los grandes latifundios en México," *Problemas Agrícolas e Industriales de México*, VIII, No. 1, 1956 (translated from the original French and recently published by the University of California Press). The data which provide the basis for my contrary interpretation are supplied by these authors themselves. This problem is discussed in my "¿Con qué modo de producción convierte la gallina maíz en huevos de oro?" which is reprinted as Chapter 15 of this volume; and it is further analyzed in a study of Mexican agriculture under preparation by the author.

10. "Capitalism and the Myth of Feudalism in Brazilian Agriculture," in *Capitalism and Underdevelopment in Latin America*.

# II

## THE EMPEROR'S CLOTHES

# 2

# SOCIOLOGY OF DEVELOPMENT AND UNDERDEVELOPMENT OF SOCIOLOGY

## Introduction

This essay examines the sociology of development currently being produced in the developed countries, especially the United States, for export to and use in the underdeveloped countries. On critical examination, this new sociology of development is found to be empirically invalid when confronted with reality, theoretically inadequate in terms of its own classical social scientific standards, and policy-wise ineffective for pursuing its supposed intentions of promoting the development of the underdeveloped countries. Furthermore, the inadequacy grows along with the development of the society which produces it. Like the underdeveloped society to which it is applied, this sociology is becoming increasingly underdeveloped.

To permit a careful and detailed evaluation of this sociology of development, I shall examine the theoretical modes or trends

1963–65. I am indebted, both for substantive and editorial help in the preparation of this study, to Nancy Howell Lee, Philip Wagner, Rodolfo Stavenhagen, Alonso Aguilar, Said Shah, and especially to Marta Fuentes Frank, David Aberle, and Barton Parks and other editors of *Catalyst*. I take full responsibility, however, for the critique and critical tone of this essay, especially as concerns the theses associated with the Research Center in Economic Development and Cultural Change and its journal, hereinafter referred to as *EDCC*, of which I am a former staff member and contributor. I have, perhaps mistakenly, not followed the good advice of some of the above-named to try to accompany my critique with a constructive alternative. But I have attempted to advance such an alternative in Chapter 1 of this volume and in *Capitalism and Underdevelopment in Latin America*.

This essay originally appeared in the Summer 1967 issue of *Catalyst*.

represented by particular writings of selected social scientists. Nonetheless, my critique extends to the whole of this sociology of development. To avoid arbitrary selection, it is convenient to permit representatives of this sociology of development themselves to select the major modes and most of the authors to be examined here. Accordingly, they are given the first word.

Manning Nash, until recently editor of *EDCC*, has said,[1]

There are, in my view, only three modes of attacking the problem of social change and economic development.

The first mode is the index method: the general features of a developed economy are abstracted as an ideal type and then contrasted with the equally ideal typical features of a poor economy and society. In this mode, development is viewed as the transformation of one type into the other. Developed examples of this mode are to be found in Hoselitz's *Sociological Factors in Economic Development*,[2] or Parsons' *Structure and Process in Modern Societies*,[3] or in some of the work of the sociologist Marion J. Levy, Jr.[4] . . .

The second mode is the acculturation view of the process of development. The West (taken here as the Atlantic community of developed nations and their overseas outliers) diffuses knowledge, skills, organization, values, technology and capital to a poor nation, until over time, its society, culture and personnel become variants of that which made the Atlantic community economically successful. Examples of this line of reasoning can be found in Moore and Feldman, *Labor Commitment and Social Change in Developing Areas*[5] [which also includes essays by Nash and Hoselitz], and in Lerner's *Passing of Traditional Society*,[6] or in the many accounts of how the Soviet Union and Japan "did it". . . .

The third mode . . . is the analysis of the process as it is now going on in the so-called underdeveloped nations. This approach leads to a smaller scale hypothesis, to a prospective rather than a retrospective view of social change, to a full accounting of the political, social, and cultural context of development. . . .

Nash's discussion of these currents in contemporary American work on economic development and cultural change is found in his introduction to a collection of essays by, among others, Everett Hagen (who first introduced his thesis in the pages of *EDCC*),[7] David McClelland (who reviewed Hagen's book in the pages of *EDCC*),[8] and John H. Kunkel (who recently discussed the third approach in *EDCC*).[9] Nash describes these authors' essays as representative of the third approach and commends them for their "dialectic of social knowledge, of confrontation of bold assertion against fact in even bolder more elegant assertion." [10] Robert Chin, co-editor of the collection, says that these writers "are performing a pioneering service." [11]

Nash's classification, summary, and evaluation of the "only three modes of attacking the problem of social change and economic development" can serve as a useful point of departure for our own examination and evaluation of these approaches. Nash is quite mistaken in claiming that these modes exhaust the possibilities of attacking the problems of social change and economic development; he is substantially correct, however, in observing that they virtually exhaust the approaches of American social scientists to these problems of vital contemporary concern.[12]

I propose, therefore, to examine and evaluate the empirical validity, theoretical adequacy, and policy effectiveness of these three approaches to the problems of development. In terms of their relative importance, we should begin with the criterion of policy effectiveness, and then consider theoretical adequacy and empirical validity, in that order. For if the recommended policy is ineffective, it renders suspect the theory from which it is derived; if the theory used is inadequate, it matters relatively little whether the claims made about particular aspects of reality are in fact empirically accurate. Contrary to the logic of the case, however, expository convenience leads me to begin with an examination of the empirical validity of each approach, for this permits us to familiarize ourselves with the approach under review. We will then proceed to the questions of theoretical adequacy and policy effectiveness in turn.

## The Ideal Typical Index Approach

The index method is an attempt to attack the problem of economic development and cultural change through the comparative statics of polar ideal types. Referring to the approach of economists generally, and to those of the World Bank in particular, Charles Kindleberger long ago labeled this mode the gap approach: you subtract the ideal typical features or indices of under-development from those of development, and the remainder is your development program.[13] We may distinguish two major variants of this ideal typical gap approach: the pattern variable approach exemplified by Hoselitz, and the historical stage approach now mostly associated with Rostow. The second variant differs from the first in that it draws on the historical experience of the developed countries to interpose stages into the gap between development and underdevelopment. A further variant of the latter, the historical variations approach of Gerschenkron, which is not examined here, draws on this same historical experience to introduce the possibility of variation into the development stages of the underdeveloped countries. Common to all three variants is the assumption that underdevelopment is an original state which may be characterized by indices of traditionalism, and that, therefore, development consists of abandoning these characteristics and adopting those of the developed countries.

### PATTERN VARIABLES

This mode is derived not only from Max Weber's conception of the ideal type in general but also from some of Weber's particular ideal types, which were later elaborated and further systematized by Talcott Parsons. Hoselitz takes the pattern variables of Parsons' *Social System*[14] and applies them to the study of economic development and cultural change.

The pattern variables, according to the *Dictionary of Sociology,* are

> types of choices open to purposive human beings; they are dichot-omies . . . each representing polar extremes. *Universalism* and *particularism* are the names of one. In other words, any individual in a situation requiring choice in his relationships with others must ask himself if he is going to act in terms of a universally accepted precept or one particular to the situation in which he finds himself. Is he going to act according to rule or in terms of particular qualities of the person towards whom he is orienting his action. Another set

is termed *achievement* and *ascription* (sometimes referred to as *performance* and *quality*) and here a person in deciding how to act focuses his attention on either the achieved aspects of the other person, e.g., his professional qualifications, or else his ascribed qualities, e.g., sex, age, social class. . . . Yet another set is known as *specificity* and *diffuseness*, and here the choice takes into account limited and specific factors, e.g., the contrast between a contract entered into, and wider diffuse obligations such as family loyalty. . . . The point of this scheme of pattern variables is to enable the sociologist to identify the typical choices made, especially of an institutionalized kind. . . . Pattern variable analysis may be used to identify similarities and differences between cultures, or it may be restricted in use to refer to aspects of society, to sub-systems of an institutionalized kind, such as political systems . . .[15]

According to Parsons any social system and any social action can be exhaustively analyzed in terms of only five pairs of pattern variables, which supposedly characterize all possible social action. These five pairs of pattern variables are the three above-defined ones used by Hoselitz, plus *affectivity* and *affective-neutrality* and *self-orientation* and *collectivity-orientation*.

Hoselitz first advanced his theory in 1953 under the title "Social Structure and Economic Growth";[16] he repeated the same thesis again (more penetratingly, he says in a footnote) in 1963 under the title "Social Stratification and Economic Development." [17] He argues that developed countries exhibit the pattern variables of universalism, achievement orientation, and functional specificity, while underdeveloped ones are characterized by their opposites—particularism, ascription, and functional diffuseness. To develop, Hoselitz counsels, underdeveloped countries should eliminate the pattern variables of underdevelopment and adopt those of development. It may be added that *EDCC* has devoted many pages to the diffusion of this approach to the study of economic development and cultural change.[18]

### Empirical Validity

Hoselitz characterizes the developed countries as universalist and not particularist. They are, as we shall see, normatively universalist. Yet the reality, the literature, and even the sociological treatment of many developed countries reveal substantial particularism. This is specifically the case for Japan,[19] France,[20] and Europe in general,[21] where the existence of particularism has been demonstrated among both upper and lower classes. Particularism is deep and widespread especially in the working class in both Europe[22] and the United States, in recent migrants from the former to the latter, and among non-white, rural, or recent rural-urban migrant groups in the United States. Moreover, much of what flies a universalist flag in the United States and other developed countries is little more than the cover for unsavory particularist private interests. We will have occasion below to observe that the developed countries export particularism to the underdeveloped ones, wrapped in such universalist slogans as freedom, democracy, justice, the common good, the economic liberalism of free trade, the political liberalism of free elections, the social liberalism of free social mobility, and the cultural liberalism of free flow of ideas such as the ones we are examining here.[23]

Hoselitz also characterizes developed countries as achievement oriented. To examine the counterpart of this pattern variable in reality, it is important to divide it into three sub-variables: reward, recruitment, and motivation. In the United States, reward within roles is indeed substantially dependent on achievement. But recruitment into roles, although perhaps substantially a matter of achievement among the middle classes, is very much based on ascription in both the high levels of business management, as Granick has shown in his comparison of American and Soviet management,[24] and among the masses of poor in the "other America," as Michael Harrington has so dramatically demonstrated. The ascription of roles, and the consequent reward, to the American Negro speaks silently and eloquently for itself through his contemporary Freedom Movement. Harrington shows, moreover, that far from becoming less ascriptive, American society, both at the top and at the bottom (and perhaps also in the middle), is becoming progressively more ascriptive.[25]

On the other hand, role recruitment in Japan is very much based on achievement, as Abegglen among others has pointed out.[26] However, the assignment of reward within the role, Abegglen argues, is highly ascriptive, being based on such factors as age, family obligations, etc. The important distinction between recruitment and reward (rarely made in discussions of achievement or ascription) and the obvious differences between Japanese and American practices in this respect would seem to explain a large part of the disagreement on this matter. For example, Bellah[27] and Levy,[28] who emphasize Japan's achievement orientation as a cause of its development, refer to role recruitment. On the other hand, Abegglen,[29] who emphasizes Japan's ascriptive pattern, is apparently thinking of reward within roles. The other achievement variable, individual achievement motivation or $n$(eed for) achievement as David McClelland calls it,[30] while increasingly confused with the Weberian category of social role assignment and reward, is quite another matter and will be discussed when we come to examine the third mode.

Thirdly, Hoselitz claims that in developed societies roles are functionally specific rather than diffuse, and that role specificity helps generate development while role diffuseness does the contrary. To assess this claim, we must first question the relevance of the specificity-diffuseness dichotomy to the structure of interaction which is being examined. Is it useful to distinguish the structure of interaction between ego and alter that is normatively defined in one diffuse role as a complex father-son, teacher-student, general-soldier, etc., relationship, from the structure of interaction in functionally specific roles which are integrated in such a way that ego is systematically father, teacher, general, etc., and alter is son, student, soldier, etc.? In a word, how important is the difference between role specificity and role diffuseness if the socially significant and dominant specific roles are collected together in one or a few individuals who wear many hats simultaneously or in quick and institutionalized succession? For the latter is the "functionally specific" role structure of the society in which, according to C. Wright Mills, the power elite dominates what President Eisenhower dubbed the military-industrial complex, and in which Douglas Dillon of Dillon Reed & Co. comes to sit in the cabinet as Secretary of the Treasury; Robert McNamara, President of the Ford Motor Company, becomes Secretary of Defense—as successor to "Engine Charley" Wilson, who gave us the *bon mot,* "What's good for General Motors is good for the country"; and in which the bulk of military purchases are from a half dozen giant corporations who employ large numbers of retired high level military officers.[31]

Our own profession is not as isolated from this role structure as Hoselitz' characterization of role specificity might suggest: Roosevelt's and Kennedy's brain trusts co-opted all sorts of American social scientists. Harvard historian Arthur Schlesinger, Jr.'s aid to the development of underdeveloped countries has so far consisted in writing the now famous White Paper on Cuba which was intended to justify the coming invasion of that country at the Bay of Pigs. He later admitted lying about the invasion in the "national interest." Stanford economist Eugene Staley wrote *The Future of Underdeveloped Countries*[32] and then planned it in the renowned Staley–[General Maxwell] Taylor Plan to put 15 million Vietnamese in the concentration camps they euphemistically christened "strategic hamlets." Since the failure of that effort at development planning, M.I.T. economic historian Walt Whitman Rostow has escalated the effort by writing *The Stages of Economic Growth: A Non-Communist Manifesto.*[33] He wrote of these stages at the CIA-financed Center for International Studies on the Charles River and has been operationalizing them on the Potomac as President Kennedy's Director of Policy and Planning in the State Department and President Johnson's chief adviser on Vietnam. It is on behalf of Vietnamese economic growth that Rostow has become the principal architect of escalation, from napalming the South to bombing the North, and beyond. Then, doubtless due to universalist particularism and achieved ascription, Eugene Rostow moves from professing international law at Yale University to practicing it at his brother's side in Washington. Meanwhile, after performing his role as Dean of Humanities at Harvard University, McGeorge Bundy becomes W. W. Rostow's superior in Washington and goes on television to explain to the misguided and incredulous why this economic development theory and policy is humanitarian (after which he goes on to direct the Ford Foundation and its influence on education and research). In the light of the manifest and institutionalized role-summation and diffuseness of these deans of humane scholarship and professors of applied social science, the clandestine direction of Project Camelot by the Department of Defense and the financing of the United States National Student Association by the CIA pale into the shadows.

However, Hoselitz' and my concern is with the economic development and cultural change of the *underdeveloped* countries. It is therefore more important to examine the reality of underdevelopment and Hoselitz' ideal typical mis-characterization of it. Hoselitz characterizes the underdeveloped countries as particularist rather than universalist. Yet normatively, underdeveloped countries are also substantially universalist. A glance at the press, radio, and much of the educational ideology of any underdeveloped country exhibits just as much universalism as do their counterparts in the developed ones. Mexico's most influential newspaper publishes more column inches about the "universalist" United States than the *New York Times* does about the whole world outside of the United States; and one American magazine, the *Reader's Digest*, which excels in getting across the American "universalist" norms and ideology, has a higher circulation in Mexico than the eight largest Mexican magazines combined.[34] What makes Hoselitz right in a sense is that this kind of universalism goes no deeper in the underdeveloped countries than it does in the developed ones; for there too it is, instead, a cover for underlying particularism. On the other hand, there are forms of universalism in the underdeveloped countries apart from the superficial façade of the particularly interested organs of public opinion formation. There are general and political strikes, decried by so many of these same observers from the developed countries; militant nationalism, which the same observers frown upon as opposed to the universal good and therefore to the particular one of this or that underdeveloped country; and widespread support in underdeveloped countries for the anti-colonial and anti-neocolonial movements, which the developed countries are combating by force of arms and universalistic-sounding propaganda about freedom, etc., in Vietnam, Malaysia, the Congo, the Dominican Republic, and elsewhere. This evidence suggests that universalism is after all quite widespread and deeply ingrained in the underdeveloped countries among groups which are not the privileged ones in command of the universalist organs of communication.

Hoselitz departs even further from reality when he says that social, economic, and political roles in the underdeveloped countries are distributed almost exclusively in terms of ascriptive norms. He specifically claims that the underdeveloped countries pay little attention to economic achievement in their determination of status and that political leadership is mainly determined by ascriptive norms.[35] Someone who had never lived in the universalist castle of American social science would be shocked to find that Hoselitz and many others characterize as ascriptive the national political leadership produced by the interminable military coups in Latin America,[36] and by the emerging "national" bourgeoisies all over Africa.[37] Yet the unreality of American popular and ostensibly scientific understanding of the world permits Hoselitz and others to suggest that Latin American political power is in the hands of some traditional landed or even feudal oligarchy. They fail to see that in all capitalist underdeveloped countries the power behind the throne, be it military or civil, rests (if it is in national hands at all) with the people who occupy the top roles in the economic organization, and particularly with those who have commercial and financial ties to the developed metropolis.[38] This metropolis is increasingly the United States—precisely the vantage point from which these social scientists make their curious observations and characterizations of the underdeveloped part of the world. In supposedly ascriptive Asia, Africa, and Latin America, many present incumbents of these top economic and political roles have achieved their positions, and done so quite recently—often more so than in the achievement-oriented developed countries of Europe and North America.[39] Thus, role assignment in the economically and politically most significant roles in underdeveloped countries is decidedly achieved and not ascribed.

It should be pointed out, however, that role assignment by achievement is also common among the lower level roles in the underdeveloped countries. This has been the case at least since mercantilist and capitalist penetration totally transformed these societies, often centuries ago. Only the social scientists from the invading metropolis seem unable to see how efficiently this penetration integrated these societies into the dominant world system and how universally the latter imposed its social organization and alienation on the people whom Frantz Fanon has called the damned of the earth.[40]

Evidently, the distribution of rewards in underdeveloped countries, at least in high-level roles, is also determined by achievement, as Hoselitz uses that term. In the monopolistic underdeveloped economies, even more than in the developed ones, financial success is determined by successful speculation and extortion, and the resulting distribution of income is even more unequal. This suggests that, contrary to what Hoselitz says, ascription counts less, and achievement more, in the distribution of reward in the underdeveloped countries.[41] (This assumes that we may call this sort of success "achievement" by our universalist standards, which the present author would not wish to do.)

Finally, Hoselitz says that roles in underdeveloped countries are functionally diffuse rather than specific. This is true in part. The poor in the underdeveloped countries, whether classified as working in the primary, secondary, or tertiary sector, do indeed practice many professions at a time, such as farmer, trader, peddler, artisan, odd jobber, thief, and provider of social security to others, in the attempt to keep body and soul together.[42] The roles at the other end of the socioeconomic scale are no less diffuse. One need only read the daily press or suffer the consequences of monopoly control in underdeveloped countries to know that the controlling roles are indeed diffuse, as Hoselitz suggests, and also that economic roles predominate in that control, as Hoselitz denies. On the other hand, it is also well to observe that a whole series of intermediate roles in underdeveloped societies, occupied by such members of the middle classes as military officers, government bureaucrats, junior executives, administrators, policemen, and others, are functionally quite specific. Their incumbents serve specific functions of making the whole exploitative system function in the diffuse but particular interest of those who have achieved control, in the same sense that the plantation administrator runs the owner's slave plantation for him. It is perhaps not surprising that it is among precisely these middle role incumbents that universalist values are predominant.[43]

In a word, if we examine the patterns of social roles in the developed and underdeveloped countries, instead of being blinded by a hand-me-down ideal typical perspective of adulterated Weberian parentage, we conclude that the characteristics Hoselitz and others attribute to developed and underdeveloped countries present a distorted and inadequate conception of social reality. This is, however, the least of the deficiencies of Hoselitz' and allied approaches to economic development and cultural change. That it is so easy to challenge the empirical validity of Hoselitz' conception of development and underdevelopment—that Hoselitz can find some particularism, ascription, and diffuseness in underdeveloped countries, whereas we can easily find universalism, achievement, and specificity there—already suggests that probably neither the one nor the other of the patterns of variables Hoselitz selects for emphasis is important for characterizing, or crucial for determining, either development or underdevelopment. It raises the suspicion that the important determining factors of development and underdevelopment are not these but others: that is, the theoretical adequacy of Hoselitz' whole approach is cast in doubt.

*Theoretical Adequacy*

Having disposed of the empirical validity of Hoselitz' claims, we may examine the theoretical adequacy of his thesis in terms of, first, his selection of roles for study; second, his selection of a social system for analysis; and third, and most important, his treatment of the social structure of development and underdevelopment.

It may be best to begin by asking how Hoselitz and I can characterize the pattern of variables or roles in underdeveloped countries so differently. Part of the answer will be found in the difference between the roles we deem important for underdevelopment and development. It appears that in Hoselitz' analysis all roles have about the same weight in characterizing and determining underdevelopment. Thus Hoselitz' prescription for development is that the maximum number of roles, almost irrespective of which they are, change from being particularist, ascriptive, and diffuse, and become universalist, achievement based, and functionally specific. The greater this quantitative change of roles from one pattern to the other, it would seem, the greater the development. My review, on the other hand, has lent more emphasis to roles at the top and some at the bottom of the economic and political stratification systems, because they are more important for development than just roles-in-general.

If social roles do not all carry the same weight or importance for development and underdevelopment, as they evidently do not, then it is not legitimate to assign them the same weights in theory. If, like Hoselitz, we construct ideal-type role patterns for development and underdevelopment (a dubious procedure to begin with) then in constructing the ideal-type we must surely assign more weight to the roles that in fact are more important for development or underdevelopment, even if they be less numerous. Yet in his characterization of both developed and un-derdeveloped societies, Hoselitz systematically evades the specific examination of the top economic and political roles. If Hoselitz lent these roles the weight they clearly have in the determination of development or underdevelopment, he would be unable to characterize as universalist, achievement based, and functionally specific a society in which the power elite of the industrial-gov-ernment-military complex pursues particularist ends; or to char-acterize as particularist, ascriptive, and functionally diffuse those countries which are governed by oligarchies with economic, polit-ical, and military power that is derived from commercial monop-oly privileges and the recurrent recourse to force of arms to protect and augment them. Still less would he be able to rest his theoretical case for development and underdevelopment on this empirical base.

Secondly, we may ask what social universe Hoselitz has in mind when he says that development is characterized by some pattern variables and underdevelopment by others. Hoselitz and many others associate particularism, ascription, and diffuseness in un-derdevelopment with the extended family, the primitive tribe, the folk community, the traditional sector of a dual society, and with the underdeveloped countries and part of the world in general. But the connection is never made with the developed part of the world nor with the contemporary dominant social organization in the world taken as a whole. Indeed, he seems to be indifferent about where change should take place, since in discussing underdevelopment he moves quite easily and almost imperceptibly from referring to one of these units to talking about another (although never, of course, to the last two). Hoselitz leaves far from clear just which is the social whole whose role patterns he would change from one set of variables to another in order to effect development. Here the theoretical inadequacy is even more glaring, for it contravenes the generally accepted rule of social and all scientific theory to look for and refer to the systemic whole in terms of which the reality (in this case underdevelopment) can be explained and changed. The social system which is today the determinant of underdevelopment certainly is not the family, tribe, community, a part of a dual society, or even, as I shall argue below, any underdeveloped country or countries taken by themselves.

The folk characteristics which were studied by Robert Redfield, and which Hoselitz seems to associate with the pattern variables of underdeveloped society, do not characterize any whole society existing today. At best, they may characterize "tribal societies," few if any of which still remain independent. Redfield himself only spoke in terms of a non-tribal folk society when he first studied Yucatan and Tepotzlan, and even then he entitled his book *The Folk Culture of Yucatan*.[44] When he later began to concentrate his attention on *Peasant Society and Culture*,[45] he took great pains to point out that peasants with folk characteristics live only in *parts* of societies inasmuch as they are peasants only by virtue of their relation to the city, whose function complements theirs within the same wider social whole that incorporates them both. Furthermore, in his study of the Guatemalan peasant community, Cantel,[46] Manning Nash himself pointed out that the appearance of the universalist, achievement oriented, and functionally specific characteristics associated with labor unionism—and their renewed disappearance after the 1954 military coup of which John Foster Dulles was so proud—must be traced beyond the boundaries of the community to the national system. In view of the well-known source of that military coup we might add that it should be traced further to the functioning and structure of the international system, never mentioned by Hoselitz, but of which Cantel, Guatemala, and all their inhabitants form integral if unhappily determined parts. Therefore, it is not a matter of empirical, theoretical, or policy indifference just which social system is selected for study and change with a view to promoting economic development. Hoselitz' selection is empirically unacceptable because he does not choose to study the system whose characteristics are the determinant ones for development and underdevelopment. Hoselitz' procedure is theoretically unsatisfactory because he does not address himself to the determinant social whole as Redfield counseled that social scientists must do.[47]

Thirdly, Hoselitz' treatment of economic development and cultural change is unsatisfactory on still more important theoretical grounds: his analysis belies its own title, "Social Structure and Economic Growth," by neglecting structure and especially the structure of underdevelopment. The previously discussed empirical and theoretical shortcomings in analyses such as Hoselitz' are of course part and parcel of this neglect. However, the failure of those using this approach to take adequate account of structure is of such far reaching importance that it requires more specific commentary of its own.

Hoselitz follows the lead of Talcott Parsons who, to commemorate the centenary of the *Communist Manifesto*, explained the theoretical significance and political consequences of his own and "modern sociological theory":

> Marx, however, tended to treat the socioeconomic structure of capitalist enterprise as a single indivisible entity rather than breaking it down analytically into a set of the distinct variables involved in it. It is this analytical breakdown which is for present purposes the most distinctive feature of modern sociological analysis. . . . It results in a modification of the Marxian view. . . . The primary structural emphasis no longer falls on . . . the theory of exploitation but rather on the structure of occupational roles. . . .[48]

The felicity of Parsons' analysis of this approach has already been empirically confirmed for us by Hoselitz' aforementioned practice of confining his attention to the arithmetic sum of social roles in general, and of forgetting about the social, political, and economic structure of a particular society under study.

Herein, Parsons, Hoselitz, and recent sociological theorists in general not only modify Marx but also depart from Weber. Parsons' structuralism and holism is confined to the analysis of a wholly abstract model of any and all real or imaginary societies and not with the study of any existing real society. However much Marx and Weber may have relied on theoretical models and ideal types, neither ever ventured to depart so far from reality. Other recent sociological theorists, mostly social anthropologists of the British structural-functionalist school, who have devoted themselves to the study of existing whole societies, fall short of the standards of classical sociology in other ways. They select small "societies" in Africa and elsewhere for study and analyze them as though they had an isolated existence independent from the imperialist system of which they formed an integral part at the time of study. Hoselitz abandons classical sociology and carries recent sociology still further. He leaves behind the structural holism of Parsons because it is not suited to any but abstract wholes. Yet he does not join the anthropologists on their field trips to study the social structure of social "wholes." Hoselitz is satisfied to abandon both holism and structuralism and to devote his attention to pattern variables. The above theorists deviate further from classical theory, which is a most serious handicap for those who would study economic development and cultural change. "Modern sociological theory" at best appeals to holism and structuralism to explain the existence of the parts, or merely to demonstrate the relations among them, but not to analyze or account for the existence of the social structure as a whole. Consequently, these theorists, who pretend to analyze economic *development* and cultural *change*, fail to direct their theoretical analysis to the past origins, the present transformations, or the future prospects of the existing social system as a system.

Yet Hoselitz and, as we shall see, the advocates of the second and third modes of analysis, all take another step beyond Parsons

—and far beyond what would have occurred to Weber in his moments of wildest fancy. They argue that to eliminate under-development and produce development it is only necessary to change particular variables, roles, or parts of the social system—that it is not necessary to change the structure of the system it-self. Logically, Hoselitz and others can take this position only if they maintain one or the other of the following: (1) that under-development and development are associated only with the char-acteristics of the simple majority of the society's roles, and not with the structure of that society; or (2) granted that develop-ment and underdevelopment are associated with the structure of the social system, the system's structure can be changed simply by changing some of its parts or their characteristics. The first violates all standards of social scientific theory; the second is contrary to all empirical reality.

The importance of the empirical and theoretical deficiency of the approach of Hoselitz and others cannot be stressed too much. The empirical evidence which has been discussed reveals that this criticism of Hoselitz' and related analyses on theoretical grounds is not based on an isolated appeal to arbitrary theoretical stand-ards. That is, the weight of the scientific standards which such analyses fail to meet lies not so much in their universal accept-ance as it does in their realism and efficacy: if Hoselitz and others had guided their observations and analyses of economic development and cultural change by these standards of struc-turalism and holism, they could not have come to the empirically erroneous conclusion that ascriptive role assignment in general is keeping underdeveloped countries underdeveloped. They would have seen not only that the crucial political and economic roles in underdeveloped countries are assigned and rewarded by achieve-ment—which is the least of it, since it is not, after all, ascription or achievement which is really important—but also that these roles and their incumbents are no more than some of the manifes-tations of the real structure of development and underdevelopment of a world-embracing system that gives rise to these roles and whose incumbents in turn serve to maintain the system and underdevelopment in particular.

*Policy Effectiveness*

Three examples may suffice to indicate that Hoselitz' policy prescriptions do not lead to the consequences he predicts. First, the existence, or the increase (if we would believe C. Wright Mills[49] or William H. Whyte[50]) of role ascription and diffuseness in business, government, and military circles in the United States has not so far turned that country into an underdeveloped one. A second piece of evidence is that the supposed achievement of functionally specific roles and pursuit of universal standards among, for instance, the business magnates and their military executors in Latin America has not so far developed their countries and still gives no signs of doing so.

Although perhaps not the most important one, a third piece of evidence against Hoselitz' thesis is particularly interesting because it is supplied by Hoselitz himself. As we saw above, Hoselitz' pattern variables of development are associated particularly with the rise of the middle classes; and such students of Latin America as John Johnson[51] in the United States and Gino Germani[52] in Argentina, among many others, have argued that the greater the social mobility and the bigger the middle class, the more development. Yet Hoselitz recently took the initiative to test this thesis by confronting it with the hard facts of reality in Latin America. There he found and wrote that the countries with the largest middle classes, Argentina and Chile, are not at all the ones with the most development.[53]

Three things however are true of middle classes in Latin America. First, their social pattern closely corresponds to the one to which Hoselitz wishes to attribute economic development and cultural change. Secondly, as in Nazi Germany and Fascist Italy, it is precisely these groups which provide the principal "popular" support for the ultrareactionary military dictatorships, as these groups again demonstrated in an impressively manifest fashion in the 1964 military coup in Brazil.[54] A third fact, which is not unrelated to the foregoing one or to the unviability of the development prescriptions of Hoselitz, Johnson, Germani, and others, is that throughout the underdeveloped countries (as well as in the United States as Gabriel Kolko has recently shown[55]), when the income of these middle classes rises it does so not at the expense of the rich but at the expense of the large masses of the poor, whose relative and often absolute income in the underdeveloped countries is thereby forced still lower.[56] Economic development and cutural change of an underdeveloped country through the promotion and rise of the middle classes (or their pattern variables) has not occurred because, among other reasons, it is physically impossible for it occur given the structure of the system: it only leads to the further underdevelopment of the majority.

### STAGES OF GROWTH

Within the first ideal typical mode, which Nash calls the index mode and which I call the gap approach, we may distinguish a second variant. Here the identification of the gap between the characteristics of development and underdevelopment includes the specification of intermediate stages and their characteristics. Although Nash mentioned Rostow in connection with his earlier work on development propensities,[57] it is preferable to take Rostow's *Stages of Economic Growth* as the example of this variant of the first mode. My review and evaluation of Rostow's and similar "stage" approaches will require less space because first, much of the criticism already made of Hoselitz applies to them as well and, second, Rostow's stages have already come in for much specific criticism from others.[58] Nonetheless, I submit that Rostow's *Stages of Economic Growth* deserves more fundamental criticism on empirical, theoretical, and policy grounds than it has thus far received.

According to Rostow,

It is possible to identify all societies, in their economic dimensions, as lying within five categories: the traditional society, the preconditions for take-off, the take-off, the drive to maturity, and the age of high mass-consumption. First, the traditional society. A traditional society is one whose structure is developed within limited production functions, based on pre-Newtonian science and technology, and on pre-Newtonian attitudes towards the physical world. . . . The second stage of growth embraces societies in the process of transition; that is, the period when the preconditions for take-off are developed; for it takes time to transform a traditional society in the ways necessary for it to exploit the fruits of modern science, to fend off diminishing returns, and thus to enjoy the blessings and choices opened up by the march of compound interest. . . . the stage of preconditions arise[s] not endogenously but from some external intrusion by more advanced societies. . . . We come now to the great watershed in the life of modern societies: the third stage in this sequence, the take-off. The take-off is the interval when the old blocks and resistances to steady growth are finally overcome. The forces making for economic progress, which yielded limited bursts and enclaves of modern activity, expand and come to dominate the society. Growth becomes its normal condition. Compound interest becomes built, as it were, into its habits and institutional structure. . . . [The] take-off is defined as requiring all three of the following related conditions: (1) a rise in the rate of productive investment from, say, 5 percent or less to over 10 percent of national income (or net national product (NNP)); (2) the development of one or more substantial manufacturing sectors, with a high rate of growth; (3) the existence or quick emergence of a political, social and institutional framework which exploits the impulses to expansion . . .[59]

Rostow's stages and thesis are incorrect primarily because they do not correspond at all to the past or present reality of the underdeveloped countries whose development they are supposed to guide. It is explicit in Rostow, as it is implicit in Hoselitz, that underdevelopment is the original stage of what are supposedly traditional societies—that there were no stages prior to the present stage of underdevelopment. It is further explicit in Rostow that the now developed societies were once underdeveloped. But all this is quite contrary to fact. This entire approach to economic development and cultural change attributes a history to the developed countries but denies all history to the underdeveloped ones. The countries that are today underdeveloped evidently have had a history no less than have the developed ones. None of them, for example India,[60] is today the way it was centuries or even decades ago. Moreover, reference to even any schoolboy world history confirms that the history of the now underdeveloped countries has been most intimately related to the history of the now developed ones for at least several centuries.

Indeed, the economic and political expansion of Europe since the fifteenth century has come to incorporate the now under-developed countries into a single stream of world history, which has given rise simultaneously to the present development of some countries and the present underdevelopment of others. However, in their attempt to construct theory and policy for the under-developed countries, Rostow and others have examined the developed countries as if they had developed in isolation from this stream of world history. It stands to reason that any serious attempt to construct theory and policy for the development of the now underdeveloped countries has to be based on the examination of the experience of the underdeveloped countries themselves—that is, on the study of their history and of the world historical process which has made these countries under-developed. Yet this task of constructing a realistic theory and policy of development has not been pursued by any of the students of economic development and cultural change who employ the modes of approach to the problem which, according to Nash, exhaust all possibilities. We see again, then, that these three approaches to studying and solving the problems of economic development and cultural change only exhaust what is done; but they do not exhaust what can be done, and least of all what must be done.

It is impossible, without closing one's eyes, to find in the world today any country or society which has the characteristics of Rostow's first, the traditional, stage. This is not surprising since the construction of Rostow's stages takes account neither of the history of the now underdeveloped countries, nor of their crucial relations with the now developed ones over several centuries past. Rostow's approach obliterates the fact that through these relations, the now developed countries have totally destroyed the pre-existing fabric of these societies (be it "traditional" or not). This was most notably the case in India which was de-industrialized;[61] Africa, where the slave trade transformed society long before colonialism did so again;[62] and Latin America, where the high civilizations of the Incas and the Aztecs were wiped out altogether.[63] The relationship between the mercantilist and capitalist metropolis and these colonies succeeded in supplanting the pre-existing—or, in the case of the *tabula rasa* situations of Argentina, Brazil, the West Indies and elsewhere, in implanting —the social, political, and economic structure they now have: that is, the structure of underdevelopment.[64]

This long relationship between the now underdeveloped and now developed countries within the same historical process did not affect only the export enclave in the underdeveloped countries, as the almost universally accepted and just as empirically and theoretically erroneous "dual" society or economy thesis has it.[65] On the contrary, this historical relationship transformed the entire social fabric of the peoples whose countries are now underdeveloped, just as in the developed countries.[66] (I shall return to this problem of the dual society or economy in the section on diffusionism below.)

If Rostow's first, traditional, stage cannot be found in any underdeveloped country today, his second stage, which contains the pre-conditions for take-off into economic development, is even more conspicuous by its absence. Characteristic of Rostow's second stage is the penetration of underdeveloped countries by influences created abroad—mostly in the developed countries— and diffused to the underdeveloped ones, where they destroy traditionalism and simultaneously create the pre-conditions that will lead to the subsequent take-off in the third stage. (This, too, is examined in the section on diffusionism.) The factual error of the second stage in Rostow's thesis is so glaring that it may be discussed briefly. As we observed with respect to the first stage, the now underdeveloped Asian, African, and Latin American parts of the world, even if they were traditional in the Rostowian sense before their contact with Europe—a dubious thesis, considering the high civilizations and technological development that had been achieved on all three continents—certainly have been and still are affected by conditions in, and penetrated by influences emanating from, the now developed metropolis. Yet these same metropolitan conditions and influences, which already have a history ranging from one to several centuries, have not brought about economic development, or even led to a take-off into de-velopment, in a single one of the "75 countries," as they came to be called at the 1964 Geneva Conference on World Trade and Development.

This Conference was called because the nearly two-thirds of the world's population living in these countries feel and know that these metropolitan imposed second stage conditions, far from furthering their economic development as Rostow and other metropolitan pundits claim, not only hinder their economic de-velopment, but even increase their underdevelopment.[67] The reason for all this is that the reality of underdevelopment, which Rostow's first and second stages obscure and even deny, is that the incorporation of these lands and peoples into the expanding mercantilist and then capitalist world system first initiated their underdevelopment; that, furthermore, their continued participa-tion in this same system still maintains and even aggravates that underdevelopment.[68] As Prime Minister Jawaharlal Nehru said, in his *The Discovery of India,*

> nearly all our major problems today have grown up during British rule and as a direct result of British policy: the princes; the minority problem; various vested interests, foreign and Indian; the lack of industry and the neglect of agriculture; the extreme backwardness in the social services; and, above all, the tragic poverty of the people.[69]

Rather than countering the authority of Rostow and most of his colleagues from the developed countries only with an appeal to the authority of Nehru and his colleagues from the underde-veloped countries, we may also appeal to empirical evidence, which is devastating for the Rostowian thesis. The evidence is from the *tabula rasa* countries that had no population at all before they were incorporated into the developing mercantilist and capitalist system. Today, more than half of both the area and the population of Latin America—especially Argentina, Uruguay, Brazil, and all of the West Indies—occupies regions which, at the time of their incorporation into the European centered mer-cantile system, were either entirely unpopulated or were repopu-lated after the rapid extermination of the pre-contact population.

None of these countries ever experienced Rostow's first stage: the mercantile metropolis did not conquer and settle these regions to institute Rostow's traditionalism, but to exploit them through the establishment of exclusively commercial mines, sugar plantations, and cattle ranches. If anything, these regions and peoples entered world history by stepping right into Rostow's second stage. But after more than four centuries, Rostowian second stage conditions and contact have not led to the third stage take-off in these regions, much less to the fourth or fifth stage of development. Today these previously unpopulated regions are just as underdeveloped as are the previously populated ones which were similarly incorporated into the world embracing capitalist system. Indeed, contrary to Rostow's conception of the second stage —and, as we will see below, contrary to most of the diffusionist thesis—the more intimate the past contact of these regions with the metropolis, the more underdeveloped they are today. Among the many examples are the ex-sugar exporting regions of the Caribbean and the Brazilian Northeast and the ex-mining export regions of Minas Gerais in the center of Brazil, of Bolivia and Peru in the Andean Highlands and of the famous Zacatecas and Guanajuato mining regions in the center of Mexico.[70]

Abundant historical evidence from the underdeveloped countries shows that Rostow's first two stages are fictional. Contemporary evidence from them shows that his last two stages are utopian. After all, if these countries now were to find themselves in the fourth stage of drive toward maturity or in the fifth one of high mass consumption, we would not call them underdeveloped —and Rostow would not have to invent his stages. What is more, while in Rostow's rendition of reality his utopian last two stages are the mere mechanical summation of the fictitious first two stages plus the third, in the unfortunate reality of the underdeveloped countries it is precisely the structure of their underdevelopment—which Rostow whitewashes with his traditionalism and externally created preconditions—and their structural relations with the developed countries, which Rostow fails to mention at all, that have for so long prevented the realization of the last two stages. By Rostow's count, we are then left only with the third stage and by my count with the second crucial flaw in Rostow's entire argument.

Rostow would have us believe that in his third stage, the take-off, he has theoretically synthesized the dynamic qualitative change between the structure of underdevelopment and that of development. However, his theory is not dynamic and he does not isolate structural characteristics or change. Least of all does he incorporate the real structure of underdevelopment and development into his theory. On the contrary, he fails to consider it altogether. Like most, but not all, stage theories of history, Rostow's is an exercise in comparative statics. While he identifies stages of development, he does not say anything about how to get from one to the other. This is no less the case for the third stage than it is for the four others. The unreality of Rostow's dynamic should not surprise us: for as we have seen, even his statics are entirely unreal; his stages correspond to no reality in the underdeveloped countries at all. How, then, could his development from one stage to another correspond to the underdeveloped world's reality?

That Rostow does not argue from structure is already suggested by the fact that he places the major burden for development in the third stage, on the mere rate of investment and growth. The conclusive evidence of the theoretical inadequacy of Rostow's stages for understanding and eliminating the structure of underdevelopment goes far beyond that, of course. In completely ignoring the history of the underdeveloped countries, Rostow necessarily completely ignores the structure of their underdevelopment. The changes in institutions and investment he posits as the take-off out of underdevelopment do not begin to affect the real structure of underdevelopment. The proof is that countries such as Argentina,[71] which Rostow claims to be taking off into development, are becoming ever more structurally underdeveloped and that, indeed, no underdeveloped country has ever managed to take off out of its underdevelopment by following Rostow's stages.

Rostow's empirical and theoretical errors extend beyond his analysis of the underdevelopment of the underdeveloped countires to his characterization of the development of the developed ones. While the developed countries are not our topic here, it is necessary at least to point out this faulty characterization of development because, like Hoselitz and others, Rostow bases so much of his policy for the underdeveloped countries on his picture of the developed ones. Rostow is particularly explicit in claiming that England was the first country to industrialize and that it did so by domestically mobilizing its own resources after having experienced certain internal structural changes. Others among the now developed countries, he says, also developed on their own except insofar as the prior development of England and others helped to create the preconditions for their take-off. Again, Rostow is wrong both on empirical and theoretical grounds. That England and other countries did not develop by relying only on their own efforts has been exhaustively proven. The English Mercantilists such as Thomas Mun,[72] had no doubt about it. Neither did Cantillon[73] or Marx.[74] Among our contemporaries, Earl Hamilton,[75] Eric Williams,[76] now Prime Minister of Trinidad and Tobago, and Basil Davidson,[77] have again demonstrated the crucial role played by the underdeveloped countries in financing the capitalization of the now developed ones. If the now underdeveloped countries were really to follow the stages of growth of the now developed ones, they would have to find still other peoples to exploit into underdevelopment, as the now developed countries did before them.

This misrepresentation of reality by Rostow must, of course, lead to (or does it follow from?) a theoretical error of the first magnitude and of vital importance for development theory and policy. This error is common not only to both variants of the first mode but also to all three modes of approach to economic development and cultural change reviewed here.[78] They each view the characteristics of development and underdevelopment as *sui generis* to the country concerned. When they proceed to the study of any structure at all, as we have already seen in the case of Hoselitz, they confine themselves to examining only parts of the domestic structure of the country concerned. In none of these modes is there an examination of the actual structure of development and underdevelopment—of the structure of the historical system which gave rise to and includes them both. As to the efficacy of the policy recommended by Rostow, it speaks for itself: no country, once underdeveloped, ever managed to develop by Rostow's stages. Is that why Rostow is now trying to help the people of Vietnam, the Congo, the Dominican Republic, and other underdeveloped countries to overcome the empirical, theoretical, and policy shortcomings of his manifestly non-communist intellectual aid to economic development and cultural change by bombs, napalm, chemical and biological weapons, and military occupation? [79]

The first or ideal typical mode of approaching problems of economic development and cultural change turns out upon examination to be empirically invalid, theoretically inadequate, and ineffective policy-wise. The fundamental reason why the whole approach must be rejected by those who would meaningfully understand and solve the problems of economic development and cultural change is that the approach, in all its variations, ignores the historical and structural reality of the underdeveloped countries. This reality is the product of the very same historical process and systemic structure as is the development of the now developed countries: the world embracing system within which the now underdeveloped countries have lived their history for centuries; it is the structure of this system which constitutes the historical cause and still contemporary determinant of underdevelopment. This structure is ubiquitous; it extends from the most developed part of the most developed country to the most underdeveloped part of the most underdeveloped country. Even if the first approach were to study the structure of underdevelopment on the domestic level of the underdeveloped countries, which as we have seen it does not, it would be unable adequately to analyze and understand that domestic structure—let alone to permit policy formulation adequate to change it. Those engaging in the first mode of analysis, and as we will see the second and third ones as well, resolutely avoid the study of the international structure of development and underdevelopment of which the domestic structure of underdevelopment is only a part. On all grounds then, empirical, theoretical, and policy, the first approach to economic development and cultural change must be rejected as inadequate.

## The Diffusionist Approach

The second mode identified by Nash views development as occurring through the diffusion of cultural elements from the developed to the underdeveloped countries. This involves, of course, acculturation to these elements on the part of the underdeveloped countries. The diffusion is seen to spread from the metropolis of the advanced capitalist countries out to the national capitals of the underdeveloped ones, and from these in turn out to their provincial capitals and finally to the peripheral hinterland.

According to this view, since development consists of and is promoted by diffusion and acculturation, underdevelopment remains because of obstacles or resistance to this diffusion. Underdevelopment is taken to be the original "traditional" state as much as it is in the first mode. There is even less inquiry into the causes and nature of underdevelopment than in the first mode. In effect, the diffusionists do not suggest to the peoples of the underdeveloped world that they inquire into and remove the causes of underdevelopment; instead they advise them to await and welcome the diffusion of developmental aid from the outside.

*Empirical Validity*

Nash emphasizes the diffusion of "knowledge, skills, organization, values, technology, and capital" as the primary factors in the second mode's view of economic development and cultural change. For expository convenience, we shall reclassify these as (1) capital; (2) technology, including knowledge and skills; and (3) institutions, including values and organization.

*Capital:* With respect to the diffusion of capital, the thesis of the second mode begins with the proposition that, being poor, the underdeveloped countries lack investment capital and therefore find it difficult or impossible to develop and thereby escape from their poverty. Therefore, the richer developed countries can, should, and do diffuse capital to the underdeveloped ones, thereby promoting their economic development. The acceptability of the initial proposition—that it is poverty which hampers the under-

developed countries' efforts at investment and development—
has been strongly challenged on theoretical grounds by Paul
Baran;[80] and this writer has supplied further theoretical and
empirical evidence which discounts this proposition.[81] I shall say
no more about this proposition here since it is the assumption—
or justification—which serves only as the starting point for the
diffusionist thesis. Instead, I shall go on to examine the thesis
itself, namely that the developed countries diffuse capital to the
underdeveloped ones and thereby aid in their development. This
thesis is upheld in the pages of *EDCC* by, among others, Martin
Bronfenbrenner,[82] and by Daniel Garnick,[83] who challenges Bronfenbrenner's argument. Whatever the disagreement between
them, however, they both agree that the developed countries actually contribute capital to the underdeveloped ones. The variety
of views on foreign aid and investment presented under Gerald
Meier's editorship in *Leading Issues in Development Economics,* by Raymond Mikesell in *U.S. Private and Government Investment Abroad,*[84] or by Benjamin Higgins, in his chapter on
"Foreign Investment and Foreign Aid" in his *Economic Development,*[85] exhibit a variety of sharp disagreements. But all these
writers, as well as others in *EDCC,*[86] seem to be in full agreement
with the proposition that the flow of capital is from the developed
countries to the underdeveloped ones. Again, the only disagreement seems to stem from the facts.

The conservative estimates of the United States Department of
Commerce show that between 1950 and 1965 the total flow of
capital on investment account from the United States to the rest
of the world was $23.9 billion, while the corresponding capital
inflow from profits was $37.0 billion, for a net inflow into the
United States of $13.1 billion. Of this total, $14.9 billion flowed
from the United States to Europe and Canada while $11.4 billion
flowed in the opposite direction, for a net outflow from the United
States of $3.5 billion. Yet, between the United States and all
other countries, that is mainly the poor, undeveloped ones, the
situation is reversed: $9.0 billion of investment flowed to these
countries while $25.6 billion profit capital flowed out of them,
for a *net inflow from the poor to the rich* of $16.6 billion.[87]

Other available statistics show exactly the same pattern of net capital flow from the underdeveloped countries to the developed ones.[88] The only trouble with these data is that they very much understate the actual flow of capital from the poor underdeveloped countries to the rich developed ones. First of all, they understate the capital flow from poor to rich on investment account.[89] Secondly, they obscure the fact that the largest part of the capital which the developed countries own in the underdeveloped ones was never sent from the former to the latter at all but was, on the contrary, acquired by the developed countries in the now underdeveloped ones.

Thus, according to the United States Department of Commerce, of the total capital obtained and employed from all sources by United States operations in Brazil in 1957, 26 percent came from the United States and the remainder was raised in Brazil, including 36 percent from Brazilian sources outside the American firms.[90] That same year, of the capital in American direct investment in Canada, 26 percent came from the United States while the remainder was also raised in Canada.[91] By 1964, however, the part of American investment in Canada that entered from the United States had declined to 5 percent, making the average American contribution to the total capital used by American firms in Canada during the period 1957–64 only 15 percent. All the remainder of the "foreign investment" was raised in Canada through retained earnings (42 percent), depreciation charges (31 percent), and funds raised by American firms on the Canadian capital market (12 percent). According to a survey of American direct investment firms operating in Canada in the period 1950–59, 79 percent of the firms raised over 25 percent of the capital for their Canadian operations in Canada, 65 percent of the firms raised over 50 percent in Canada, *and 47 percent of the American firms with investments in Canada raised all of the capital for their Canadian operations in Canada and none in the United States.* There is reason to believe that this American reliance on foreign capital to finance American "foreign investment" is still greater in the poor underdeveloped countries, which are weaker and more defenseless than Canada. This, then, is the source of the flow of capital on investment account from the poor underdeveloped countries to the rich developed ones.

Thirdly, these data take account neither of the well known de-cline in the underdeveloped countries' relative participation in world trade, nor of the deterioration of the terms of trade which is currently costing the underdeveloped countries far more capital than their net or gross receipts of investment and loans from de-veloped ones.[92] (Net receipts, as was noted above, are negative to begin with.) Fourthly, these data on the flow of investment capital leave out of account the still larger flow of capital from the underdeveloped countries to the developed ones on other service accounts. In 1962 Latin America spent fully 61 percent of its foreign exchange earnings on services that were supposedly rendered to it by the developed countries. Half of this, or 30 percent of the total, was accounted for by officially registered profit remittances and debt service. The other half was composed of Latin American payments to the developed countries, which means mostly the United States, for transportation and insurance, travel, other services, donations, transfer of funds, and errors and omissions (in registered capital flows). Moreover, Latin Amer-ica's loss of capital on service accounts is increasing over time: while in 1961–63 it was 61 percent, in 1956–60 it had been only 53 percent.[93] This capital outflow amounts to 7.3 percent of Latin America's Gross National Product, or 10 percent if we add the 3 percent of GNP lost by recent years' deterioration in the terms of trade; and this equals two and three or more times the capital that "capital poor" Latin America devotes to net investment for its own development.[94] Other kinds of capital loss by the underdeveloped countries are not included in these calculations, such as the notorious brain drain, or outflow of hu-man capital that was financed by the poor countries for the subsequent benefit of the rich. Who, we may ask, is diffusing capital to whom?

Beyond the question of the amount and direction of capital diffused, there is the problem of the kind and consequences of foreign aid and investment in underdeveloped countries. That metropolitan investment in and control of primary sector produc-tion in underdeveloped countries (in, for example, sugar, bananas, minerals, and most spectacularly petroleum) has notably failed to develop the underdeveloped countries, but has instead interposed a whole series of obstacles to their development, has by now surely been sufficiently documented to be obvious even when viewed from the developed countries themselves.

Foreign investment in the industrial and service sectors of underdeveloped countries raises further questions. It is far from clear that even this investment helps underdeveloped countries to develop. Nonetheless, with few exceptions, writers from the developed countries have failed to question, much less to analyze, the supposed benefits of this foreign investment to underdeveloped countries. Economists and statesmen from the underdeveloped countries, on the other hand, are increasingly challenging these supposed benefits and are going on to analyze the obstacles to industrialization and economic development created by foreign investment. For example, a congress representing thirty-four Schools of Economics in Latin America recently concluded that:

> Direct foreign investment has many unfavorable effects on the balance of payments, on economic integration and on capital formation in our countries; it determines in great measure the character and direction of our foreign trade, stimulates monopolistic competition, absorbs or subordinates weaker national firms, etc. For all these reasons it is necessary to adopt ways and means that can impede these negative effects.[95]

Arturo Frondizi wrote during his successful electoral campaign for the presidency of Argentina:

> It is not amiss to remember that foreign capital usually acts as an agent which perturbs the morality, the politics, and the economy of Argentina. . . . Once established thanks to excessively liberal concessions, foreign capital obtained bank credits which permitted it to expand its operations and therefore its profits. These profits are immediately sent abroad as if all of the investment capital had been imported by the country. In this way, the domestic economy came to strengthen foreign capitalization and to weaken itself. . . . The natural tendency of foreign capital in our country has been, in the first place, to settle in areas of high profits. . . . When Argentinian effort, intelligence, and perseverance created an independent economic opportunity, foreign capital destroyed it or tried to create difficulties for it. . . . Foreign capital had and has a decisive influence in the social and political life of our country. . . . The press

is usually also an active instrument of this process of submission.
. . . Foreign capital has had special influence in the political life of
our nation, allying itself with the conservative oligarchy . . . those
who are tied to foreign capital by economic ties (directors, bureaucratic personnel, lawyers, newspapers that receive advertisements,
etc.) and those who, without having economic relations, end up
being dominated by the political and ideological climate created by
foreign capital.[96]

Octaviano Campos Salas, before he became Minister of Industry
of Mexico, summarized the consequences of foreign investment:

A) Private foreign capital takes over high profit sectors permanently,
expelling or not permitting the entry of domestic capital, by relying
on the ample financial resources of its home office and on the political power which it sometimes exercises. B) The permanent takeover
of important sectors of economic activity impedes domestic capital
formation and creates problems of balance of payments instability.
C) Private direct foreign investment interferes with anti-cyclical
monetary and fiscal policy—it comes when there are expansions and
withdraws during depressions. D) The demands by private foreign
investors for concessions to form a 'favorable climate' for investment in the receiving countries are unlimited and excessive. E) It
is much cheaper and more consistent with the underdeveloped
countries' aspirations to economic independence to hire foreign
technicians and to pay royalties for the use of patents than to accept
the permanent control of their economies by powerrul foreign
consortia. F) Foreign private capital does not adapt itself to development planning.[97]

It is not, then, indisputably obvious that the underdeveloped
countries would be still more underdeveloped if they were not
visited by foreign capital.[98] Evidently, not any and all diffusion,
even of capital, let alone of other things, is an aid to economic
development.

*Technology:* Technology is diffused only in part. However, the
problem is not, as the diffusionists would have us believe, one of
insufficient quantity of technology diffused, and still less one of
cultural resistance to its acceptance and employment in technologically backward areas. The problem of technology and its
diffusion arises out of the same monopoly structure of the eco-

nomic system on the world, national, and local levels. During the course of the historical development of the capitalist system on these levels, the developed countries have always diffused out to their satellite colonial dependencies the technology whose employment in the colonial and now underdeveloped countries has served the interests of the metropolis; and the metropolis has always suppressed the technology in the now underdeveloped countries which conflicted with the interests of the metropolis and its own development, as the Europeans did with the irrigation and other agricultural technology and installations in India, the Middle East, and Latin America; or as the English did with industrial technology in India, Spain, and Portugal.[99] The same is true on the national and local levels in which the domestic metropolis promotes the technology in its hinterland that serves its export interests and suppresses the pre-existing individual or communal agricultural and artisan technology that interferes with the use of the countryside's productive and buying capacity and capital for metropolitan development.

Throughout this historical process the metropolis has maintained a high degree of monopoly over industrial production and technology which it has relinquished only when it had already established an alternative source of monopoly in heavy industry; this latter it is slowly beginning to relinquish in our day now that it has developed a still newer source of technological monopoly in electronics, synthetics, cybernetics, and automation in general. Far from diffusing more and more important technology to the underdeveloped countries, the most significant technological trend of our day is the increasing degree to which new technology serves as the basis of the capitalist metropolis' monopoly control over its underdeveloped economic colonies.

Some of the facts of technological diffusion, which sharply contrast with most of the diffusionist faith, were recently analyzed by the American business magazine, *Newsweek*, under the title "The U.S. Business Stake in Europe":

> To knowledgeable Europeans, in fact, the technical lead of the big U.S. companies is the most disturbing facet of the dollar invasion. In the future, a French study committee recently concluded, competition over prices will give way to competition in innovations, and

the pace will be so hot that only firms of international size—that is, American ones, chiefly—will survive. . . . European industries will function more and more under foreign licensing agreements; they will become subsidiaries of U.S. parent companies, which will sell them their know-how and manage Europe's production. . . . French politicians and publications of the right, left, and center have been accusing the U.S. of economic colonization, satellization, and vassalization. . . . A company chairman in Brussels sums up: "We are becoming 'pawns manipulated by U.S. giants'". . . . An Olivetti executive discussing alternatives to the GE [General Electric] deal . . . [declared] "But even if we had merged with Machines Bull in France and Siemens in Germany (which later signed a licensing agreement with RCA [Newsweek]), we still would have been dwarfed and eventually put out of business by the U.S. giants. . . . Research costs are too high. The transatlantic technological gap is a fact of life. . . . We studied a European solution very carefully. . . . There is no European solution to these problems.[100]

Contrary, then, to what the diffusionist would have us believe, the hard fact of technological diffusion, as these members of the developed European business community are well aware, is not the essentially simple matter of diffusing technological development aid from the more developed to the less developed countries. Still less, of course, is the problem of technological diffusion and economic development one of cultural resistance derived from traditionalism or from Hoselitz' pattern variables. If these strong and developed European economies cannot find a European solution to the real developmental problem posed by the technological gap (rather than to the fancied one of the diffusionists), what hope do the weak and underdeveloped economies caught in the same system have to find such a solution?[101] It is surely no accident that among European and previously underdeveloped countries, it is only in the socialist countries—the Soviet Union and China—that a "solution to these problems" has been found.

*Institutions:* The past, present, and future diffusion of institutions and values from developed to underdeveloped areas is a fact beyond question. The construction of an entire theory of economic development on this foundation is another matter. In addition to Manning Nash, who is probably best classified in this category— although he rejects diffusionism in its crudest "pitchforking"

form as he calls it—theorists concerned with the developed countries' diffusion of institutions and values, and the underdeveloped
recipients' resistance to them, have been well represented in the
pages of *EDCC*.[102] Technically, diffusionist theory might deal
with the diffusion of any kind of institutions or values. In practice,
however, the diffusionist school has concentrated its attention
on the diffusion of old-fashioned or newfangled liberalism
(though they rarely call it this)—which is, indeed, most of what
has been diffused from the metropolitan to the now underdeveloped countries during the last century. Consequently, I shall
concentrate attention on the diffusion of liberalism, in its economic, political, and social forms. Moreover, the pattern variables
of universality, achievement orientation, and functional specificity
with which Hoselitz identifies economic development are little
more than liberalism recast into technical sounding jargon. This
is what Hoselitz apparently would like to see diffused to transform underdevelopment into development. Does diffusionism
constitute an adequate development theory, and does the diffusion of liberalism or of anything else serve as an effective economic
development policy?

Economic liberalism was and is diffused, not in general, but
under very specific and particular circumstances. Its exportation
from the metropolis is an expression of the particular interests
of those who diffuse it, as its importation by the underdeveloped
countries is an expression of the particular interests of those
who are acculturating to it. The specific circumstances of and
particular interests in the diffusion and acculturation of liberalism,
like anything else, were and still are determined by the structure
and development of the economic, social, and political system
within which it occurs. The German economist Friedrich List
reported in the 1840's that an American Supreme Court Justice
had observed, in regard to one of liberalism's most important
tenets, that like most of Great Britain's other products, the free
trade doctrine was produced primarily for export.[103] A few years
later, U.S. President, General Ulysses S. Grant observed that

for centuries England has relied on protection, has carried it to
extremes, and has obtained satisfactory results from it. There is no

doubt that it is to this system that it owes its present strength. After two centuries, England has found it convenient to adopt free trade because it thinks that protection can no longer offer it anything. Very well, then, Gentlemen, my knowledge of my country leads me to believe that within two hundred years, when America has gotten all it can out of protection, it too will adopt free trade.[104]

President Grant only erred by a century: since World War II, that is, since it achieved the unrivaled industrial supremacy and near monopoly in the world which Britain had attained a century before, the United States both directly and through its controlling influence in international agencies, such as GATT, the International Monetary Fund, and the World Bank, has been most adamant in exporting free trade. Free trade, like free enterprise, is protective monopoly under another name—as Frederick Clairmonte has so well shown.[105]

The circumstances and interests leading to the underdeveloped countries' ready acculturation to international free trade and domestic economic liberalism in the nineteenth century—and to free trade in technology and free enterprise in the twentieth—can be summarized just as clearly:

> The doctrine of liberalism, imported from Europe, thus found fertile ground in our country [Chile] and grew vigorously. It constituted the theoretical basis to re-enforce the interest of the controlling forces, inasmuch as it represented and expressed its desires.[106]

Another more specific and thorough observation is worth quoting at length:

> The pressure groups who controlled the economic policy of the country were decidedly freetraders: they were more freetrader than Courcelle-Seneuil, the famous and respected leader of doctrinaire freetradism: they were definitely more Catholic than the Pope. . . . The mining exporters of the North of the country were freetraders. This policy was not fundamentally due to reasons of doctrine —though they also had these—but rather to the simple reason that these gentlemen were blessed with common sense. They exported copper, silver, nitrates and other minerals . . . they were paid in pound sterling or dollars. . . . It is hard to conceive of an altruism or a farsighted or prophetic vision which would lead these

exporters to pay export and import duties with a view to the possible industrialization of the country.

Veliz goes on to describe how the agricultural and livestock exporters and the big import houses operated in terms of the same logic. He adds:

> Here then is the powerful coalition of strong interests which dominated the economic policy of Chile during the past century and part of the present one. None of these three had the very least interest in Chile industrializing. They monopolized the three powers at all levels; economic power, political power, and social prestige.[107]

Aldo Ferter finds the same pattern in nineteenth-century Argentina:

> The merchants and livestock owners, who were the dynamic forces in the development of the littoral, were chiefly interested in the expansion of exports. Free trade thus became the philosophy and practical policy of these groups. . . . Free exports also meant freedom to import.[108]

Ferrer returns to discuss the Argentina of our day after its supposed take-off into industrialization during the 1930's and 1940's, and after the expulsion of Peron and the abrogation of his policy in the 1950's by these same groups and their foreign, now primarily American, allies who instituted the policy of the International Monetary Fund instead:

> In January of 1959, Argentina began the application of a stabilization plan. . . . At the same time the exchange rate structure was liberalized, and the peso was devalued. . . . Devaluation has become, moreover, a tool of economic policy explicitly designed to change the domestic price structure in favor of the export sector. . . . The difficulties of this kind of readjustment, in view of the objective conditions obtaining in the Argentinian economy as well as in the world market, are reflected in the fact that stagnation has not been overcome and that the rigidities of the economic system which determine it, far from being on the way to solution, have become even more serious. . . . The financial and monetary policy . . . has been accompanied by a strongly regressive redistribution of income. . . . There has been a strong business contraction. . . . The deficit in the balance of payments and the government budget and

the rise in price have not been resolved. . . . In fact, the stabilization plan and the recommendations received from abroad have simply served as a tool in the hands of the sectors who saw their immediate and long term interests served by the impact of the policy followed on the distribution of income and the *backward* structural adjustment of the Argentinian economy.[109]

Two additional well known examples are instructive as to how economic liberalism in the domestic economies of the underdeveloped countries promotes monopoly and thereby the underdevelopment of the majority. One example is the nineteenth-century breakup, in the name of liberalism, of communally held Indian land, its distribution into private ownership and consequent monopoly concentration during the epoch of liberal reform—a concentration which far exceeded that of the autocratic colonial times.[110] Another example is the currently ever greater monopoly concentration of finance, commerce, industry, and (still) of land in underdeveloped countries under the aegis of the "free" world's "free" enterprise.[111] It is clear then that the diffusion and acculturation of economic liberalism between the developed (or developing) metropolitan countries and their underdeveloped satellites—as well as that within the underdeveloped countries—is a response to interests, and produces consequences which can be summed up in a single word: monopoly. Contrary to the elaborate classical and neo-classical theoretical economic edifice that was carefully built up in Manchester (the first city to enter the modern industrial age!) and which is still being assiduously exported and imported by interested parties, the diffusion of economic liberalism has quite consistently contributed its significant share to the establishment, maintenance, and strengthening of economic monopoly, both on the national and international levels. Through this monopoly, economic liberalism has contributed to the economic development *of those who diffuse it*; to, as the United Nations Economic Commission for Latin America calls it, the limited "outward-oriented development" [112] of the capitals of the underdeveloped countries; and to ever more underdevelopment for the world's majority who were and are liberally forced to suffer its consequences.

The diffusion of political liberalism which accompanied and

followed the spread of economic liberalism cannot be said to be very different. Since the consequences of the diffusion of political liberalism are clear in the above analysis of economic liberalism, and since they are explicit in our daily newspapers, it is unnecessary to rely on Lenin's analysis of the relations between economic and political power and institutions in his *The State and Revolution*, or to go into it here.[118] The only remark that needs to be made is that the relations between economic and political power —again discussed by President Eisenhower in terms of the "military-industrial complex" [114] and by C. Wright Mills[115]—are even more intimate in the underdeveloped countries than they are in the developed ones which are discussed by Lenin, Eisenhower, and Mills.

Although it does not go by that name, we may also observe the diffusion of and acculturation to "social liberalism." This modern liberalism takes the form primarily of promoting "social mobility" and "middle classes" in the underdeveloped countries. Like the others, social liberalism is advertised as leading to a more open, democratic society capable of greater and faster economic development. We have observed above that Hoselitz' pattern variable approach lends support to this thesis, and that Johnson and Germani, among many others, propose the promotion of middle classes and of social mobility as development theory and policy. Johnson diffuses it from the United States,[116] and Germani acculturates to it in Argentina when he writes under the title of "A Strategy for Promoting Social Mobility." [117] Like economic and political liberalism, social liberalism is, however, more aptly described as individual liberalism. It is the liberty of a few individuals to move, to monopolize, and thereby restrict the development of the economic, political, and social whole. Those persons in underdeveloped countries who have migrated from country to city or moved from a lower economic and social status to a higher one often say in one way or another that they have made their own individual reform or revolution. In so doing they express not only the conservatism which reflects their desire to maintain their newly gained position but also a fundamental social scientific truth which seems to escape the attention of diffusionists and others: "social" mobility is really *individual* mobility and does not transform social structures: rather, a change in the social structure may render possible *social* mobility and economic development.

As with the other liberalisms, the evidence is accumulating (supplied in part by Hoselitz himself, as we saw above)[118] that the diffusion to the underdeveloped countries of the institutions and values of social liberalism is highly selective at both the diffusing and acculturating ends. The selective diffusion is determined by the structure of the international system, including the structural relations of the sending and receiving societies and sub-societies within it. Far from aiding the development of the underdeveloped countries, social liberalism hinders it. As we noted above, social mobility and the rise of the middle classes in the underdeveloped countries renders the distribution of income not more but less equal;[119] and it provides economic and political support not for changing but for maintaining and reinforcing the structure of the economic, political, and social status quo.[120]

## Theoretical Adequacy

As with our examination of the first mode, our review of the empirical validity of propositions in the second mode offers a good vantage point from which to evaluate their associated theoretical formulations. Like the first mode, the diffusionist approach suffers from serious theoretical shortcomings because of its failure to take adequate account of the determinant structure and development of the social system within which diffusion, acculturation, and economic development and cultural change take place. Perhaps the most important theoretical fault of diffusionism is that it is premised on dualism instead of on structural and developmental holism. In the pages of *EDCC*, the theory of dualism itself has been most explicitly advanced and defended by Benjamin Higgins,[121] who rejects the social dualism of Boeke[122] only to argue that dualism has a technological and economic basis. Reflecting its widespread acceptance, dualism is explicitly expressed in *EDCC* by writers and reviewers who span the globe.[123]

Although explicit reliance on the dual society or economy thesis is usually reserved for the analysis of underdeveloped countries alone, the dualist thesis is implicit in the entire analysis of development reviewed here.

All three modes of analysis seek to analyze both the differences between developed and underdeveloped countries as well as the inequalities within the latter by attributing separate and largely independent economic and social structures to the developed and underdeveloped sectors, each with its own separate history and dynamic, if any. (Frequently, as we have seen, the one part is denied any history at all.) Jaques Lambert for example argues in his *Os Dois Brasis* [The Two Brazils] that

> the Brazilians are divided into two systems of economic and social organization. . . . These two societies did not evolve at the same rate . . . they are separated by centuries. . . . The dual economy and the dual social structure which accompanies it are neither new nor characteristically Brazilian—they exist in all unequally developed countries.[124]

In this sense, the plantation or mining sector of an underdeveloped country is viewed as an enclave of the developed metropolitan economy on foreign soil. The "enclave" is presumed not to be a real part of the supposedly isolated subsistence economy of the underdeveloped country itself; and it is thought to exercise little if any economic and social influence on this isolated sector in the present, and none in the past.[125] Similarly, in a supposedly somewhat less underdeveloped country, part of the population, usually the indigenous inhabitants, are said to be outside the market economy and marginal to the national society and to the world as a whole.[126] This conception of a dual economy and society, whether the duality be attributed to cultural, social, technological, economic, or other causes, then gives rise to the diffusionist theory and policy regarding the diffusion of capital, technology, and institutions.

The dualist theory and the diffusionist and other theses based on it are inadequate because the supposed structural duality is contrary to both historical and contemporary reality:[127] the *entire* social fabric of the underdeveloped countries has long since been penetrated and transformed by, and integrated into, the world embracing system of which it is an integral part. The facts of this penetration have been presented and the thesis of the consequent transformation and integration has been persuasively argued for Meso-America by Eric Wolf;[128] for India by Marx,[129] Dutt,[130] and Desai;[131] for China by Owen Lattimore;[132] for Africa by Woddis,[133] Suret-Canale,[134] and Mamadou Dia;[135] and even for Indonesia, the birthplace of dualism, by Wertheim and Geertz,[136] the latter formerly a research associate of Higgins and now a colleague of Hoselitz.

More specifically, as Eric Wolf [137] has taken great pains to point out for Meso-America and this writer for Brazil,[138] it is not true, as diffusionists and others implicitly or explicitly maintain, that the isolation of indigenous peoples, peasants and others, declines over time until they are completely integrated in the national society, which then is no longer dual. On the contrary, the degree of integration and other aspects of the relationship which these peoples have with others at home and abroad varies in ways which are determined primarily by the structure and development of the national and international capitalist system, and secondarily by these peoples' own very partially successful efforts to defend themselves against the exploitative consequences of this system.

Dualism is not only theoretically inadequate because it misrepresents and fails to analyze the capitalist system on the international, national, and local levels, but also because it fails to adhere to the standards of holism, structuralism, and historicity. Dualists contravene holism in explicitly setting up two or more theoretical wholes to confront a single social whole which they cannot or will not see. As for structuralism, dualists fall far short because if they see and deal with any structure at all it is at best the structures of the parts. They do not deal with, and even deny the existence of, the structure of the whole system through which the parts are related—that is, the structure which determines the duality of wealth and poverty, of one culture and another, and so on. As to the historical development of the social phenomena they study, dualists and diffusionists either deny any history to one part altogether or, observe its ongoing social change without the historical perspective necessary to interpret it adequately; and they steadfastly abstain, of course, from giving any consideration whatsoever to the historical development of the social system of which diffusing donor and acculturating recipient are but parts. Little wonder then that diffusionists and other dualists who only look at appearances misunderstand their significance and misjudge their consequences for economic development and cultural change.

As Marx said, science would be pointless if the outward appearance of things were to correspond to their inner significance. Thus the task of social scientific theory, which dualist and other advocates of the three modes reviewed here fail to pursue, is not to see how different the parts are, but on the contrary, to study what relates the parts to each other in order to be able to explain why they are different or dual. If the policy of economic development and cultural change is really meant to eliminate these differences—or the undesirable ones among them—then its task must be to change the relationships that produce these differences: that is, it must change the structure of the *entire* social system which gives rise to the relations and therefore to the differences of the dual society.

The unfortunate, though not inexplicable, fact is that the theory and policy reviewed here is moving away from this task. With their supposedly structural and historical ideal typical approach, the disciples of Weber are leaving their teacher's scientific scope and method behind and dedicating themselves to no more than its cruel caricature. Similarly, dualists and diffusionists-acculturationists are corrupting the vision and work of one of their principal teachers of recent times, Robert Redfield. In creating the ideal type of the folk community, and in analyzing diffusion along the folk-urban continuum,[139] as well as in his later works on the relations between high and low culture,[140] Redfield, no doubt unintentionally, encouraged contemporary students of economic development and cultural change to adopt a dualism and diffusionism which he himself rejected in his later years.

Redfield taught that in situations of culture contact diffusion is never a one-way affair. In this respect, then, the diffusionist emphasis on diffusion from the metropolis to the periphery, and the virtual exclusion of the reverse is a departure from Redfield, as well as being unacceptable on other theoretical grounds. Moreover, although Redfield was far from being a structuralist (although he spared no pains to emphasize the need for holism in social scientific theory), he did call our attention to the structural determination of mutual diffusion between, for instance, high and low culture within a single social system. Nonetheless, Redfield's lessons seem not to have come to the attention of that majority of diffusionists who employ his terminology while distorting his ideas.

Finally, it was Redfield more than anyone else in recent times who insisted that there are no peasants without the city to which they are tied and which defines them as peasants, and that there can be no city without its peasants or their equivalent.[141] It is clear, then, that at least the later Redfield himself recognized and emphasized the *holistic interdependence and unity* of the dual ideal typical poles and social sectors he made so popular. It may be lamentable that Redfield did not extend this holism to the larger social system and to historical evolution, although his concern with the relations between high and low culture in his last years may have been a step in that direction. It is certainly more than lamentable, however, that so many of his diffusionist and dualist followers have abandoned their mentor's empirical realism and scientific holism and have substituted the most simplistic and crassly nonholistic diffusionism.

*Policy Effectiveness*

As a policy of economic development and cultural change diffusionism has been largely ineffective. The centuries long contact and diffusion between the metropolitan countries and the now underdeveloped ones has failed to result in the economic development of the latter. Nor has any diffusion from the capitals to the provinces of the underdeveloped countries brought about the development of these hinterlands. New technology may have increased diffusion beyond that of certain times in the past but surely not beyond the diffusion of initial contact times which, far from initiating the development of, initiated the underdevelopment of the now underdeveloped countries. More diffusion, per se, does not generate more development. Moreover, the diffusion which follows in the train of new roads, buses, transistor radios, etc., is not increasing the economic development of the recipient regions. Often it has helped to sink them into even deeper and more hopeless underdevelopment.

Conceived in its present form, diffusionism is inherently ineffective as a policy of economic development and cultural change. For it is not so much diffusion which produces a change in the social structure as it is the transformation of the social structure which permits effective diffusion. Development, underdevelopment, and diffusion are all a function of the social structure. In order for the underdeveloped parts of the world to develop, the structure of the world social system must change—on the international, national, and local levels. This structural change, however, cannot be brought about by diffusion. On the contrary, the structure of the system itself on all these levels determines the amount, nature, direction, and consequences of the past and present diffusion—a diffusion which has so far produced development only for the few and underdevelopment for the many, and by all indications will continue doing so. Consequently, the structure of this system has to change in order to permit development for all and to permit diffusion to contribute to that development.

## The Psychological Approach

Nash introduces the third approach as the one "most profitably pursued," and which leads to "smaller scale hypotheses, to a prospective rather than a retrospective view of social change." Furthermore, Nash writes:

> These papers I commend to your attention as examples of the dialectic of social knowledge, the confrontation of bold assertion against fact, and the incorporation of more general fact in ever bolder, more elegant assertion.[142]

Nevertheless, a year later, comparing the psychological (and to some extent the first) mode of approach with his own second mode as published in *EDCC*, Nash seems to have had second thoughts:

> The "specific factor" analysis of social requisites (like lack of entrepreneurship, low achievement motivation, particularism, capital

shortage, etc.) is not likely to provide anything systematically relevant to an understanding of growth. . . .[143]

When Nash says that this mode of analysis leads to smaller scale hypotheses, he is quite right, as we will see below. However, it should be noted here that the first two modes were seen to be inadequate precisely because the scale of their theory and hypotheses is already too small to treat adequately the dimension and structure of the social system which gives rise to both development and underdevelopment.

As any historian of social thought will recall, Marx turned Hegel on his head and substituted historical materialism for idealism. Further, he worked with relatively large-scale theory and hypotheses which he derived from his examination of the capitalist system as a whole as he saw it. Being a true holist, Marx was led—inevitably as Parsons pointed out above—to the observation that exploitation is a necessary basis of this system and to the conclusion that such a basis generates the polarization of the system. Since this conclusion was not palatable to Social Democrats such as Weber and Durkheim, whose disciple Parsons became, they set out to construct an alternative theory of the social system by starting with its parts rather than with the whole—a procedure which, as Parsons says, inevitably de-emphasizes exploitation and makes the system appear to be not polarizing or disintegrative but integrative instead. Nonetheless, although Weber and Durkheim intentionally and explicitly abandoned the approach, conclusions, and policy of Marx, they still retained strong emphasis on the determinative importance of social structure, and in the case of Weber especially, of history as well. Even Hoselitz, being directly as well as via Parsons a disciple of Weber, and an advocate of the first mode of analysis, retains considerable interest in the role of social structure (he even puts it in his title) despite the attraction that the third mode approach of David McClelland, although apparently not of Everett Hagen, holds for him.[144]

The pioneering service, as Nash's co-editor Robert Chin calls it, of these latter students of economic development and cultural change is precisely that they drop all pretense and practice of social scientific structuralism. They "Freudianize" Weber to such an extent that they no longer follow him at all. In fact, they specifically deny the importance of social structure and reject structural analysis. Although Hagen puts the word "social" into his title, he is quite frank in his preface in explaining that his theory is not social at all but rather psychological—or really psychiatric.[145] McClelland, reviewing Hagen's book in *EDCC*, agrees: he calls it "A Psychological Approach to Economic Development," albeit one which he finds to be not up to his own standards.[146] Not to be outdone, McClelland is quite explicit in telling his readers that not the social structure as Weber had it, nor even assignment of and reward in social roles based on achievement (as in Hoselitz' view), but only a high degree of individual motivation or need for achievement is the alpha and omega of economic development and cultural change:

> In its most general terms, the hypothesis states that a society with a generally high level of *n* Achievement will produce more energetic entrepreneurs who, in turn, produce more rapid economic development . . . it must satisfy us to have learned that high *n* Achievement leads people to behave in most of the ways they should behave if they are to fulfill the entrepreneurial role successfully as it has been defined by economists, historians, sociologists. . . . The whole view of history shifts once the importance of the achievement motive is recognized. For a century we have been dominated by Social Darwinism, by the implicit or explicit notion that man is a creature of his environment, whether natural or social. Marx thought so in advocating economic determinism, in arguing that man's psychology is shaped in the last analysis by the conditions under which he must work. Even Freud thought so in teaching that civilization was a reaction to man's primitive urges and to the repressive force of social institutions beginning with the family. Practically all social scientists have in the past generations begun with society and tried to create man in its image. Even Toynbee's theory of history is essentially one of environmental challenges, though he recognizes that states of mind can create internal challenges.[147]

In his contribution to the volume edited by Nash and Chin, Mc-Clelland goes on to be even more explicit.

What is needed is a glacial shift in Western and particularly American social thinking. Ever since Darwin, social scientists have almost unconsciously started with the premise that the environment is primary and that the human organism somehow learns to adapt to it. . . . Consequently if one wants to change anything really fundamentally, he must start by modifying material arrangements in the environment which in turn will gradually re-shape institutions and eventually ideas. Yet the evidence, as in the present instance, is very strong that it is just as often and perhaps more often initiated the other way around. . . . This is just one more piece of evidence to support the growing conviction among social scientists that it is values, motives, or psychological forces that determine ultimately the rate of economic and social development. . . . *The Achieving Society* suggests that ideas are in fact more important in shaping history than purely materialistic arrangements.[148]

We have returned full circle to Hegel. Except that McClelland's prescriptions for progress are not quite Hegel's. In his book's final chapter entitled "Accelerating Economic Growth," McClelland summarizes his prescriptions in his sub-titles: "Increasing Other-Directedness and Market Morality"; "Increasing *n* Achievement"; "Decreasing Father Dominance"; "Protestant Conversion"; "Catholic and Communist Reform Movements"; "Effects of Education on *n* Achievement"; "Reorganizing Fantasy Life"; "Utilizing Existing *n* Achievement Resources More Effectively"; and he offers a final recommendation:

> So we end on a practical note: a plan for accelerating economic growth through mobilizing more effectively the high *n* Achievement resources of a developed country to select and work directly with the scarcer high *n* Achievement resources in underdeveloped countries particularly in small and medium scale businesses located in provincial areas. . . .[149]

This new pioneering service was undoubtedly inspired by Weber's emphasis on values in *The Protestant Ethic and the Spirit of Capitalism*[150] and reinforced by Schumpeter's emphasis on entrepreneurship in *The Theory of Economic Development*.[151] The post-World War II revival of academic interest in economic development was soon followed by a return to the letter if not to the spirit of Weber and Schumpeter. Books and articles on the role of religion and values in economic development appeared in great numbers, not a few of them in *EDCC*, as cited above.[152] Simultaneously, Harvard University set up a Research Center in Entrepreneurial History and a journal, *Explorations in Entrepreneurial History*. Papers on entrepreneurship as a crucial factor in economic development and cultural change were published in *EDCC* and elsewhere.[153] The increasing evidence against the supposed role of the Schumpeterian entrepreneur in economic development, not only in underdeveloped countries but even in the nineteenth-century United States,[154] has not prevented the psychological idealizers of economic development from going on to advance theories such as those of Hagen and McClelland. Nor has it prevented *EDCC* from following in their footsteps to publish an entire series of studies reinterpreting the world to show the supposed importance of the achievement motive.[155] Furthermore, *EDCC's* reviewer of *The Achieving Society*, S. N. Eisenstadt, concludes:

> the fact that in discussing this book, we are confronting it with Weber's work, is the measure of the importance of the problems raised by McClelland's endeavor. . . . McClelland has given a very stimulating and important work which anybody interested either in the broader problem of the impact of motivational orientation on society or in the more specific problem of economic development cannot ignore.[156]

To his and *EDCC's* credit, John H. Kunkel has recently evaluated this "pioneering service":

> As long as man's activities are considered to be a function of values or personality, little attention need be directed to the immediate surrounding social environment, since it is not so much the present social structure as that of the past which is most involved in the formation of values and personality. The delineation of societal prerequisites of economic development, according to this view, can accomplish no more than prepare the ground for industrialization years, if not decades, in the future. However, as soon as behavior is considered to be a function largely of the surrounding social structure, both past *and* present, which affects behavior through the continuously operating determination of reinforcing and discriminative stimuli, the present social system takes on great importance. The

behavioral prerequisites of economic development can be created only through alterations of the social structure, or certain elements of it, viewed broadly and including the economic system of a society. . . . There is no foundation, on theoretical grounds, for the pessimistic outlook concerning the capacity of the underdeveloped countries to industrialize in a short period of time. Pessimistic conclusions regarding the time necessary for the preparation of the right psychological conditions for economic development are based, essentially, on an incorrect conception of man and on the disregard of principles of behavior formation and maintenance derived from experimental psychology.[157]

Nevertheless, in his contribution to the collection of papers edited by Nash and Chin which exemplify this third mode approach, Kunkel's criticism is based largely on psychological principles and limited essentially to methodological criticism of the third mode's empirical assertions.[158] So is Eisenstadt's criticism in his review of McClelland's book.[159] Furthermore, Kunkel's proposed alternative in his contribution to *EDCC* is limited to suggesting that behavioristic methodology can overcome the methodological shortcomings of the approach exemplified by Hagen and McClelland.[160] In this connection, Kunkel rightly observes:

Hagen makes much use of personality as an "internal state" of individuals. The characteristics of the "internal state" are derived from psychoanalytic theory, and then used to support the theory and the hypothesized relations among observed facts and inferred characteristics. When psychoanalytic concepts and theories are used in the study of economic development, problems of validating the concepts make any casual generalization difficult to test and accept on bases other than faith. . . . The casual analysis is inadequate. Hagen infers causes from effects, but no evidence is presented to validate the inference made. . . . McClelland postulates a variety of needs as components of a person's "internal state," but this method of analysis involves inferences from behavior (e.g., the writing of stories based on TAT pictures) which are difficult to validate, in order to explain the data collected by McClelland and his associates.[161]

Both Kunkel and Eisenstadt find that the work of these students of economic development and cultural change is deficient in that it fails to establish a methodologically adequate efficient cause between the supposedly causative psychological states and the supposedly derivative economic development. Kunkel's purpose in his contribution to *EDCC* is to provide such an efficient causative relation which is not dependent on untestable inferences about internal states of mind.[162]

Whatever the methodological merits or demerits of Kunkel's resort to behaviorism, it is as limited to generating small scale hypotheses, as Nash calls them, and to recommending small scale changes as is the methodology it seeks to substitute. Kunkel himself concludes:

> If it is true that striving behavior, like any other, is shaped through differential reinforcement [such as reward and punishment by parents, as Kunkel tells us elsewhere], there is no reason why an internal state . . . should have to be postulated as an essential element in the analysis of economic development. . . . Various selected elements of the societal environment are amenable to change today, thereby making possible the shaping of behavior patterns necessary for economic development. . . . Since usually only a few aspects of the societal environment can be altered, present efforts to create behavioral prerequisites must begin on a small scale.[163]

This suggests that, to evaluate the theoretical adequacy of the third mode approach, we must bring still other criteria to bear, such as the historicity and holistic structuralism by which we already examined the first two approaches.

As editor of a collection of works which exemplify the third mode, Manning Nash holds that of the three modes he is able to visualize, this third one is "most profitably pursued." One of its profitable aspects is that it leads "to a prospective rather than a retrospective view of social change." That is, as we may infer, Nash thinks that the social scientists working in terms of the third mode are performing a pioneering service not only because they abandon Weber's structuralism, leaving Bert Hoselitz behind as well—and he after all not only retains some structuralism but also is world renowned as an economic historian—but also because in not looking back, these pioneers leave behind them Weber's retrospective and historical approach and analysis.

However, Nash does not confine himself simply to lauding

this effort and to recommending that students of economic development and cultural change forget about the past history of the underdeveloped countries concerned. Instead, he goes on to deny that the underdeveloped countries have any history. The third approach, he says, poses three main theoretical problems:

> 1. To systematically take account of the varieties of *traditional* societies, 2. To seek out the sources of resistance . . . among the various species of *traditionality*, 3. [To study why a society may or may not come] to rest somewhere between its *initial base* and modernity.[164]

In other words, underdeveloped societies have no history, they have traditionally been the way they are now, which is underdeveloped. This is indeed a "bold assertion"; but once it faces "confrontation with fact" this claim is clearly revealed to be a falsification. How could Nash make such an assertion after having done the fieldwork for his doctoral dissertation in a community descended from a people who are world renowned for their history, the last seventy years of which he studied, and after having entitled his book *Machine Age Maya*?[165] How is it a pioneering service for the practitioners and champions of the third mode to take less and less account of the history of the underdeveloped countries they presume to study (especially after having delved into it here and there themselves), and finally to end up denying that the underdeveloped countries and underdevelopment even have history? For whom is this a pioneering service?

The answers emerge if we apply the criterion of structural holism to the question of the theoretical adequacy of the third mode approach and if we inquire into the effectiveness of the policy of economic development and cultural change to which this approach gives rise.

Kunkel correctly notes in regard to both the theory and the policy of the third mode that "little attention need be directed to the immediate surrounding social environment since it is not the present social structure which matters." But the critic of this approach is hardly as explicit and clear as its exponent, McClelland himself: "Ideas are in fact more important in shaping history than purely materialistic arrangements . . . of his [man's] environment, whether natural or social." The third mode of approaching economic development and cultural change, then, represents perhaps the ultimate step in pioneering progress away from classical scientific structural holism. The present economic, social, and political structure does not matter at all: There is no need to change the contemporary status quo.

What, then, according to these purveyors of dialectic social knowledge (as Nash terms their service) is to be done; and how effectively and for whom does their policy of promoting economic development and cultural change work? McClelland tells us what is to be done: "Increasing *n* Achievement" . . . "Protestant Conversion" . . . "Education" . . . "Reorganizing Fantasy Life." As McClelland himself recognizes, not only Marx, but even such progressive students as Spencer, the father of Social Darwinism, Toynbee, the father of neo-Thomism, and Freud, the father of individual psychiatry, and all of their intellectual children, never were progressive enough to believe and maintain that so deeply ingrained a social and economic condition of society could be changed simply by having more of its individuals taught to get a hold of themselves and raise their need for achievement, as McClelland would have it; or by not letting themselves be beaten down by adversity, as Hagen would have it; or even by having teachers and parents tell children more hero stories so that when the latter grow up they might be heroic developers themselves. This degree of progress and progressiveness had to await the coming of David McClelland and his disciples.

McClelland gives credit to one source of co-revelation of his vision of economic development and cultural change: the Communists, particularly the Chinese ones.[166] They receive no credit for following the teachings of Marx or other social scientists, the validity of whose theory McClelland denies; no credit for changing any economic, social, or political structure, the need for which change McClelland denies; nor any credit for making a revolution, which McClelland does not deem worthy of mention. Instead, they receive credit for realizing and putting into practice the truth that ideas and *n* Achievement promote economic development: the Chinese are achieving faster economic development than the Indians, McClelland points out.[167] On the basis of what economic, social, and political structure, he doesn't say: the Chinese have more $n$ Achievement and $n$ Power.[168] According to McClelland, it does not matter how that structure determines the distribution of power and the direction of achievement. Despite this generous bow to the Chinese Communists, we need no great insightfulness to discern the allegiance and effectiveness of an economic development policy which—following the example of such highly motivated members of the Cambridge, Massachusetts, academic community as W. W. Rostow,[169] McGeorge Bundy, Arthur Schlesinger, Jr., and perhaps David McClelland himself— promotes $n$ Achievement and reorganization of fantasy life within the existing economic, social, and political structure, at home or abroad.

In complimenting the Communists, McClelland fails to give due credit where it really belongs. It is Frank Buchman and his worldwide movement for Moral Rearmament (MRA) who preached precisely the policy of economic development and cultural change now clothed in academic gown by David McClelland. His policy advice to developers is to take their eyes off and leave as is the economic, social, and political structure of the status quo; prepare instead each man for himself, to rearm morally and spiritually to face the difficult road of economic development, cultural change, and social progress that lies ahead. The political character and effectiveness of this development policy is amply demonstrated by its practitioners who include such renowned practical dialecticians, progressive servants, and self-declared MRA supporters as ex-Chancellor Adenauer of Germany, ex-Premier Kishi of Japan, ex-Prime Minister Tshombe of Katanga and the Congo, and the second President of Brazil after the 1964 military coup, General Costa e Silva.

## Conclusion

Having examined the three modes of approach to and analysis of the problems of economic development and cultural change separately, we can briefly evaluate them conjointly. What first forces itself into view is the wide and deep similarity in the extent of the three modes' empirical inaccuracy, theoretical inadequacy, and ineffectiveness of policy. Yet this similarity should not surprise us. It is no more than the reflection of their fundamental similarity in points of departure, both ideologically and analytically. Thus, the first mode is ideal-typical in that it sets up the supposedly typical characteristics of development. The second mode concerns itself with how these typical characteristics of the first mode are supposedly diffused from the developed countries to the underdeveloped ones. Finally, the third mode, and herein lies its pioneering service, tells us how the typical characteristics that are identified in the first and diffused according to the second mode are to be acculturated by the underdeveloped countries if they wish to develop. This, in a nutshell, is the sum total of this received theory and analysis of economic development and cultural change; it is the alpha and omega of the possibilities that Manning Nash can visualize: it is thanks to this limitation of his, if not of theory and reality, that Nash manages to arrive at the third mode, as he says, "via the argument of residue."

The pioneers of these three modes have progressed; to social dualism, they have added sociological dualism. Their whole theory and theorizing is split down the middle. They see one set of characteristics, take note of one social structure if any; construct one theory for one part of what has been one world economic and social system for half a millennium, and construct another pattern and theory for the other part. And all that in the name of universalism. They argue that one part of the system, Western Europe and Northern America, diffuses and helps the other part, Asia, Africa, and South America, to develop. They similarly argue that those national metropolises of these three continents that have already received the benefits of this diffusion in turn help pull up their own hinterland behind them. They argue that the take-off by the underdeveloped countries and their national metropolises is hindered by the drag on them of their slow and backward hinterlands. Curiously, though fortunately, except for the most irresponsible among them, they do not argue similarly that the take-off and development of the world capitalist metropolis in Europe and North America is hindered by the drag of its underdeveloped hinterland in Asia, Africa, and Latin America. They ask where the capital for the development of the national metropolises of the underdeveloped countries is to come from and say it must and will come from the developed countries; which is wrong, since in fact it comes from the domestic internal colonies of these national metropolises. They ask where the capital for the development of the already developed countries came from and say it came from themselves; which is also wrong since much, and at the time the critical part, of it came from the consequently now underdeveloped countries. As with most of the remainder of the developed countries' universalism, the theoretical universalism of their social science is a pretense and a sham. If we may borrow something from the arsenal of this mode's pioneers, the theorists of all three modes of economic development and cultural change who like to call themselves universally theoretical dualists, are intellectual and political schizophrenics.[170]

To render the real significance and value of this highly developed conventional wisdom still clearer, we may characterize it —no less exhaustively than Nash summarizes it—by the caricature of the twin mythological supports of the society that produced it, which Steinberg put on the cover of a *New Yorker*: Santa Claus and Sigmund Freud. American society rests on and revolves around these twin gods, Steinberg suggests, and we may add, so does the ideology of economic development and cultural change which that same society produces and exports. How are the people in the underdeveloped countries to achieve economic development? By waiting for Christmas and then accepting the gift of diffusion from Santa Claus in the North. What gift does Santa Claus bear for the peoples of the underdeveloped countries? The latest message from Sigmund Freud. If only the people of the mythically characterized underdeveloped world will, as we did, learn to worship at the altar of these twin Gods, they too will change culturally and develop economically. Can it be any wonder that the people of the real underdeveloped world must, and will, look beyond what some others dream possible to find a theory of economic development and cultural change which is empirically congruent with, theoretically adequate for, and politically acceptable to, their reality, needs, and desires?

The direction in which to look for an alternative theory of

economic development and change that is more adequate for the underdeveloped countries is suggested by the common shortcomings of the three-part approach of received theory reviewed here. Firstly, where this approach is empirically wrong about the past and present reality of the underdeveloped part of the world, the developed part of the world, and the world as a whole; an adequate alternative theory will have to come to terms with the history and contemporary reality of development and underdèvelopment. Secondly, where the approach is theoretically inadequate because it cannot identify the determinant social whole, because it takes account neither of the history of the underdeveloped part nor of its relations with the developed part, and least of all of the world as a whole, and because it does not conform to the structure of that world's social system; an alternative theory must reflect the structure and development of the system which has given rise to, now maintains, and still increases both structural development and structural underdevelopment as simultaneous and mutually produced manifestations of the same historical process. Thirdly, where the development policy of this approach is ever more politically conservative and counsels accepting the structural status quo with folded hands while waiting for others' gifts with open hands, an alternative policy for economic development and cultural change will have to be politically ever more revolutionary and help the peoples of the underdeveloped countries to take the destruction of this structure and the development of another system, into their own hands. If the developed countries cannot diffuse development, development theory, or development policy to the underdeveloped countries, then the people of these countries will have to develop them by themselves. These three modes of approach are the emperor's clothes, which have served to hide his naked imperialism. Rather than fashioning the emperor a new suit, these people will have to dethrone him and clothe themselves.

## NOTES

1. Manning Nash, "Introduction, Approaches to the Study of Economic Growth" in "Psycho-Cultural Factors in Asian Economic

Growth," (Issue Editors: Manning Nash and Robert Chin), *Journal of Social Issues*, Vol. 29, No. 1 (January 1963), p. 5.

2. Bert F. Hoselitz, *Sociological Factors in Economic Development* (Glencoe: The Free Press, 1960). Hoselitz is the founder and editor of *EDCC*.

3. Talcott Parsons, *Structure and Process in Modern Societies* (Glencoe: The Free Press, 1960).

4. See especially, Marion J. Levy, Jr., "Contrasting Factors in the Modernization of China and Japan," *EDCC*, Vol. 2, No. 3 (October 1953); reprinted in S. Kuznets, W. E. Moore and J. J. Spengler, eds., *Economic Growth: Brazil, India, Japan* (Durham: Duke University Press, 1955). Levy refers to a related theme in his "Some Aspects of Individualism and the Problem of Modernization in China and Japan," *EDCC*, Vol. 10, No. 3 (April 1962).

5. Wilbert Moore and David Feldman, *Labor Commitment and Social Change in Developing Areas* (New York: Social Science Research Council, 1960).

6. Daniel Lerner, *The Passing of Traditional Society: Modernizing the Middle East* (Glencoe: The Free Press, 1958).

7. Everett Hagen, "The Theory of Economic Development," *EDCC*, Vol. 6, No. 3 (April 1957); also see his *On the Theory of Social Change* (Homewood: Dorsey Press, 1962).

8. David McClelland, "A Psychological Approach to Economic Development," *EDCC*, Vol. 12, No. 3 (April 1964); and *The Achieving Society* (Princeton: Van Nostrand, 1961).

9. John H. Kunkel, "Values and Behavior in Economic Development," *EDCC*, Vol. 13, No. 3 (April 1965).

10. Manning Nash, "Introduction," pp. 5–6.

11. Robert Chin, "Preface, A New Social Issue," *Journal of Social Issues, op. cit.*, p. iii.

12. A 111-page essay by Seymour Martin Lipset entitled "Elites, Education, and Entrepreneurship in Latin America," was unfortunately not available to me in time to be included in this review. In this essay, Mr. Lipset, who is probably the most technically skillful and influential contemporary American political sociologist, masterfully constructs a misinterpretation of Latin American development out of all the major and most of the minor empirical, theoretical, and policy errors criticized here. The essay has since been published as Chapter 1, "Values, Education, and Entrepreneurship," in Seymour M. Lipset and Aldo Solari, eds., *Elites in Latin America* (New York: Oxford University Press, 1967).

13. Charles P. Kindleberger, "Review of *The Economy of Turkey; The Economic Development of Guatemala; Report on Cuba,*" *Review of Economics and Statistics,* Vol. 34, No. 4 (November 1952).

14. Talcott Parsons, *The Social System* (Glencoe: The Free Press, 1951).

15. Jeffery Duncan Mitchell, *Dictionary of Sociology* (London: Routledge and Kegan Paul, 1967), pp. 130–131.

16. Bert F. Hoselitz, "Social Structure and Economic Growth," *Economia Internazionale,* Vol. 6, No. 3 (August 1953); reprinted in *Sociological Factors in Economic Development,* Chapter 2. This is not to say, of course, that this approach exhausts the work of Hoselitz, which on the contrary ranges exceptionally widely over the fields of sociology, economics, history, etc. On the other hand, this part of Hoselitz' work organizes and summarizes a very wide range of work by other social scientists.

17. Bert F. Hoselitz, "Social Stratification and Economic Development," *International Social Science Journal,* Vol. 16, No. 2 (1964).

18. In addition to the already cited article by Levy, see for instance, "India's Cultural Values and Economic Development: A Discussion," *EDCC,* Vol. 7, No. 1 (October 1958); Clifford Geertz, "Religious Belief and Economic Behavior in a Central Japanese Town: Some Preliminary Considerations," *EDCC,* Vol. 4, No. 2 (January 1956).

19. James Abegglen, *The Japanese Factory* (Glencoe: The Free Press, 1958).

20. Nicole Delefortrie-Soubeyroux, *Les dirigeants de l'industrie française* (Paris: Armand Colin, 1961).

21. David Granick, *The European Executive* (Garden City: Doubleday, 1962).

22. Ferdynand Zweig, *The British Worker* (Harmondsworth: Penguin Books, 1952); *The Worker in an Affluent Society: Family Life and Industry* (London: Heinemann, 1962); Raymond Williams, *Culture and Society 1780–1950* (Harmondsworth: Penguin Books, 1961).

23. Frederick Clairmonte, *Economic Liberalism and Underdevelopment—Studies in the Disintegration of an Idea* (Bombay and London: Asia Publishing House, 1960).

24. David Granick, *The Red Executive* (Garden City: Doubleday, 1960).

25. Michael Harrington, *The Other America, Poverty in the U.S.* (New York: Macmillan, 1963); Gabriel Kolko, *Wealth and Power in America: An Analysis of Social Class and Income Distribution* (New York: Praeger, 1962).
26. James Abegglen, *The Japanese Factory.*
27. Robert Bellah, *Tokugawa Religion* (Glencoe: The Free Press, 1957).
28. Marion J. Levy, "Contrasting Factors in the Modernization of China and Japan."
29. James Abegglen, *The Japanese Factory.*
30. David McClelland, *The Achieving Society.*
31. C. Wright Mills, *The Power Elite* (New York: Oxford University Press, 1956); Fred J. Cook, *The Warfare State* (New York: Macmillan, 1962); also see Tristan Coffin, *The Armed Society* (Baltimore: Penguin Books, 1964).
32. Eugene Staley, *The Future of Underdeveloped Countries* (New York: Harper, 1964).
33. Walt Whitman Rostow, *The Stages of Economic Growth, A Non-Communist Manifesto* (Cambridge: Cambridge University Press, 1962). The recent *New York Times* profile of Rostow observes: "Since McGeorge Bundy and Bill D. Moyers left the White House, Mr. Rostow, a former professor at the Massachusetts Institute of Technology, has been emerging as the White House spokesman on foreign affairs. . . . He now organizes and attends the President's Tuesday luncheon conferences. Secretary of State Dean Rusk, Secretary of Defense Robert S. McNamara and the White House Press Secretary, George Christian, are usually the only other guests." *New York Times*, April 13, 1967.
34. Pablo González Casanova, *La Democracia en México* (Mexico: Era, 1965), p. 202.
35. Bert F. Hoselitz, "Social Stratification and Economic Development."
36. John J. Johnson, ed., *The Role of the Military in Underdeveloped Countries* (Princeton: Princeton University Press, 1962); *The Military and Society in Latin America* (Stanford: Stanford University Press, 1964); Edwin Lieuwen, *Arms and Politics in Latin America* (New York: Praeger, 1960); *Generals and Presidents, Neo-Militarism in Latin America* (New York: Praeger, 1964).
37. Frantz Fanon, *Les damnés de la terre* (Paris: Maspero, 1961). Published and mistranslated as *The Wretched of the Earth* (New York: Grove Press, 1966).

38. José Luis Ceceña, *El Capital Monopolista y la Economía de México* (Mexico: Cuadernos Americanos, 1963); Ricardo Lagos, *La Concentración del Poder Económico en Chile* (Santiago: Editorial del Pacífico, 1961); Carlos Malpica, *Guerra a la Muerte al Latifundio* (Lima: Ediciones Voz Rebelde, 1963); Jacinto Oddone, *La Burguesía Terrateniente Argentina* (Buenos Aires: Populares Argentinas).

39. See for instance, José Luis de Imaz, *Los que Mandan* (Buenos Aires: EUDEBA, 1964).

40. Frantz Fanon, *The Wretched of the Earth*. The degree of capitalist penetration of underdeveloped countries was observed long ago by Rosa Luxemburg in *The Accumulation of Capital* (New York: Monthly Review Press, 1964), especially Section Three, pp. 329–467. I have explored the same in *Capitalism and Underdevelopment in Latin America* and Chapter 14 of this volume.

41. United Nations Economic Commission for Latin America, *The Economic Development of Latin America in the Postwar Period* (New York: United Nations, 1963), E/CN. 12/659.

42. United Nations Economic Commission for Latin America, *The Social Development of Latin America during the Postwar Period* (New York: United Nations, 1963), E/CN. 12/660.

43. Theodore R. Crevanna, ed., *Materiales para el Estudio de la Clase Media en América Latina* (Washington: Unión Panamericana, 6 volumes, 1950–1951); Marshall Wolfe, *Las Clases Medias en Centro América: Características que Presentan en la Actualidad y Requisitos para su Desarrollo* (New York: United Nations) E/CN. 12/CCE/Rev. 2; and United Nations, *The Social Development of Latin America*; John L. Johnson, *Political Change in Latin America: The Emergence of the Middle Sectors* (Stanford: Stanford University Press, 1958).

44. Robert Redfield, *The Folk Culture of Yucatan* (Chicago: University of Chicago Press, 1941); "The Folk Society," *American Journal of Sociology*, Vol. 52, No. 4 (January 1941).

45. Robert Redfield, *The Little Community and Peasant Society and Culture* (Chicago: University of Chicago Press, 1960); also see *The Primitive World and Its Transformations* (Ithaca: Cornell University Press, 1955).

46. Manning Nash, *Machine Age Maya* (Glencoe: The Free Press, 1958).

47. Robert Redfield, *The Little Community*.

48. Talcott Parsons, "Social Classes and Class Conflict in the Light

of Recent Sociological Theory," in *Essays in Sociological Theory* (Rev. ed.; Glencoe: The Free Press, 1954), p. 324.

49. C. Wright Mills, *The Power Elite.*
50. William H. Whyte, Jr., *The Organization Man* (New York: Simon and Schuster, 1956).
51. John J. Johnson, *Political Change in Latin America;* "The Political Role of the Latin, American Middle Sectors," *The Annals of the American Academy of Political and Social Science,* Vol. 334 (March 1961).
52. Gino Germani, *Política y Sociedad en una Epoca de Transición* (Buenos Aires: Paidós, 1962); *Política e Massa* (Belo Horizonte: Publicaçôes de Revista Brasileira de Estudos Politicos, 1960).
53. Bert F. Hoselitz, "Economic Growth in Latin America," *Contributions to the First International Conference in Economic History,* Stockholm 1960 (The Hague: Mouton & Co., 1960).
54. Andrew Gunder Frank, "Brazil; The Goulart Ouster," *The Nation,* April 27, 1964.
55. Gabriel Kolko, *Wealth and Power in America.*
56. Aníbal Pinto, "Concentración del Progreso Técnico y de sus Frutos en el Desarrollo Latinoamericano," *El Trimestre Económico,* Vol. 32, No. 125 (January–March 1965). See also his *Chile: Una Economía Difícil* (Mexico: Fondo de Cultura Económica, 1965).
57. Walt Whitman Rostow, *The Process of Economic Growth* (New York: Norton, 1952).
58. Most of the criticism of Rostow's book has, however, been superficial and largely limited to quibbling about details in the characterization of his stages. This superficiality is notably evident in the "Appraisals and Critiques" of "The Rostow Doctrine" by Meier, Kuznets, Cairncross, Habakkuk, and Gerschenkron in Gerald Meier, ed., *Leading Issues in Development Economics* (New York: Oxford University Press, 1964). It is revealing of the narrowness of American economics that Meier, whose book has been very favorably reviewed for its purported breadth of issues and appraisals did not include the probably most penetrating criticism of Rostow so far by Paul A. Baran and Eric Hobsbawm, "The Stages of Economic Growth," *Kyklos* (Basel), Vol. 14, Fasc. 2 (1961).
59. W. W. Rostow, *The Stages of Economic Growth,* pp. 4, 6, 7, 39.
60. R. Palme Dutt, *India Today and Tomorrow* (London: Lawrence & Wishart, 1955); A. R. Desai, *Social Background of Indian*

*Nationalism* (Bombay: Popular Book Depot, 1959); Jawaharlal Nehru, *The Discovery of India* (New York: John Day, 1946); V. B. Singh, *Indian Economy Yesterday and Today* (New Delhi: People's Publishing House, 1964).

61. *Ibid.*
62. Basil Davidson, *The African Slave Trade* (Boston: Atlantic-Little Brown, 1961); and Jack Woddis, *Africa, The Roots of Revolt* (London: Lawrence & Wishart, 1960).
63. Eric Wolf, *Sons of the Shaking Earth* (Chicago: University of Chicago Press, 1959).
64. Sergio Bagú, *Economía de la Sociedad Colonial. Ensayo de Historia Comparada de América* (Buenos Aires: Ateneo, 1949); Celso Furtado, *The Economic Growth of Brazil* (Berkeley: University of California Press, 1963); Aldo Ferrer, *The Argentinian Economy: An Economic History of Argentina* (Berkeley: University of California Press, 1967); Aníbal Pinto, *Chile, Un Caso de Desarrollo Frustrado* (Santiago: Editorial Universitaria, 1958); Andre Gunder Frank, *Capitalism and Underdevelopment in Latin America*; Ramiro Guerra y Sánchez, *Sugar and Society in the Caribbean* (New Haven: Yale University Press, 1964).
65. J. H. Boeke, *Economics and Economic Policy of Dual Societies* (New York: Institute of Pacific Relations, 1953); Jaques Lambert, *Os Dois Brasis* (Rio de Janeiro: Ministerio da Educação e Cultura, n. d.). See also footnote 121.
66. Paul A. Baran, *The Political Economy of Growth* (New York: Monthly Review Press, 1957); Andre Gunder Frank, *Capitalism and Underdevelopment in Latin America*. See also footnote 120.
67. See United Nations Conference on World Trade and Development (Geneva: 1964), U.N. Document Series, E/CONF. 46, and especially the Report by the Secretary-General cited in footnote 92.
68. Paul A. Baran, *The Political Economy of Growth*; Gunnar Myrdal, *Rich Nations and Poor* (New York: Harper & Brothers, 1957), also issued under the title *Economic Theory and Underdeveloped Regions*; Yves Lacoste, *Les pays sous-developpés* (Paris: "Que Sais-Je?," Presses Universitaires de France, 1959); Frantz Fanon, *Les damnés de la terre*; Andre Gunder Frank, *Capitalism and Underdevelopment in Latin America*.
69. Quoted in Paul Baran, *The Political Economy of Growth*, pp. 149–150.
70. Andre Gunder Frank, "The Development of Underdevelopment."

71. Aldo Ferrer, *The Argentinian Economy*; and "Reflexiones Acerca de la Política de Estabilización en la Argentina," *El Trimestre Económico*, Vol. 30, No. 120 (October–December 1963). "Two Argentinian scholars have recently written doctoral dissertations under Professor Walt Rostow at the Massachusetts Institute of Technology, attempting to identify in the economic history of their own country his series of stages of economic growth. The period of Pre-Conditions, they thought, was completed by 1914 when the railway net was finished and the entire rich area of the Pampas had been brought into pastoral or agricultural use. But somehow development did not follow, and the Take-Off did not occur, again by their reckoning, until 1933. What they did in this situation was to invent a wholly new stage of growth, or rather non-growth, for the Argentinian case, which they called The Big Delay. Even their Take-Off, moreover, has not been followed by rapid progress. Writing in 1959, the experts of the United Nations Economic Commission for Latin America [said], '. . . Since the time of the great world depression . . . per capita production has increased at an average rate scarcely half the rate of the increase registered between the beginning of the century and the onset of the depression.' It appears, then, that Argentina had in fact attained a relatively high level of income by the earlier part of the century and that in more recent decades . . . the Argentine experience has been characterized by delay, stagnation, and—to take another word from the ECLA economists—'strangulation'."—Carter Goodrich, "Argentina as a New Country," *Comparative Studies in History and Society*, Vol. VII (1964–1965), pp. 80–81.

72. Thomas Mun, *England's Treasure by Forraign Trade, or the Balance of Our Forraign Trade Is the Rule of Our Treasure* (Oxford: Basil Blackwell, 1959), first published in 1664.

73. Richard Cantillon, *Essai sur la nature du commerce en général*, edited, with an English translation and other material, by Henry Higgs (New York: Augustus Kelley, 1964).

74. Karl Marx, *Capital*, Vol. III (Moscow: Foreign Languages Publishing House, n. d.).

75. Earl J. Hamilton, "American Treasure and the Rise of Capitalism," *Economica* (London), No. 27 (1929); *American Treasure and the Price Revolution in Spain, 1501–1650* (Cambridge: Harvard University Press, 1934); *War and Prices in Spain 1651–1800* (Cambridge: Harvard University Press, 1947). See also the ex-

tension of this work by P. Vilar, "Problems of the Formation of Capitalism," *Past & Present*, November 1956.

76. Eric Williams, *Capitalism and Slavery* (Chapel Hill: University of North Carolina Press, 1944); reprinted by Russell & Russell, New York, 1963; and issued in paperback by André Deutsch, London, 1964.

77. Basil Davidson, *The African Slave Trade; Old Africa Rediscovered* (London: Gollancz, 1959).

78. The same error also applies to a further variant which is associated particularly with Alexander Gerschenkron, *Economic Backwardness in Historical Perspective* (Cambridge: Belknap Press of Harvard University, 1962). Gerschenkron introduces variations into the ideal types of development. He reasons that since the pattern of development of the latecomers, such as Germany, differs from that of those which developed earlier, it is only reasonable to suppose that the pattern of those still later—that is the still underdeveloped countries—will differ even more from the already established pattern and stages of growth. This analysis might indeed seem to be a major advance over the others. But it is not. As with the other proponents of the first mode, there is no hint in Gerschenkron that the underdeveloped countries also have a history which requires study; nor is there any hint that their history and their relations with the now developed countries are much more important for any serious attempt to understand and remove the causes of underdevelopment than is the study of the history of the developed part of the world, whose experience has been quite different. Gerschenkron's variety of the first mode must, therefore, also be judged inadequate.

79. The *New York Times* profile comments: "Mr. Rostow is an architect of the United States policy in Vietnam, and proud of it."— *New York Times*, April 13, 1967. "W. W. Rostow once explained the State Department's rationale behind the arms race in the 1950's as forcing the USSR to 'waste' her resources for military purposes and thus denying her the use of these resources to sustain her growth rate."—Two Labor Economists, "Tasks of the American Labor Movement," *Monthly Review*, Vol. 18, No. 11 (April 1967), p. 12. Is this also the rationale for the stages of growth Mr. Rostow is proud to impose on Vietnam and China in the 1960's?

80. Paul A. Baran, *The Political Economy of Growth*.

81. Andre Gunder Frank, *Capitalism and Underdevelopment in Latin America*.
82. Martin Bronfenbrenner, "The Appeal of Confiscation in Economic Development," *EDCC*, Vol. 3, No. 3 (April 1955); "Second Thoughts on Confiscation, *EDCC*, Vol. 11, No. 4 (July 1963).
83. Daniel H. Garnick, " 'The Appeal of Confiscation' Reconsidered: A Gaming Approach to Foreign Economic Policy," *EDCC*, Vol. 11, No. 4 (July 1963); and "Further Thoughts on Confiscation," *EDCC*, Vol. 12, No. 4 (July 1964).
84. Raymond F. Mikesell, ed., *U.S. Private and Government Investment Abroad* (Eugene: University of Oregon, 1962).
85. Benjamin Higgins, "Foreign Investment and Foreign Aid," in his *Economic Development* (New York: Norton, 1959).
86. Chi Ming-Hon, "External Trade, Foreign Investment, and Domestic Development: The Chinese Experience 1840–1937," *EDCC*, Vol. 10, No. 1 (October 1961).
87. Harry Magdoff, *The Age of Imperialism* (New York: Monthly Review Press, 1969), p. 150.
88. Keith B. Griffin and Ricardo French-Davis, "El Capital Extranjero y el Desarrollo," *Revista de Economía* (Santiago), Vol. 83–84 (1964), pp. 16–22; and Chapter 9.
89. *Ibid.*; José Luis Cecena, *El Capital Monopolista y la Economía de México* (Mexico: Cuadernos Americanos, 1963); and Michael Kirdon, *Foreign Investments in India* (London: Oxford University Press, 1965).
90. Claude McMillan, Jr., Richard F. Gonzales, with Leo G. Erickson, *International Enterprise in a Developing Economy. A Study of U.S. Business in Brazil*, M.S.U. Business Studies (East Lansing: Michigan State University Press, 1964), p. 205.
91. This and the following data on Canada are taken or computed from A. E. Safarian, *Foreign Ownership of Canadian Industry* (Toronto: McGraw-Hill Company of Canada, 1966), pp. 235, 241.
92. Report by the Secretary-General of the Conference, "Towards a New Trade Policy for Development," *Proceedings of the United Nations Conference on Trade and Development* (New York: United Nations, 1964), E/CONF.46/141, Vol. II, pp. 9–13, 42, and other documents of the Conference. It should be noted (cf. p. 13) that in comparing the underdeveloped countries' loss of capital due to declining terms of trade with the "net inflow of all

types of finance (loans, investments and grants-in-aid)," the United Nations calculate the latter "including private re-investment," that is, including the investment capital that does not flow in at all, net or gross, but is generated in the underdeveloped countries themselves.

93. See Chapter 11, "Invisible Foreign Services or National Economic Development?"

94. The 7.3 percent is computed from the $6,195 million service expenditures in *ibid.* as a percentage of the $84,458 million GNP in 1962 reported in United Nations Economic Commission for Latin America, *Estudio Económico de América Latina 1963* (New York: United Nations, 1964), E/CN.12/696/Rev. 1, p. 6. This document is also the source of all the data used in the computations of the articles cited in footnote 93. The 3 percent is computed from United Nations Commission for Latin America, *El Financiamiento Externo de América Latina* (New York: United Nations, 1964), E/CN.12/649/Rev. 1, p. 33.

95. Relatorio de la III Reunion de Facultades y Escuelas de Economía de América Latina, Mexico, June 21–25, 1965. Published in *Presente Económico* (Mexico), Vol. 1, No. 1 (July 1965), p. 63, and in *Comercio Exterior* (Mexico), Vol. 15, No. 6 (June 1965), p. 439; and *Desarrollo* (Colombia), No. 1 (January 1966), p. 7–9.

96. Arturo Frondizi, *A Luta Antiimperialista* (São Paulo: Editora Brasilense, 1958); a translation of *Petroleo y Política* (Buenos Aires: Editorial Raigal, 1955).

97. Quoted in Cámara Textil del Norte, "Las Inversiones Extranjeras y el Desarrollo Económico de México," *Problemas Agrícolas e Industriales de México*, Vol. 9, No. 1–2 (1957).

98. For more detailed analysis of this problem, see: José Luis Ceceña, *El Capital Monopolista y la Economía de México*, Fernando Carmona, *El Drama de América Latina, El Caso de México* (Mexico: Cuadernos Americanos, 1964); Arturo Frondizi, *A Luta Antiimperialista*; Silvio Frondizi, *La Realidad Argentina* (2nd ed.; Buenos Aires: Praxis, 1967), Vol. I; Hamza Alavi, "U.S. Aid to Pakistan," *Economic Weekly* (Bombay), Special Number (July 1963); Chapters 8 and 9 of this book; *Capitalism and Underdevelopment in Latin America*; and "Foreign Investment in Latin American Underdevelopment from Colonial Conquest to Neo-Imperialist Integration," in David Horowitz, ed., *Containment and Revolution*, (Boston: The Beacon Press, 1967).

99. Analysis of this process may be found for instance for India in the work cited in footnote 60; for Latin America in footnote 62; for China in footnote 132; for Spain, in José Larraz, *La Epoca del Mercantilismo en Castilla* (*1500–1700*) (2nd ed.; Madrid: Atlas, 1943); for Portugal in Alan K. Manchester, *British Preeminence in Brazil, Its Rise and Decline* (Chapel Hill: University of North Carolina Press, 1933).

100. "The U.S. Business Stake in Europe," *Newsweek*, March 8, 1965, pp. 67–74.

101. See Andre Gunder Frank, particularly the last part of "Capitalist Development of Underdevelopment in Brazil" in *Capitalism and Underdevelopment in Latin America*. Also see "The Growth and Decline of Import Substitution in Brazil," *Economic Bulletin for Latin America* (New York: United Nations), Vol. 9, No. 1 (March 1964).

102. Manning Nash, "Social Prerequisites to Economic Growth in Latin America and South East Asia," *EDCC*, Vol. 12, No. 3 (April 1964); Burkhard Strümpel, "Preparedness for Change in Peasant Society," *EDCC*, Vol. 13, No. 2 (January 1965); S. N. Eisenstadt, "Breakdowns of Modernization," *EDCC*, Vol. 12, No. 4 (July 1964); William N. Parker, "Economic Development in Historical Perspective," *EDCC*, Vol. 10, No. 1 (October 1961); S. N. Eisenstadt, "Sociological Aspects of the Economic Adaptation of Oriental Immigrants in Israel—A Case Study in the Problem of Modernization," *EDCC*, Vol. 4 (April 1956); and others.

103. Friedrich List, *National System of Political Economy* (Philadelphia, 1856).

104. Quoted in Pedro Santos Martínez, *Historia Económica de Mendoza durante el Virreynato* (Madrid: Universidad Nacional del Cuyo, 1959), p. 125, and retranslated from the Spanish by the author.

105. Frederick Clairmonte, *Economic Liberalism and Underdeveloped Countries*.

106. Max Nolff, "Industria Manufacturera," in *Geografía Económica de Chile* (Santiago: Corporación de Fomento de la Producción), Vol. III, pp. 162–3.

107. Claudio Véliz, "La Mesa de Tres Patas," *Desarrollo Económico* (Buenos Aires), Vol. 3, No. 1–2 (April–September 1963), pp. 237–242.

108. Aldo Ferrer, *The Argentinian Economy*, p .56.

109. Aldo Ferrer, "Reflexiones acerca de la Política de Estabilización en la Argentina," pp. 501–514. Emphasis in the original.

110. Antonio García, *La Democracia en la Teoría y en la Práctica, Una Tercera Posición Frente a la História* (Bogota: Editorial Iqueima, 1951), and *Bases de la Economía Contemporanea, Elementos para una Economía de Defensa* (Bogota, 1948); Moisés Gonzales Navarro, ed., *Vallarta en la Reforma* (Mexico: Ediciones de la Universidad Nacional Autónoma, 1956); and *La Colonización en México, 1877–1910* (Mexico, 1960); Jesús Reyes Heroles, *El Liberalismo Mexicano* (Mexico: Universidad Nacional Autónoma, Facultad de Derecho, 3 Vols., 1957–1961).

111. See works cited in footnotes 38, 56, and 66.

112. United Nations Economic Commission for Latin America, *The Economic Development of Latin America in the Postwar Period,* and other publications.

113. V. I. Lenin, "The State and Revolution," in *Selected Works* (Moscow: Foreign Languages Publishing House, n. d.), Vol. II, Part 1.

114. Quoted in Fred J. Cook, *The Warfare State.*

115. C. Wright Mills, *The Power Elite.*

116. John J. Johnson, *Political Change in Latin America: The Emergence of the Middle Sectors.*

117. Gino Germani, "Estrategia para Estimular La Movilidad Social," *Desarrollo Económico* (Buenos Aires), Vol. 1, No. 3 (1962).

118. Bert F. Hoselitz, "Economic Growth in Latin America."

119. Aníbal Pinto, *Chile: Una Economía Difícil,* and his "Concentración del Progreso Técnico y sus Frutos en el Desarrollo Latinoamericano." Also see Gabriel Kolko, for the United States.

120. See Chapter 23 of this book; Rodolfo Stavenhagen, "Seven Erroneous Theses about Latin America," *New University Thought,* Vol. 4, No. 4 (Winter 1966/67); Claudio Véliz, "Social and Political Obstacles to Reform," *World Today* (London), January 1963, reprinted in Oscar Delgado, ed., *Reformas Agrarias en América Latina* (Mexico: Fondo de Cultura Económica, 1965).

121. Benjamin Higgins, "The 'Dualistic Theory' of Underdeveloped Areas," *EDCC,* Vol. 4, No. 2 (January 1956); also see his *Economic Development.*

122. J. H. Boeke, *The Structure of the Netherlands Indian Economy* (New York: Institute of Pacific Relations, 1942); *The Evolution*

*of the Netherlands Indies Economy* (New York: Institute of Pacific Relations, 1946); and the definitive *Economics and Economic Policy of Dual Societies.*

123. P. T. Ellsworth, "The Dual Economy: A New Approach," *EDCC*, Vol. 10, No. 4 (July 1962); Walter Elkan, "The Dualistic Economy of the Rhodesias and Nyasaland," *EDCC*, Vol. 11, No. 4 (July 1963); Samir Das Gupta, "Underdevelopment and Dualism—A Note," *EDCC*, Vol. 12, No. 2 (January 1964); Tsunehiko Watanabe, "Economic Aspects of Dualism in the Industrial Development of Japan," *EDCC*, Vol. 13, No. 3 (April 1965).

124. Jaques Lambert, *Os Dois Brasis*; see also his new book, *L'Amérique latine* (Paris: Presses Universitaires de France, 1963).

125. The classic argument of the enclave economy is that of J. H. Boeke.

126. Pablo González Casanova, *La Democracia en México*, and many other works. The Guatemalan government's "Seminario de Integración Nacional" carries the entire idea in the organization's very name.

127. See review of Rostow's work above, and *Capitalism and Underdevelopment in Latin America*, especially the section entitled "Capitalism and the Myth of Feudalism in Brazilian Agriculture." For further criticism of dualism in general and of the particular dualist theses of Jaques Lambert and Celso Furtado about Brazil and of Pablo González Casanova about Mexico, see Chapters 20 and 21.

128. Eric Wolf, *Sons of the Shaking Earth.*

129. Karl Marx, "British Rule in India," in *On Colonialism* (Moscow: Foreign Languages Publishing House, n. d.).

130. R. Palme Dutt, *India Today and Tomorrow.*

131. A. R. Desai, *The Social Background of Indian Nationalism.*

132. Owen Lattimore, "The Industrial Impact on China 1800–1950," *First International Conference of Economic History*, Stockholm 1960 (The Hague: Mouton & Co., 1960).

133. Jack Woddis, *Africa, The Roots of Revolt.*

134. Jean Suret-Canale, *Histoire de l'Afrique Occidentale* (Paris: Editions Sociales, 1961).

135. Mamadou Dia, *Réflexions sur l'économie de l'Afrique noire* (Paris: Présence Africaine, 1960).

136. W. F. Wertheim, *Indonesian Society in Transition, A Study of*

*Social Change* (2nd rev. ed., The Hague and Bandung: W. van Hoeve Ltd., 1959); and Clifford Geertz, *Agricultural Involution, The Process of Ecological Change in Indonesia* (Berkeley: University of California Press, 1963).

137. Eric Wolf, *Sons of the Shaking Earth*, and "Types of Latin American Peasantry," *American Anthropologist*, Vol. 57, No. 3 (June 1955).

138. *Capitalism and Underdevelopment in Latin America.*

139. Robert Redfield, *The Folk Culture of Yucatan*, and *The Little Community and Peasant Society and Culture.*

140. Robert Redfield, *Human Nature and the Study of Society, Papers of Robert Redfield*, Margaret Park Redfield, ed. (Chicago: University of Chicago Press, 1962).

141. Robert Redfield, *Peasant Society and Culture.*

142. Manning Nash, "Introduction" in "Psycho-Cultural Factors . . . ," pp. 5–6.

143. Manning Nash, "Social Prerequisites to Economic Growth . . . ," p. 242.

144. Bert F. Hoselitz, "Role of Incentives in Industrialization," *Economic Weekly* (Bombay), Vol. 15, Nos. 28, 29, & 30, Special Number (July 1963).

145. Everett E. Hagen, *On the Theory of Social Change.*

146. David McClelland, "A Psychological Approach . . ."

147. David McClelland, *The Achieving Society*, pp. 205, 238, 391.

148. David McClelland, "Motivational Patterns in Southeast Asia with Special Reference to the Chinese Case," *Journal of Social Issues*, Vol. 29, No. 1 (January 1963), p. 17.

149. David McClelland, *The Achieving Society*, pp. 391–437.

150. Max Weber, *The Protestant Ethic and the Spirit of Capitalism* (London: G. Allen & Unwin, 1930).

151. J. A. Schumpeter, *The Theory of Economic Development* (Cambridge: Harvard University Press, 1934).

152. See footnote 18.

153. For recent examples see Alec P. Alexander, "Industrial Entrepreneurship in Turkey: Origins and Growth," *EDCC*, Vol. 8, No. 4, Part 1 (July 1960), and Arcadius Kahan, "Entrepreneurship in the Early Development of Iron Manufacturing in Russia," *EDCC*, Vol. 10, No. 4 (July 1962).

154. W. Paul Strassman, *Risk and Technological Innovation: American Manufacturing Methods in the Nineteenth Century* (Ithaca: Cornell University Press, 1959); and "The Industrialist," in John

J. Johnson, ed., *Continuity and Change in Latin America* (Stanford: Stanford University Press, 1964).

155. Norman N. Bradburn and David Berlew, "Need for Achievement and English Industrial Growth," *EDCC*, Vol. 10, No. 1 (October 1961); Juan B. Cortes, "The Achievement Motive in the Spanish Economy Between the 13th and 18th Centuries," *EDCC*, Vol. 9, No. 1 (October 1960); James N. Morgan, "The Achievement Motive and Economic Behavior," *EDCC*, Vol. 12, No. 3 (April 1964).

156. S. N. Eisenstadt, "The Need for Achievement," *EDCC*, Vol. 11, No. 4 (July 1963), p. 431.

157. John H. Kunkel, "Values and Behavior in Economic Development," pp. 276–277.

158. John H. Kunkel, "Psychological Factors in the Analysis of Economic Development," in the same issue of *Journal of Social Issues*.

159. S. N. Eisenstadt, "The Need for Achievement."

160. John H. Kunkel, "Values and Behavior . . ."

161. John H. Kunkel, "Psychological Factors . . . ," pp. 72–73, 82. For a similar criticism also see S. N. Eisenstadt, "The Need for Achievement."

162. This effort is reminiscent of the famous but unsuccessful attempt to remedy functionalists' accounting for the existence of institutions through reliance on teleology by George C. Homans and David M. Schneider in their *Marriage, Authority, and Final Causes. A Study of Unilateral Cross-Cousin Marriage* (Glencoe: The Free Press, 1955). Rejecting the final cause of societal equilibrium as an explanation for an institution's existence, Homans and Schneider sought to substitute an identifiable efficient cause, though strangely their "efficient cause" was an internal state— that is, another final cause similar to the ones criticized here.

163. John H. Kunkel, "Values and Behavior . . . ," pp. 275, 277.

164. Manning Nash, "Introduction . . . ," p. 4. Emphasis supplied.

165. Manning Nash, *Machine Age Maya.*

166. David McClelland, "Motivational Patterns in Southeast Asia . . . ," and *The Achieving Society*, pp. 412–413.

167. David McClelland, *The Achieving Society*, p. 423.

168. David McClelland, "Motivational Patterns . . ."

169. "Mr. Rostow's former university colleagues on the old Kennedy White House staff . . . are savagely critical of his increasing influence, and they condemn his aggressive intellectualism as self-

serving opportunism that consoles the President but tends to mislead him, particularly on Vietnam."—*New York Times*, April 13, 1967.

170. Further theoretical limitations of the functionalist part of this social science theory are examined in Chapter 3 of this book.

# 3

# FUNCTIONALISM AND DIALECTICS

The treatment by Pierre van den Berghe of "Dialectic and Functionalism: Toward a Theoretical Synthesis" in the October 1963 issue of the *American Sociological Review* provides excellent points of departure for an examination of some elementary but fundamental aspects of functional and dialectical analysis which that author did not see fit to mention and of which functionalists generally show little or no awareness in their functionalist analysis of society or in their social analysis of functionalism.

The article cited claims to find four points of convergence, overlap, or synthesis between functionalism and dialectics. These are (1) that both approaches are holistic; (2) that they converge in the role they assign to conflict and consensus, to integration and disintegration; (3) that they share an evolutionary notion of social change; and (4) that both theories are fundamentally based on an equilibrium model. Although examining functionalism and dialectics at these four points of supposed convergence cannot constitute the scientifically important step toward fruitful, balanced, theoretical analysis of social structure and social change, which the cited author claims for his "synthesis," it can permit us some clarification of the theoretical assumptions, empirical basis, and policy implications of functionalism and dialectics. It can also afford us some insight into the real limitations of any attempted synthesis.

---

1964–65. Fernando Henrique Cardosa and Rodolfo Stavenhagen, Latin American sociologists whose life and work in underdeveloped society have been so fruitful, were helpful in the preparation of this paper. The paper was originally published as "Functionalism, Dialectics, and Synthetics," in the Spring 1966 issue of *Science & Society*.

## Holism

Both functionalism and dialectic theory are holistic. But here the resemblance ends. Functionalist holism and dialectical holism differ from each other in at least three elementary but fundamental ways: First, in their approach to the whole; second, in the questions they ask of the whole; and third, in the whole they select for study.

The levels of abstraction of functionalist holism and dialectical holism are altogether different. Dialecticians, even bad ones, necessarily begin with a particular existing society and go on theoretically to analyze it and its transformation in its entirety. Even the best functionalists, on the other hand, almost always eschew the study of a whole society. In the few instances in which they do analyze the whole, they either leave reality aside altogether or depart from functionalist theory.

The archetype of contemporary holistic functionalist analysis of the whole is, of course, that of Talcott Parsons. But Parsons' functionalist analysis of the social system is not even intended to be an analysis of any existing social system in particular. Parsons' holism, if we can call it that at all, is an analysis of an abstract whole, or of a wholly abstract supposedly universally valid model of any and all existing or imaginary societies. Accordingly, the holistic functional interrelations he so meticulously traces out are those of a construed model and not those of any known society. Lest we be unwittingly misled into thinking otherwise by taking the abstract for the concrete, the world's other most renowned contemporary functionalist authority, Claude Levy-Strauss, goes to great pains to be explicit: he says that he works only with a functionalist *model*, and he submits that all functionalists do and must do likewise, believe it or not. Indeed, no one, to our knowledge, has ever tried to make a holistic Parsonian analysis of any really existing society, least of all of our own, and were anyone foolish enough to try, Levy-Strauss forewarns him, he must surely fail. There is no overlap or even convergence here with dialecticians who try to study our real society—and still less with the best of them who succeed.

Most functionalists, Parsonian and otherwise, who have studied reality at all, have, of course, limited their holistic attention to a part of the society of their choice and to how it is functionally related to the whole of that society. The relatively few of the better functionalists, such as Malinowski, Radcliffe-Brown, Evans-Pritchard, Meyer Fortes, Raymond Firth, Max Gluckman, Fred Eggan, or Edmund Leach, who are not Parsonians and who *have* devoted their attention to a whole existing society, have found it necessary to retreat from functionalism and to leave quite a large gap between their description of the many parts of the society's concrete social reality and their analytic demonstration that, and how, all of these parts are functionally related to each other (and not to anything else) in an equilibrated whole—a gap which, as many of their own disciples have shown, is bridged by little more than their own and their readers' functionalist faith. Still, no amount of faith has so far been enough to lend any functionalist the necessary equipment or courage to attempt such a holistic analysis of our own society or hardly even to come to grips with the relations between their favorite subjects of study and our society. Radcliffe-Brown, for instance, never did his countryman Cecil Rhodes justice. Reading the former, one would never know the latter or his work existed. A world of difference, certainly, from Marxist dialecticians.

Perhaps a still more important difference between the holism of functionalism and that of dialectics is that they do not ask the same question at all about the whole. Functionalism appeals to holism only to explain the parts, while dialectics appeals to holism to explain the whole—and thereby the parts. Even at their best, functionalists and their theory do not attempt, or even pretend, to analyze, explain, account for, understand, and least of all to predict the existence—and still less the appearance or disappearance—of a particular social system or structure. On the contrary, just like their theory, functionalists always take the existing social structure as given and for granted; and both their theoretical and apparently practical interest in it are limited to the analytic value that structure may have in explaining the existence of the particular institutional parts to which functionalists like to limit their scientific study.

More explicitly, we may note that functionalists like Merton, Davis, Durkheim, Radcliffe-Brown, and others began their holistic functionalist study of social reality in trying to account for the existence of particular social institutions (but never of the social system or structure itself) by reference to these institutions' function in the social system. After that attempt failed, they retreated to the less ambitious task of showing how these institutions function within the system.

The initial attempt of functionalists to explain or account for the existence of particular institutions by reference to their function in the social system failed, of course, because of its quite unacceptable teleological foundation, as philosopher-critics such as Hempel and Nagel analytically showed that it must and as the sophisticated debate on cross-cousin marriage between Levy-Strauss, Homans and Schneider, and the latter's critics amply confirmed empirically. Moreover, even if despite Homans and Schneider's valiant attempt and failure, it were possible to substitute a motivational or other efficient cause of an institution for the classical but unacceptable teleological final cause of social integration or pattern maintenance, the attempt to account for an institution's existence by its function would still flounder on the obstacles of its own *post hoc, ergo propter hoc* argument.

Recognition of this Achilles' heel of functionalist theory has led many functionalists to shift the battle to a front where they are less vulnerable. Instead of maintaining their efforts to account for the existence of an institution by virtue of its function, they now only seek to show how it is functionally articulated with other parts of the social system. In pursuit of this more limited end, functionalism has indeed proved to be a useful tool in expert hands. But in this sense also, Marx himself must be termed a functionalist if we recall, for example, his suggestion that "religion is the opiate of the people." Indeed, in this more limited sense and scope, the identification and analysis of social function is an integral part of Marxist or any other dialectic analysis of society. As Kingsley Davis pointed out recently, and to paraphrase John Maynard Keynes, in the long run we are all functionalists. Therefore, to attempt to synthesize functionalism and dialectics at this point is not to advance beyond but only to misrepresent

Marxist dialectical and other analyses of society and their commonality with any social science.

But this shift of functionalists to the examination of only the function of a particular institution, when it is not theoretically and practically linked to scientific advance on all other fronts, as it is among the better Marxists, in turn renders functionalists vulnerable in another way. For thereby they abandon holism. After all, what makes functionalism holistic is either that it deals with the whole or at least that it interprets the part in terms of the whole. But when functionalists, like economists, relegate general equilibrium theory to the first paragraph of their analysis (or more usually even forget about it altogether) and when they resort to partial equilibrium analysis to relate one part of the social system to only one or a few other parts, then they abandon even the holistic base of any possible synthetic edifice.

Thus, there is a big difference in the question that functionalism and dialectics ask of the whole. Functionalists, if they do not abandon the universally accepted scientific precept of holism altogether, only ask of the whole how it explains the part. Of the whole itself they ask no questions at all; they do not ask why it exists or how, where it came from or what is happening to it; they do not ask whether they like it or not; they simply accept the whole system as it is, gladly taking its social structure as they find it. At their best, they try to understand and, perhaps, to reform a part. In Marxism, in contrast, the *sine qua non* is precisely first to analyze and explain the origin, nature, and development of the entire social system and its structure as a whole, and then use the understanding of the whole' thus gained as the necessary basis for the analysis and understanding of its parts. Therein lies its claim to holism. How wholly different then are functionalism and dialectics in this respect as well, and how spurious is any attempted synthesis.

A third sense in which the holistic similarity of functionalism and dialectics is not real and only verbal is the whole they choose to study and the criterion of selection they use to choose it. Asking the right question, as the saying goes, is more than half of getting the right answer; and asking the wrong question—such as choosing the wrong whole—assures never getting the right answer at all. As is well known and even termed a virtue by some, there is no stricture in functionalist theory or practice against choosing any old whole to work in. Family, club, community, industry, nation, free world, imaginary social systems are all fair game. And the criterion of selection among them is more often than not simply personal interest or convenience. Even when the best of functionalists wish to find and eliminate the cause of social evil, unhappiness, ignorance, crime, poverty, exploitation, underdevelopment, war, or whatever, they unabashedly try and even claim to find it in the structure of the tribal or folk community, traditional family—and, increasingly, even in the low-achievement individual. One might be led to suppose that the theoretical and empirical relevance to this task of the analysis of one social whole as against another is of no practical relevance at all. Still, we might ask why functionalists' convenience, or at least their deeply revealed preference, is to look into precisely these wholes for answers to mankind's pressing problems. Be that as it may, anyone engaged in such holistic study who can still maintain even the world perspective of his daily newspaper must surely see how empirically wrong, theoretically inadequate, and practically absurd it is to look for the causes and still less the remedies of our ills in the social structure of only a supposedly isolated community, of only one part of a supposedly dual society, of only a supposedly national society, of only a third part of a world which Wendell Willkie already rightly termed as one.

Marxists, of course, encounter the empirically and theoretically determinant whole in the single worldwide capitalist system, and the better of them in the structure of the world society which harbors not only capitalism, but now also socialism. No sensible Marxist would, in the name of historical materialism—which is not the same as economic determinism, though they are often confused—suggest that the productive structure of, or differences in access to, the means of production within the family, the community, or even only the modern state is the basic determinant of class conflict, of historical evolution, or of anything else. The reason is, of course, that the criterion of selection by Marxist dialecticians of the determinant social whole for study is not determined in turn by their own convenience or desires, but rather by social reality itself. Contrary to what is so often said of them in some circles, in this respect at least, Marxists, unlike some others, do not substitute their wishes for reality. Instead, they take reality as it is, but finding it unacceptable, work to change it; and being holistic in viewing the part as it is determined by the whole, they do not seek to change the part in isolation. Unlike functionalists, they seek to promote social change, instead, by changing the social structure of the whole which is determinant of the part.

Our elementary examination of functionalism and Marxist dialectics thus shows that there are fundamental differences in the holism of the one and of the other. The first synthesis of functionalism and dialectics is entirely vitiated by the fact that they do not at all refer to the same whole, or ask the same question of it, or go about answering it in the same way.

### Integration and Conflict

The second proposed synthesis of functionalism and dialectics is based on their supposed convergence on social integration and social conflict. The fact is that functionalists explicitly or implicitly reject any tendency toward long-run social disintegration; and functionalist theory assures us that there is, and indeed must be, a long run tendency toward social integration in all existing social systems. But functionalist analysis does not, and due to its own short-run basis cannot, present any empirical evidence in support of the supposed fact of long run integration. Whence, then, do functionalists draw their analytical support for the supposed necessity of integration and the associated supposed impossibility of disintegration?

No less an authority than Talcott Parsons deals with this problem very succinctly and, thereby, also clarifies the real disjunction and imaginary synthesis between functionalism and the dialectical treatment of social integration. "Social Classes and Class Conflict in the Light of Recent Sociological Theory" explained that

[Marxists] treat the socioeconomic structure of capitalist enterprise as a single indivisible entity rather than breaking it down analytically into a set of distinct variables involved in it. It is this analytical breakdown which is for present purposes the most distinctive feature of modern sociological analysis. . . . It results in a modification of the Marxian view . . . the primary structural emphasis no longer falls on . . . the theory of exploitation but rather on the structure of occupational roles. . . .

Therefore, he continues, "conflict does not have the same order of inevitability." From this it follows, as Parsons notes several pages later, "that stratification is to an important degree an integrating structure in the social system. The ordering of relationships in this context is necessary to stability." Thus, the analytic basis of the supposed necessity for integration which functionalists pose could not be clarified more than it is by Parsons: if we start with the parts and work up to but never get to the social whole—as Parsons, other functionalists and modern sociologists in general do—then internal social conflict takes on the appearance of being integrative. Only by beginning with the social whole and breaking it down into its parts, as Marxists do, does conflict appear to be ultimately disintegrative as well. Chinese students of the problem have recently put it succinctly: Do two combine into one, or does one split into two? Which is true in fact depends on whether reality is in fact an integrated whole or only a series of isolated parts. That is, these authorities seem to agree that if in reality we face an integrated whole capitalist system, then we face its disintegration.

True to his functionalist persuasion, van den Berghe tells us in his aforementioned article, "Dialectic and Functionalism: Toward a Theoretical Synthesis," that "the usefulness of the integration or equilibrium model suggests that it must be salvaged. . . . A minimum of integration must certainly be maintained for any social system to subsist" (p. 697). We might ask just what the model is useful for if Parsons had not already supplied the answer in no uncertain terms: "It results in a modification of the Marxian view. . . . The primary structural emphasis no longer falls on the theory of exploitation." Why integration is necessary and the model must be salvaged is made explicit on the following page: "I believe that it is correct to speak of a long-range tendency toward integration . . . rather than scrapping the model, however, we must try to modify it." Like the existing social system, the functionalist model of it must be salvaged and may not be scrapped. After all, as Talcott Parsons pointed out, it is useful for withdrawing emphasis from exploitation.

The supposed synthesis of functionalism and dialectics, which takes the analysis of conflict from dialectics and adds it to functionalism, only slights functionalists in denying their analysis of social conflict, adds nothing new to functionalist theory, and distorts Marxist dialectics and its treatment of social conflict and cohesion beyond all recognition.

Functionalists have always incorporated a part of social conflict into the very basis of structure-functionalist theory. We need only recall Simmel on conflict, Gluckman on custom and conflict, Leach on political systems, Durkheim and Merton on alienation, or even the most integralist of functionalists, Radcliffe-Brown on joking relationships or mothers' brothers. However, the function of social conflict for functionalists is only social integration. All other social conflicts—revolution and social disintegration—are off-limits for functionalist theory and practice.

Given this limitation of functionalism, something of additional value could indeed be found in Marxist dialectics. Unlike functionalism, of course, Marxist dialecticians analyze disintegrative social conflict as well and incorporate its existence and consequences into dialectic theory. Moreover, also inconsistent with functionalists but not with reality, dialecticians distinguish among kinds and degrees of social conflict instead of indiscriminately assigning it all more or less the same theoretical weight. Thus, Marxist dialecticians also can and do incorporate non-disintegrative conflict into their theory. To take only one instance, though not an unimportant one, Marxists clearly see the class relationship as socially integrative insofar as, following Durkheim's famous suggestion and Parsons' above-quoted one, the process of production is organized through the cooperation of classes in the division of labor. It is not for nothing that Marxists place so much emphasis on the social nature of production. But this recognition does not prevent Marxists or dialectic theory from also seeing the associated non-social nature of capitalist distribution of the product, the consequent interference in the productive process by the same monopoly structure which promotes it, and the resulting disintegrative class conflict. It is precisely this ability to recognize and deal with such contradiction which makes Marxist theory dialectic and fundamentally different from functionalism. Is this the aspect of dialectic theory then which is to be salvaged in and from functionalism? No! The dialectics of conflict and opposition is precluded by and excluded from functionalism altogether.

The point of the *dialectics* of conflict and opposition is the holistic interpenetration of opposite poles—the unity of opposites —within the whole which makes it two and yet one, dualist and yet holistic. Thus, Marxist dialectics sees social classes, like other opposites, as existing only in cohesive yet conflicting relation to each other, and not in mechanical addition to each other as functionalist stratification theory does. The point is then the interpenetration of integration and disintegration, of structure and change, and dynamically of the negation of the negation. In functionalism there is none of this. In the proposed "synthetic" treatment of social integration and conflict, the attempt is not so much to synthesize functionalism with dialectics as it is to salvage functionalism at any cost, even if that distorts not only dialectic theory but also denies due credit to functionalist practice.

### Evolution

Functionalism and dialectics also do not converge but rather diverge in the matter of evolution. As they have with social conflict, functionalists have long since incorporated social change into the very heart of functionalist analysis of society. Much of the fame of Raymond Firth, Max Gluckman, Fred Eggan, Edmund Leach, and even of the most renowned of structuralists, Malinowski and Evans-Pritchard, rests precisely on their analysis of social change. There surely was social change in Tikopia, Bantu Africa, American Indian country, Highland Burma, the Trobriands, and Nuerland. Were their functionalist students speaking dialectic prose without knowing it? The answer surely is that they were not.

These and other functionalists have long been talking about social change. But they have not been talking about evolution, and much less have they sought to subject it to dialectic analysis. As they do with social conflict—and as Raymond Firth made clear with craftsmanlike precision in his first Presidential address, entitled "Social Organization and Social Change," to the Royal Anthropological Institute—functionalists limit their analysis of social change to that which is determined by and takes place *within* the existing social structure of the system. They leave out of consideration change *of* the social system and its structure. Indeed, they must, since in their theory the social structure is the source of change and not, as in Marxist theory, change the source of the social structure. That is why quite a number of functionalists themselves, like Dahrendorf and Leach, have for some time felt that functionalist theory has a utopian yet conservative bias and that they should bring us out of it by reforming the theory—without, however, scrapping any of its structural fundamentals. Any attempt to equate the functionalists' social change within the social structure with evolutionary change both within and of the system, is certainly stretching the classical definition of evolution beyond all recognition not only of Morgan and Engels, but also of Gordon Childe, Leslie White, and Julian Steward. Though not excluding such cyclical and random or spontaneous change, evolutionary change is both quantitatively and qualitatively different. According to Marxist understanding of evolution, not only does the social structure permit or give rise to some social change as in the functionalist conception, but more importantly the ongoing process of social change determines the social structure of the moment. Social change and evolution are not seen as abstract but mechanistic succession of thesis, antithesis, and synthesis of anything, but rather as the real simultaneous existence within particular social reality of its past, present, and future. And the most important source of the most important change and evolution is the whole's dialectic division into opposites. How, then, could functionalism analyze the evolution of the social whole if, as we saw, it does not even pretend to study the whole?

## Equilibrium

The sum total of functionalist holism, integration, and change within the system is that functionalist theory is an equilibrium model. As Raymond Firth also noted in the already referred to essay on social organization and social change, functionalist analysis of that change is premised on the notion of equilibrating social choice of the varying but limited alternatives set by the existing social structure and on the resulting equilibrating cyclical social change within that stable and unvarying social structure. It is quite otherwise with dialectics. Far from being only cyclical and limited by the structure, in dialectic theory not to mention reality social change is more spiral-like and transforms the structure of society. Where then, we may ask, is the convergence of functionalism and dialectics on equilibrium, and where the synthesis? The answer is on page 704 of Mr. van den Berghe's synthesis: "Functionalism and the dialectics converge on an equilibrium model which is compatible with the assumption of long-range tendency toward integration." That is, the convergence lies in the assumption of integration and the synthesis is based on the distortion of dialectics and on the ignorance or omission of its and Marxism's *sine qua non*, that social reality includes its own disequilibrating negation and that the social whole contains the disequilibrating structural seed of its own evolution and transformation.

In order to achieve "a theoretical synthesis" of functionalism and dialectics, functionalists must leave dialectics shorn of its theory and analysis of the formation, existence and transformation of the determinant social whole. They must deny the identification of this process with historical materialism as untenable, dismiss dialectical division and interpenetration of opposites as confused, and regard extra-systemic stimuli as incompatible with dialectics. Having done all this, we can only hope that functionalists will indeed do what Mr. van den Berghe declares himself "prepared to do," that is to "abandon the term 'dialectic'" (p. 701). If functionalists once abandon not only dialectics but also its name, what will there be left to synthesize? Only the fifth and final matter left pending, "modern sociological theory" itself.

## Conclusion

The quite synthetic functionalist attempt at synthesis reviewed here is a significant example of the supposition in "modern sociological theory" that all scientists—functionalists, Marxist dialecticians, and others alike—are free to pick and choose and synthesize their methods of scientific classification and analysis precisely as it suits their personal fancy or social convenience. The resulting synthetic product is a magnificent example of the scientific fruits of this methodological liberty. But scientific, like other freedom, is limited by reality and not illimited by fancy. As both Marxist Western "materialist" and non-Marxist Oriental "idealist" philosophers have so painfully pointed out, true liberty lies in the recognition and management of reality. Though many of us, functionalists, Marxists, and others, agree that existing functionalist theory is inadequate for analyzing, let alone changing, social reality as we experience and know it, this does not give functionalists synthetic license to do with functionalist and scientific theory as they please. Where would Marxists end up if they were to leave behind the bounds that dialectic reality imposes on their choice of analytic method, or functionalists if they were to escape from the limitations that functionalist theory and reality impose on their analysis of the latter, or physicists if they left behind the universe and atom? Perhaps, like some proud metaphysicians, both ancient and modern, they would all leave our poor suffering world to others' devices and achieve the grand final synthesis of whole, integrated, evolving synthetic angels equilibrating on four or more synthetic pins.

# 4

# ECONOMIC POLITICS
# OR POLITICAL ECONOMY

We Latin American economists who are concerned about the inadequate ability of our science in its present state, and consequently of our own ability, to offer the proper cooperation to the peoples of Latin America in their goal of attaining economic and social development, consider it essential that teaching and research in economic science in Latin America use new approaches and take other directions. We are taking advantage of the debates and resolutions of the Third Meeting of Faculties and Schools of Economics of Latin America to make available to our Latin American economist colleagues for their information and judgment our points of view on teaching and research in economics in Latin America.

The Third Meeting of Faculties and Schools of Economics of Latin America began its work under the following auspices:

1965. In a 1965 meeting of Latin American economists held in Mexico, professors Andre Gunder Frank of the National University of Mexico, and Arturo Bonilla of the National School of Agriculture of Mexico, drew up and submitted for the consideration of their colleagues a report which stated the need for new approaches in teaching and research in economic science in Latin America. The authors later revised this document in order to submit it to Latin American economists for study and revision. Concurrence was sought with the aim of presenting the document to professors and students of economics as a set of formulations which might stimulate the replacement of the inadequate techniques and methodologies which still prevail in our educational and research institutions. Nearly 100 professional economists from 17 Latin American countries (whose names and institutional affiliations appear at the end of this chapter) signed the document before its publication and its subsequent use to reform the curriculum in several Latin American economics departments. The original title of the document was "Necesidad de Nuevos Enfoques en la Enseñanza e Investigación de la Ciencia Económica en América Latina."

It is we, the economists of the underdeveloped countries, who have the duty to formulate a body of knowledge based on observation and experience by arranging these facts in a logical order which will permit us to derive conclusions of general validity. . . . The constant subordination to advances in economics in the Anglo-Saxon countries explains the apparent inability of Latin American economists to formulate a rigorous and logical body of knowledge applicable to the mechanics of growth, instead of limiting themselves to the rather thankless task of pretending that reality adapts itself to obsolete theoretical molds. . . . We must achieve a rational explanation of the fact that some countries grow and others do not, and that development occurs only at a particular historical juncture and not at another. . . . We must determine which are the mechanisms that prevent the international diffusion of economic development through trade and why this latter has turned into the instrument that most serves to accentuate the differences between rich and poor countries.

We agree with the general report of the Third Meeting of Faculties and Schools of Economics in its outline of the principal problems of Latin America, in that:

The main obstacles that hinder and deform Latin America's economic development are of a structural nature and are therefore linked to basic aspects of the domestic economy and to the dependence vis-à-vis foreign power. Furthermore, both often influence each other reciprocally.

The slow and unstable rate of Latin American economic development is due less to the lack or scarcity of productive resources than to the faulty utilization of investment potential, a substantial part of which is wasted in the form of luxury consumption and unproductive investments and expenditures, and which escapes abroad because of an unfavorable rate of exchange and the negative effect of the international movement of capital.

Inflation and the disequilibrium in the balance of payments must be dealt with outside of orthodox monetary formulas; this does not imply an underestimation of the importance of financial problems or of the need for a good monetary and credit policy.

Direct foreign investments produce unfavorable effects on the balance of payments, on the integration of the economy, and on the formation of capital. They influence foreign trade unfavorably, encourage monopolistic competition, and displace and subordinate many domestic entrepreneurs.

Planning cannot be a substitute for structural reforms, which really should precede the former as well as emanate from it.

All these concerns are a consequence of the ever-graver problems faced by Latin American countries in their attempt to attain economic and social development.

Therefore, as was stated in the opening session of the Third Meeting of the Faculties and Schools of Economics: "It is for this reason that the fundamental task of this Conference must be to devise the basis which will permit the structuring of a specifically Latin American theory of economic development, which is the rallying cry of the younger generation."

*We therefore consider* it indispensable:

To construct by whatever means possible an economic theory for Latin America and other backward countries that can explain the causes and the phenomena which have brought about, and which maintain and generate, the stagnation of Latin America and its distorted development. This theory should be founded not so much on approaches, theories, and methodologies based on an alien reality, but rather on the historical experience and present-day reality of a Latin America which, ever since the Conquest, has been incorporated into the world expansion of the capitalist system. In its first phase this incorporation was mercantile and it subsequently generated the industrialization of the presently developed countries at the expense of inhibiting the industrialization of Latin America, Asia, and Africa, and of condemning their economies to a state of underdevelopment. Logically it devolves primarily on us, the economists and other scholars of Latin America and of other underdeveloped countries, to carry out the bulk of this task as an undeferrable scientific necessity and as a moral responsibility to our peoples.

The Third Meeting of the Faculties and Schools of Economics of Latin America has resolved that:

The analysis of the problems of Latin American development requires its own theory, which without reflecting on the constructive contributions which it can gather from other countries, should arise basically from the systematic observation and analysis of Latin American problems. The theory of development formulated in highly industrialized countries does not adequately explain such problems, and consequently cannot serve as a basis for a strategy and a policy capable of dealing with them successfully.

*We consider that* in the teaching and research of economic science in Latin America there remain obstacles to the attainment of the proposed goals, such as:

—The indiscriminate and uncritical teaching of theories originating in a reality alien to that of Latin America.

—The existence of curricula in some faculties and schools of economics which do not yet include a chair in Economic Development; and where such chairs do exist they are not accorded the status that so important a subject merits. To make things worse, the fact is that in such courses of study the nature of underdevelopment is not rigorously analyzed.

—Departments, curricula, and even research programs generally divide the subjects up in such a way as to hinder both the scientific and didactic examination of the structural and dynamic relations among the various economic, political, social, and cultural characteristics of Latin America and an overall analysis of the structure and character of the capitalist system in Latin America.

—There is an inadequate treatment of the economic problems of each Latin American country; and, to make matters worse, no attention is paid to the situation in the other countries of the Latin American area, due to the lack of knowledge of what is happening in countries as a whole, which prevents seeing their similarities as well as their individual differences. In studying the underdevelopment of Latin America and the obstacles which hinder its economic and social development, either the analysis is based on economic theories alien to the Latin American reality which, furthermore, even contradict the facts cited above, or this Latin American reality is examined in a descriptive and superficial way, confusing its institutional manifestations with its nature and its structural character. Specifically, teaching and even research rely on static models of free competition which, even taking into account institutional rigidities such as those pointed out by the monopoly theory and the Keynesian theory, presuppose an equili-brating and rationalizing tendency, despite the fact that Latin American economies increasingly live in and suffer from an essentially monopolistic system which generates, in a dis-equili-brating and chaotic way, development for the few and under-development for the many.

—Thus monopoly has yet to receive the attention it deserves as a problem of underdevelopment, even though it played a very important role in the colonial stage (foreign trade and a ban on the establishment of industry) and though in our day, in its new forms, it takes on ever-increasing significance as a factor of under-development.

—The monetarist illusion often prevails, and inflation is studied as the cause of development in Latin America instead of con-sidering it a consequence of underdevelopment. Neo-classical and Keynesian models are used, which, even if adapted as much as possible to our realities and needs, are not truly and adequately applicable to the economic and political structure in which the foreign trade and financial relationships of Latin America are evolving. The reason for this is that they take no notice of the penetration of direct and portfolio foreign investment in the economy and their impact on monetary and fiscal policy. Neither do they take into account the deformations which monetary and fiscal policy produce in the concentration of power and income and therefore in the growing obstacles to development.

—In teaching courses on international trade, business cycles, monetary and fiscal theories, agricultural economics, and other courses, as many theories are drawn on as there are authors. The courses begin with theories of developed countries; at most an attempt is made, at the conclusion of a course, to adapt the Latin American reality to these theories, rather than taking Latin American reality as the context and point of departure and then going on to look for and find wherever possible the necessary theoretical instruments for its analysis. Consequently neither in-ternational trade nor business cycles are seen as they were and are in underdeveloped countries.

—There is insufficient initiative and boldness in the revision of curricula overloaded with microeconomic and Keynesian analysis, the former already transcended and useful only in very specific cases, and the latter not applicable to our reality.

—As for demographic studies, Neo-Malthusianism, through the so-called theory of population explosion, plays an ever more important role in a false attempt to explain the causes of underdevelopment. In every way it evades the fact that if the population cannot earn a livelihood, it is not due to its rapid growth, but to the form of social organization which is to an ever-greater degree incapable of guaranteeing to the population forms and means which can guarantee and improve its standard of living.

—Economic planning is confused with sectoral or regional programming; and, moreover, an attempt is made to find in such programming the panacea for all the economic problems of our times, just as the free trade doctrine was regarded in the last century.

—The curricula do not sufficiently or rigorously prepare students in such subjects as economic research, statistics, mathematics, accounting, administration, and fiscal, monetary, and banking techniques. An attempt is frequently made to correct these deficiencies with remedies that contain deformations in economics, such as positivism and methodologism. The former attempts to reduce truth to the narrow framework of that which it is possible to show statistically or manipulate mathematically. The latter confuses methodology with theory, attempting to convert methods into objectives of knowledge instead of using them for the study of the historical and social background of the problems of underdevelopment, as well as of development, that the Latin American economies have.

—Thus inadequate courses of study in the subjects mentioned above serve to exacerbate the tendencies of positivism and methodologism. This leads to taking as parameters and fixed variables precisely those economic, political, and social factors which are changing or which should be modified if adequate Latin American economic development is to be attained, steering us away from the broad, structural, and historical approach which is fundamental to the elaboration of a theory of development based on Latin American reality. The deformations of positivism and methodologism have become more pronounced in teaching and are due to the conscious or unconscious intent of evading the responsibility which we, as intellectuals, have toward our peoples in regard to truths already discovered or yet to be discovered. Improved teaching of these subjects will only be significant, will only have meaning and potential, as a function of the approach which we are proposing in order to understand the causes of underdevelopment in Latin America, and it will have practical utility to the extent that it aids in finding the economic theory which must be constructed if Latin American development is to be attained.

—There is a tendency to follow the neo-classical pattern of isolating economic phenomena, minimizing the social character of classical political economy, and thus isolating the study and practice of the profession of economics from the life of our peoples and from our social responsibility to them.

—The growing foreign influence exercised through institutions, professors, curricula, research programs, scholarships for study abroad, and financing from certain developed countries, like other forms of technical assistance, encourage and contribute to the deformations we have pointed out, especially to positivism and methodologism in teaching and research in economics. Not only that: they frequently exert ideological influence and even interfere in political policy in Latin American universities.

From all the above we can deduce—as confirmed by the Second Commission of the Third Meeting of Faculties and Schools of Economics of Latin America—that "the studies which can best explain the process of our development will be those that include and give proper emphasis to factors of really fundamental importance, such as the manifold influence of foreign dependence, the effects of concentration of wealth and income on production, consumption, market formation, and the process of accumulating capital, as well as the inflexibility and inefficiency in economic policy which arise from the institutional structure."

Therefore, we, as Latin American economists who are conscious of these needs and defects in teaching and research in the faculties and schools of economics in Latin America, *recommend that:*

We economists and other Latin American scholars devote ourselves to elaborating an economic interpretation of Latin American history, inasmuch as in order to be able to understand, analyze, and overcome present Latin American underdevelopment, we must approach our problems in a totally new way, not based on the classic theory of international trade, but rather taking historical and present-day reality as its point of departure, objectively studying and analyzing in their totality the Latin American economic and political relations with now-developed countries, turning our sights to the objectives and goals of classical political economy, and dedicating ourselves as Latin American economists to the analytical and objective, rather than descriptive and emotional, study of the most important characteristics of Latin American underdevelopment and development which constitute its historical heritage and present reality, such as:

—The highly monopolistic structure of foreign and domestic trade.

—The extremely important but rarely studied role of the banking and financial sector in Latin American underdevelopment and development.

—Foreign investment and its economic and other implications in Latin America.

—The partially successful and frequently frustrated attempts of the present character of Latin American industrialization, especially in its monopolistic integration with overseas countries, its de-Latin-Americanization, and the impact these produce on small and medium industry.

—The concentration of land ownership and its ties to the oligopsonic and oligopolic character of trade in agricultural products and other sectors of economic activity.

—The continuing and growing deformation of the Latin American economic structure, particularly with respect to the alarming growth of the tertiary sector, which is generally unproductive, relating it to the underemployed population in this sector.

—The causes and consequences, for both development and underdevelopment, of the imbalances provoked by geographic centralization and regional impoverishment as signs of internal colonialism.

—The brakes on Latin American development caused by the social stratification and the class structure.

—To summarize, and this is decisive: it is necessary to study the nature and role of monopolies in the power structure, as related to the economic underdevelopment and development of Latin America.

Inasmuch as the goals indicated are difficult to reach, and in order to propose possible ways to attain them, *we recommend that the faculties and schools of economics of Latin America should:*

—Give first order of importance in their curricula and research programs to the historical interpretation of the Latin American economy, to economic underdevelopment, and to the present forms in which these phenomena appear in the various countries and in the area as a whole, so as to give students a better appreciation of the real problems.

—Assign a secondary status to Keynesian macroeconomics and especially to neo-classical microeconomics, which is the rank they really deserve in the curricula, giving top priority to the introduction of studies of political economy.

—Take from orthodox macro- and microeconomics whatever they can contribute to the elaboration and teaching of a theory founded on experience and reality, for the explanation of development and underdevelopment instead of, as is frequently done, adding to the essentially static theories of classical macroeconomics and microeconomics a few afterthoughts on development, and few or none on the causes of Latin American underdevelopment.

—Be conscious of these theoretical needs, even at the risk of making mistakes sacrificing the minute precision of macro- and microeconomic theories and of methods such as mathematics, econometrics, and statistics; and instead have the courage to confront the reality of Latin American underdevelopment with their own intellectual and financial resources.

—Make use of their present courses and, where necessary, introduce courses in international trade, industrial economics, agricultural economics, economic history and geography, monetary and fiscal policy, etc., for the objective study and scientific analysis, rather than a merely theoretical treatment or superficial description, of these aspects of Latin American reality, beginning with an analysis in their historical and contemporary context of

Latin America's foreign trade relations with today's developed countries and of the influence which these have had and continue to have on the distortion of these economies and in the under-development of the area, as well as an analysis of other economic relations with developed countries of a financial, technological, and political character; a study of the dangers of foreign invest-ment and foreign technological dependence, insofar as they bring with them growing de-Latin-Americanization, monopolization, and even industrial stagnation. At the same time it is necessary to study agricultural monopolization of land, water, technology, and of the commercialization of agricultural products, the interde-pendence among all of these, as well as their relations with so-called internal colonialism, which generates regional and sec-toral polarization, resulting in the development of part of the economy at the cost of the ever more acute underdevelopment of many rural regions and some urban zones; and it is necessary to study the growing inequality in distribution of wealth and income, and the effects of all these tendencies on class structure, distribu-tion of power, and social stratification.

—Include in their curricula more subjects in the fields of history and the other social sciences; strengthen their relations with the faculties and schools that teach these subjects, such as those of history or the political, geographical, social, anthropological, and psychological sciences, etc.; encourage these faculties and schools to revise their own curricula and research programs in the spirit of considerations and recommendations of this document.

—Promote round tables, conferences, meetings, studies, etc.; promote contacts with other universities in Asia, Africa, and Latin America, and also with those of developed countries, in order to analyze very doubtful theses which are nevertheless generally ac-cepted in developed countries, such as:

a) The so-called theory of the population explosion and its implications for economic backwardness.

b) The thesis according to which only by receiving foreign capital is it possible to achieve economic development.

c) The character and form of the so-called technical, economic, and financial aid from developed countries to underdeveloped countries.

d) Free trade as the only formula which guarantees the development of backward countries.

e) Unrestricted free enterprise as the necessary and only condition for industrialization.

In any case, these and many other doubtful theses which have originated in developed countries require a careful examination by us, in accordance with the purpose we have set forth.

—Link teaching with research to a much greater degree so as to bring the preparation and academic work of students and teachers closer to the reality and context of their countries and peoples, carrying out research sponsored by and in cooperation with government ministries and other public institutions in their countries, as an integral part of their study and research programs, but without prejudice to university autonomy or the principles which it involves, such as academic freedom and independence of research.

—The faculties and schools of economics in Latin America, in carrying out their long-overdue task of forming cadres to raise their own scientific and teaching level, must send to study abroad persons of such maturity and experience as to permit them judiciously to choose those studies that may be useful and to reject those which hinder the attainment of the goal of developing in their own countries a science of economics more adequate to the Latin American reality and *problematique,* thus sending abroad fewer inexperienced and immature young people who lack this capacity for judgment and selection.

The faculties and schools of economics in Latin America, as a part of their program for training cadres and for improving their own qualifications, must send more people to Asia, Africa, and of course Latin America for study, to profit from experiences and instruction springing from a reality more similar to our own. They must become acquainted with problems and efforts toward economic and social development carried out in these countries; this would mean sending fewer people to study in already developed metropolitan countries that are currently experiencing other problems and providing other lessons.

*We support* the proposal of the Second and Third Meetings of Faculties and Schools of Economics of Latin America to establish an Association of Faculties and Schools of Economics of Latin America as a permanent body.

*We recommend* that this Association establish permanent and special committees charged with:

—Promoting periodic meetings of faculties and schools.

—Facilitating an exchange of professors, students, and lecturers among the faculties and schools of economics of Latin America, in both regular and special courses, summer and winter.

—Establishing contacts with similar associations and with faculties and schools of economics in the countries of Asia and Africa with a view toward promoting a permanent exchange of professors, students, curricula, and above all of journals and other research works.

—Fighting for the defense of university autonomy and academic freedom, denouncing to the affiliated faculties any violation of this autonomy that might be inflicted on any one of them.

—Financing the Association and its activities principally through resources contributed by the faculties and schools of economy of Latin America and other Latin American sources. A list of Professors and Researchers who have signed this declaration to signify their support, with names, country, and institutional affiliation (for identification purposes only) follows.

**Argentina:** Raúl Arturo Ríos (Universidad Nacional de Córdoba); Silvio Frondizi (Universidad Nacional de Buenos Aires).

**Bolivia:** César A. Vázquez (Secretaría Nacional de Planificación).

**Brazil:** Jairo Simoes (Universidad de Bahía); Caio Prado Júnior (Universidad de São Paulo); Cid Silveira (Universidad do Brasil).

**Colombia:** Gumersindo Serje (Universidad de Cartagena); Iván Colorado (Universidad de América); Alfonso Delgadillo Parra (Universidad de América); Pedro Amaya Pulido (Universidad Distrital Francisco José de Caldas); Simeone Mancini (Universidad Nacional); José Consuegra (Universidad de Cartagena).

**Chile:** José Valenzuela Feijoo (Universidad de Concepción); Cristóbal Fasce Henry (Universidad de Concepción); Alexis Guardia Basso (Universidad de Concepción); Julio López Gallardo (Universidad de Concepción).

**Dominican Republic:** Marcio Mejía-Ricart (Universidad Autónoma de Santo Domingo).

**El Salvador:** Alejandro Dagoberto Marroquín (Universidad de El Salvador).

**Guatemala:** Raúl Sierra Franco (Universidad de San Carlos); Salvador Sánchez Aguillón (Misión Conjunta de Programación para Centroamérica).

**Haiti:** Gérard Pierre-Charles (Université de Haití).

**Honduras:** Jorge Arturo Euceda G. (Universidad Nacional Autónoma de Honduras); Marco Virgilio Carías (Universidad Nacional Autónoma de Honduras); Andrés C. Dávila (Universidad Nacional Autónoma de Honduras); Irma Roberta Díaz (Universidad Nacional Autónoma de Honduras); Diego I. Turcios L. (Universidad Nacional Autónoma de Honduras); Miguel Angel Funes Cruz (Universidad Nacional Autónoma de Honduras).

**Mexico:** Lucas de la Garza González (Universidad de Nuevo León); Sebastián Villanueva de la Rosa (Universidad Autónoma de Puebla); Juvencio Wing Shum (Escuela Nacional de Agricultura); Remigio Jasso (Escuela Nacional de Agricultura); Guillermo Garcés Contreras (Instituto Politécnico Nacional); Genero Arce (Universidad de Sinaloa); María del Refugio de Montero (Universidad de Sinaloa); Ismael Diarte Pérez (Universidad de Sinaloa); Rigoberto Elenes Bringas (Universidad de Sinaloa); Oscar González (Universidad de Sinaloa); Octavio Guerrero Bernal (Universidad de Sinaloa); Manuel Inzunza Sains (Universidad de Sinaloa); Silvia Millán Echegaray (Universidad de Sinaloa); Roberto de la Mora Zatarain (Universidad de Sinaloa); José Luis Ceceña Cervantes (Universidad de Sinaloa); Pedro Pérez Montes (Universidad de Sinaloa); Raúl Ramírez Quintero (Universidad de Sinaloa); María de la Luz U. de Cristerna (Universidad de Sinaloa); Félix Espejel Ontiveros (Uni-

versidad Nacional Autónoma de México); Eduardo Botas Santos
(Universidad Nacional Autónoma de México); Juan Brom (Uni-
versidad Nacional Autónoma de México); Alonso Aguilar (Uni-
versidad Nacional Autónoma de México); Fernando Carmona
(Universidad Nacional Autónoma de México); José Luis Ceceña
(Universidad Nacional Autónoma de México); Rodolfo Puiggros
(Universidad Nacional Autónoma de México); Manuel López
Gallo (Universal Nacional Autónoma de México); Graciela
Wright (Universidad Nacional Autónoma de México); Gustavo
Cerna (Universidad Nacional Autónoma de México); Víctor
Barceló (Universidad Nacional de México).

**Nicaragua:** Raúl Castellón D. (Universidad Nacional Autónoma
de Nicaragua); Fernando Robleto Marcenaro (Universidad Nacional Autónoma de Nicaragua); Eduardo Conrado Gómez (Universidad Nacional Autónoma de Nicaragua); Constantino Pereira (Universidad Nacional Autónoma de Nicaragua).

**Panama:** Rubén D. Herrera (Comisión Económica para América
Latina).

**Paraguay:** Roberto Jadue Seba (Corporación de Fomento).

**Puerto Rico:** Paquita Pesquera de Mari (Universidad de Puerto
Rico); Antonio J. González (Universidad de Puerto Rico); José
Herrero (Universidad de Puerto Rico).

**Uruguay:** Samuel Lichtensztejn (Universidad de la República
de Uruguay); Jorge Iristy (Universidad de la República de Uruguay); Carlos Quijano (Universidad de la República de Uruguay).

**Venezuela:** D.F. Maza Zavala (Universidad Central de Vene-
zuela) Rafael Martínez Pérez (Universidad Central de Vene-
zuela); Manuel Rodríguez Mena (Universidad del Zulia); Leticia
Díaz de Zabala (Universidad del Zulia); Rafael Zabala (Universi-
dad del Zulia); Diego Hernández D. (Universidad del Zulia);
José Romero Coronel (Universidad del Zulia); Rubén Carlos
Margheritti (Universidad del Zulia); Narciso Hernández Bravo
(Universidad del Zulia); Gastón Parra (Universidad del Zulia).

# 5

## TRIPLE DELUSION

[*The November 1964 issue of* Monthly Review *printed "The Triple Revolution," a document published in the spring of 1964 by a distinguished group calling itself the Ad Hoc Committee on the Triple Revolution that has attracted a great deal of attention and discussion in the most varied quarters. As the* Monthly Review *editors summarized it, "The three strands of the triple revolution, according to the Ad Hoc Committee, are the 'Cybernation Revolution,' the 'Weaponry Revolution,' and the 'Human Rights Revolution.' The first is increasing productive capacity to an almost unlimited degree and doing away with the need for human labor. The second has already eliminated war as a method of settling international conflicts. And the third is a worldwide movement for social and racial equality. Taken together, they demand radical changes in attitudes, policies, and institutions . . ." The editors asked any readers to comment.*]

Alexis de Tocqueville pointed out that the real nature and evils of a country are best seen from its colonies. Viewing the American-centered world capitalist system from its colonies then, it may readily be seen that the "Triple Revolution" is a snare and a delusion. As seen from Vietnam, the Congo, Cuba, or any other capitalist economic colony or ex-colony, the real attributes of the supposed cybernetic, weaponry, and human-rights revolutions distinctly appear as the metropolitan capitalist delusions they are. Furthermore, the metropolitan attribution of a technological base to "revolution" and the solution of man's problems is easily unmasked as a counter-revolutionary attempt, like

---

1964. This piece originally appeared in the January 1965 issue of *Monthly Review*.

so many others before it, to snare the colonial world's exploited and oppressed people into forsaking their real human revolution for the vain hope of metropolitan technological solutions for their growing misery. More so even than their fallacious conclusions—rightly criticized already by workers in the capitalist metropolis—it is important for the peoples of all the world to reject the Ad Hoc Committee's even more fallacious and pernicious *premise* of triple "revolution."

It is but a cruel hoax on the world's starving millions to argue as the Committee does that cybernetic and nuclear development is doing away with the need for human labor to obtain a decent living. On the contrary, in the train of this metropolitan "revolution," per capita food production in Asia, Africa, and Latin America (excluding the socialist countries) has fallen and continues to fall since before the Second World War. The vast majority of the people in the capitalist world have to labor ever more to consume ever less. Nor do cybernetic and nuclear developments promise industrialization to the peoples of the capitalist world. On the contrary, the structure and development of capitalism promise to turn cybernetics, just like standardization, the assembly line, electricity, the steam engine, and other developments of the industrial "revolution" into metropolitan capitalist instruments for the exploitation and further underdevelopment of its colonies. Like British industrialization and the de-industrialization of India in the past, American cybernetic and nuclear development in the present has already begun to stunt industrialization in the colonial economies and frustrate their people's development efforts by placing the colonial economies ever more firmly under the control of the imperialist metropolis.

It is a sacrilegious affront to its victims for the Ad Hoc Committee to claim that a weaponry "revolution" has already eliminated war as a method of settling international conflicts at a time when the Committee's government is unabashedly waging cruel foreign colonial wars for "humanitarian" reasons in Vietnam, the Congo, Cuba, and elsewhere—and by its own admission using especially the first of these wars as a testing ground for weaponry development designed for later use against other peoples' human-rights revolutions. Yet still more to be condemned is the Committee's suggestion, apparently all too shared in other quarters as well, that the technological development of nuclear weapons has eliminated the need of external and internal colonial peoples to use arms to defend and liberate themselves from continued capitalist exploitation, now further refined by cybernetic and weaponry developments. Are the peoples of Vietnam, the Congo, and Cuba really to be snared into renouncing weaponry "revolution"? American capitalism's nuclear blackmail of the colonial and socialist peoples is already morally indefensible enough without aggravating it by nuclear delusions.

There is a world "human-rights revolution" indeed. But the Ad Hoc Committee's relegating it to playing second fiddle to supposed technologically based cybernetic and weaponry "revolution" is a clear—however well intentioned—attempt to subvert the real human-rights *revolution* into superficial reforms designed to save capitalism and its exploitation. This is far from the first time in the history of capitalism that the masters have told the slaves that the masters' new weapons make revolution inadvisable and that the masters' new technology now renders this human revolution unnecessary anyway. As seen from the colonies, the Committee is only adding its voice to the already resounding pseudo-scientific refrain from the capitalist metropolis that metropolitan science and technology will bring peace and plenty to all—that is, if only capitalist freedom to exploit in the "free world" be preserved, if necessary at the price of some reforms, but inevitably at the cost of ever increasing physical and cultural starvation for the majority of the capitalist world's people. No, in the colonies it is clear that the real human rights revolution is the colonial war which has been shamelessly imposed on the capitalist world's oppressed but which is accepted and fought by them with dignity.

# 6

## MR. HEILBRONER'S RHETORIC AND REALITY

"The exposure of the NSA-CIA tie would deeply hurt the enlightened, liberal, internationalist wing of the CIA." So, according to *Ramparts*, went the most "pathetic" of the

> arguments put forward by NSA's current officers as to why the CIA-NSA relationship should be kept secret . . . CIA Covert Action Division No. Five, after all, was not in the business of assassinating Latin American Leftists; it was supporting liberal groups like NSA, groups with international programs in the best tradition of cultural changes between countries.[1]

*Ramparts* comments: "The twisted sickness of this Orwellian argument should speak for itself. Yet it is extraordinary, and frightening, that it could be so easily made by the talented young

1967. This essay was prepared as a comment on Robert Heilbroner's "Rhetoric and Reality in the 'Revolution of Rising Expectations,' " at the invitation of the organizers of a conference on American foreign policy held at Estes Park, Colorado, in March 1967. Both Mr. Heilbroner's paper and my comment were to be delivered orally.

Mr. Heilbroner's paper was later published as "Counterrevolutionary America" in the April 1967 issue of *Commentary* and then in a collection of the conference proceedings entitled *Struggle Against History: U.S. Foreign Policy in an Age of Revolution*, edited by Neal D. Houghton (New York: Simon & Schuster, 1968). My paper is presented here for the first time: I could not deliver it at the conference because the U.S. State Department refused me a visa; *Commentary* rejected the essay when it was submitted as a comment on Mr. Heilbroner's paper; and the editor and publishers of the conference proceedings presented the author with the choice of publishing a version they had politically edited beyond recognition or not publishing the essay at all. I chose the latter course and now publish the comment as it was originally prepared, with page references to Mr. Heilbroner's original mimeographed version.

liberals at the head of NSA. One would think that the idea of 'an enlightened wing of the CIA' would be an obvious contradiction in terms." [2]

Nonetheless, Mr. Heilbroner has just told us:

All this confronts American policy-makers and public opinion with a dilemma of a totally unforeseen kind. On the one hand, we are eager to assist in the rescue of the great majority of mankind. . . . On the other hand, we seem committed, especially in the under-developed areas, to a policy of defeating communism . . . thus we have on the one side the record of Point Four, the Peace Corps, and foreign aid generally; and on the other, Guatemala, Cuba, the Dominican Republic, and now Vietnam.[3]

As Mr. Heilbroner would have it, we are also faced with two wings of the State Department or of American policy-makers generally; an "enlightened, liberal, internationalist wing" with a good record of foreign aid to underdeveloped countries generally, and a wing of "blind anti-communism" (page 13) which assassinates not only Latin American leftists but also Vietnamese children. In Mr. Heilbroner's rhetoric there is a choice between the two, and for his part he chooses the former. Reality, I suggest, is far different and offers other options. How is it then that a distinguished liberal of acknowledged talent such as Mr. Heilbroner does not see the "obvious contradiction in terms" within his rhetoric and between it and reality? The answer is, I suggest, twofold: (1) This liberal rhetoric cannot come to terms with the reality of the historical development and contemporary class and colonial structure of the world capitalist or imperialist system; and (2) in the face of the real, as distinct from the rhetorical, contradictions of this system, American intervention in "Cuba, the Dominican Republic, and now Vietnam" has—as a matter of record—been launched and escalated precisely by the "enlightened, liberal, internationalist wing" of the American bourgeoisie and its government.

Though Mr. Heilbroner records numerous but isolated truths, he seems neither to see the record nor to grasp the contradiction. Accordingly, he systematically fails to understand and explain (1) the real causes and structure of underdevelopment; (2) the real alternatives facing the underdeveloped countries, which render development possible only under socialism; and (3) the resulting inevitability of United States opposition to the development efforts by the peoples of the underdeveloped countries. Mr. Heilbroner's rhetoric may be contrasted with the reality of these three issues in turn.

1. For Mr. Heilbroner, the principal, immediate task for the peoples of the underdeveloped countries is modernization (pp. 2, 7, 11). Modernization and development in the underdeveloped countries are stimulated and supported by the developed countries through foreign aid and other measures (pp. 2, 9). The major obstacles emphasized by Mr. Heilbroner for their wellnigh universality are population growth (pp. 4, 7) and "inertia and traditionalism" (p. 3). Beyond these, the obstacles are said to vary from place to place: the lack of "underpinnings of nationhood" in Africa; "the miasma of apathy and fatalism, superstition and distrust" in Asia; and "obsolete social institutions and reactionary social classes where landholding rather than industrial activity is still the basis for social and economic power" in Latin America (p. 2). Thus in Mr. Heilbroner's view, "political discipline" and "economic coercion" are not yet reality in the underdeveloped countries, but only the prospects held out by communist and radical regimes (p. 8). Only in China, by his calculation, do people eat less and live more bitterly than five hundred years ago (p. 6); and the deterioration in the standard of living is not a reality for Mr. Heilbroner but has only a substantial chance of occurring in the future (p. 7). Accordingly, though Mr. Heilbroner suggests it, he does "not recommend such a calculus of corpses" (p. 7), which would compare the costs of the status quo yesterday and today with the costs of the alternative that would permit development. Indeed, Mr. Heilbroner disregards the whole history of the world since the expansion of mercantile capitalism and maintains "that the social physiology of these nations remains so depressingly unchanged" (p. 3), that "the multitudes of the underdeveloped world have only in the past two decades been summoned to their reveille" (p. 4), that some of them had experienced a "revolution of rising expectation" (p. 4), and that most of them still remain the victims of "in-

ertia and traditionalism" (p. 3). The present urgency in responding to the revolution in rising expectations, Mr. Heilbroner tells
us, derives from "the population problem" and "the need to avert
political unrest" (p. 4). Before we go on to examine the option
which Mr. Heilbroner derives from this picture of the underdeveloped world, we may briefly turn to the reality of underdevelopment.

In reality, the now underdeveloped countries have long since
been incorporated and integrated into the single world embracing
the mercantile and industrial capitalist system, to whose development they contributed and still contribute with cheap labor
and raw materials or, in a word, with investible surplus capital.[4]
In this process—that is, in the process of capitalist development
and of the economic development of the capitalist metropolis in
Europe and North America—the social physiology of Asia, Africa,
and Latin America has been totally and remarkably uniformly
changed into what it is today, the structure of underdevelopment
which among these peoples was created by and is still consolidated
by the development and structure of the world capitalist system.
It is in capitalism then, and not in population growth or inertia
and traditionalism that the fundamental cause of underdevelopment resides. This is equally true of Africa, Asia, and Latin America, which are distinguished by the remarkable uniformity of their
structure of underdevelopment rather than by differences of nationhood, fatalism, and institutions.[5] In none of these has landholding been the principal basis for social and economic power
since their incorporation into the capitalist system. In all of
these, on the contrary, power has come to rest primarily in the
control of commerce and that control has been and still is substantially exercised by and on behalf of the interests of the
bourgeoisie in the capitalist metropolis and its junior partners
in the therefore underdeveloped countries.[6]

This process has resulted in a truly incalculable number of
corpses, physical, cultural, and spiritual, in Asia, Africa, and
Latin America. Entire civilizations have been wiped out, cultures
destroyed, and countless millions have met an untimely death
which liberated them from miseries that were previously unknown. Not only in China, but for the last two centuries in

India, and certainly for the last century in Africa and Latin America, the absolute level of living of the majority of people has declined. However much the expectations of some may have risen during the last two or three decades, per capita food production in non-socialist Asia, Africa, and Latin America has declined (3 percent in Asia excluding China and 7 percent in Latin America in the period 1934–38 to 1963, according to United Nations Food and Agricultural Organization data), and the distribution of income has become markedly more unequal in these regions. Absolute consumption of the majority of the people has declined so alarmingly as to threaten heretofore unknown famine on continental scales in Asia, Africa, and Latin America.[7] Not the rhetoric of rising expectations but the reality of falling consumption is at issue. In the face of this reality, the peoples of the underdeveloped countries have not been apathetic in the past and are not fatalistic today. Though our historians have scarcely seen fit to record it, people have rebelled in the past; and though our social scientists have largely failed to note it, they will revolt tomorrow—not against traditionalism and non-capitalist institutions, but rather against the capitalist system. The choice they face is not, as Mr. Heilbroner and others would have it, between the greater or lesser cost of development, but is between devoting the already existing sacrifice by the many for the perpetual benefit of the few or using the same sacrifice for an economic development which benefits the many and frees them from this sacrifice in the future.

2. After thus painting a historically and structurally inadequate picture of underdevelopment and posing the possibility of "communist"—meaning socialist—development for the underdeveloped countries, Mr. Heilbroner sets out the alternatives for the peoples of the underdeveloped countries, as he understands them. Beginning with the "need to avert political unrest," Mr. Heilbroner suggests that "mounting political restiveness enjoins the speediest possible time schedule for development" (p. 4). "But how to achieve haste?" he asks (p. 5). The African state at least "may suffer capitalist, communist, military or other kinds of regimes during the remainder of this century, but whatever the nominal ideology in the saddle," the problem and by implication the

solution is the same (p. 7). It is "not communism or capitalism that establishes much of the tone and tension of international relations" and that is decisive for Mr. Heilbroner (p. 11). It is modernization or traditionalism. And "there is certainly no inherent necessity that the revolutions of modernization be led by communists" (p. 8). In Southeast Asia and in Central and South America "there is the possibility that the task of modernization may be undertaken by non-communist elites," and in Greece, Turkey, Chile, Argentina, and Mexico "the existing political and social framework [is] sufficiently adaptable, so that considerable progress may now be hoped for without resort to violence" (p. 7). In all these underdeveloped areas development can be undertaken, according to Mr. Heilbroner, by a non-communist elite led by "a Gandhi, a Marti, a pre-1958 Castro" or even by the army (p. 7), which according to the post-1958 Castro now militarily occupies its own country everywhere in Latin America and in many other underdeveloped countries as well. How, Mr. Heilbroner asks (p. 8), can a non-communist elite persevere in this task? By having "to offer a philosophical interpretation of its role as convincing and elevating" as the "philosophy," "vocabulary," "view of history," "psychological assurances," and "unquestioning faith" "that communism finds its special strength," for it is through these, Mr. Heilbroner supposes, that "communism" has been able "to reach and rally the anonymous mass of the population [and] that is *the* great accomplishment of communism" (p. 4). It is after posing these supposed options that Mr. Heilbroner can then "suppose that most of Southeast Asia and much of Latin America were to go communist" and can "think it fair to claim that the purely *military* danger posed by such an eventuality would be slight" (p. 9). That is, having rhetorically posed these options contrary to all reality, Mr. Heilbroner can then envisage a simple choice to go communist or not, a simple exercise of this choice without the transfer of power by recourse to violence, and—as we shall observe in the third part of our discussion below—without the military intervention by the imperialist bourgeoisie in the United States.

The real choice facing the people of the underdeveloped countries today is not one between the cost of modernization in pursuit of one ideology and that of another. A calculus of corpses would certainly be recommendable if it could estimate the sacrifice that the majority of the people of the underdeveloped countries now make—for nothing, or rather for the benefit of the few who rule them. The option is not whether to increase the sacrifice or not. The question is whether this sacrifice shall continue to benefit the few and to grow for the many, or whether this same sacrifice shall be channeled into an economic, social, cultural, and psychic development for the benefit of the masses of the people and of man as a whole. Being the historical source and the contemporary cause of underdevelopment, capitalist class and colonial exploitation must be eliminated to permit such development.

Capitalism or socialism is, therefore, the central issue after all. And "non-communist"—that is, capitalist—elites are not capable of leading, or even accompanying, this transformation of the social physiology of the underdeveloped countries. If the pre-1958 Castro showed that non-communist leadership can begin this process, then the experience with reality of the post-1958 Fidel showed that a mass-based movement interested in and capable of achieving state power and eliminating the capitalist class and colonial structure is inherently necessary for the historic process of modernization and development to proceed. Marti, who died in 1898, did not live to face this necessity. Gandhi died after a life devoted to the support of the capitalist class and structure, both at home and abroad, which has since sunk India into the ever profounder underdevelopment and foreboding disaster.[8] As for Atatürk and Nasser (whom Mr. Heilbroner also mentions as possible examples), the former certainly failed to develop or to provide for the future development of Turkey, and the latter, unlike Fidel, has not yet demonstrated his capacity to proceed with the development of the United Arab Republic and its people. And the reason is, as the contrast with Cuba and China today vividly demonstrates, that the essential factor in development today is the political movement of the masses of the people who push forward, leaving others to say, in the words of the old refrain, "I am their leader; I must follow them." Yet with all his idealistic rhetoric about philosophical leadership, Mr. Heilbroner leaves the Prince of Denmark out of his Hamlet when he deals with rhetorical apathy and fatalism instead of real popular force.

3. Finally, turning to the metropolis of the imperialist system, Mr. Heilbroner claims that the loss of its investments in the underdeveloped countries is economically easily supportable by the economy of the United States and that therefore "I [Mr. Heilbroner] do not myself believe that the corporate elite is particularly war-minded" (p. 10). Since "the nations of Europe, most of them profoundly more conservative than America in their social and economic dispositions, have made their peace with communism . . . ," Mr. Heilbroner suggests that "we can except a similar scaling down of our position in history" (p. 12).

In Mr. Heilbroner's rhetoric, he visualizes the possibility that the underdeveloped countries simply choose to "go" nationalist or communist, that in this process, or rather simple change, "the threats of a military or economic kind would not be insuperable" (p. 10) to the United States whose economic structure and political institutions could and would remain essentially untouched, that the dangers would be "above all those of an American hysteria," and that this danger can be averted and this adjustment made by mere changes in "our attitudes," firstly in "a continuation of the gradual thawing and convergence of American and Russian views and interests" and secondly in "the public airing of the consequences of our blind anti-communism for the underdeveloped world" (pp. 12–13).

Mr. Heilbroner's rhetorical options and solutions betray his failure to grasp the reality of the class and colonial structure of the capitalist system. It may be that the loss of American investment abroad "should be manageable economically" for the American economy or its people as a whole. What should be is not however the case, because the ownership of this investment is vested in, and the bulk of the benefits are appropriated by, a very small group of very large monopoly corporations and their owner-managers, who cannot manage, economically or politically, without the maintenance—indeed, the expansion—of these private benefits and of the system that makes them possible. In fact, by 1957 three hundred American corporations owned 88 percent of American investment abroad and of these, forty-five firms owned

57 percent.[9] Since then the degree of concentration has certainly risen further. Moreover, today trade not only follows the flag but it follows investment itself. In 1964 foreign sales by American corporations amounted to $168 billion, of which $88 billion were by wholly or substantially owned foreign subsidiaries abroad, $25 billion were from exports, and the remainder from other investments. Yet in that same year domestic sales of all movable goods were $280 billion, making foreign sales nearly a third of total sales of movable goods. The sum of exports and federal purchases for military expenditures to defend the "Free World" at home and abroad amounts to 20 to 50 percent of total sales in each American manufacturing industry—except farm machinery in which it is less, and the aircraft and ordnance industries in which it is more. But here also the bulk of the sales are concentrated in a relatively small number of corporations. Moreover, the share of total output devoted to military and foreign buyers is steadily increasing. During the last ten years, while domestic sales of American manufacturing industries increased 50 percent, the foreign sales of American-owned factories increased 110 percent. Finally, the concentration of profits is greater still than that of sales. Thus for the major American corporation foreign operations account for a still greater share of their total profits than of their total sales, and this share may easily reach and even exceed 100 percent of their profits. Socialist revolution in the underdeveloped countries and the elimination or radical transformation of the foreign economic activities of the major American monopoly corporations would therefore be of considerable interest to the "corporate elite" and would in fact require very far-reaching readjustments in the class and colonial structure of the monopoly capitalist American economy.

If some American liberals do not perceive this structure of the system and its implications, others understand it all too well. Thus, Dean Acheson already noted in 1944, while he was Assistant Secretary of State in the *liberal,* Democratic administration of Franklin Delano Roosevelt,

> under a different system in this country you could use the entire production of the country in the United States. I take it the Soviet Union could use its entire production internally. If you wish to con-

trol the entire trade and income of the United States, which means the life of the people, you could probably fix it so that everything produced here would be consumed here, but that would completely change our constitution, our relations to property, human liberty, our very conceptions of law. And nobody contemplates that. Therefore, you find you must look to other markets and those markets are abroad.[10]

Are we to believe that, after he became Secretary of State in the administration of F.D.R.'s former Vice-President, Mr. Acheson lost sight of the structure of this system and the need to sustain it, and that he thoughtlessly administered the Department, the Point Four program, and foreign aid generally for the benefit of the underdeveloped countries? The answer was provided by, among others, Eugene Black, for many years the President of the World Bank and now ex(?)-liberal, Democratic President Johnson's adviser on Asian development problems, and proposed administrator of the $1 billion President Johnson offered for his Southeast Asian development program in his famous Baltimore speech:

Our foreign aid programs constitute a distinct benefit to American business. The three major benefits are: (1) Foreign aid provides a substantial and immediate market for U.S. goods and services. (2) Foreign aid stimulates the development of new overseas markets for U.S. companies. (3) Foreign aid orients national economies toward a free enterprise system in which U.S. firms can prosper.[11]

Are we then to believe that the Mekong River development project "for" Southeast Asia represents the dove wing and escalation in Vietnam the hawk wing of L.B.J.? The Vice-President in charge of Far Eastern operations of the Chase Manhattan Bank —associated with the *liberal* Republican Rockefellers—answers: "In the past, foreign investors have been somewhat wary of the overall political prospects for the [Southeast Asia] region. I must say, though, that the U.S. actions in Vietnam this year—which have demonstrated that the U.S. will continue to give effective protection to free nations of the region—have considerably reassured both Asian and Western investors." [12]

It is clear then that not only in "Guatemala, Cuba, the Dominican Republic, and now Vietnam" but also in Iran, the Congo, and elsewhere any attempt to transform the structure of under-development into one of development necessarily meets armed resistance by the bourgeoisie whose center and *liberal* leadership is now in the United States. Accordingly, there is indeed an "inherent necessity" that these attempts at modernization and development be revolutionary and that they be violently opposed by counter-revolutionaries. In a word, the United States is engaged in the Vietnamization of Asia, Africa, and Latin America with all its inevitable implications and consequences. This necessity inheres in the class and colonial structure of the capitalist system itself, irrespective of whether "the corporate elite is particularly war-minded" or not. No less in the metropolis of the system than in its economic, political, and structural colonies does the revolution of this real, as distinct from rhetorical, contradiction involve not simply a change in attitude and ideology but a change in class structure. And this involves the mobilization of the masses of the people, as they are now mobilized in Vietnam and as Mr. Johnson feared that they threaten to become mobilized in Santo Domingo, Watts, and elsewhere. Contrary to Mr. Heilbroner's suggestion, the question is not whether this would "effectively alter the present balance of military strength in the world," but rather how such popular movement at home and abroad will alter the political balance of the capitalist system. This is the real issue; and if I may, I should like to pose it in the words of a promoter of modernization you all know: "The people, and the people alone, are the motor force in the making of world history. . . . All views that overestimate the strength of the enemy and underestimate the strength of the people are wrong" (*Quotations from Chairman Mao Tse-tung*, pages 86 and 118). We must be thankful to Mr. Heilbroner for his masterful use of a rhetoric which exceptionally clarifies its own limitations, as another modernizer put the issue, not only to explain reality but to change it.

## NOTES

1. *Ramparts*, March 1967, p. 38.
2. *Ibid.*

3. Robert L. Heilbroner, "Rhetoric and Reality in the 'Revolution of Rising Expectations,' " p. 9.

4. See Paul A. Baran, *The Political Economy of Growth* (New York: Monthly Review Press, 1957).

5. The view which locates the obstacles to development in social and psychological factors is challenged in extenso in Chapter 2. An alternative explanation is advanced in *Capitalism and Underdevelopment in Latin America*, and in Chapter 1 of this volume.

6. *Ibid.*

7. Cf. Andre Gunder Frank's "Hunger: A Statistical Note," *Canadian Dimension*, Winnipeg, Vol. 5, No. 8 (1967), which relies on data from the FAO publication, *The State of Food and Agriculture, 1964*, pp. 16 and 108.

8. Cf. E. M. S. Namboodiripad, *The Mahatma and the Ism* (2nd ed., New Delhi, 1959); Rajani Palme Dutt, *India Today* (2nd rev. ed., Bombay, 1949); and the summary of various appraisals, edited by Martin Deming Lewis, *Gandhi, Maker of Modern India?* (Boston: D. C. Heath and Co., 1965).

9. This and the following data are all from Harry Magdoff, *The Age of Imperialism* (New York: Monthly Review Press, 1968).

10. Quoted in William Appelman Williams, *The Tragedy of American Foreign Policy* (New York: Delta, 1962), p. 236.

11. Quoted in Magdoff, *The Age of Imperialism*, p. 176.

12. *Ibid.*

# 7

# LIBERAL ANTHROPOLOGY VS.
# LIBERATION ANTHROPOLOGY

Che Guevara, upon being asked what, as a writer, one could do for the Revolution, answered that he used to be a doctor. The issue is not whether medicine or anthropology is less useful or relevant than other fields of human endeavor. The issue is the responsibility of the anthropolo*gist*. His responsibility is to use anthropology only as far as it is sufficient, while doing whatever is necessary to replace the nearly worldwide violent, exploitative, racist, alienative capitalist class system, which embraces most anthropologists and the people they study. Appeals to truth (Berreman) and for a humanistic approach (Gjessing) are insufficient liberal critiques of the liberal support which most anthropologists give and the benefits they derive from the system they serve. Anthropologists more than anybody can be expected to know that values, mythology, science, and other facets of culture are intimately related to the structure of the society—even if many anthropologists like to observe this fact only among other people and societies. Berreman and Gjessing, who devote most of their essays to negating the possibility of doing value-free anthropology, would therefore seem to be beating an anthropologically dead horse.

Suggestions that anthropologists abandon the integrity of their discipline (Gjessing) to overcome the limitations of specializa-

1968. This essay originally appeared in the May 1968 issue of *Current Anthropology* (Montreal), a special issue on responsibility in anthropology. It was prepared as a commentary on three papers which were contributed to a "Social Responsibilities" symposium: "Is Anthropology Alive? Social Responsibility in Social Anthropology" by Gerald D. Berreman, "The Social Responsibility of the Social Scientist" by Gutorm Gjessing, and "New Proposals for Anthropologists" by Kathleen Gough.

tion and individual field work (Gough), though perhaps necessary, are also far from sufficient. Gjessing goes on to claim that economists, political scientists, and sociologists have largely replaced anthropologists and that American anthropology is now closer to reality than its European counterpart. But insofar as this is true it does not mean that Gjessing's proposal to do interdisciplinary work in their footsteps offers any solution: For these liberal social "scientists" and their techniques now simply serve American imperialism better and more efficiently than the perhaps more outmoded children of an earlier imperialism (Gough and Gjessing). Thus, in his introduction to *Social Science Research on Latin America*, sponsored by the Social Science Research Council, the anthropologist Charles Wagley[1] observes that in the United States for the last three decades

> Latin America has also been neglected by our scholars who in the end must provide the basic data for academic and public consumption. As much as Africa, Latin America has been in many ways a "dark continent." This situation is now changing. There is a new public interest in Latin America stimulated by a realization of its importance to our own national interests. The National Defense Education Act supports the study of Spanish and Portugese and of Latin American society. The Alliance for Progress has . . . dramatized the importance of the region to us. Private foundations have supported research on the study on Latin America. . . .

The same can surely be observed in the sudden spurt of African studies in the United States, which must be traced less to the Africans' increasing "independence" from Europe than to their American-imperialism-sponsored growing dependence on the United States. The participation of anthropology, not to speak of applied anthropology, in this transfer of the "white man's burden" across the Atlantic is evident, and its scientific and political results are predictable.

Project Camelot was not an isolated event, and the widespread hue and cry against direct Defense Department employment of social scientists rather misses the point that virtually the whole of the "free" world's social science is in effect one huge imperialist Camelot project, whoever pays for it. Politically naive though not so innocent liberal social scientists may not be aware of why their research is financed and how their results are used. But, as William Domhoff shows in *Who Rules America?*,² the uses and abuses of social science and scientists are well known to the bourgeois upper class trustees of the quite correctly named Carnegie, Rockefeller, and Ford foundations, *et al.*, and of the perhaps less revealingly named major American universities (who liberally exchange their presidents Rusk, deans Bundy, and finances with each other and the U.S. Department of State). No less uninterested in a "free" worldwide Camelot project is the Panel of the Defense Science Board—National Academy of Sciences of the United States which cogently observes:

In recent years the Department of Defense (DOD) has been confronted with many problems which require support from the behavioral and social sciences. . . . The Armed Forces are no longer engaged solely in warfare. Their missions now include pacification, assistance, "the battle of ideas," etc. All of these missions require an understanding of the urban and rural populations with which our military personnel come in contact—in the new "peacefare" activities or in combat. For many countries throughout the world, we need more knowledge about their beliefs, values, and motivations; their political, religious, and economic organizations; and the impact of various changes or innovations upon their sociocultural patterns . . . [Innovating in] conventional social science methodology . . . is one of the happy cases in which there is substantial overlap in the interests of both DOD and the academic community producing the research. . . . [W]e believe that DOD has been singularly successful in enlisting the interest and services of an eminent group of behavioral scientists in most of the areas relevant to it. . . . On the other hand, the DOD could probably make improvements by assuming more responsibility for stating its needs in terms which are meaningful to the investigator rather than the military. To ask people to do research in "counter-insurgency," "guerrilla warfare," etc., not only produces a less than enthusiastic reaction but also provides no basis for insight into the ways in which they might contribute. . . . The behavioral science community must be made to accept responsibility for recruiting of DOD research managers. . . . The following items are elements that merit consideration as factors in research strategy for military agencies. *Priority Ordered Research Undertakings:* 1 . . . methods, theories and training in the social and behavioral sciences in foreign countries

. . . 2 . . . programs that train foreign social scientists . . . 3 . . . social science research to be conducted by independent indigenous scientists . . . 4 . . . social science tasks to be conducted by major U.S. graduate studies centers in foreign areas . . . 7 . . . studies based in the U.S. that exploit data collected by overseas investigators supported by non-defense agencies. The development of data, resources and analytical methods should be pressed so that data collected for special purposes can be utilized for many additional purposes . . . 8 . . . Collaborate with other programs in the U.S. and abroad that will provide continuing access of Department of Defense personnel to the academic and intellectual resources of the free world . . .[3]

Similarly aware are the nearly 500 intellectuals from seventy countries who at the January 1968 Cultural Congress unanimously proclaimed in an "Appeal of Havana"[4] to all intellectuals of the world:

> We recognize that this enterprise of domination assumes the most diverse forms, from the most brutal to the most insidious, and that it operates at all levels: political, military, economic, racial, ideological, and cultural; and we also recognize that this undertaking is carried on with enormous financial resources and with the help of propaganda agencies disguised as cultural institutions.
>
> Imperialism seeks, by the most varied techniques of indoctrination, to ensure social conformity and political passivity. At the same time, a systematic effort is made to mobilize technicians, men of science, and intellectuals generally in the service of capitalistic and neo-colonialist interests and purposes. Thus, talents and skills which could and should contribute to the task of progress and liberation become, instead, instruments for the commercialization of values, the degradation of culture, and the maintenance of the capitalist economic and social order.
>
> It is the fundamental interest and the imperative duty of intellectuals to resist this aggression and to take up, without delay, the challenge thus posed to them. What is required of them is support for the struggles for national liberation, social emancipation, and cultural decolonization for all the people of Asia, Africa, and Latin America, and for the struggle against imperialism waged in its very center by an ever greater number of black and white citizens of the United States; and to enter the political struggle against conservative, retrograde, and racist forces, to demystify the latter's ideologies and

to attack the structure upon which these rest and the interests they serve . . .

This commitment must begin with an unqualified rejection of the policy of cultural subjection of the United States, and this implies the refusal of all invitations, scholarships, employment, and participation in programs of cultural work and research, where their acceptance could entail collaboration with this policy.

For two reasons, West European and North American anthropologists can best fulfill this responsibility by working in their own societies. One reason is that, although their work abroad serves the interests of imperialism, it does not serve the interests of the colonized peoples among whom the metropolitan anthropologists work. Nor is it likely to. According to Gjessing (quoting Myrdal), mighty political changes, not autonomous reorientation, redirect scientific work. But contemporary political changes are not redirecting metropolitan anthropologists or other scientists to work in the interest of the colonized people, except insofar as they bring these scientists to work toward the destruction of imperialism in the metropolis and thereby toward the liberation of the people everywhere. A second reason for working at home is that, on the other hand, the imperialist metropolis is witnessing mighty political changes which can direct some anthropologists into responsible work at home—as participants in the liberation movement there.

For those North American anthropologists and others who would take this responsibility seriously, Barbara and Alan Haber[5] have summarized several implications:

(1) The movement must be seen as a utility—which helps us define what we do and without which our work loses political relevance . . . If our personal aspirations or professional work precludes our doing things that are safe or respectable, then we are kidding ourselves about our politics. (2) High status and respect and rewards in the professional establishment are foreclosed. We must expect job instability, the likelihood of getting fired periodically, the danger of increasing difficulty in finding jobs. (3) A radical cannot see his loyalty as being to the profession or institution in which he works. Our loyalty is to our political comrades and to the political aims for which we are organizing . . . Obviously this presents a moral dif-

ficulty because others will assume we have traditional loyalties . . .
We are not intellectuals above it all who say the truth to whomever
will listen or asks: we are *partisans* . . . (4) Radicals cannot accept without reservation the code of ethics and responsibility of
their professions. Ethics are not abstract ideals. They are sanctifica-
tions of certain types of social relations, purposes, and loyalties
[which is no news to anthropologists so long as the reference is to
other peoples' ethics rather than their own]. Conventional ethics
entrap us into support of things which we do not support politically and into loyalties which conflict with our own values and
politics. . . .

North American and West European anthropologists who
recognize these facts about their society and who are prepared
to accept the concomitant responsibility can and must draw on
their special skills to serve the movement in three ways. By
analyzing the shoddiness of the emperor's social scientific clothes,
these anthropologists should, like Gough, display imperialism in
its ideological nakedness and denounce those of their colleagues
who continue to enjoy the physical comforts that their pseudo-
scientific suit affords them. Among other things this involves
showing, contrary to Gjessing, that the theoretical and political
limitation of Firth and his followers is not that their theory of
social organization only deals with changes generated inside
rather than outside the social structure. First it means, like Gough
but not Gjessing, showing the real limitation of imperialist-
fathered anthro(a)pological theory and theorists to be that they
arbitrarily define villages or tribes as social systems and invent
theoretical categories like "folk" to hide the naked truth of
economic exploitation and cultural alienation of "my" people by
the real determinant social system, which is imperialism. The
second limitation to be exposed is that this theory is naively or
intentionally restricted to analyzing social change *in* but not *of*
the imperialist and capitalist system. And if, as some anthropologists would have it, the social—including economic and
political—structure really determines culture and ideology, then
the socially responsible anthropologist can go on to analyze why
most of his colleagues prefer studying change in to promoting

change of their own society; is it false consciousness or class consciousness, or what?

A complementary task of the responsible metopolitan anthropologist is to help the movement by pursuing research and developing theory required and requested by the political movement at home. If the responsible metropolitan anthropologist's field work techniques are any good, then let him use them in community studies to analyze the social structure of his own society for a political movement that promotes the necessary social change of that society. This task offers a host of research problems not only in "the other America" but also in the bourgeois anthropologist's own America and Europe. Thirdly, the politically committed and active anthropologists, like the guerrilla doctor who treats his wounded comrades, can draw on his expertise to help the liberation movement at home by doing specific social research jobs for his comrades—rather than for publication. Finally, the anthropologist can become a real partisan—an intellectual revolutionary rather than a revolutionary intellectual. Many metropolitan anthropologists, disregarding mighty political changes, will of course not redirect their work but will persist with their field work abroad. These anthropologists might suitably take a cue from de Tocqueville who one hundred and thirty years ago observed that the true nature of the metropolis is best seen from the perspective of its colonies.

Anthropologists from the economically, politically, and culturally colonialized—and therefore underdeveloped—countries must also work at home for the same reasons. They may be assured that as long as imperialism persists, metropolitan social science including anthropology will never analyze their societies or the imperialist system for them. Still less will it develop the (underdeveloped countries') problem-oriented anthropology Gjessing asks for. If the world view is at all derived from social structure, then only the formerly or still colonialized peoples of the underdeveloped world and the internally colonialized Afro-Americans are likely to find the necessary perspective. For those who would truly seek that perspective, the way has been pointed out by the apostle and practicing anthropologist of the damned of the earth, Frantz Fanon.[6]

> Now, precisely, it would seem that the historical vocation of an authentic national middle-class [mistranslation of "bourgeoisie" from the French original] in an under-developed country is to repudiate its own nature in so far as it is bourgeois, that is to say that in so far as it is the tool of capitalism, and to make itself the willing slave of that revolutionary capital which is the people.
>
> In an under-developed country an authentic national middle-class [bourgeoisie] ought to consider as its bounden duty to betray the calling fate has marked out for it, and to put itself to school with the people: in other words to put at the people's disposal the intellectual and technical capital that it has snatched when going through the colonial universities. But unhappily we shall see that very often the national middle-class [bourgeoisie] does not follow this heroic, positive, fruitful and just path; rather, it disappears with its soul set at peace into the shocking ways—shocking because anti-national—of a traditional bourgeoisie, of a bourgeoisie which is stupidly, contemptibly, cynically bourgeois.

In Asia, Africa, and Latin America responsible anthropologists must be moved by the mighty political changes in these continents; they must become conscious of the responsibility of the intellectual as defined in the "Appeal of Havana"; and they must fortify themselves by the moral commitments demanded by Haber and Fanon. Then, rather than metropolitan anthropologists, however responsible or committed they may be, it is the anthropologists and others from the underdeveloped countries who will be most likely to build the theoretical framework in which change and stability are complementary factors (asked for by Gjessing). Among other research problems, this involves analyzing how class structure and indeed culture and personality in Asia, Africa, Latin America, and also North America are formed and deformed by the world capitalist colonial, neo-colonial, and internal-colonial structure. These same anthropologists from the underdeveloped rather than from the developed countries must also become partisans and activists in the liberation movements of their own countries and begin to work on the many facets of a "research project devoted to the problem of how poorly armed guerrillas might more effectively resist a brutal and devastating military technology" (mentioned by Berreman citing Chomsky). This in turn involves, among other things, studying how the colonial and class structure and their contemporary transformation generates not only counter-insurgency but insurgency as well, and thanks to what grievances which sectors of the population can at particular times and places be politically and militarily mobilized in the long war to destroy the violent, exploitative, racist, and alienating capitalist system, and in the liberated areas to build a truly free and humane society.

This endeavor requires more than the simple study of anthropological medicine. It calls for the practice of that medicine, following the example of Che Guevara and thousands like him, including also some anthropologists, in Vietnam and elsewhere. Then the counter-insurgency formula of ten anthropologists for each guerrilla (cited by Berreman) will surely have to yield to a victorious popular insurgency formula of ten thousand guerrillas with each anthropologist worthy of the name.

## NOTES

1. Charles Wagley, "Introduction," in Charles Wagley, ed., *Social Science Research in Latin America* (New York: Columbia University Press, 1964), p. 3.
2. G. William Domhoff, *Who Rules America?* (Englewood Cliffs, N.J.: Prentice Hall, 1967).
3. Defense Science Board, National Academy of Sciences, "Report of the Panel on Defense Social and Behavioral Sciences" (Williamstown, Mass., Berkshire Summer Study, July 5–14, 1967), pp. 33, 38, 40–43, 52.
4. "Appeal of Havana," in "Proceedings of the Cultural Congress of Havana," *Granma*, January 21, 1968.
5. Barbara and Alan Haber, "Getting by with a Little Help from Our Friends," *Our Generation*, Vol. 5, No. 2 (1967), pp. 95, 96.
6. Frantz Fanon, *The Wretched of the Earth* (New York: Grove Press, 1966), pp. 122–123.

# III

## ECONOMIC IMPERIALISM

# 8

## AID OR EXPLOITATION?

Does American aid and investment contribute much or little to, or even hinder, Latin American economic development? The recent argument between the Brazilian and American embassies on this question invites analysis and comment. The Brazilian viewpoint, expressed by its embassy in Washington (in the charge of Roberto Campos de Oliveira) is that American aid is small and not altruistic. The American answer, delivered by U.S. Ambassador Lincoln Gordon in a lecture before the National Economic Council of Brazil, is that in exporting capital the United States incurs great sacrifice and contributes significantly to the economic development of Brazil.

Unfortunately, if subjected to non-diplomatic analysis, the reality of the economic relations of the United States and Brazil, or any other Latin American country, appears much less pleasant than either Ambassador suggests. In the following, I summarize the arguments of the two Ambassadors on each of the topics discussed, appending my own comment.

### Amount of Capital Transferred

*Brazil:* The real amount of resources the United States offers Brazil is smaller than generally imagined both because it should be measured in funds transferred rather than in those committed and because the return flow of amortization and interest payments must be deducted from the gross.

*United States:* The American Ambassador does not understand

---

1963. This essay originally appeared in Portuguese in *Jornal do Brasil* (Rio de Janeiro), March 23, 1963. It is reprinted from the November 16, 1963, issue of *The Nation*, where it appeared as "Brazil: Exploitation or Aid?"

why the Brazilian Embassy lends importance to the distinction between authorizations and disbursements, since the United States keeps its promises and thus makes the gap between the two only a matter of time. He also feels it is confusing and bad economics to deduct the amortization and interest payments from gross transfers because it deprecates the American capital's contribution to the construction of steel mills, hydroelectric plants, etc., while it is in Brazil. Moreover, American capital improves the Brazilian balance of payments. Measuring this way, it would appear that the flow of capital is not from the United States to Brazil, but rather from Brazil to the United States.

*Comment:* In reality, the net contribution of United States capital to Brazil is neither large nor small, but negative. The Brazilian Embassy's distinction between commitment and disbursement is easy to understand if one considers that, of the promises made at Punta del Este, some funds were canceled by the U.S. Congress and Executive, others are disbursed by private firms not bound by government agreement, and all of them are contingent on Brazilian compliance with United States demands about expropriation, International Monetary Fund financial policy, etc. For the balance of payments and the exchange rate, transfers, not promises, are significant.

The "appearance" that, if amortization and interest are counted, the outflow of capital is really from Brazil to the United States instead of vice versa unfortunately reflects reality quite accurately. Official Brazilian figures for the years 1947–60 indicate an inflow of $1,814 million in new investment and loans and an outflow of $2,459 million in remittance of profits and interest. Adding an estimated $1,022 million of "services," largely representing clandestine remittances, total outflow becomes $3,481 million, or nearly twice the inflow, and the net outflow $1,667 million.

This outflow from Brazil is by no means a historical accident or a result only of Brazilian calculations. An ECLA study shows that in no decade of the past century has the total flow of goods and services out of Brazil been smaller than the flow into Brazil. Turning to other parts of Latin America (Argentina, Chile, Peru, Venezuela, Colombia, Mexico), U.S. Department of Commerce

figures for the period 1950–61 show net new private U.S. investment as $2,962 million and remittances of profit and interest
thereon of $6,875 million, or well more than double the amount,
for a net withdrawal of $3,913 million. U.S. aid and loans of
$3,384 million and repayments and interest thereon of $1,554
million (to date, with more of course to come in the future),
still leave a net capital movement to the United States of $2,081
million.

But in these calculations the flow *to* Brazil, such as of surplus
food, is measured in often inflated, so-called market prices that
the U.S. seller sets himself, while the flow *from* Brazil is measured
in dollars actually bought by Brazil. Additionally, these data do
not include most of the Brazilian and other national private
capital, currently often estimated at $10 billion for Latin America,
which is transferred abroad (such as to the famous Swiss and New
York banks). The real effective drainage of capital from Brazil
and the other capital-poor countries is thus even larger than
appears from the above official figures. It is difficult to see how the
American Ambassador imagines this constant American drain of
funds from Brazil to be helping Brazil's balance of payments. It
is, instead, a principal source of balance-of-payments deficits.

To speak of American capital, public or private, going into the
development of basic heavy industry in Brazil is more than misleading. Under the Alliance for Progress, especially, the emphasis
of American public capital investment in Latin America is on
education and health—latrine-building, as it has been aptly
dubbed. U.S. private capital, as the daily experience of anyone can
attest, prefers the export, processing, and service industries—
Coca-colonization, in a word. Far from contributing to Brazil's
industrialization, this investment, no less than more traditional
investment in raw materials extraction, serves to keep the economy
underdeveloped. Indeed, it deforms the economy into one ever
less able to develop by increasingly absorbing Brazilian capital
and misdirecting it. Often an initial sum of capital brought from
the United States by an American firm is supplemented, or even
multiplied, by borrowing Brazilian capital from local U.S. banks
with Brazilian deposits, or from Brazilian banks, or even from
the Brazilian government. The combined capital is then invested

not where it will best serve the interests of Brazil's development, but where it will serve the interests of the American firm's development. The earnings that are not shipped home are then reinvested in Brazil, often not by building new productive facilities, but by buying up or buying into existing Brazilian installations and thus transferring their direction into American hands also.

Now, the Brazilian "expropriation" proposal offers American investors government aid in withdrawing their capital from less profitable public utilities and transferring "a minimum of 80 percent" into much more profitable industries. Thus, American capital, with financial and technical advantages due to its international connections and with additional special privileges granted by the Brazilian government "to attract foreign capital," progressively de-nationalizes Brazilian industry, misdirects Brazilian investment, integrates the weaker Brazilian economy increasingly with the stronger American one—on which it thus becomes dependent—and thereby adds further to Brazil's balance-of-payments difficulties.

## Degree of United States Sacrifice

*Brazil:* Between 1940 and 1962 American aid to Brazil has meant little or no sacrifice to the United States. Half the total comes from the Export-Import Bank, which consistently makes profits. Another 35 percent represents the supply of agricultural surpluses under Public Law 480. American aid was tied to the purchase of American goods and was part of a program to develop foreign markets for goods that were surplus at home and could thus contribute to the utilization of excess capacity in the export industry.

*United States:* The manner of financing is unimportant. Had American funds not been used in this way, they could have been put to some other use. Tying American aid to the purchase of American goods is natural and does not reduce the value of the aid, since useful aid must reflect itself ultimately in the transfer of real goods. In general, since the marginal capital-output ratio in the United States is higher than in Brazil, the investment of

American capital in Brazil instead of at home really represents a considerable loss to the American economy. The excess-capacity argument could carry some weight only if the American economy had been chronically depressed since the war, which has not been the case.

*Comment:* American aid and investment are no sacrifice, but an instrument for obtaining considerable Brazilian riches and for preserving the present monopolist structure of the American economy. The capital-output ratio is quite irrelevant to the issue. American firms do not invest in Brazil in a sector with the average of the latter's marginal capital-output ratio, and they do not draw their investment funds from such a sector of the American economy. Much more relevant to the firms are their profits in Brazil and their excess capacity at home. An American business commission in Brazil observed that "profits in Brazil are normally much higher than in the United States. It is not uncommon that a factory pays for itself in one or two years"—that is, makes a profit of 100 percent or 50 percent per year. These rates, however, refer only to profit on total capital invested. Since part of that total represents capital borrowed from Brazilian sources at low cost, and another part represents reinvestment of such earnings in the years following the original introduction of capital, it is similarly not uncommon that the real rate of earnings on American capital in Brazil is in thousands of percent per annum.

Turning to the U.S. economy, unemployment has not fallen below 5 percent in several years and the minimum rate keeps rising. The excess installed capital capacity of these same large export firms is several times that percentage, whatever the average marginal capital-output ratio may be for the economy as a whole. For them, export and foreign earnings are a necessity, not a sacrifice. And as the Alliance for Progress makes so eminently clear—consider, for instance, the public statement by three of its official spokesmen, including David Rockefeller, that the Alliance should improve conditions for American invest.ent in Latin America—the purpose of U.S. government aid is to pave the way for the economic activity of this same private U.S. capital.

Just as U.S. government purchase of surplus agricultural products and their subsequent shipment abroad as "food for peace" supports the increasing monopolization and therefore excess capacity of U.S. agriculture, government "aid" money provides the credits for foreign purchase of increasingly monopolized U.S. industry. At the same time, the strings attached to the money are designed to maintain or improve the political and economic climate abroad for this same U.S. economic activity. That also explains the tying of loans to purchases of U.S. goods. For real goods could be transferred through multilateral trade, if the U.S. government did not wish to avoid helping Brazil to trade more with Western Europe—let alone with the socialist countries. And the development of U.S. balance-of-payments difficulties only increases these same American needs.

### Gains and Losses from Trade

*Brazil:* The terms of trade have been turning to the disadvantage of Brazil. Between 1955 and 1961, the prices paid for Brazilian products have fallen considerably, and the prices of American exports have risen. The result has been a loss to Brazil greater than the total of all aid since World War II.

*United States:* The argument of the Brazilian Embassy about the terms of trade is mistaken. In less professional circles, these price changes are described as a "process of exploitation" by the industrialized countries, especially the United States. Had the Brazilian Embassy chosen 1947–49, instead of the high-price 1950–53 base, it would have come to the opposite conclusion. In each decade since 1920 the terms of trade were worse for Brazil than they are at present, and only in the 1950's were they better. One might equally well talk of "presents" made to Brazil in the twelve years since 1950. The majority of serious students are highly skeptical of long-term generalizations about tendencies inherent in the terms of trade. Regarding the question, "Are coffee prices today too low?", simply as economists we would have to answer, "No." The idea that the industrialized nations in a certain sense "owe" the nations who export primary commodities a certain level of terms of trade seems neither reasonable nor desirable. There is no conspiracy to deteriorate the terms of trade. On the contrary, competition to sell is greater than ever.

*Comment:* Brazil and other poorer countries are falling increasingly behind the already industrialized ones. The economic relations between the two, taken as a whole, are quite evidently a contributing, if not the crucial, factor in this loss by the underdeveloped, raw-materials exporters. The countries which were able to avoid or break this relation have also been able to avoid this loss. If in the 1930's and 1940's the terms of trade were less favorable to Brazil, this was in good part due to the depression and the war and because Latin America generally acceded to American pleas to keep raw materials prices lower than they might have been as their contribution to the war effort. The higher prices in the years 1950–53 were, of course, due to the Korean War, during which this same American ideological argument carried less weight abroad; and since that time these prices have indeed fallen again. It thus seems difficult to accept the thesis that the prices of the 1950's constituted a gift to Brazil.

Instead, serious economists *can* demonstrate that the terms of trade, as part of the economic relationship taken as a whole, are too low, even at their highest, to prevent the exploitation and permit the development of Brazil and other poorer countries. Thus the idea that the developed countries owe something to the underdeveloped ones seems quite reasonable and desirable unless one still wishes to advance the argument that the "hidden hand" regulates economic relationships. This is an argument long used to hide the fact that the general standard of living in Brazil, and in almost all other poor countries, was *higher before* they became entangled in the relationship of "trade," "aid," and especially of "foreign investment" than it is today. Moreover, rather than competition, monopoly and cartels, protected by suprastates such as the European Common Market, NATO, the petroleum industry, etc., and of course rising prices, are the trend in the industrialized world today. And these arrangements most certainly are conspiratorial and prejudicial to the underdeveloped world.

## Effects of United States Capital in Brazil

*Brazil:* U.S. aid money has been well used by Brazil. The rate of growth of income per capita has been one of the highest in Latin

America for the decade 1950–61. There is no better index of adequate use of foreign aid than the achievement of a high growth rate. More than 90 percent of imports have been accounted for by essential raw materials, basic foodstuffs, and equipment and parts.

*United States:* The substantial contribution of U.S. public and private capital to Brazilian economic growth in general, and especially to desirable structural change toward manufacturing, import substitution, and increased export capacity, refutes the clichés about the "process of exploitation."

*Comment:* Both Ambassadors misdirect their analysis and exaggerate the effects of U.S. aid, which in reality retarded Brazilian economic growth. Evaluating the use of American aid, as does the Brazilian Embassy, by reference to the Brazilian growth rate is unacceptable. As the Brazilian note points out, recent per capita growth in most Latin American countries has been largely zero or negative, while in Brazil it has been 3 percent for the period since World War II and 3.9 percent since 1957. However, as the Minister for Planning, Celso Furtado, points out, the most important economic development in Brazil occurred during the 1930's when, due to the depression, American export of capital and goods reached its lowest point and Brazil changed over from importing all of its capital equipment to producing it at home. And during this crucial take-off into economic development, the per capita rate of growth registered was 0.3 percent. Thus, the significant index of good use of foreign and domestic resources for Brazil is not, as the Brazilian Ambassador suggests, the growth rate, as much as it is the creation of a national productive capacity, especially in heavy industry, and initially for the domestic market. American aid and investment decidedly does not contribute to this process.

It is perhaps his use of an incorrect criterion which permits the Brazilian Ambassador to go on to make his strange claim that the "aid" resulted in the import of goods important for Brazil's economic development. For a country of continental proportions with every conceivable raw material, and perhaps the greatest agricultural potential on this globe, it seems indeed a strange argument to claim that Brazil is putting its resources to good use when it imports "essential" raw materials and "basic" foodstuffs, instead of importing equipment and technology which would permit it to develop that potential. Much of the "equipment and parts," to say nothing of the remaining 10 percent of imports, should undoubtedly have also been produced nationally.

Even disregarding the negative consequences of foreign aid and investment, their contribution to total investment in Brazil is, contrary to the American Ambassador's claim, minuscule and easily forgone. According to a Brazilian estimate for the years 1950–54, all foreign (including American) investment amounted to 1.32 percent of Brazilian Gross National Product, or 8.2 percent of total investment in Brazil. For the period 1955–59, a Brazilian estimate of the share of foreign investment is 2 percent of gross and 2.8 percent of net investment. But, as we saw earlier, large parts of even this small "contribution" of foreign capital are no contribution at all, since much of this capital was Brazilian to begin with and is foreign only in ownership, control, and earnings. It is evident, therefore, that Brazil could easily find national capital that would more than substitute for so small a foreign addition to her total investment, and dispense at the same time with the damages inflicted by foreign investment on its economic development.

The American Ambassador's assertion that U.S. capital has contributed to desirable structural change in the Brazilian economy is even less founded in reality. Rather, American capital has contributed to the already much too great concentration of capital in São Paulo to the prejudice of the other regions, especially of the Northeast. Similarly, capital has flown into the export, processing, and service industries to the disadvantage of basic industries and Brazil. Tariff exclusion of relatively inessential products has drawn national, but proportionally especially foreign, capital into the production of these same relatively inessential, but protected, products. The American Ambassador's "import substitution" is therefore at best a two-edged sword. But even this substitution of specific imports does not necessarily contribute to the reduction of imports as a whole. On the contrary, if this investment goes into certain kinds of processing, it makes "essential"—as the Brazilian Ambassador observes in another context—the import of more raw materials. If it helps to shift the distribution of income to groups with higher propensities to import, it increases imports as a whole. As for increasing export capacity, to which the American Ambassador also refers, Brazilian capacity to export non-raw materials remains notoriously low. And using scarce resources to increase Brazil's capacity to export *raw materials* is certainly a most questionable policy.

## Economic Policy for Brazil

*United States:* The serious problem for Brazil is the expansion of export earnings. Since it cannot hope to regain the predominant position in the coffee, cocoa, and sugar markets already lost to new producers, Brazil should follow the example of Japan which, when faced with declining earnings from textile exports, expanded into shipbuilding and electronics. Following a similar policy, Brazil could expand its exports of iron ore, meat, and manufactured products. And in order not to cut itself off from technological progress and thereby from economic progress, Brazil should continue to invite foreign investment.

*Comment:* Brazil's urgent need at this time is not still more outward-directed, but rather inward-directed, economic development. Far from emphasis on exports, as the American Ambassador suggests, this requires regional and sectoral economic integration and additional basic industry for national needs. Least of all does it imply or permit using the resources urgently needed for that national task to expand two lines of raw material exports—iron ore and meat—to serve the needs of the already industrialized countries.

It is difficult to see how the American Ambassador draws the lesson he does for Brazil from the example of Japan. Japan expanded into shipbuilding and electronics, but Brazil is to expand into iron ore and meat. Moreover, Japan is at a quite different stage of economic development than is Brazil. The export market Japan was losing was in textiles, not in coffee. How did that country achieve this degree of industrialization and development? Not by pursuing the policy the American Ambassador prescribes for Brazil, but by doing precisely the opposite. In fact, Japan is the crucial example among the capitalist economies, as the Soviet Union is among the socialist, of a country which, in order to achieve the take-off into economic development in a world of already industrialized and imperialist countries, began by isolating itself substantially from foreign trade and totally from foreign investment and control. Neither country found it necessary, let it be noted, to permit such foreign investment in order to take advantage of the technology of the industrially more advanced countries. Only *after* they had forged an economic structure and their own control of it, which permitted them to take advantage of more intimate economic ties with already advanced countries, did Japan and the Soviet Union enter into such relations. Thus, Japan indeed does provide the example most relevant to Brazil's present economic organization, but the national stance it points to is one of independence, not one of dependence. Let it be noted, however, that on this road Japan also became an imperialist power itself, with all that implies.

## Conclusion

The two Ambassadors, although both highly reputable economists of similar training, evidently have quite different official views of Brazilian-American economic relations. As they themselves imply in their reference to the diplomatic schizophrenia of defending abroad what one denounces at home, and vice versa, their differences may probably be traced to the circumstances and interests of the two countries, of the two worlds, of the rich and of the poor, whose diplomatic representatives they are. The American describes a relationship in which Big Brother selflessly provides much of the capital, technology, and good advice (like that of the Ambassador himself), which the little brother, Brazil, needs to grow up into an independent industrialized adult. Though Americans do not really owe Brazilians anything, they incur considerable sacrifices on Brazil's behalf; and any gains they may derive are quite accidental and extraneous to the relation. Finding it difficult to accept this rosy picture, the Brazilian suggests instead that the real importance of U.S. aid is to the U.S. economy itself, that the hand-in-aid gives only little and that even this and more is taken away in trade by the other hand. Still, being the official diplomatic representative of, among other influential groups, Brazilian groups which benefit from current Brazilian-U.S. relations, the Brazilian Embassy paints a picture that is not altogether dark.

Dispensing with diplomatic polity, but still confining the discussion largely to the topics selected by the Ambassadors, the comments of the present author suggest that, in its current form, this relation is neither "very" nor "slightly" beneficial, but instead definitely prejudicial to Brazil. Far from contributing capital to, and improving the structure of, the Brazilian economy, the United States draws capital out of Brazil and with what remains gains control of Brazilian capital and channels it into directions that increase Brazil's dependence on the United States and hinder Brazil's economic growth. The terms of trade form neither an accidental nor an extraneous but an integral part of this process. Far from pointing the way to Brazil's industrialization and development, the American Ambassador's recommended policies—emphasis on private enterprise, foreign investment, more raw-materials exports, etc.—would maintain Brazil's position as an underdeveloped, dependent economy. It thus appears that the United States takes away with both hands; the picture is neither rosy nor neutral, but quite dark.

The picture would emerge still darker or pitch-black if the analysis were extended beyond the selected topics to include the entire economic relationship between Brazil and the United States. Consider, for instance, the imposition, on threat of withholding short-term credits, of the policy of the International Monetary Fund. Supposedly to reduce balance-of-payments deficits, this policy calls for reducing exchange restrictions and thus permitting more transfer of capital out of Brazil; Brazilian devaluation to make the cruzeiro cheaper and the dollar dearer; supposedly anti-inflationary measures which shift income from the poor to the rich, thereby weakening domestic production and increasing the demand for imports—all of which result in new balance-of-payments deficits, new loans, and new dosages of the same IMF medicine.

One might ask why, if all this "aid" is really so damaging to

Brazil, does Brazil permit and even seek it? Again, the answer is to be sought in the very Brazil-U.S. relationship itself. First, of course, the relationship does reward *some* Brazilians with profits and power. These groups then apply this same power to efforts to maintain the relationship. Second, with time Brazil becomes so dependent that breaking away involves such high costs in the short run—whatever the long run gains—that many other groups, and especially any government, are loath to accept them. Thus, in the short run, failure to receive credits to refinance the already existing debt would force a cut of imports that are necessary in the same short run, because in the meantime the same economic relationship has destroyed or prevented the creation of productive capacity that would obviate these imports. If, going a step further out of the relationship, American investments are threatened, the short-term cost, as the case of Cuba demonstrates, is the stoppage of all trade. In a word, Brazil and other countries find themselves in a kind of debt-slavery relationship not unlike that of the peasant with his moneylender-landlord the world over, a relationship in which the very exploitation appears to make its own continuance necessary.

Finally, for what it may be worth, and as the analysis by the American Ambassador and in part that by the American-trained Brazilian Ambassador demonstrated, the United States also supplies the economic science—and the ideology as well—that tries to pretend this exploitative relationship is really necessary and desirable.

# 9

## MECHANISMS OF IMPERIALISM

*It is madness for one nation to expect
disinterested help from another.*
—George Washington

*The United States does not have friends; it has interests.*
—John Foster Dulles

In the previous essay, I examined the official Brazilian and United States views of economic relations between the two countries as presented by Roberto de Oliveira Campos, then Brazilian Ambassador in Washington and now the minister in charge of economic policy in the military dictatorship which took power in April, and by Lincoln Gordon, then and now American Ambassador to Brazil. My conclusions were that both official views are wrong: the United States does not help Brazil a lot (Gordon) or a little (Campos), but rather exploits Brazil unmercifully and stunts and distorts its economic development. In this essay I propose to probe more deeply into these questions, especially in the hope of throwing light on a few of the numerous and often hidden mechanisms of which the imperialist countries make use in their relations with the colonial and semi-colonial countries of the underdeveloped world.

### The Flow of Capital from Brazil to the United States

It is widely believed that the United States and other developed capitalist countries contribute more capital to the under-

1964. This essay originally appeared in the September 1964 issue of *Monthly Review*. It was written in answer to a long letter from a reader who had taken serious exception to the essay reprinted as the previous chapter.

162

developed countries than they receive from them. Nonetheless, all available statistics, including those compiled by the official agencies of the developed countries themselves, show precisely the opposite, as we saw in the previous chapter.

My present purpose is not to dwell further on the amount of the capital transfer from Brazil and other countries to the United States. Instead it is proposed to inquire into some of the reasons for and sources of this—for Brazil and others—so prejudicial capital flow. When the facts finally force American business, political, and unfortunately also academic, spokesmen for American capital to admit the existence of this capital flow from the poor underdeveloped countries to the rich developed ones, they often try to defend it in the following terms: Either it is said that the direction of the flow is the result of the accidental or deliberate choice of a year or set of years in which the return flow on past investment happens to be greater than the outflow of new investment; or it is said instead (and sometimes in addition) that this drainage of capital from the poor underdeveloped countries really helps them to develop and that it is normal and logical that the capital flow into the investing and lending country—in this case into the United States—should be greater than the capital flow out of it because, after all, profits and interest legitimately earned abroad must be added to the amortization and repayment of the original investment.

The facts of economic life completely vitiate this American logic. If the disparity between capital inflow from and outflow to Brazil is as normal and legitimate as its defenders claim, then why is it that according to the late President John F. Kennedy the capital inflow to the United States from the underdeveloped countries in 1960 was $1,300 million and the capital outflow from the United States to the same countries $200 million, while in respect to the advanced countries of Western Europe the outflow from the United States ($1,500 million) exceeded the inflow ($1,000 million) by a wide margin? [1] Why does *U.S. News & World Report* of December 25, 1961, using Department of Commerce data, find the same pattern to obtain for the five-year period 1956–61, that is, a ratio of inflow to the United States to outflow from the United States of 147 percent for Latin America,

164 percent for the underdeveloped world as a whole, and 43 percent for Western Europe? To eliminate still further the possibility that this disparity may be due to accidentally comparing years of low current outflow and high return flow of previous outflows, we may add up (as the Department of Commerce never does) the officially registered capital flows into and out of the United States for each year from 1950 to 1961 as reported in the *Survey of Current Business* and find that the total capital outflow is $13,708 million and the "corresponding" inflow $23,204 million, or an inflow/outflow ratio of 177 percent.[2] Are we to believe that it is normal and legitimate that profits and interest earned by the United States in weak underdeveloped countries are very much greater than in the strong developed ones, the United States included?

The disparity between capital inflows and outflows is more realistically explained by examining, as I propose to do in the following paragraphs, the source and composition of these flows than by appeal to any simplistic theories. In the first place, the argument that it is only logical for capital inflows to the United States to exceed outflows because, after all, the latter must earn a profit is premised on the unstated but erroneous assumption that official capital inflows into the United States are earnings on capital the United States previously sent abroad. As a matter of fact, much of the capital on which Americans "earn" profits in Brazil is Brazilian in origin and American only in ownership, control, and earnings. The Brazilian origins of "American" capital are manifold. We here take note of only those which fall under the titles of loans, concessions, and foreign exchange privileges.

Direct loans from the government's Bank of Brazil to American firms and to mixed American-Brazilian consortia are common in industry, commerce, and agriculture. In 1961, the two giant American worldwide cotton merchants, SANBRA and Anderson & Clayton, received $54 billion cruzeiros in loans from the Bank of Brazil, or 47 percent of that bank's entire agricultural and industrial loan portfolio.[3] By re-loaning this money (at higher interest rates, of course) to wholesalers and producers of cotton whom they thereby control; by buying up harvested stocks, storing them in government provided bins, and speculating with them later; by monopolizing important sectors of organization and distribution—these American firms use *Brazilian* capital to control much of the Brazilian domestic and export cotton market (as they also do that of many other countries) and to ship the profits home to the United States. Swift, Armour, and Wilson (recently involved in a public scandal for having partly exported and partly held back for a higher price the meat consigned to them by the government for storage and sale to the public), the A. & P.'s subsidiary American Coffee Company, and other American monopolies similarly derive fat profits from using Brazilian capital to monopolize critical sectors of the domestic and export markets. American banks like the ubiquitous National City Bank of New York, insurance companies, and other financial institutions evidently work almost entirely with Brazilian capital, loan much of it to American non-financial firms in Brazil, and then serve as a channel to send their own and others' profits on this Brazilian capital "back" home.

In the public utility sector especially, the ownership and earnings of so-called American capital are based, not on original investment of capital, but on concessions, exorbitant use rates, and other privileges. The capital is provided by Brazil. In 1907, the São Paulo Light Co. (now merged with the Rio Light, Rio Gas, Brazilian Telephone, and other companies in the Brazilian Traction Co.) took over a concession already granted to two Brazilian individuals until 1950 and then got it extended to 1990. In 1923, by engaging an ex-President as its lawyer to fight a legal battle through several courts up to the Supreme Court—still staffed by the ex-President's appointees—the company, contrary to the stipulations of its contract, obtained an extension of the concession for its telephone subsidiary. Later the concession of the gas subsidiary was also extended. For its starting capital São Paulo Light issued bonds for $6 million. It then took over the already existing streetcars and associated properties. Following the usual procedure, the various light companies financed expansion of service to new areas by assessments on, and more recently by loans from, the communities to be served, while equipment was purchased out of earnings from exorbitant public utility rates. Even so, as any user can testify, service always lags far behind demand (electricity rationing is now normal in Rio and sometimes reaches blackouts of five hours daily). Through political influence and bribery, the company managed to delay the construction of competing facilities at one site for fifteen years. In 1948 the company received $90 million in loans from the International Bank, for which it obtained a guarantee from the Brazilian government. Part of this foreign exchange was used, of course, not to import new equipment, but to convert cruzeiro earnings into dollars for remittance to the United States. To avoid showing exorbitant profits, the company increased its registered capital base by issuing stock dividends to its owners. Between 1918 and 1947, Brazilian Traction made profits of $550 million, of which $165 million were sent home. Now that public utilities have become unprofitable relative to other industries and now that the Brazilian government wants to take them over in order to permit the expansion of needed service, the American owners bring all possible diplomatic and other pressure to bear in usually successful attempts to obtain once again the remaining equipment's value several times over through "expropriation." [4]

Addressing the Brazilian Senate in 1953, President Vargas' Treasury Minister said, "I have to declare that foreign capital . . . demands guarantees to enter the country, greater guarantees to remain in it, and still greater ones to withdraw from it. Therefore, it does not seem desirable for any country and still less for Brazil." [5] After establishing a state petroleum company and threatening to do the same with electric power, the Vargas government was, owing to foreign and domestic pressure, replaced by one which proposed the "creation of a climate favorable fór the investment of foreign capital in the country." To this end the Superintendency of Money and Credit (SUMOC) issued Instruction 113 according to which, in the words of the President of the Federation of Industries of the State of São Paulo, "foreign firms can bring their entire equipment in at the free market price . . . national ones, however, have to do so through exchange licenses established in import categories. In this way there was created veritable discrimination against national industry. We do not plead for preferential treatment but for equal opportunities." [6] Moreover, foreign firms were permitted to import used equipment (often already depreciated for tax purposes at home), while Brazilians could import only new machinery. As a result, Brazilians, who on this basis were unable to compete with foreign firms and/or who were unable to get assignments of foreign exchange from the Central Bank, were forced to combine with non-Brazilians who, though they might not contribute much of any capital to the common enterprise, could contribute and capitalize on special privileges as foreigners. Ten years after Vargas, President Goulart was still forced to observe:

> In fact it is incomprehensible—and much less justifiable—that in this time of renewed heavy burden for the people, innumerable superfluous or easily dispensable products which are consumed mainly by the richer classes continue to enjoy the benefits of an exchange rate of 475 cruzeiros [the market rate was then 800 cruzeiros]. The same exchange rate as for petroleum products and other basic goods is enjoyed by extract of whisky and of Coca-Cola. . . . The disappearance of our scarce foreign exchange resources occurs not only through imports. The concession of exchange privileges to remit foreign exchange destined for the payment of unessential services causes the same harmful effects to our balance of payments.[7]

It is worthy of note that, "fascist" or "communizing" or not, as Presidents Vargas and Goulart respectively have been termed by the foreign press, the effective power of these Presidents was evidently insufficient to combat the forces, inside and outside their own governments, which benefit from and fight to maintain those privileges which accrue to small but powerful foreign and domestic interests at the cost of national development. There are, of course, influential Brazilian interests which willingly cooperate in this provision of Brazilian national capital to American firms so long as, in association with this powerful ally from the North, they can participate in some of the spoils.

*Effects on Brazilian Economic and Industrial Structure*

Spokesmen for the supposed advantages of American investment for Brazil often claim that the distribution of American investments and loans among productive sectors in the receiving country contributes to that country's economic development, and that the resulting import substitution is converting the Brazilian economy into one capable of self-sustained overall economic growth. The facts support neither of these contentions.

We have already noted in part what kind of contribution American owned, *but not supplied*, capital makes to Brazilian development in the trade and public utilities sectors which, according to the Department of Commerce, absorb 43 percent of the total. Of the 791 American firms in Brazil in 1960, we must certainly call into question the allegedly essential contribution to the development of its economy made by the 125 import, export, and other commercial houses; the banking, insurance, real estate, and other financial institutions, which are 64 in number; petroleum distribution (by the worldwide petroleum monopoly of notorious fame); retailing (such as Sears and Roebuck, which outside the United States is a luxury chain); and publishing, advertising, hotels, cinema, and other services (including towel supply), which account for 77 more dubious contributions to a solid basis for Brazilian economic development.[8] Coca-Cola at least built or equipped a manufacturing plant.

As for the 54 percent of American capital which the Department of Commerce attributes to manufacturing, no detailed breakdown is given. In 1959, light consumer goods industry accounted for 48 percent of foreign, including American, manufacturing in Brazil, of which approximately 20 percent was in the food and beverage sector, including seventeen bottling and ice cream firms.[9] Even the 40 percent of United States investment which the Department of Commerce attributes to basic industry is not telling. To serve as a base for self-sustained industrialization and growth, investment must, all will agree, produce the materials and equipment—steel, machinery, trucks, tractors—necessary for expanded production. But the bulk of this investment is in the automotive industry, and there it does not produce primarily trucks and tractors which are needed for development purposes but which are not immediately profitable; rather, it seeks maximum profits in the production of passenger cars for the high-income market.

In general, then, American enterprises in Brazil tend to produce non-essentials, and they do so largely with Brazilian capital.

But this is not all. The composition of foreign investment and its effects on the structure of the Brazilian economy are crucial to the maintenance of underdevelopment there. It is often claimed that American investment in Brazil results in import substitution which creates Brazilian capacity for autonomously directed and self-sustained economic development. Examining only American investment in the most basic sectors, we find, unfortunately, that the facts demonstrate largely the opposite. It is characteristic of American investment in Brazil and elsewhere that the giant investing corporations set up only a part of a particular productive process abroad and keep a critical, though it may be a smaller, part under their immediate control at home. The archetype of this arrangement is the Brazilian assembly plant of an American corporation which is made to depend on the import from the parent corporation of the basic equipment needed, of its spare parts and replacements, often of critical components, especially the highly tooled ones, of critical raw materials, associated patents, technicians, transport, insurance, and, above all, of the technical and organizational schema of the productive process.[10] Significantly, this arrangement also serves to eliminate any existing or potential Brazilian markets for inventive engineering and ties Brazilian technological development to the American economic structure; the reason is, of course, that the solutions to technical problems are already engineered into the productive process in the United States and are exported to Brazil in the form of the technological organization established there.

The Brazilian economy is tied still further to the stronger American economy when American interests "cooperate" with Brazilian capital in joint enterprises, or when American firms farm out part of the productive process to local suppliers of components. While the propaganda has it that the United States is stimulating private enterprise and economic development, the reality is that American corporations use Brazilian capital for their own purposes, transferring part of the risk and cost of demand fluctuations to the local supplier, channeling Brazilian capital into the provision of goods and services which maximize the American corporations' profits, and binding the Brazilian economy increasingly to themselves in particular and the American economy in general. Moreover, American influence thus increases not only in the Brazilian economy but also in Brazilian political life; and, interestingly, in view of the claims about import substitution, this process results in increasing American determination of the composition even of Brazilian imports. Brazilian exports, of course, have been largely in American hands. Thus, what to Americans may appear as "the natural process of import substitution" appears to Brazilians, other than those directly cooperating in the process, as what it is: the progressive domination of the Brazilian economy and the strangulation of its capacity for national development.

Particularly noteworthy in Brazil, Argentina, Mexico, and India, but increasingly visible elsewhere in the underdeveloped world, is the ever greater emphasis on medium and light consumer goods industries. These are economically and technologically dependent on the monopoly corporations of the imperialist countries for many of their capital goods and for parts. Thus the imperialist domination and the national dependence which have produced much of the apparent growth of the postwar years and the real stagnation of the present and future for these, the most industrialized of the capitalist underdeveloped countries, is the direct and inevitable result of their participation in the imperialist system— whose structure and development necessarily produces these results.

The problem of imports is compounded by that of exports which are not keeping pace. The United Nations Economic Commission for Latin America (ECLA) notes that, subtracting petroleum, Latin American exports have risen only 40 percent since 1938, while world trade has doubled and the trade of the developed countries has tripled. ECLA notes further, "that the deterioration of Latin America in world trade is one of the most important points of strangulation of its economic and social development." [11] Add to this the drain of capital out of Brazil and the misuses of its own resources engendered by foreign investment, and the result is Brazil's chronic balance of payments deficit. Now come the foreign loans.

These loans, we are asked to believe, are also development-producing. The fact is that to an increasing extent they are deposited in New York banks to cover the dollar needs of Americans in Brazil. As Simon Hanson has repeatedly pointed out in his *Latin American Letter* (for American businessmen) and in *Inter-American Economic Affairs* (Summer 1962), Alliance for Progress dollars are destined to serve as the source of the foreign exchange needed by Brazil to buy out American owned (but as we saw, not supplied) capital in Brazilian public utilities, and to pay for imported equipment, materials, technicians, and service "needs" that (as we also saw above) American corporations have built into the Brazilian economy's underdeveloped structure. As these loans come with economic and political strings attached, Brazil thus loses control of critical sectors of her economy to foreign interests on foreign investment, domestic production, export, import, and loan accounts. These levers of control integrate the weaker Brazilian economy ever more into the stronger American economy, render the oligarchic Brazilian allies of American interests ever more dependent on the United States, and structure *under*development all the more firmly into the very foundations of Brazilian society.

Beyond these considerations, some observations about recent features of American aid in Brazil may be illuminating. It is well to note that, though included in the dollar totals of aid, loans under Public Law 480, euphemistically called "Food for Peace," do not supply a single dollar but consist rather of cruzeiros derived from the sale in Brazil of American surplus wheat which, like all other "dumping," competes unfairly with and inhibits the development of Brazilian wheat production.

The major American-financed capital project in Brazil, the Volta Redonda steel mill, was, in fact, built by the United States during the Second World War to provide steel in Brazil for the United States' own wartime needs: Brazilians have been paying for the mill ever since. As for the much heralded aid for the development of the "depressed Northeast," the governor of one of its states has publicly pointed out that with a population of 25 million and one of the world's lowest standards of living, this area received $13 million from the Alliance for Progress while the state of Guanabara (including the city of Rio de Janeiro) with

4 million inhabitants and the highest per capita income among Brazil's twenty-two states was allocated $71 million. The governor of this latter state, it just so happens, is the presidential candidate of the ultra-right economic interests, the Brazilian Barry Goldwater, who spends his American-supplied dollars on parkways marked "works of the government of Carlos Lacerda" and on other projects, such as forcing slum dwellers to move out to "John Kennedy village" located twenty miles out of town, while burning down their houses in the center of town to make room for a new tourist hotel. That's development!

## Underdevelopment, Industrialization, and Foreign Investment

Finally, we will briefly broach what is undoubtedly the most difficult but the most important matter of all, the economic history of underdevelopment and development, and the role of foreign trade and investment therein. The events in this history which are critical for the understanding of the problems under discussion are universally known, albeit all-too-conveniently forgotten, in certain circles.

The expansion of metropolitan mercantilism and capitalism to Latin America, Africa, and Asia wrought the destruction of productive and viable agricultural and also industrial economies on these continents and most notoriously in Mexico, Peru, West and East Africa, and India. Arriving mostly by force of arms and establishing alliances in these societies (and in newly established ones such as Brazil) with old and newly created exploitative oligarchies, the metropolitan economies reduced the large bulk of the world's people to levels of abject poverty that they had never suffered at the hands of their previous own or foreign masters. In our times, it has become fashionable to call these societies "underdeveloped," as though they have always been this way. The developing metropolitan powers pillaged the peoples in these political and economic colonies of capital which they used to industrialize their own economies. By incorporating them into what is now known euphemistically as the world market, they converted these now *underdeveloping* economies into appendages of their own. As we have seen above, this process continues unabated in our day.

Lest it be thought that the United States is only a newcomer to this exploitative process which produces development for some at the expense of underdevelopment for others, it is well to remember that the initial industrial capital of the Northeastern United States was derived largely from the slave trade and from the products of Southern slavery. Though the forms have been modernized, the content and the effects of the expansion of capitalism in contemporary times remain essentially what they always have been; the level of living of the majority of the people is still *falling*. The United Nations Food and Agricultural Organization (FAO) supplies part of the evidence. Taking per capita food production in 1934–38 as 100, in the three crop years 1959/60, 1960/61, and 1961/62, it was 99, 100, and 98 in Latin America, Africa, and Asia (excluding the socialist countries) respectively; while it was 113 for the world as a whole, and 145 for the countries universally known for the failure of their agriculture, the Soviet Union and Eastern Europe.[12] But these figures tell only part of the story. The other part lies in the combination of low or negative economic growth rates with the increasing *inequality* of the distribution of income in countries for which estimates are available, such as Brazil, Argentina, Mexico, and India. The result is that while foreign and domestic exploiters enrich themselves, the masses of the people in the underdeveloping countries are suffering an absolute decline in their per capita incomes.

This essay has been an attempt to report on a few of the mechanisms of imperialist exploitation of underdeveloped countries. It is not, and is not intended to be, a substitute for inquiry into the structure and transformation of the imperialist system. But even these structurally derived mechanisms of imperialism in action, though no doubt familiar to practicing imperialists and allied businessmen and diplomats, are all too unfamiliar to many of those who would combat imperialism. Yet an understanding of contemporary imperialism in action is essential to the theoretical base necessary for any successful struggle against the system. And there are many more such mechanisms of imperialism in action.[13] But even where reports of economic mechanisms of imperialism exist, they are usually studies of individual firms, industries, incidents, etc. Not only do these make tedious, if necessary, reading, as those who have followed this report this far will have found out; but in the absence of more inclusive and quantitative information on such matters as real profit rates and totals, concessions, financial control, imperialist-nationalist joint ventures, etc., we can reach only a very inadequate understanding of even these mechanisms of imperialism. It is hoped, therefore, that students in the underdeveloped countries, as well as in underdeveloped regions and sectors of the industrialized nations, will increasingly report on the hard facts of imperialism.

## NOTES

1. Cited in *O Estado de São Paulo*, April 12, 1963.
2. These totals can be computed from the following issues of the *Survey of Current Business:* November 1954, pp. 9, 13; August 1955, pp. 18, 20; August 1957, p. 25; August 1959, p. 31; August 1961, pp. 22, 23; August 1962, pp. 22, 23.
3. Reported by Congressman Jacob Frantz in Congressional debate and cited in *O Semanario*, May 30–June 6, 1963.
4. See: Paulo F. Alves Pinto, *Antologia Nacionalista*, Vol. 2, cited in Barbosa Lima Sobrinho, *Marquinas para transformar cruzeiros em dolares*, and Sylvio Monteiro, *Como Atua o imperialismo ianque?*
5. Quoted in Osny Duarte Pereira, *Quem faz as leis no Brasil?*, p. 97.
6. Quoted in Jocelyn Brasil, *O Pao, O Feijao, e as Forzas Ocultas*, p. 125.
7. *O Semanario*, September 26, 1963.
8. Barbosa Lima Sobrinho citing Editora Banas, in *O Semanario*, September 26, 1963.
9. Editora Banas, *Capital extranjero no Brasil.*
10. Much the same pattern in Latin American petroleum, mining, steel, automotive, machine building, and other industries was noted and criticized by the American observer John Gerassi in *The Great Fear* (New York: Macmillan and Company, 1963).
11. *Jornal do Brasil*, January 22, 1964.
12. FAO, *The State of Food and Agriculture, 1962*, p. 15 of Spanish edition.
13. Hamza Alavi has recently reported on some others in his "U.S. Aid to Pakistan," *Economic Weekly* (Bombay), Special Number (July 1963), reprinted in French as "Pakistan: le fardeau de l'aide américaine" in *Révolution* (Paris).

# 10

## LATIN AMERICAN ECONOMIC INTEGRATION

Recent years have witnessed the birth and development of two Latin American free trade zones, one in South America and one in Central America. Any superficial resemblance these may have to the European Common Market should not lead us to expect the current steps toward economic integration in Latin America to reproduce the European results. Even apart from the fact that a free trade zone is a much weaker form of integration than a common market, the circumstances in Latin America are quite different, especially as regards the area's low degree of economic development and high degree of imperialist economic dependence.

For the time being, there is virtually no intra-regional trade in South America, to say nothing of Central America. Therefore, the most important, if not only, significance of a free trade zone, customs union, or similar arrangement is the creation of a potential market large enough to attract and justify investment in Latin American industrialization. The free trade zone is thus defended by many of its proponents, who recall Adam Smith's dictum that the division of labor depends on the extent of the market. But history shows that the extent of the market, in turn, depends less on its territorial extension than on the income of its consumers. Hence increasing the breadth rather than the depth of the market is at best only a minor step in the right direction and at worst, as will be argued here, a premature step which will impede the larger and more necessary step. What is really needed is to solve the problem of poverty and low productivity, especially in agriculture. Even if we leave aside for the moment

1962–63. This essay originally appeared in the September 1963 issue of *Monthly Review*.

the human needs and welfare of the people and consider only effective demand and supply in the industrial sector, history still provides ample evidence for the primary importance of solving the problem of agriculture. The successful industrialization of Western Europe was evidently dependent on the revolution in European agriculture as well as, of course, on the colonization of the now underdeveloped continents of the world. But the priority of depth over breadth of the market, of solving the problem of agricultural productivity, is attested to equally by the failure to date of attempts to industrialize such countries as Brazil and Mexico. Brazil already has a market of continental proportions. It has built in São Paulo the largest industrial complex in Latin America. But having failed even to attack its agricultural problem, notoriously one of the world's most serious, Brazil remains a very underdeveloped and non-industrialized country. Mexico, whose revolution fifty years ago produced what was before Cuba the most far-reaching agricultural reform in Latin America, stopped her land reform short and failed to release large parts of the potential productivity and energy of her rural people. As a result, Mexico's industrialization and economic development drive has also stopped short. The truth is that to foster industry and economic development, Latin America must transform its agriculture; and to do that it must in turn radically alter its entire internal and external political, economic, and social structure. Economic integration, especially integration of the present economic structures of its various countries with each other, will not solve the problem.

What, then, *will* integration do—and what will it prevent? It will, notwithstanding "provisions" to the contrary, attract capital to the centers that are already most industrialized and not to those that are least so. Indeed, to the extent that the capital will come from inside Latin America, integration will draw capital out of the poorer and into the richer regions, just as has already happened in the development of Brazil. It will widen also the gap between country and city, and it will certainly not benefit the large mass of peasants. It will, in short, make the rich richer and the poor poorer, relatively, certainly, and absolutely as well, if Latin-American developments in the past ten years, even without a common market, are any guide. The thesis that a free market equalizes incomes, or even prices, among its sectors is a myth that was invented by the rich while they were exploiting the poor.

Nor is this all. Given the present economic structure of Latin America, local capital is scarce; given the present political structure, foreign capital is "welcome." The industrial capital that the economic integration is supposed to attract would therefore in large part, and in Central America obviously almost wholly, have to come from abroad, especially the United States. But the principal aim of investment capital is of course to benefit the investors. And it does. According to U.S. Department of Commerce calculations, during the 1950's the total amount of money sent from Latin America to the United States as "earnings" on U.S. investments in the region was double the value of the investments. Latin American calculations show an even higher rate of return. For example, the Joint Brazil-U.S. Economic Commission estimated that withdrawals to the United States between 1939 and 1952 came to sixty-one (yes, 61) times the amount of long-term investment. Thus economic integration of Latin America under present circumstances will not only draw capital from the poor to the rich in Latin America itself. It will also make the poor Latin Americans poorer and the rich North Americans richer.

Matters are still worse. Economic integration carries with it special privileges for firms inside the integrated region. They receive tariff protection, often tax and credit privileges, and in Central America virtually total monopoly positions. In many if not all cases the quality of their products will be poorer and their prices higher than those of comparable imported goods. The Latin American consumer will therefore lose by the arrangement. Such short-term losses from infant-industry protection are justified and even welcome if the sacrifices involved will bring or at least contribute to long-term benefits. But, as we have already seen, the long-term effects of integration in Latin America are likely to be unfavorable. Thus current steps toward integration involve short-term sacrifices to be followed by greater long-term sacrifices.

The truth is that countries which have successfully industrialized in the past have done so without foreign investment and "aid." Outstanding examples are Japan and the Soviet Union, not to speak of the countries of Western Europe. The countries that have been the recipients of heavy foreign investment have remained non-industrialized and underdeveloped. The only apparent exceptions are the United States, the British Dominions, and Israel. But in all these cases foreign immigration accompanied the foreign capital, and all the benefits went to the immigrants and none to the natives. The exceptions thus seem to prove the rule. It will be interesting to see if foreign aid to a *socialist* country, such as Yugoslavia, Cuba, or Eastern Europe, will result in economic development. It has been suggested that, because a socialist country can control its economy and thus can channel the aid into development-producing industrial projects, foreign capital can aid a socialist country to develop where it fails to do so in a capitalist country. If this argument is well taken, then economic integration will also benefit Latin America only if it comes *after* the respective countries' conversion to socialism, and not before.

If Latin American economic integration will not make a positive contribution, will it serve to *prevent* economic development? The political implications of the move to integration suggest that it will, to the extent that it proceeds before rather than after fundamental change. The United States used to oppose the Latin American Free Trade Zone project. The Kennedy administration is supporting it. Why? United States involvement in Latin America used to be based principally on the client relation maintained with the commercial bourgeoisie in each country, while the latter maintains a similar client relation with its own landowning class. This triple alliance long served the interests of all the partners and permitted the U.S. to follow a divide-and-rule policy in which it maintained a bilateral relation with each country separately. Integration threatened the stability of this arrangement. Now, underlying economic, social, and political developments are increasingly threatening the stability of this form of alliance anyway. The growth of national, mostly light, industry and the concomitant development of a national industrial bourgeoisie in some countries, along with a relative shift of interest of American capital from extractive to secondary and tertiary industries in Latin America have altered the economic relations.

This, along with social mobility and the growth of middle classes, which have become the pivots of the electoral process, as well as the declining relative power of the landowner, have changed national political alignments. For these reasons, American policy, as the Alliance for Progress makes amply clear, has been to shift its reliance away from the "feudal" landowner toward strengthening of ties with the newer groups interested in maintaining the status quo. Economic integration measures strengthen the hand of these new groups relative to that of the landowners while tying (through American investment and "aid") these groups increasingly to the United States. At the same time, of course, integration opens the doors to that same American investment in secondary and tertiary industry. Above all, in the context of a continent in flux, the Latin American Free Trade Zone contributes to political stability. It strengthens existing groups, excepting the "feudals," and creates others with an interest in preserving the status quo. Thus, the Free Trade Zone has, from the American point of view, become desirable: the more successful this project, the less desirable and necessary are alliances with military dictators like Trujillo, Duvalier, and Stroessner. Less desirable because their very dictatorial power affords them, domestically, a certain degree of independence from U.S. management; and less necessary because the political weight of the new domestic forces created by integration affords political stability and an opportunity for the U.S. to play one group off against another. "Divide and rule" no longer operates by dividing one country from another as much as by dividing one class and interest group from another. But U.S. domination remains the same.

If economic integration contributes to class division, will it also in the long run contribute to progress by increasing class struggle? To the extent that integration does foster industry even if not industrialization, it adds to the growth of the industrial working class. That class, it might be argued, will then ultimately destroy the alliance which keeps Latin America underdeveloped. The evidence in Latin America so far, however, is that industrial workers, especially organized industrial workers, far from being a progressive force, have been a conservative element. They too have been a relatively privileged group, an aristocracy of the proletariat, which derives its privileges from the present economic structure and thus has an interest in preserving it. Except in special cases, only the peasants in Latin America have a large and independent revolutionary potential. And economic integration will indeed intensify their exploitation. Thus, in the last as in the first analysis, it is in destroying the existing agricultural structure, and not in integrating the present industrial structure, that the key to Latin America's future lies. Only that step can and will lead to genuine industrialization.

# 11

## INVISIBLE FOREIGN SERVICES
## OR NATIONAL ECONOMIC
## DEVELOPMENT?

While the United Nations Conference on Trade and Development (UNCTAD) looks at the underdeveloped countries' capital
loss and shortage through their terms of trade and their failure to
receive real aid from the developed capitalist countries, these
are "invisibly" draining much more capital out of the underdeveloped countries on "service" accounts such as profit remission,
debt service, foreign transport and travel, capital transfers, and
other "services."

The case of Latin America is illustrative. In 1961–63, that continent (excepting Cuba) spent 61.5 percent (by 1966 about
65 percent) of its total foreign exchange earnings to pay for invisible foreign services rendered to it by the imperialist capitalist
metropolis. (See table.) In dollars of potentially investible capital,
this is U.S. $6,000 million, or more than 7 percent of Latin
America's GNP. By comparison, the much emphasized deterioration of Latin America's terms of trade since the Korean War
period cost it 3 percent of its GNP in 1962,[1] and the investment
in human capital represented by Latin America's total expenditures, public and private, for education from kindergarten through
university was only 2.6 percent of GNP.[2] Who knows what, by
further comparison, total net investment in all capital is?

Thus, the chronic balance of payments deficit, inadequate import capacity, and underdevelopment of Latin America and other

---

1965. This is a slight revision of an article which first appeared in Spanish
in *Comercio Exterior* (Mexico: Banco Nacional de Comercio Exterior), Vol.
XVI, No. 2 (February 1966).

### Earnings and Expenditures of Foreign Exchange in Latin America Without Cuba

| | Millions of $ | % |
|---|---|---|
| *Earnings* | | |
| 1. Merchandise exports (a) | 8,596 | 85 |
| 2. Service exports (b) | 1,481 | 15 |
| 3. Current foreign exchange earnings (c) | 10,077 | 100 |
| *Expenditures* | | |
| 4. Services | 6,195 | 61.5 |
| 5. Profits (d) | 1,438 | 14.3 |
| 6. Debt service (e) | 1,506 | 14.9 |
| 7. Freight and insurance | 998 | 9.9 |
| 8. Foreign travel | 598 | 5.9 |
| 9. Other services (f) | 564 | 5.5 |
| 10. Donations | 163 | 1.6 |
| 11. Funds transferred abroad | 637 | 6.3 |
| 12. Errors and omissions (g) | 309 | 3.1 |
| 13. Merchandise imports FOB (h) | 7,381 | 73.2 |
| 14. Raw materials and intermediate goods | 2,583 | 25.6 |
| 15. Fuels | 583 | 5.8 |
| 16. Consumer goods | 1,314 | 13.0 |
| 17. Subtotal | 10,675 | 105.9 |
| 18. Capital goods | 2,768 | 27.5 |
| 19. Other imports | 133 | 1.3 |
| 20. Total expenditures | 13,479 | 134.7 |

*Source*: United Nations Economic Commission for Latin America, *Estudio Económico de América Latina 1963* (New York, 1964), E/CN.12/696/Rev. 1. Lines 1 and 2—page 38; line 5—p. 242; line 6—p. 45; line 7—p. 238; line 8—p. 239; lines 9 and 10—p. 244; line 11—p. 247; line 12—p. 231; lines 14, 15, 16, 18, and 19—p. 58; lines 3, 4, 13, 17, and 20—computed.

*Notes to the Table*

(a) Preliminary data, which include net non-monetary gold.
(b) Preliminary data, which refer to gross earnings for non-financial services.
(c) These are the current earnings from the export of goods and of services, as they appear on page 38 under the title "total capacity to buy." Pages 43 and 45 show, for the total of current earnings, the slightly higher figure of $10,203 million, instead of the $10,077 million of page 38 on which the figures in this table are based.

(d) These profits are "the earnings from direct investments," plus the "income from other investments," as these appear on page 242. The percentages are computed on the basis of total current export earnings. Page 243 gives a percentage of 13.8 percent for net outflow of these earnings, which is slightly lower than the 14.3 percent computed here. Page 45 refers to 10.7 percent "profits on direct investments." It is important to note that all of these percentages underestimate the true amount of profits taken out of Latin America by foreign companies. Typically, a considerable part of company profits are disguised in the company books and, therefore, in the balance of payment reports, under entries such as costs and payments for merchandise, technical personnel, patents, trade marks, etc. Other profits are hidden through the quite common practice of overbilling imports into and underbilling exports from Latin America.

(e) This refers to total expenditures and includes: interest on loans ($348.1 million) and amortization of the long-term debt ($1,157.9 million). These are preliminary data.

(f) "Other services" include transactions which are registered, according to the definitions of the International Monetary Fund, in the following two ways: (1) Government transactions not included in the other sections of the balance of payments. These include civil and military expenses of foreign governments in Latin America (credit) and similar expenses of Latin American governments abroad (debit) which are not registered as official donations. And (2) other services, which include all service transactions not included in other sections of the balance of payments, such as insurance (excluding on merchandise shipments, which are included under "freight and insurance"), personal income, management fees, stock brokers' commissions, agents' fees, subscriptions to wire services, movie rentals, real estate rentals, etc.

(g) "Errors and omissions" is a common category in balance of payments reports. Errors and omissions represent the balance between the sum of financial movements individually computed and the total. Each year the flow of capital represented by "errors and omissions" is unfavorable to Latin America. The cited ECLA source comments on page 247: "But generally the negative errors and omissions occur, in all probability, in the area of capital operations, and are not due to an overestimate of capital inflow, but, rather, to an underestimate of capital outflows."

(h) The amount of merchandise imported is labeled FOB—that is, excluding freight—by the quoted source. Freight costs are found under the heading of services. Nevertheless, the percentages of various types of merchandise are not so enumerated. It is not clear, therefore, if these include transport or not. If freight costs are already included, it would be necessary to subtract them by reducing the percentages of the total by approximately 10 percent. The percentages of imported merchandise are listed by the source as percentages of the total of products imported. As this is $7,381 million, and the total current income is $10,077 million, it was necessary to compute 73 percent of the percentage given to find the percentage which they represent of current foreign exchange earnings.

underdeveloped regions appears in clearer perspective when we observe that of its total current earnings of foreign exchange Latin America has to spend 61 percent on payment for non-merchandise services alone (line 4 of the table) and that these services plus the import of raw materials, consumer goods, and fuels cost Latin America 106 percent of its foreign exchange earnings (line 17). Consequently, to finance its import of capital goods, Latin America is now resorting to foreign investment and external debt financing that further hinder its economic development.

The United Nations Economic Commission for Latin America (ECLA) argues that "the large long-term increase of the balance of payments deficit since 1950 can be attributed to three principal causes: (1) the much greater increase in the value of imports compared to the increase in the value of the exports, (2) the income received by foreigners on their Latin American investments . . . (3) travel expenditures . . . transport costs . . . expenditures for other services"; and since it regards the increase of expenditures for services (factors two and three above) as low, it concludes that "the worsening of the terms of trade can be considered as the factor which contributed most, directly and indirectly, to increasing the Latin American balance of payments deficit." [3] It is worthwhile noting that ECLA, like many others, refers more to the *rise* of these expenditures and the *increase* of the deficit, than to the *amount* of the expenditures and to the *cause* of the deficit. Yet the amount of these expenditures on "invisible" services and their contribution to the cause of the balance of payments deficits are so large that they themselves demand much more attention be devoted to them than in the past. The intent of this article is to begin to do so.

As far as is known, the total amount of Latin America's foreign exchange expenditures on service account have never been added up, in spite of the fact that they have for a long time been of concern to the Latin Americans.[4] ECLA now supplies data that permits totaling the Latin American expenditures on service and other accounts, in order to discover several "invisible" obstacles to Latin American development. ECLA itself has begun this analysis, not only by furnishing all the statistics on the expenditure of foreign exchange, but also by comparing, albeit separately, the expenditures on travel and the amortization and interest payments on the external debt with current foreign exchange earnings. Yet ECLA has not added up these components of foreign exchange expenditures; nor has it compared them, so totaled, with current foreign exchange earnings. To do so, it is necessary to depart somewhat from traditional balance of payments accounting procedures, and to include both expenditures on current and on capital account on the debit or currency outflow side. This procedure reveals the real magnitude of the expenditure of foreign exchange on services compared to the amount of foreign exchange available from current export earnings. The same procedure also reveals an important cause of Latin America's balance of payments deficits, inadequate import capacity, underdevelopment, and growing resort to external financing.

According to ECLA's data for 1962, Latin America, excluding Cuba, is obliged to spend 61 percent of its total current earnings from all exports on expenditures on service account (line 4 of the table). At the same time, only 15 percent of these same foreign exchange earnings represent the sale of Latin American services (line 2), the largest part of which are tourist and other services rendered by Mexico and Panama, thanks to their special circumstances. This means that the overwhelming majority of the Latin American countries obtain practically no earnings from the sale of services to foreigners. Nevertheless, Latin America as a whole spends more than three-fifths of its current foreign exchange earnings in payments for services. Consequently less than two-fifths remain available for the purchase of foreign goods. Moreover, the proportion of current foreign exchange income absorbed by service charges rose from 53 percent in 1956–60 to 61 percent in 1961–63 and continues to increase.[5] Perhaps this *increase* of foreign exchange expenditures on invisible service account seems small to ECLA when compared to the more notorious deterioration of the terms of trade to which ECLA attributes the largest part of the increase in Latin America's balance of payments deficit. Nevertheless, the *existence* of the balance of payments deficit and inadequate import capacity of Latin America must be largely attributed to the enormous, though scarcely known, proportion of its earnings which the region is obliged to spend on "invisible" services.

The importance of expenditures on service account in Latin America's balance of payments becomes even more significant when we consider that the region has a *balance of trade surplus* on goods account. In 1962 the value of merchandise imports, including those bought on credit, was $7,381 million (line 13). Merchandise exports were $8,596 million (line 1), and total exports of goods and services were $10,077 million (line 3). However, because of the $6,195 million which was spent on services (line 4), total expenditures were $13,479 million and produced a balance of payments deficit equal to 35 percent of Latin America's earnings of foreign exchange on current account (line 20). The more equitable terms of trade, which Latin America and the other "75 countries" demanded at Geneva, would no doubt reduce the deficit in Latin America's balance of payments, and they might thus remove some obstacles to its economic development. However, an improvement in terms of trade would under no circumstances eliminate Latin America's balance of payments deficit, its low import capacity, and the obstacles to its economic development that have their origins in the burden of the 61 percent of its current earnings spent, not on merchandise, but on services.

Half of Latin America's expenditures on service account and nearly one-third of its loss of foreign exchange earnings on current account are profit remittances of foreign investors and service of the external public debt. Profits repatriated by foreign investors absorbed 14.3 percent (line 5) of foreign exchange earnings in 1962, while in 1961 and 1963, according to the same official source, they were 1 percent higher. It is important to note, as is observed in note (d) of the table, that these figures underestimate the true outflow of profits. Another 14.9 percent went to service the external public debt (line 6). Freight on foreign carriers used up 10 percent of the foreign exchange earned by Latin America, and trips abroad consumed an additional 6 percent (lines 7 and 8). Other services and other capital transfers abroad absorbed 16.5 percent (lines 9–12). When totaled, all these expenditures add up to the impressive sum of 61 percent of total foreign exchange earnings. In other words, the 29 percent of Latin

American foreign exchange earnings absorbed by profit remittances and debt service (lines 5 and 6), plus the 11 percent of
foreign exchange outflow represented by donations, funds transferred abroad, and errors and omissions (lines 9, 10, 11, and note
g) absorb 40 percent of Latin America's foreign exchange earnings. This means that the outflow of capital on *financial* service
account alone is considerably larger than Latin America's balance
of payments deficit, which is 35 percent of its foreign exchange
income on current account.

The relationship between Latin America's expenditures on
service account and its balance of payments deficit and inadequate
import capacity emerges more clearly still when we analyze the
composition of merchandise imports and the conditions under
which they are imported by Latin America. Six percent of all
foreign exchange income is spent on fuel purchases (line 15).
Most of these expenditures, no doubt, are for Venezuelan oil sold
to Latin Americans by foreigners who charge the notoriously
high prices established by the international petroleum cartel.
Another 26 percent of Latin America's foreign exchange earnings
is used in the purchase of raw materials and intermediary products
(line 14). A part of these materials, like copper, aluminum, and
other metals, are probably also produced in Latin America and are
sold to Latin America by foreigners who transfer the profits realized on these sales to their homeland abroad. Another serious
problem is that Latin America spends 13 percent of its foreign
exchange earnings on the purchase of consumer goods, of which
8.3 percent of the total are non-durables, largely foodstuffs (line
16 and its source). Although some of these foodstuffs are sold at
subsidized prices (which compete seriously with national production), they are shipped to Latin America in high-cost foreign
bottoms, which in the case of bulky products like wheat absorb a
large part of the price.

The 61 percent spent on services plus the expenditure on the
above-mentioned imports cost Latin America 106 percent (line
17) of its total earnings of foreign exchange on current account.
These obligations and expenditures mean, in other words, that
even before importing a single unit of the capital goods which are
so important for its economic development, Latin America must

face a balance of payments deficit equal to 6 percent of its current foreign exchange earnings. How then can Latin America import capital goods, which represent 38 percent of its merchandise purchases, 27 percent (28 percent with the 1 percent of unclassified other imports) of current foreign exchange earnings, and 20 percent of total imports, and which increase the balance of payments deficit from 6 percent to 35 percent of its current foreign exchange earnings?

At first glance it might appear—and this is the studied opinion and serious advice of numerous official and academic economists —that the solution to these payments, import, and development problems can be found by looking for foreign financing. In fact, Latin America has resorted to foreign debt and investment finance in its attempt to face and solve these problems. With what results?

Thanks to external debt financing, servicing the foreign debt absorbed 5 percent of Latin America's foreign exchange earnings in 1955–56, 11 percent in 1956–60, and 16 percent in 1961–63.[6] Yet the high cost of servicing the debt contracted through the Alliance for Progress has hardly begun to be paid and will inevitably raise this cost still higher. Already, according to an Associated Press news release dated April 5, 1966, the "Export-Import Bank takes out, annually, $100 million more than it grants in loans" to Latin America. Latin America thus finds itself in a vicious downward spiral, which sinks it deeper each year in a dilemma that must end in crisis.

Resort to direct foreign investment to finance imports of capital goods for industrialization inevitably has grave consequences for Latin America. These consequences far exceed the 14 percent foreign exchange earnings absorbed by officially admitted foreign profit remittances (line 5), a substantial portion of the 16 percent absorbed by other services and capital transfers (lines 9–12), and the large share of freight and insurance charges that are intimately tied to these foreign private investments. Here I shall insist only on two further consequences that are particularly relevant to the present discussion. I shall not deal with others, such as the progressive de-Latinamericanization of Latin American industry, the channeling of investments in directions that are of interest to foreigners but that are not necessarily conducive to Latin America's economic development, and the increase of foreign influence on the economy and even on the political life of Latin America.

One related and grave consequence of recourse to foreign investment financing is that investment is not channeled to areas which reduce the Latin American need to import the capital goods and technology required by its own economic development. This has been pointed out by ECLA in reference to Brazil: "The outstanding aspect of the inflow of foreign capital for the expansion and diversification of industry was not so much its volume as its orientation; that is, it was channeled, in the case of public capital, into strategic sectors of the economy, and in the case of private capital, into the sectors where the import substitution prospects are most promising." However, "to sum up, in the light of the study of the main sample items, it may be concluded that no real substitution process took place in respect of capital goods as a whole." Moreover, "as far as the results of continued import substitution are concerned, it may be said, in broad terms, that it would tend to slow down economic growth." [7]

Foreign investment finance thus does not so much increase Latin America's capacity to produce the capital goods that are so necessary for its economic growth, as it creates a growing need for new imports which intensify Latin America's dependence on the exterior. Foreign investment, like the external public debt, increases foreign control of the scarce income and resources of Latin America.

The other onerous consequence of resorting to foreign investment and external debt finance is that they increase the rigidity of the import structure. Foreign investment in commerce and industry, and the control they place in foreign hands, result in foreign determination of the organization of Latin American industry, of the raw materials used, of the components and the technical processes employed, so that even the imports required by the industrial process of production in Latin America are also increasingly determined by foreigners. Thus, to resort to foreign investment finance means to put in foreign hands the control over the selection of goods and services which Latin America purchases abroad. In consequence, foreign investment finance threatens a vicious spiral analogous to that of foreign debt finance.

The 6 percent of Latin America's total income of foreign exchange that is spent on service account, plus a large part of the funds used for such merchandise imports as foreign fuel and raw materials, are taken out of Latin America's income by decisions of foreigners serving interests that are foreign to Latin America. The economic system whose structure causes and whose development aggravates this prejudice to Latin American interests by foreign ones causes the most serious difficulties for Latin American economic development. Any attempt to resolve or face these difficulties by the same foreign financial operations that created this dilemma in the first place, condemns Latin America to sink in it deeper and deeper. This suggests that the solution to this problem of the rising merchandise imports and especially of the increasing expenditures on service account that Latin America cannot afford must be sought in another direction.

If Latin America and other underdeveloped regions would themselves render a larger portion of the services they need instead of buying them abroad; if they would finance more of their development with their own resources; if they would have recourse to alternative and cheaper sources of foreign loan finance; and if they would supply themselves with more of their own shipping, insurance, advertising, and other services—then the underdeveloped regions would have more of their foreign exchange available to import the goods needed for, and more of their domestic capital left over to permit the finance of, their own economic development and national welfare, than they do now by importing invisible services.

## NOTES

1. Computed from United Nations Economic Commission for Latin America, *El Financiamiento Externo de América Latina* (New York: United Nations, 1964), E/CN.12/649/Rev. 1, p. 33.
2. International Institute for Educational Planning, *Problems and Strategies of Educational Planning: Lessons from Latin America* (Paris, 1964), p. 63.

3. United Nations Economic Commission for Latin America. *El Financiamiento Externo de América Latina*, p. 70.

4. The Count of Revillagigedo, Viceroy of New Spain, noted "the freight charges, dues, taxes and other charges which the European merchants brought with them." Luis Chávez Orozco, ed., *El Comercio Exterior y su Influjo en la Economía de la Nueva España (1763)*, Vol. 4 of the Collección de Documentos para la Historia del Comercio Exterior de México (Mexico: Banco Nacional de Comercio Exterior, 1930), p. 43. Also *El Ferrocarril* (Valparaiso, Chile), in 1868 complained "of the monopoly which has considerably diminished our profits, charging them, additionally, with freight charges, commissions, and other taxes invented by English traders." Quoted in Hernán Ramírez N., *Historia del Imperialismo en Chile* (Santiago: Austral, 1960), p. 83.

5. Percentages are computed by the author from ECLA data for these years. The data for each component of these expenditures on service account are from the page reference for that component cited in the sources of the accompanying table.

6. United Nations Economic Commission for Latin America, *El Financiamiento Externo de América Latina*, p. 45.

7. United Nations Economic Commission for Latin America, "The Growth and Decline of Import Substitution in Brazil," *Economic Bulletin for Latin America* (New York), Vol. IX, No. 1 (March 1964), pp. 38, 51, 57.

# 12

# THE ECONOMICS OF
# MILITARY GOVERNMENT

Brazil's gorilla President Castello Branco aptly celebrated the first anniversary of the successful coup with a military parade in Brasilia. In Washington, Secretary of State Dean Rusk, not to be outdone in enthusiasm, celebrated the occasion on March 25 by telling a House of Representatives panel, according to UPI, that before April 1964 Brazil

> was gravely threatened by continual economic and political deterioration . . . Since then, the situation has changed dramatically for the better. Political stability has been restored. The climate which helped the Communists and other extremists infiltrate and exercise disproportionate influence has given way to one which inhibits violence or extreme action. ·

The very same day, in Rio de Janeiro, Niceu Cruz César, the General Director of the National Department of Employment and Wages of Brazil's Ministry of Labor, told the ultra-conservative daily *O Globo*:

> In São Paulo the whole industry is in crisis, especially the metal-lurgical and textile industries, which produce 1000 new unemployed

---

1965. This essay was originally published as "Brazil: One Year from Gorillas to Guerrillas," in *The Minority of One* (July 1965). It was prepared on the first anniversary of the military coup and reports on the economic events which arose out of the coup. But it may also be suggested that these events are the culmination of the economic and political process of the preceding years. A colleague from a North American university told me that in his official capacity as adviser to the Brazilian government he had drawn up the economic plan whose partial execution is represented in the measure and effects described below. He added that the Americans had been waiting for this opportunity for years; unfortunately, bureaucratic obstacles in the American government prevented their taking full advantage of it.

per day. . . . Business in general declines day by day. . . . Not only in São Paulo is there economic crisis and growing unemployment but in all of the Northeast as well.

The very next day, guerrilla uprisings occurred in three separate places in Brazil's southern state of Rio Grande do Sul.

Let us look into the stark Brazilian reality behind the official American enthusiasm.

The military government for the defense of democracy and political stability began by throwing 46,000 people in jail, most of them without charge or warrant. Large landowners, protected by the army and police, availed themselves of the long awaited opportunity to eliminate local peasant leaders, hundreds of them never to be seen or heard from again. Once the heat and confusion of battle were over, police and military authorities cold-bloodedly began the systematic torture of political prisoners. Several of this writer's personal friends suffered this fate, and one of them escaped to tell about it. An army sergeant, unenthused about his officers' "defense of democracy," was castrated and left to die of the resulting gangrene. A Catholic priest was dying in prison from lack of medical attention for his prison-caused illness.

One of the new government's first acts was to abrogate the Constitution, and, at the point of a bayonet, to ram an "Institutional Act" through parliament denying sixty-seven of its members their seats and political rights. The act also opened the door to military intervention in state governments and to a possible removal of their governors. Several states have since had such experiences. In addition, the act withdrew, for ten years, civil and political rights from hundreds of leading citizens, including three ex-presidents and such internationally respected scholar-statesmen as Prof. Josué de Castro, the former Director of the United Nations Food and Agricultural Organization and author of *The Geography of Hunger*, and Celso Furtado, former Minister of Planning, who is now teaching at Yale University.

With the Congress tamed and opposition muted, the next step was to revoke the mild land-reform law. Then, having taken care of this most pressing business in rural areas, the government turned to the city, withdrawing public subsidies of wheat, petroleum, newsprint, and imports for the state-owned Petrobras Oil Company; the price of bread and gasoline rose by 100 percent in one stroke. Transportation costs rose correspondingly.

This much "political stability" and "economic progress" had been achieved during the first two months of April and May 1964. It was only the beginning.

Under the guise of economic progress and the need to contain inflation, the Brazilian military government assiduously followed the economic policy pressed on it by the International Monetary Fund and the United States government. This was the price for international loans. The military government also had to satisfy such domestic commercial and financial interests linked to American trade as could assure it of however small internal support. No wonder that by August the Banco Nacional de Comercio Exterior (National Bank of Foreign Trade) of the government of Mexico was able to report in its monthly review, *Comercio Exterior:*

> the political events that have recently developed in Brazil are strongly reflected in the economic situation. . . . The economic activity of the country has slowed down. . . . Bank credit to the private sector has been restricted. . . . Government expenditures, especially investments, have been severely cut. . . . Industry was the first to feel the effects when their orders fell off. . . . For the first time there exists the specter of unemployment in alarming proportions—coming to several hundred thousand.

During the first half of the year prices had officially risen 42 percent compared to the 30 percent of the corresponding months of the Goulart administration; and Carlos Lacerda, the ultra-reactionary governor of Guanabara and number one civilian supporter of the military coup, disclosed that this official rate by far underestimated the real inflation in his city of Rio de Janeiro. Making foreign imports dearer for Brazilians and Brazilian exports cheaper for foreigners, the exchange rate had been lowered several times in succession. By October, the import dollar had risen from its April level of 2,400 cruzeiros to a new level of 4,600 cruzeiros. Exporters of coffee, however, many of them American companies, are protected by a special high rate for the dollars earned abroad that they sell to the Bank of Brazil.

While coining such disingenuous terms as "disinflation" and "regenerative inflation," the government printed money which by November exceeded by 25 percent the amount the Minister of the Treasury had "foreseen." By December, the stock of money had increased to 154 percent of what it had been on March 31, the first day of the military coup. This surpassed by 70 percent the amount the Minister of Planning had "planned." *Comercio Exterior*, the already quoted official source of the Mexican government, noted in its December issue that "interest rates go from 48 percent to 72 percent per year. . . . As could not fail to happen, these high costs are transferred to the consumer, thus causing a rise in the cost of living. . . . Prices are rising continually and ever faster." By September, the official rate of inflation for the year had risen to 60 percent; by December to 86 percent. *Comercio Exterior* noted that inflation in Brazil was by far the highest in Latin America.

Of course, the government had not been idle in the face of this inflation which, as always, makes the poor poorer and the rich richer. To meet its own increased needs for purchasing power, and to reduce the effective demand for food and other essentials, the government has sharply increased sales taxes on consumer goods. It reasons, perhaps, that this does not hurt the poor much since they are too poor to consume much anyway, and thus do not have to pay much of the tax.

At the same time, to fight inflation in still another valiant way, as *Comercio Exterior* observes in its October issue,

> the government sent businessmen a circular in which it recommends that they abstain from granting wage increases which they think distort the wage structure. . . . The circular holds . . . that periodic wage raises in accord with the increase in the cost of living encourage inflation. . . . Moreover, banks have been instructed not to grant . . . loans to those firms whose wage agreements are not in accord with the standards established by the government.

Why might these firms grant such distorted wage increases in the first place, one may ask. Because of union-organized worker pressure, of course. But the government has played safe and has also been helpful in warding off this inflationary danger; it has taken over and installed its own military overseers in 409 labor unions, 43 federations of labor unions, and 4 union confederations.

The economic "progress" on the side of prices has had its counterpart on the side of production and employment. In August, *Comercio Exterior* reported that Brazilian steel output had fallen by 50 percent. With most of its capacity idle and mills shutting down, this underdeveloped country, which previously had to import steel, domestic production not meeting the needs, now exports steel and looks for still more foreign buyers. The major Rio daily, *Correio da Manha,* reported on January 31, 1965, that of the 350,000 textile workers in Brazil, 50,000 are unemployed. All over the country large industrial firms, not to mention small ones, report no production for the past month or two, or more. According to *Comercio Exterior:*

> The Brazilian press announced, on February 12, that numerous industrial and commercial enterprises of the country, particularly in São Paulo, have declared themselves bankrupt or are about to do so. . . . In the last few days at least three large business firms which operate with capital between 1 million and 400 million cruzeiros have gone broke. . . . Brazilian textile producers also warn that soon all of the textile factories of the country will have to close their doors for lack of markets.

These and other similar setbacks add up to a 3 percent decline in total production, and a 6 percent decline in per capita income (as against the goal of the Alliance for Progress of a 2.5 percent rise of capital income). The following summary of the situation *Correio da Manha* published on January 31 under the title, "Deflation through Declining Production."

> Production is being reduced; and in the proportion that this happens, prices rise vertically. Consumption has been restricted. The people's buying capacity hardly suffices for food subsistence. Discouraged by the ghost of imminent failure, the businessman has begun to live without horizons, downed as he is by the financial storm that is sweeping the country. . . . In fact, production is declining. But unfortunately, with it is also declining one of the world's great nations . . . As may be verified, everything was done calculatedly, coldly, with the purpose of reducing the production which, on one side, is affected by the drastic shortage of current capital (absorbed by the

government) and by the abrupt reduction of bank credit, and, on the other side, by the reduction of consumption forced by the merciless rise of all the prices. Ministers of State and public officials then run to the television to try to explain what nobody understands . . .

In order better to understand, one has to look even closer at the corroding Brazilian coin, which Secretary Rusk and the American press find to be so shiny. Such has been the American enthusiasm for the military takeover that President Johnson at once offered aid on an unprecedented scale. In addition, *Comercio Exterior* reported as early as July 1964 that a "new expiration date for the foreign debt" has been set and that "two more loans from abroad" have been secured for Brazil.

The Brazilian Superintendency for the Development of the Northeast (SUDENE), which had been established by one-time Minister of Planning Celso Furtado, was taken over lock, stock, and barrel by the American aid administration. An American official of a United Nations agency told me, after his May 1964 trip to Brazil, that at long last the State Department's aid program for the desperate Northeast of Brazil was receiving real cooperation fom the local authorities.

One would expect concrete results of this idyllic U.S.-Brazilian cooperation; and in fact concrete results there were. One involved Roberto Campos de Oliveira, President Goulart's Ambassador to the United States. In 1963, he had signed, without his government's authorization, an agreement for Brazil to purchase the Brazilian properties of the American and Foreign Power Company for about $70 million. Both the price and the other terms of the transaction were considered unduly favorable to the American company. The equipment involved in the transaction was old. It had been financed mostly by Brazilian capital. It had long since been depreciated and, with the extremely high public utility rates, the Brazilian users had paid for it several times over. Little wonder that a hue and cry went up against the deal from circles of diverse political orientation. Hanson's *Latin American Letter*, which is published in Washington in the interests of American business (if not specifically of the utility branch), wrote in 1963 that if Brazil actually yielded in this transaction to American diplomatic and economic pressure, it would become the laughing-stock of Latin America. Understandably enough, President Goulart delayed the final purchase and tried to renegotiate its terms.

Comes the "Revolution" of 1964, Roberto Campos de Oliveira is promoted to Minister of Planning; and, as the Mexican government's bank reports, the purchase is consummated for $135 million, plus $17.7 million "compensation" for the delay in fulfilling the 1963 agreement. Including interest, the total price is calculated to come to several hundred million dollars. Both Hanson's *Latin American Letter* and *Comercio Exterior* suggested that the United States must have presented an ultimatum to the Brazilian government to "expropriate" the eleven electric concessions of the American company. . . . Well, Hanson proved to have been wrong: events have not made anyone laugh; some have been brought to smiles, others to tears.

Or to take another instance of U.S.-Brazilian economic cooperation. The American Hanna Mining Company had bought out an English gold mining company and had acquired concessions in the State of Minas Gerais involving what are believed to be the world's largest known deposits of high-grade iron ore. To extract this ore more profitably, the Hanna Company had petitioned the Brazilian government for an authorization to construct its own private port south of Rio de Janeiro. The petition was refused on the grounds that it was obviously and flagrantly contrary to the national interest.

Comes the "Revolution," and the petition is revived and granted. The new Chief of the General Staff of the Brazilian Armed Forces, Peri Belaquiva, a veteran leader of the anti-Goulart forces, resigns in protest, but this does not suffice to rescind the national giveaway. Commented *Comercio Exterior* for December:

> The [Brazilian] government has authorized the construction of a private seaport by the American mining company Hanna . . . This constitutes a privilege which will transform the Hanna Co. into an absolute master of the internal mineral market of the country; it will also end up eliminating the firm Vale do Rio Doce, a public enterprise producing minerals, which occupies the seventh place in the world in terms of export volume . . .

With such arbitrary advantages extracted by American business, the problem arose of protecting them against possible measures by a future Brazilian government that would be more responsive to the interests of its own people, and less to those of foreign enterprises. Thus the present government proposes to reinforce its own brand of democracy by obliging all political parties and candidates for public office to pledge that they would uphold any international agreements concluded in the past.

The favoritism intended to create what the U.S. calls "a better investment climate" was not exhausted in a few giveaways such as cited above. General fiscal measures have been adopted that turn Brazil into an oasis for foreign speculators. Thus, the new government removed several (never effectively enforced) restrictions on the remittance of profits abroad; set import and foreign exchange provisions improving foreigners' "competitive" (read monopolistic) advantage over Brazilian firms in introducing industrial equipment; and promised in the future to count profits earned in Brazil as part of the original foreign capital on the basis of which profit remittance abroad is computed. Such, then, are the measures which the American government hails as providing the investment climate necessary for America to help Brazil develop and which the new Brazilian government terms desirable. The Mexican government's Foreign Trade Bank, which itself welcomes American capital, observed: "The law about the remittance of profits abroad did not result in the foreseen entrance of dollars but rather in substantial exit . . . During the first half of the year, the capital inflow was less than the outflow."

The brighter future, which President Johnson sought when he recently asked American businessmen to bring home more capital to aid the American balance of payments, was written, if not on the wall, at least in the pages of the *Correio da Manha* which in January suggested that any Brazilian businessman would drop his enterprise at the first corner for a handful of dollars. Since then, one Brazilian firm after another went into real receivership or bankruptcy. Interested in nothing but development and progress, the American monopolies are drawing on their ample resources to offer the Brazilian a handful of dollars; at an accelerating rate American companies are buying out their Brazilian ex-competitors at bargain basement rates.

Under the title "Brazilian Firms Sold to Foreigners," *Comercio Exterior* of February 1965 reported:

The press of São Paulo informs—on February 4—that there is much ill feeling in response to the news that the national firm Mineraçao Geral do Brazil, is to be liquidated, following the steps of other Brazilian industrial firms which are being sold to foreigners . . . The owner . . . [pleaded necessity] in view of the crisis the firm had to face because of the weakening of the internal market. The sale, which will be to the Continental Company, will be for $70 million, with guarantees by international financial organs. To justify himself, the owner of Mineraçao Geral said that in a weak market like that of Brazil, the decline in supply which would result if the firm were to leave the market, would produce unforeseeable consequences for the economy of the country. To avoid having to close his business, he chose to convert into dollars the most important steel company in the country which has an annual production of 300 thousand tons of steel, or more than 12 percent of the national total.

Only a few days later, the American Ambassador, Lincoln Gordon, said in Brazil's Presidential Palace that the United States "reaffirms its promise of help" and that "the Brazilian authorities are making solid and continuous efforts to apply the principles of the charter of Punta del Este." There can be little wonder, then, that American Big Business, its government, and its press are so jubilant about the bright economic prospects in Brazil. And there can be no wonder that Brazilians are taking to the hills as guerrillas to reconquer their country from the Americans and their gorillas.

### Postscript

UPI reported on October 31, 1965, that one American businessman in Brazil told them that "we understand that Minister of Planning, Roberto Campos, and the one of Finance, Octavio Bulhoes, will remain in their posts. That is good. They are very well regarded here and abroad"; and that another told them, "Let's be frank, in Washington they don't like to admit it, but the majority of businessmen understand that between a dictatorship and a wavering democracy, business is better under a dictatorship."

# 13

## THE STRATEGIC WEAKNESS
## OF THE JOHNSON DOCTRINE

The Johnson Doctrine was made loud and clear at the beginning of American military occupation of Santo Domingo. The Doctrine quite simply states that American military power will seek to prevent the establishment of any new government it does not like, and that it will use all that is necessary and available to "nip in the bud" the development of another Cuba.

Yet the Johnson Doctrine is not new. It is no more than the explicit statement, in today's circumstances, of the policies and practices of Johnson and his predecessors. It is the restatement and continued application of the Truman Doctrine, the Eisenhower Doctrine, the Kennedy Doctrine—"the Policy of Containment."

After the unsuccessful application, during World War II, of the Churchill Doctrine (which sought to delay Soviet influence by delaying the "second front" in the West), Churchill bequeathed the Doctrine of Containment to President Truman at Fulton, Missouri, in 1948. (We might note that it found its literary expression in George Kennan writing in *Foreign Affairs*, under the name of Mr. X.) Its immediate application can be seen in the suppression of popular liberation movements: by force in Greece and Turkey and by other means in France and Italy. It was not North Korea's supposed "military invasion," but its growing economic strength and force of example, as well as the prior failure to contain the revolution in China, which transformed

---

1965. This article originally appeared in the December 1965 issue of *Progressive Labor*. It was written before the occurrence of three series of events which confirm its theses: (1) The OAS occupation of Santo Domingo; (2) Watts; and (3) the new wave of American refusals to fight in Vietnam.

the Policy of Containment to one of attack, the physical destruction of North Korea, and the attempt to escalate the Korean
War into the heart of China. Eisenhower ran his election campaign on the promise to retreat from this initiative and to return
to containment, pure and simple. He even resisted the pressure
to attack China again in 1954, but he *contained* in Guatemala,
Iran, and Lebanon.

When Kennedy took over the presidency and the Policy of
Containment, the postwar economic recovery of imperialism had
so increased economic deterioration in many countries, particularly
those of Latin America, as to rouse new popular desires for change.
True to the Policy of Containment, Kennedy adopted the policy
of "if you can't beat them, join them"—and "redirect *their* movement to *your* advantage." He gave the old policy and tactics a
new name—Alliance for Progress.

In the Congo, Kennedy had to both join and beat Lumumba
and Tshombe. And, of course, when he could not *join* popular
movements for change at all, as in Cuba and Vietnam, he tried
to beat them. Thus, when Johnson took over from Kennedy, he
also took over the latter's, Eisenhower's, and Truman's Doctrines
and Policies of Containment.

In most economically colonialized countries the economic situations become worse and worse—their industrial and service sectors
are being increasingly monopolized by the imperialist countries;
per capita food production in Asia, Africa, and Latin America
is declining; the domestic distribution of income is becoming increasingly unequal; and in many of these countries the absolute
income of the majority of the people is declining. At the same
time popular political consciousness is increasing and national
liberation movements are getting up renewed steam. The experience of Cuba has shown that a democratic revolution need not
take long to become a socialist one. The example of the heroic
people of Vietnam is showing that self-reliant and determined
popular national liberation movements can checkmate imperialism's moves to join them and/or beat them.

In the face of these developments, Kennedy did not just sit in
his White House rocking-chair anymore than Johnson confines
himself to his accustomed Capitol Hill "politicking." Beyond

implementing its Policy of Containment through its strategy of nuclear blackmail, the United States has long since built up a worldwide network of multilateral military pacts and programs under NATO, CENTO, SEATO, the attempted NEATO, the Pact of Rio de Janeiro (which might be called a so-called LATO), and the many bilateral agreements within and without these, such as those with Japan, India, and the countries of Latin America.

The internal contradictions of imperialism are increasingly weakening NATO, despite the absence of real or military threat in its region; CENTO never worked well but it has never had to face a critical test; SEATO has vanished except in name and has been replaced by direct U.S. occupation of Vietnam; NEATO was stillborn, though Korea was occupied long before the pact was even conceived; LATO was dormant until the Dominican crisis, when the United States attempted to inject it with new vigor through the creation of a first temporary then permanent multilateral military force, under the auspices of the Organization of American States. We are today witnessing the birth of its little brother, a sort of "CATO," in Central American steps toward the creation of a unified military command under American tutelage.

Over this entire period the Pentagon has done its best to build up "professional" armies, particularly in Latin American countries, by bringing their officers to the United States for long periods of military and ideological training, by establishing military bases abroad, and by sending its own military advisory missions and military equipment abroad.

So far, though formally the weakest, in reality the internally strongest of the American multilateral military arrangements is the Latin American one, and its newborn offspring—the Central American Military Pact (CAMP). (Its strength, of course, lies in that the inter-American system includes only one great power and many entirely dependent and subservient governments.) However, in the face of the relative weakness and instability of the multilateral arrangements, bilateral military cooperation has until now proved the most fruitful, even if some of America's military partners (and especially particular American-trained officer groups or individuals) do get out of hand, once in a while.

During the period of its development, this American international military system has also undergone important changes of purpose and direction. It is directed decreasingly against the Soviet Union and increasingly against China. (The Soviet Union's complacency in the face of the American Policy of Containment has been offset by Chinese, as well as other, encouragement of national liberation movements.) This change is reflected in the accelerating shift of emphasis from the Atlantic to the Pacific theater of operations, and in the U.S. military build-up in the Indian Ocean, on the Indian subcontinent, and in Southeast Asia.

More important, U.S. military thinking has paralleled the development of national liberation movements and is increasingly preparing to "face and fight the enemies" who are threatening to "subvert" the stability and survival of allied governments from within. This shift in American military emphasis represents the adaptation of the Policy of Containment to changing circumstances, rather than its abandonment. This became most evident when Kennedy brought "special warfare" General Maxwell Taylor out of retirement and into the Armed Forces Chiefs of Staff, and when he intervened in Cuba, the Congo, and Vietnam. Kennedy, in fact, made this shift evident and explicit when he said that American military aid to Latin America, which he doubled in his first year of office, is no longer given to combat a non-existent external enemy, but rather is exclusively to fight internal challenges to the existing order—be they short-term urban popular uprisings or long-term rural guerrilla movements.

The Pentagon and sometimes the State Department have offered their tutelage to military coups in Honduras, Ecuador, Brazil, and Bolivia, as well as to attempted coups in Uruguay and elsewhere. Beyond that, the Kennedy Doctrine expressed itself in ever-increasing American military intervention against Venezuela and Colombia.

The Kennedy Doctrine was an extension of the Truman and Eisenhower Doctrines. The Johnson Doctrine then, is the further extension of these imperialist doctrines. In Latin America it is the extension and adaptation of the imperialist Pan- or Inter-American doctrines of Monroe, Blaine, Teddy Roosevelt, and even of Wilson and FDR. The "liberal" presidents spoke with honeyed words of "neighborliness" and "alliance"; Teddy "walked softly and carried a big stick"; Lyndon treads heavily and carries a big stick. He has no choice; these doctrinal differences between imperialist presidents have probably been due more to differences in objective circumstances than to subjective temperaments. Like his predecessors, Johnson may be putting his own name and mark on the doctrine, but he is doing it under the conditions created during the era in which he governs.

It is sometimes said that "men make history"; that Napoleon, Lenin, or Mao did it with their genius and that Johnson is doing it with his vanity and stupidity. Perhaps. But history also makes men and creates the circumstances in which they may accelerate or retard the process of its development. The Johnson Doctrine took shape after he assumed the presidency and, without regard to the demands of humanity or world opinion, repressed the seemingly mild and innocent demands of Panamanian students in January 1964. The Doctrine was spelled out more clearly soon after when Johnson's "watch-over-Latin America" appointee, Thomas Mann, announced that not all military coups were alike after all. The United States, he clarified, would welcome some military take-overs and not others.

In April 1964, President Johnson himself hurried to welcome the coup in Brazil, even before the military had succeeded in getting the constitutional president to resign. Then followed the elaborate U.S. preparations, in close cooperation with the armies of Argentina and Peru, to reverse the possible victory of a Socialist-Communist coalition in the September presidential elections in Chile. Since the coalition did not win, the plans did not have to be put into practice. In the meantime, however, it was necessary to douse the popular brushfire in the Congo by airlifting Belgian and mercenary troops to the scene in U.S. planes.

In Vietnam, perhaps the first application of the Johnson Doctrine was to dispatch "special warfare expert" General Maxwell Taylor as Ambassador to Saigon. And the next was the escalation of the war, the bombing of the North, and then the massive reinforcement of American troops. The most recent applications are the increase in the draft and the less publicized logistic and quartermasterly preparations for further escalation.

In Venezuela and Colombia, all the while, American military "advisers" have quietly followed in the footsteps of their colleagues in Vietnam, growing in the thousands and carrying the war to the people of those countries' rural regions. Thus, the Johnson Doctrine did not so much emerge but has been more clearly defined in Santo Domingo.

In recent months, circumstances have obliged President Johnson to reaffirm the American imperialist practice of speaking explicitly and treading heavily and spectacularly. The popular uprising in Santo Domingo obliged Johnson to send 40,000 American troops and to vitalize and mobilize the entire inter-American diplomatic and military system to combat what he called a movement led by fifty-eight Communists. Johnson's words were as loud as his actions were clear. He had no choice, he said; he could not and would not sit by and permit any internal popular movement to take even incipient steps that might lead to another Cuba. Any such popular action within any country, he claimed, constitutes aggression, is covered by the Rio de Janeiro military pact against external aggression, and must be met by inter-American multilateral military force *if possible* and by North American unilateral military repression and occupation of the country in question *if necessary*.

In reality, Johnson only repeated from his desk what Kennedy had said from his rocking chair: Any domestic political activity abroad that is unsavory to American imperialist taste constitutes external aggression and will be met by all due American military force. Sent to Latin America to explain, roving Ambassador Averell Harriman added a further clarifying note in a press conference in Montevideo: The Doctrine of Non-Intervention in other countries' internal affairs he said, has been *outmoded by events*. It has been replaced by the Kennedy and Johnson Doctrine of undisguised massive military intervention. In Vietnam, events have obliged Johnson to multiply American ground forces, using not only "special forces" but also ordinary troops and soon preparing to draw on the call-up of reserves and the speed-up of new draftees.

Johnson explained these acts in Vietnam and laid bare, in a recent press conference, the essential reasoning behind his words about Santo Domingo. We must and will resort to any means at our disposal to prevent "our" expulsion from Vietnam, Johnson said, because if a popular movement there can throw us out, despite our massive effort to keep our promise to stay, it will be a signal to the people of all other lands, first in Southeast Asia, and then elsewhere, *that it can be done*; and then he added, they will do it, *they will throw us out everywhere.* Events have obliged Johnson, the leader of the counter-revolution, to explain what every true revolutionary has always known.

It may be well, nonetheless, to make some of the lessons to be drawn from these developments explicit.

The imperialist system is global and integral. Washington's policy is and must be to preserve it (as far and as long as possible) by trying to contain all movements of liberation. All postwar imperialist doctrine has been a reflection of the threat to the system and of the policy to contain it. Doctrinal differences have been small and essentially responses to changing circumstances. The Johnson Doctrine is no exception. One piece of evidence is that the American people voted against Goldwater but got most of his doctrine anyway. Johnson has made the Goldwater Doctrine his own because circumstances have forced him to.

The unity of the imperialist system means that events in Vietnam have repercussions, as Johnson rightly observes, in Santo Domingo, Harlem, Watts, everywhere, in accord with imperialist interests everywhere. Thus, the global extension of imperialism, which constitutes its strength, produces the global interests and needs which constitute its weakness. The more the imperialist system develops, the weaker it becomes.

Today imperialism is strategically weak. Washington recently said that it will not be thrown out of Vietnam by force of arms. Maybe. But Vietnam indicates that Washington is impotent against the force of men. Imperialism cannot contain popular movements wherever its interests demand and its needs command. Therein lies imperialism's fundamental strategic weakness.

A determined and self-reliant popular national liberation movement with a clear, long-range aim, though in a small country such as Vietnam, has shown itself to be unbeatable on its own ground. Washington knows it, and admits it. Johnson even says that imperialism's defeat in Vietnam would be the signal for its final knock-out round.

Imperialism could not face, let alone beat, several "Vietnams" at once. Therefore, as Johnson makes excessively clear in Vietnam, imperialism must resort to all possible means of containing the advance of this liberation movement, even if this containment can be no more than an attempt to salvage a stalemate, or if American presence in Vietnam need be even more limited to the indefinite occupation of a few coastal fortresses.

Therefore, also, as Johnson makes equally clear in Santo Domingo, imperialism must seek to nip in the bud any and all popular movements elsewhere before they can develop not only into another Cuba, but, as Johnson says, even into another Vietnam.

Let us examine how imperialism can succeed or fail, liberation fail or succeed.

Imperialism's strategic weakness in the face of popular liberation movements is growing. Almost all popular movements in Asia, Africa, and Latin America today are necessarily nationalist, anti-imperialist, and especially anti-American. This renders the Kennedy policy of controlling and containing these movements (by joining them) increasingly difficult to execute, increasingly dangerous for imperialism, because they may get out of hand. This situation is reflected in the anti-imperialist pronouncements of the self-styled neutralist leaders of Asia and Africa, and it has been well described by J. Gerassi, former Latin American editor of *Time* and *Newsweek*, in his book *The Great Fear: The Reconquest of Latin America by Latin Americans*. The reasons are deeply inherent in the contradictory structure and uneven development of the imperialist system itself and are beyond the scope of this discussion, though I have analyzed some of them in *Capitalism and Underdevelopment in Latin America*.

If imperialism cannot control and contain these popular movements by joining them itself, it must either seek to control them indirectly by having the national bourgeoisies join them; or, if this is too dangerous or impossible, imperialism must try to beat them directly, as in Santo Domingo.

The national bourgeoisies, however, in Latin America at least, also find it increasingly difficult and even more dangerous to control and contain people's movements by joining them, as I have sought to explain in my book.

On the one hand, the same development of imperialism and underdevelopment of its economic colonies that makes most popular movements necessarily nationalist and anti-imperialist also renders the underdeveloped dependent bourgeoisies of these countries less and less able to lead or even join a national liberation movement. On the other hand, Cuba has taught them that joining a popular liberation movement may be a short step to their own rapid undoing; and if they still harbor any doubts, American imperialism doesn't.

Containing popular movements by joining them has become so difficult economically and so dangerous politically for the Latin American bourgeoisies that, like Johnson in Santo Domingo, most of them have had no choice but to beat them with military coups. Even the famed democratic governments of Betancourt in Venezuela and Belaunde in Peru first try to hush up popular movements so that word does not get around as it does from Vietnam; then they try to beat them with their own resources; and finally, as in Venezuela today and Peru tomorrow, they call for United States military "advice" missions. If the "advice" and equipment prove insufficient to contain the popular movement, as in Venezuela and Colombia, American troops must begin to fight. This increases American weakness and makes it much more conspicuous. As Fidel Castro noted in his "First of May" speech, American intervention in Santo Domingo is not a sign of imperialist strength, but of its weakness.

American imperialism's strategic vulnerability to popular liberation movements increases with every step it takes to combat them. American support, or even installation of unpopular governments (which cannot contain poverty), multilateral and bilateral pacts, American military bases and missions, escalation from military advice to covert intervention to outright combat (as in Venezuela and Colombia and military occupation as in Santo Domingo)—in short, the "Vietnamization" of Latin America—may contain the national liberation movements for a time, but only at the cost of deepening American imperialism's strategic weakness and paving the way to its ultimate doom.

With all its military might, the United States is already short of ships, planes, and combat divisions to police all the world's oceans and continents and to shuttle its fighting equipment and men back and forth from Vietnam to Santo Domingo to the Congo to the world. Perhaps American industry can produce more conventional warfare equipment and possibly the American people can be persuaded to pay for more ships, tanks, planes, helicopters, new types of guns, bombs, and gas and other means of combating popular forces all over the world. But American men will be much less easily persuaded to fight and die, or their families to let them go, in order to pursue an anti-popular war which not even the American propaganda machine and advertising genius has been able to sell to its people.

An ever larger number of Americans are learning that their participation in these wars is not only personally costly and immoral but merely aids the exploitation of others abroad by the same American monopolies that exploit the "Other America" at home. As the imperialist system is one and indivisible, its contradictions and strategic weakness will make themselves felt at home as well as abroad. In a vain attempt to allay or at least delay the repercussions of its growing strategic weakness, American imperialism is desperately trying different solutions:

1. To draw on other countries' troops—Congressman Ford just suggested those of Taiwan—to fight in Vietnam.

2. To construct a viable international Latin American military force under U.S. command to combat domestic popular movements in any and all countries of that continent.

3. To draw on its technical tactical power by throwing conventional weapons aside and threatening nuclear bombs.

4. To adapt the Policy of Containment of popular movements in the capitalist countries by carrying imperialist attack to the socialist countries.

What are the consequences, and what are the responses from the popular forces?

Though the strategy of ruling by pitting Africans or Asians against each other has served imperialism very well in the past, it will, however, be self-defeating in Vietnam and the rest of Southeast Asia. If the Vietnamese will no longer fight for the

U.S. cause in Vietnam, how will Koreans or Taiwanese be per- suaded to do so? Their deployment can only increase and advertise imperialism's strategic weakness more.

Latin America now has established guerrilla movements in Venezuela, Colombia, Peru, Guatemala, Ecuador, and Honduras with more to come in Brazil, Bolivia, Santo Domingo, Haiti, and elsewhere. The more widespread and deep-rooted they become, the more they are coordinated with each other—as is occurring on the Venezuelan-Colombian border—and with multi-form popular movements in their own countries and elsewhere. The more guer- rilla and other popular movements adopt socialism—and not lim- ited objectives—as their goal, and devote themselves to this same political education of the people among whom they work; the more they stimulate and teach the people to develop their own leadership (instead of accepting only that of the guerrillas or in- tellectuals); then the more will these guerrillas and other popular movements in Latin America checkmate the United States' strat- egy of relying on international Latin American military forces of containment; the more will they expose the fundamental weakness of this U.S. strategy; and the more will they oblige U.S. imperial- ism to send its own troops to "Vietnamize" Latin America as well. This implies a long war for Latin Americans but still greater strategic weakness for imperialism.

Nonetheless, if imperialism has its strategic weakness, it also has its tactical strength. As Vietnam lays bare the global strategic weakness of imperialism, so does Santo Domingo illustrate its isolated tactical strength. If the popular forces of the world do not learn from the Dominican and other experiences and do not move to pit their strategic advantage against imperialism's tactical one, the people's final victory over imperialism will take more time and cost more blood than necessary. The following lessons, at least, may be drawn from this experience.

Limited and short-term popular objectives can (do) not take advantage of popular strategic strength and thus run the serious risk of placing the popular forces at a tactical disadvantage vis-à- vis imperialism. The more limited and short-term a popular move- ment's objectives, the easier it is for imperialism and its local al- lies to make limited concessions, to join the movement, and to neutralize it or even turn it to the service of imperialist interests.

The limited constitutional objectives of the Caamaño forces did not exclude the *Trojan horse* of the Organization of American States which, once admitted into the island as a negotiating agency, began to undermine and corrode the popular forces' bargaining position and power.

Having once recognized the OAS as a bargaining agency, Caamaño has had to make greater concessions than he would have had to make to the American invaders or their domestic military henchmen. Limited and short-term popular objectives also increase imperialism's ability to mobilize to beat the popular movement if it cannot be contained by joining it. Constitutional short-sightedness permitted the Americans to land troops unmolested, to save the Imbert troops from sure defeat, and then to increase American control of the city, and to consolidate Imbert's military and police control of the country.

The unplanned spontaneity of armed uprising in Santo Domingo also failed to take advantage of popular strategic strength and played into the hands of imperialism. The fundamental tactical weakness of such spontaneous uprisings and the corresponding tactical advantage of reaction were demonstrated in the classic examples of Paris, Shanghai, and elsewhere; and they have been evidenced again in Puerto Caballo in Venezuela, and Santo Domingo. The isolation and spontaneity of these uprisings renders them highly vulnerable to repression. Johnson says that they will be repressed, and his actions show that they can be repressed.

To constitute a step toward the attainment of far-off popular objectives, the momentarily heightened popular consciousness and mobilization of an uprising must be harnessed into a long-term movement that is conscious of its objectives and strength. Otherwise, the popular disillusionment that may follow an unsuccessful uprising can retard the revolutionary process.

The contrast between Santo Domingo and Vietnam could not be greater, nor the lesson clearer. Imperialism is tactically strong but strategically weak. To counter imperialism's technical tactical power, the people must draw on their combined popular strategic strength. Isolated uprisings with limited objectives cannot defeat imperialism even locally. They are likely to cost much blood without achieving even their short-term objectives. The contribution they can make depends on their ties to the popular movements with far-reaching objectives, which can and do challenge imperialism's strategic weakness.

In Vietnam the desperate United States attempt to substitute bombs for men has failed to stop the resolutely confident liberation forces who know their own strength and imperialism's weakness. The same American attempt must and will be made to fail elsewhere.

To avoid paying the consequences of trying to mobilize its own population to fight unpopular anti-peoples' wars abroad, U.S. imperialism is increasingly thrown back on its weakest weapon—blackmail of the socialist countries by conventional attack on North Vietnam and nuclear threats to China. The strength or weakness of this imperialist strategy is not, of course, for imperialism itself to decide—that decision also lies with the socialist countries.

The socialist countries must make unequivocally clear to American imperialism that any further attempt to escape its own weakness or bolster its eroding power in its underdeveloped backyard by escalating unsuccessful containment into a counter-revolutionary attack on an already liberated socialist country, will mean destruction of its own hearth and home. Events in Vietnam prove that any socialist failure to draw its line at its borders and to clarify this point for the United States can weaken, or destroy, the freedom of the already liberated socialist countries themselves. Socialist indecision on this point cannot aid liberation or preserve freedom; it can only make liberation more costly or destroy freedom. The inviolability of the socialist countries is the essential complement of the popular liberation movements of the exploited peoples which are the penultimate nail in the imperialist coffin.

The final destruction of U.S. imperialism falls to the people of the United States themselves. Though this end may not be in sight at home, the present task of all progressive forces in the U.S. is clearly enough staked out by events in other parts of the imperialist system. The events in Vietnam, Santo Domingo, the Congo, Cuba, Berlin, and elsewhere are themselves the strongest beacons guiding the American people along the path of political clarification and progressive action. They make it increasingly clear to more and more Americans that "*Americanism*" *is imperialism.*

The war in Korea was a foretaste of the American peoples' coming revulsion to and rejection of the disruption of their communities and lives as they left home and went to fight peoples' movements in many distant lands. U.S. imperialism's need to send its own men to fight popular movements abroad increases and lays bare a similar popularly based strategic weakness at home. Then, if U.S. imperialism cannot substitute arms for men, and its men will not fight for its cause, what can it do?

The principal task of all truly progressive forces at home therefore seems to be to take advantage of this popularly based imperialist strategic weakness by working in two allied directions: political education of the people in general, and popular mobilization of the "Other America"—and relating both with world events in the imperialist system as a whole.

The American people, who are virtually the only ones who still don't know that imperialism exists, must be taught. Progressive or radical political education must accompany the recruitment and dispatch of American soldiers to Vietnam, Santo Domingo, the Congo, and must explain to the people what is being done there and why they must not go. It must impress on the people that serious consequences must follow from the government's attack on the socialist countries. It must go beyond liberalism's appeal to morality, condemning killing in Vietnam and "appeals to reason" to stop nuclear threats against the socialist countries. It must appeal to socialist understanding of the nature of the system that obliges Americans to kill in Vietnam and that threatens nuclear destruction of others and themselves. It must relate one to the other and both to the restiveness of the "Other America" at home.

It is particularly important to explain how exploitation, underdevelopment, and poverty abroad are systematically related to exploitation, discrimination, and poverty at home—how the Vietnamese fight for liberation now is therefore related to the Afro-American fight for *Freedom Now*. The educational road for Americans does not lie, then, in following Max Gordon, former editor of the *Daily Worker*, who, in replying to the editors of *Monthly*

*Review* (December 1963) tried to write imperialism out of existence, or in following James Farmer, head of CORE, who is trying to disassociate the liberation movement in Vietnam and the civil rights movement in the United States. The road of political education, on the contrary, is to establish the connection between them.

In political education, as in popular movements today, limited short-term goals designed to attract the many to a cause which has a weak foundation points the way to defeat. The road to victory lies in understanding and moving the fundamental causes of the deep-seated problems of the peoples' lives.

The other principal immediate task of progressive forces in the U.S. today is to help the civil rights movement to travel farther and faster along the road of the Afro-American Freedom Now liberation movement. At home, no less (and perhaps more) than abroad, United States' imperialism's great strategic weakness lies in its inability to contain self-reliant and confident popular movements that combat it with far-reaching goals. The experience in Latin America and in the Southern United States shows that imperialism can all too easily join popular movements of short-term and limited aims, contain their force, and divert the direction of their development. The real progressive service of such movements can only be to lead to others with bigger aims, greater vision, and stronger foundations.

From Montgomery to Selma the popular movement in the South has shown that imperialism's problem and weakness at home does not lie at the city lunch counter or in the rural and small town South. At home, United States imperialism's political strategic weakness lies in the urban ghetto which it produces North and South; and its inhabitants know it better than anyone. It is here that the American popular movement must organize to pursue its far-reaching demands. U.S. imperialism's strategic weakness lies in its inability to meet these popular demands economically or to contain these movements politically at home or abroad at once.

The greatest strategic weakness of imperialism lies in its own existence!

## Postscript

Listening in from Latin America, Senator Fulbright's recent declarations sound like the forging of a double-edged sword in a cat's paw and are all the more dangerous for that. On the surface, Senator Fulbright's condemnation of America's military intervention in Santo Domingo seems to contradict his recent sugary words of praise for the military government of Brazil and its intervention in Santo Domingo. If, as the *National Guardian's* October 2 editorial suggests, Representative Selden's interventionist resolution in the House was prompted by Senator Fulbright's apparently anti-interventionist words in the Senate, then perhaps the Representative and other Americans do not understand what appears to be going on behind the scenes of the Senator's flowery oratory. Nonetheless, Fulbright's own words, while in Brazil, afford us a hint, and recent events in that country and elsewhere in Latin America seem to confirm it: we are witnessing the forging of an iron cat's paw with the sword of Damocles.

While on a recent official mission to Brazil, Fulbright already foreshadowed his Senate declaration when he said that it is unfortunate for the United States to have to intervene unilaterally in other countries of the American continent, and it would be interesting to consider forming an Inter-American Trade Zone reaching from Alaska to Patagonia, and that Brazil played a very important praiseworthy role in the inter-American military intervention in Santo Domingo.

No sooner did Fulbright leave Brazil than did the Argentine Chief of Staff, General Ongania, arrive to talk with the Brazilian Minister of War, Costa e Silva. Frontiers between Alaska and Patagonia should no longer be economic or even political, they agreed; the frontiers are ideological. After the generals' declarations had caused an uproar in Uruguay and Chile, and though they denied the existence of the treaty, they admitted that they had come to an "agreement" to coordinate their military forces to intervene anywhere in the American continent where these ideological frontiers might be threatened by subversion. Economic and political events in Uruguay, it was hinted, are creating such circumstances. Argentina then announced that it is being "threatened" by the invasion of a 500-man guerrilla force coming from Paraguay.

First Brazil's Foreign Minister, speaking in Rio de Janeiro, and then Brazil's Minister of Planning, speaking at a diplomatic reception in Moscow, publicly said that Chile's President Frei should watch his step lest he go the way of Goulart—who was deposed from Brazil's presidency by the government they represent. In the meantime, the United States is building military "missile" bases up and down the coast of Brazil and beginning the manufacture of weapons and even of K-rations in that country; and the Pentagon has announced a big increase in arms shipments to Argentina.

The cat's paw is being readied to strike: and Senator Fulbright's oratory and, perhaps unwittingly—or is it wittingly?—Representative Selden's Resolution (which is now drawing the Latin American's anti-interventionist fire) are providing the smoke-screen. Brazil has evidently replaced Argentina again as the United States' "favorite ally" in Latin America, but now as part of an economic, political, and military maneuver of much vaster proportions and far-reaching implications than ever before. Brazil was once the vanguard of independent foreign policy in Latin America, which has now passed to the President of Chile who is being forewarned of following in Goulart's footsteps.

Under Brazil's new Americanophile government, the giant of Latin America has already come out against the newly strengthened Latin American common market proposal of Chile's President Frei. Now Brazil is espousing the earlier American proposal, already launched as a weather balloon at the 1964 Geneva Trade Conference (GTC), of an inter-American trade zone—the one from Alaska to Patagonia. Having failed at its attempted independent imperialism, under the flag of an independent foreign policy, during the governments of Quadros and Goulart, the Brazilian bourgeoisie has resigned itself to the role of sub-imperialism (as Rui Mauro Marini calls it) as the principal junior partner of the United States in Latin America. If Brazil is to get the left-overs at the oratory-crowned imperialist banquet, then the United States' other faithful ally, Argentina, must be thrown at least the crumbs. Like imperialism itself, however, sub-imperialism transcends eco-

nomic and national boundaries and reaches the "ideological boundaries" which the bourgeoisie's military arm is prepared, or being
prepared, to defend by force.

With American intervention in Vietnam and Santo Domingo
already straining at United States capacity on the home and propaganda fronts, what can be more "logical" than liberally· to condemn further American unilateral intervention with its own troops
which prepares for automatic inter-American multilateral intervention with Latin American troops where possible, and heap
liberal praise on Brazilian intervention with Brazilian troops in
Latin American affairs? If such "un-American" countries as Chile,
Mexico, and Uruguay threaten to be uncooperative at the coming
Rio de Janeiro conference of the Organization of American States
(OAS) and not support the United States and Brazilian proposed
formation of a permanent OAS inter-American military force for
intervention in sovereign Latin American states, then what can be
more prudent than to prepare the Brazilian cat's and the Argentinian kitten's paws for such military action by direct deals with
these independent states; and to invite other kittens to join the
charmed circle of cat's paws if and when they wish?

Where there is smoke there is fire. Behind his liberal smoke-
screen, Senator Fulbright and others seem to be well on the way
to forging a Latin-manned sword of Damocles to be held over the
heads of Latin America's people—a sword in an iron cat's paw—
to be liberally swayed by whom? What more can we expect of
Kennedy, Humphrey, Fulbright, and any other *good* liberals?

# IV

## INTERNAL COLONIALIST AND CLASS POLITICS

# 14

## DIALECTIC, NOT DUAL SOCIETY

Under the title, *Third World? Which Third World?"* (*Revolution*, Vol. 1, No. 7 of the English Edition), Pierre Jalée correctly analyzed imperialism to show that there is no Third World or way, and importantly warned that this expression which has found such wide currency among imperialists and even would-be Marxists is little more than an insidious cover for the introduction of neo-colonialism by the former and of revisionism by the latter, which, as Togliatti himself[1] foretold in 1928 if not today, comes to much the same thing. My purpose here is to suggest that the very same can be said and must be understood about the "dual society" thesis whose explicit and implicit currency is perhaps still more widespread and insidious than that of its Third World twin. *There exists no dual society in the world today and all attempts to find one are attempts to justify and/or cover up imperialism and revisionism.* As Jalée quotes Vietnam's Le-Duân as saying,[2] today "the task is reduced to a choice between two roads: the non-capitalist road of development or the capitalist road." All non-socialist societies, dual or otherwise, are fully integral and integrated parts of the imperialist system and their liberation from its exploitative and underdeveloping effects is possible only under a Marxist-Leninist strategy of combating imperialist capitalism in all non-socialist societies; it is not possible to oppose capitalism vainly in one part or "sector" while encouraging and supporting it in another sector of a supposedly "dual" society.

Pierre Jalée notes that "the fact that imperialism has an essential internal contradiction between exploiting and exploited

---

1964. This article was written especially for *Revolution*, which ceased to exist before the article could be published.

countries does not remove any of its unity. This unity is indeed the fruit of this contradiction, without which imperialism would not be imperialism"—or capitalism, we might add. Jalée concludes,

> if we have directed our attacks against the expression "Third World," it should be understood that it was not to begin a quarrel of linguists. To accept too easily the term, to introduce it into ordinary language, means to introduce insidiously the idea that the group of countries about which we have spoken constitutes a particular entity, a world in itself, in regard to which the theories and reasoning applied to the group of capitalist countries and to the group of socialist countries should be revised, adapted, and more or less adulterated. Unconsciously, this is attacking the universality of Marxist doctrine and the unity of the revolutionary struggle on a world scale.[8]

If these words about the Third World are quoted here at length, it is because word for word they are just as true about the dual society. The modern version of the dual society thesis had its birth in the interpretation of Indonesian society by J. H. Boeke in 1942. This Dutch sociologist and his economist followers maintained that only part of Indonesia had been colonized by his countrymen while the largest part had been left more or less to its own devices. Indonesia had become a dual society, he said, in that its modern, capitalist, export sector had been created by and incorporated into the metropolitan (that is, imperialist) economy as a metropolitan enclave on Indonesian soil, while the majority of Indonesia's people had been left to continue their age-old and traditional subsistence economy quite outside of the metropolitan-centered world imperialist or capitalist system.

A typical recent dualist interpretation of underdeveloped countries is that of the famous French geographer, Jaques Lambert, who significantly chooses to call his book *The Two Brazils.* Lambert maintains, quite erroneously as we shall see, that

> the dual economy and the dual social structure which accompanies it are neither new nor characteristically Brazilian—they exist in all unequally developed countries. . . . The Brazilians are divided into two systems of economic and social organization which are as

different in levels as in styles of life. These two societies did not evolve at the same rate and did not attain the same face; they are not separated by a difference in their natures but by differences in age. . . . In the course of the long period of colonial isolation, there was formed an archaic Brazilian culture . . . a culture which . . . maintains in that isolation which still continues the same stability as the indigenous cultures of Asia or the Near East. . . . Between the old Brazil and the new there are centuries of distance.

In his review of Lambert's book, Brazil's most renowned progressive sociologist, who calls himself a Marxist, Florestan Fernandes, called it "one of the best sociological syntheses so far written about the formation and development of Brazilian society."

This idea of a dual society has gained universal acceptance among bourgeois students of underdeveloped countries in Asia, Africa, and Latin America who like to interpret the evident internal income and other social differences within these "unequally developed" countries as being caused by the retention of "traditional" ways in "archaic" sectors and by the introduction and acceptance of "modernism" in the "advanced" sectors of each of these countries. But the same interpretation of a dual society has crept into Marxist analysis of the underdeveloped world as well, often in the form of the supposition of the conservation of feudalism in one part and the introduction of capitalism into another part—each part or sector's organization being independently determined within itself and having its own separate dynamic—of society in these underdeveloped countries. Both in the bourgeois and the supposedly Marxist version of the dual society thesis, one sector of the national economy, which is claimed to have once been feudal, archaic, and underdeveloped as well, took off and became the now relatively developed advanced capitalist sector while the majority of the population stayed in another sector which supposedly remained as it was in its traditionally archaic, feudal, underdeveloped state. The political strategy usually associated with these factually and theoretically erroneous interpretations of development and underdevelopment is for the bourgeois the desirability of extending modernism to the archaic sector and incorporating it into the world and national market as well, and for the Marxists the desirability of completing the capitalist penetration of the feudal countryside and finishing the bourgeois democratic revolution.

If, as Pierre Jalée argues, the Third World is excluded by the existence of a single and unitary capitalist world in which "imperialism [that is, capitalism] has an essential contradiction between exploiting and exploited" without which it would not be itself, then this same dialectic unity also excludes the possible existence of the aforementioned dual societies. Far from development and underdevelopment and differences in "levels as in styles of life"—to return to Lambert—being due to the supposed existence of a dual society with "two systems of economic and social organization," either in the imperialist capitalist world as a whole or in any of its national states, these differences—and all of underdevelopment—must be traced to the dialectical unity of a single capitalist system whose contradictory and exploitative nature produces these differences. Underdevelopment, far from being due to any supposed "isolation" of the majority of the world's people from the modern capitalist expansion, or even to any continued feudal relations and ways, is the result of the integral incorporation of these people into the fully integrated but contradictory capitalist system which has long since embraced them all.

It is imperialist capitalism's essential internal contradiction between exploiting and exploited countries, to recall Pierre Jalée's words again, which has been and still remains the source and cause of the simultaneously and dialectically related development of economic development and underdevelopment. As today's Prime Minister of Trinidad, Eric Williams, noted twenty years ago in his important and accurately titled book, *Capitalism and Slavery*, and as Cortez himself already recognized when he conquered Mexico in 1520, metropolitan expansion in the Americas, whatever the various names under which it was organized, rested primarily on African, indigenous American, and originally also European, slave labor. The newly settled areas such as Brazil, the West Indies, and the Southern United States, whose migrants, largely African slaves imported by the metropolis itself, were destined to the production of sugar, cotton, cocoa, etc., for that metropolis, were almost by definition fully penetrated by and integrated into the world mercantilist-capitalist system from the very beginning. But the already densely settled areas of Asia, Africa, and Latin America, many of them previously occupied by societies of high civilization, were no less quickly and fully penetrated by and integrated into the by then worldwide capitalist system once the latter invaded and conquered them by force to provide the metropolis with labor, capital, and markets.

To extract the fruits of their labor through pillage, slavery, forced labor, free labor, raw materials, or through monopoly trade —no less today than in the times of Cortez and Pizarro in Mexico and Peru, Clive in India, Rhodes in Africa, the "Open Door" in China—the metropolis destroyed and/or totally transformed the earlier viable social and economic systems of these societies, incorporated them into the metropolitan dominated worldwide capitalist system, and converted them into sources for its own metropolitan capital accumulation and development. The resulting fate for these conquered, transformed, or newly established societies was and remains their de-capitalization, structurally generated unproductiveness, ever-increasing poverty for the masses —in a word, their underdevelopment.

Those people in the underdeveloped countries who were not or are not at any one time incorporated into the capitalist system's market as visibly direct sellers of labor or buyers of products are not for all that unintegrated into, isolated from, or marginal to the capitalist system. Theirs is another fate which is a no less necessary result of the essential internal contradiction of the capitalist system. Though according to the erroneous and insidious dual society thesis they have been unaffected by, or are at least marginal to, the capitalist system, these people have been and still are being deprived of their land and the livelihood it afforded them by the world-engulfing expansion of that capitalist system; they have, as in India, seen imperialism destroy the organization of irrigation, handicrafts, industry, and trade as well as the livelihood they derived from these; they have witnessed the capitalist system produce its sometimes sudden, sometimes slow, but always inevitable world, national, and regional shifts in supply and demand for their former output of spices, sugar, cocoa, coffee, tea, rubber, gold, silver, copper, tin, and other raw materials, and of industrial goods as well, which for months, years, decades, or even centuries transform whole populations of once independent producers or dependent workers into the "floating" or "marginal" bare- or non-subsistence populations of the capitalist system's ubiquitous underdeveloped rural and urban slums and ghettos.

Thus the underdevelopment of the Brazilian Northeast, for instance, today one of the world's poorest regions, the plight and struggle of whose twenty-five million people was made famous around the world by Francisco Julião and his Peasant Leagues, is not due to the "isolation," "archaic culture," and "feudal regime" that Lambert and many others, including unfortunately too many supposed Marxists, attribute to it. On the contrary, the Brazilian Northeast's underdevelopment must be traced to the essential internal dialectic contradiction of the single unitary mercantilist-then-capitalist system whose sixteenth-century depression of the Brazilian sugar and slave economy, seventeenth-century depression of the Brazilian sugar economy, nineteenth-century sacrifice of slavery to the British textile interests and shift of the Brazilian metropolis to the southern coffee-producing region, whose continued reliance on other means to extract capital from the Northeast for the benefit of the world and the Brazilian metropolis, caused, maintains, and still deepens the structure of the Northeast's underdevelopment from which there can be no escape short of the escape from the imperialist and capitalist system itself.

With respect to the all-embracing nature of the capitalist system, if not in all of her strategy for combating it, Rosa Luxemburg was undoubtedly right in her time, to say nothing of ours, when in *Accumulation of Capital* she argued that capitalism had long since penetrated, incorporated, and transformed even the most "isolated" or "marginal" outposts of this planet. As even such bourgeois economists as Sweden's Gunnar Myrdal and the United Nations' Raúl Prebisch have emphasized the capitalist world, or one might say the entire capitalist society, is inexorably divided into exploiting developed metropolis and exploited underdeveloped periphery. This metropolis-periphery division rests on capitalism's essential internal contradiction between exploiting and exploited and, in the present as in the past, simultaneously gives rise to economic development for some and underdevelopment for most. But far from having failed to reach the "isolated," "marginal," "non-capitalist" subsistence sector of supposedly dual societies, this contradiction of capitalism produced and maintains the underdevelopment of that sector of capitalist but dialectically divided society, however archaic, feudal, or isolated-seeming it may be. To speak of a "Third World" or a "dual society" in our day produces and is utter confusion.

Capitalism's essential internal contradiction between the exploiting and exploited appears within nations no less than between them. And imperialism's consequent essential structure of the exploitative relations between the developing metropolis and the underdeveloping periphery is partially duplicated within each society, each nation-state, and indeed within their regions and sectors. In each underdeveloped country it is today its national metropolis which had and has the greatest contact with the world metropolis. Simultaneously and consequently, these national metropoles, and of course the world capitalist metropolis as well, maintain an exploitative relationship with their respective provincial peripheries which is an extension of the relationship the world capitalist metropolis maintains with them. On the regional and sectoral levels as well, the provincial commercial centers, which are in the economically disadvantageous position of a periphery with respect to the national and international metropoles, are for their own part in turn an exploiting metropolitan center to their respective rural hinterlands. The metropolis of each of these levels is of course intimately tied to and dependent on the metropoles of other levels. They differ in their exploitative roles within the capitalist system which ties them to each other and to their peripheries in that the central metropolis, with its worldwide hinterland which includes the national and regional metropoles, has a dominating dependence on the others while the national and regional metropoles have a relatively less dominating and more dominated dependence. In the metropolis-periphery relationship of each of these levels, as in that of the international one which engulfs them all, the metropolis sucks capital out of the periphery and uses its power to maintain the economic, political, social, and cultural structure of the periphery and its peripheral metropoles and therewith to maintain as long as possible the capitalist imperialist system which permits this exploitation. The essential internal contradiction of the capitalist system as a whole, while permitting the relative development of some, thus produces and maintains the underdevelopment of others on the international, national, regional, sectoral, and local levels. On any of these levels, therefore, the only escape from this underdevelopment is socialist escape from the capitalist structure which necessarily produces and maintains that underdevelopment. There is no dual society and no third way.

As Pierre Jalée's analysis of the exclusion of the Third World also holds for the dual society, so do his conclusions limiting the policy alternatives to those of capitalism and socialism hold equally for the political policy necessary to escape from that capitalism and underdevelopment into socialism and development. No less than the Third World position, the dual society thesis, which explicitly or implicitly claims the existence of two or more independently determined sectors in a single really dialectically united/divided society, consciously or unconsciously attacks, revises, adapts, adulterates the "universality of Marxist doctrine and the unity of the revolutionary struggle on a world scale." Though, as Jalée suggests, Frantz Fanon may have erred terminologically in using the term Third World, he certainly did not fall into the insidious trap of the dual society or have any illusions about the possibility of a third way. On the contrary, perhaps more than any other of our contemporaries, Fanon recognized, clinically studied, and emphasized the thoroughness and totality of capitalism's colonial penetration into the heart and soul of the underdeveloped countries it has corrupted. And Fanon did not fail to warn most emphatically that any attempt to rely on a national bourgeoisie to pursue an independent third way out of imperialist colonial underdevelopment is bound to corrupt the society still further and to end in disastrous failure. The national bourgeoisie, where it can be said to exist, and indeed the entire national metropolis and capitalist system on which it thrives, are necessarily so inextricably integrated into the imperialist system and the exploitative metropolis-periphery relationship it imposes on them that it cannot possibly escape from and can only extend and deepen the resulting underdevelopment.

Frantz Fanon was explicit in saying that the national bourgeoisie phase in the history of the underdeveloped countries is useless and that once this bourgeoisie has been consumed by its own contradictions it will be necessary to begin again from zero. It may be suggested that indeed Fanon himself fell into substantive error at this point: as it is never possible to turn history back, it will not be possible to start over again at the zero at which the national bourgeoisie began. On the contrary, though the national bourgeoisie in combination with popular forces can in some places still contribute to some forms of liberation, the bulk of historical experience, Fanon's own work, and unadulterated Marxist analysis show that the action of the "national" bourgeoisie in underdeveloped countries today necessarily strengthens, instead of weakens, those countries' links with imperialism, promotes still greater and deeper structural underdevelopment, and thus increases the final cost of liberation—or, to retain Fanon's simile, on balance advances the underdeveloped country to *below* zero before real national liberation is possible. This national bourgeois phase in the underdeveloped countries today must therefore be eliminated where possible or at least shortened, rather than prolonged in the name of the subsistence of a dual society or the existence of a third way.

Undoubtedly the bitterest experience with the underdevelopment produced by these imperialist-dominated "national" bourgeoisies and economies is that of Latin America, which has already suffered from and underdeveloped under it for decades if not for a century and a half. Unfortunately, more bitter than this experience has been that of almost all of Latin America's Communist parties which, armed among other things with the dual society thesis, if not with the third world view, have an almost unblemished record of total and unquestioning support of these national bourgeoisies in the name of a mythical—or, to use Fanon's word, caricature—pursuit of the bourgeois revolution in the dual society at home, and in effect if not in name, Third World independence from imperialism abroad, and which have a clean record of total and often disastrous failure. Loyal and fervent supporters of President Goulart, less anxious to organize the masses for liberation than even some admittedly entirely bourgeois economic and political groups, the Brazilian Communist Party now shares with its compatriots the political repression of the recent fascist military coup whose easy victory was the inevitable fruit of the Brazilian Communist Party's and others' consistently erroneous and disastrous policy. And this Party, like others of its brother Communist parties in Latin America, recently rushed into the forefront of those who vociferously criticize as "divisionist" precisely those parties which seek to rely on Marxism-Leninism to advance that revolutionary struggle against capitalism in the underdeveloped countries whose early initiation, though it may not produce liberation overnight, can and will provide the only possible escape from underdevelopment.

## NOTES

1. *Revolution*, Vol. I, No. 11.
2. *Revolution*, Vol. I, No. 1, p. 7 of the French edition.
3. *Ibid.*, p. 3.

# 15

## CAPITALIST LATIFUNDIO GROWTH IN LATIN AMERICA

### On the Subject of Feudalism

We invite the reader to consider the following problem and to contemplate the significance of the solution we offer for an examination of the Ibero-American *problématique*: Connect the nine points drawn here with a single line of four (not five) continuous and straight segments. In looking for the solution the reader will verify that he does not find any, as long as he stays within the square and limited frame that the nine points appear to impose on us. The solution is that we must emerge from this limited and self-imposed frame thusly:

Similarly, if we are to understand the Latin American *problématique* we must begin with the world system that creates it and go outside the self-imposed optical and mental illusion of the Ibero-American or national frame.

This is what we shall do to face Rodolfo Puiggrós' warning and challenge "not to mistake the point of departure in explaining

---

1965. This is the author's part of a debate with Rodolfo Puiggrós, which was published in successive issues of *El Gallo Ilustrado*, supplement to *El Día* (October 31 and November 28, 1965).

current capitalist feebleness and the existing possibilities for passing to a higher order." These are the words with which he ends his comments "On the Subject of Feudalism" in his examination of "The Modes of Production in Ibero-America." We shall also answer Roger Bartra who, in his examination of "Pre-Capitalist Societies" does us the honor of placing us on the "Left," only later to exclude us from it, quoting us and linking our name with those of others who "do not appear to have a 'dialectically dual' understanding of reality" and among whom "the old bourgeois theses are hidden."

Puiggrós again asks the question concerning "the mode of production initiated by Hispanic colonization of America. Was it feudal, was it capitalist, or what was it?" "Common sense, more than science," he tells us, "is reluctant to admit that the Spaniards came to our continent as bourgeoisie to organize capitalist societies." It seems to us, rather, that common sense is reluctant to admit that they came as feudal lords to organize feudal societies, that they had economic interests and means in Spain to finance an extremely costly enterprise that would benefit feudal holdings— that is, closed economies—overseas. Furthermore, not only common sense, but Mr. Puiggrós himself is reluctant to admit such speculation. He tells us: "The commercial bourgeoisie of the manufacturing cities of Spain and Italy discovered America. . . . It was not the lords of Castille; it was not feudalism. Their opposition to Columbus' project is well known."

Going on with his argument, Puiggrós maintains that "the important thing is to determine whether the modes of production of the colonial epoch show as a rule, not merely exceptionally, the following characteristics [listed by Puiggrós and to which we shall return below]. . . . Since we have not discovered these dominant characteristics, we wonder on what arguments those people rely who declare our countries to have been capitalist from their birth."

In answer to Puiggrós, we, who declare Ibero-America to be capitalist not only from its birth but from its conception, answer that we support our case not so much on arguments as on facts, something which Puiggrós does not do. When we present ourselves on the field of battle armed with the seven characteristics

Puiggrós himself has chosen as the most important ones—and they are not those we would have chosen—we find that our honorable and fierce adversary does not appear, since he merely tells us that he did not discover his favorite characteristics and does not even tell us why, nor where he sought for them, nor much less what he found instead. Thus we find ourselves obliged to present arms alone: The first characteristic, whose existence Puiggrós considers it important to determine, but whose presence he cannot see, is "the accumulation and reinvestment of capital." Looking somewhat beyond the points of the narrow Latin American framework, we verify, and all the facts show, that this characteristic *was* present on a large scale: the accumulation of Ibero-American capital and its investment in Europe. His second characteristic is "developed mercantile production, not the simple production of surplus in a subsistence economy." This was precisely the most outstanding characteristic of the mercantile system in the colonial epoch. Third: "The existence of capitalists and workers." These were present on both sides of the Atlantic, especially capitalist Europeans using Ibero-American workers and capital. And so on with the four remaining characteristics, as the reader can verify for himself. As for us, we prefer to leave the field of battle chosen by our adversary but on which he did not appear; and, armed with facts, we shall go in search of him wherever he may be.

## Anecdotes and Facts

To lend "attention to the export of precious metals and tropical products," is, for Puiggrós, to indulge in "academic aberrations, with no more value than an anecdote." It was not thus for the Spaniards and other Europeans. They did not any the less speak the truth for speaking anecdotically. In fact, Columbus was of the opinion that "the best thing in the world is gold . . . It can even send souls to heaven"; Cortés, on arriving on these shores [Mexico], informed an Indian: "We, the Spaniards, suffer from a disease of the heart for which there is only one specific remedy: gold"; the Franciscan friars and Bishop Mota y Escobar observed that "Where there is no silver, the gospel does not enter," and "Where there are no Indians, there is no silver." Nonetheless, though we go along with the colonial chroniclers who characterized mining as the "nerve and substance" of the Ibero-American economy, we shall not labor the point here but rather shall proceed to another question raised by Puiggrós.

He maintains that "commerce, and even certain investments in mines, manufacturing [*obrajes*], and colonial business enterprises did not . . . reform the agrarian regime, nor did they promote important domestic accumulations of capital." The entire weight of the argument rests on the key words "reform" and "domestic." There were, undeniably, large accumulations of Ibero-American capital—accumulation within the enterprises and accumulations within the global system, but in Europe. As was recognized by the merchants and mercantilist statesmen of the period, and by economists from Smith to Marx, and as is recognized today by those who have not lost all contact with historical and current reality, it was precisely this and other such primary and later capital accumulation, extracted from mines, plantations, haciendas, and Ibero-American and overseas trade, which permitted metropolitan capitalist development and condemned Ibero-Americans and other human beings of this earth to the capitalist feebleness of so-called underdevelopment.

Puiggrós also asks if these mercantile and capitalist events "reformed the agrarian regime" in Ibero-America. The answer is *no*; they *formed* it. Puiggrós himself, as someone who knows his own country, speaks of "the farming-cattle-raising capitalism of the Argentine littoral . . . [which] arose as a function of sales to the market, to the foreign market in the first instance." Puiggrós warns us: "Let us not be so foolish as to judge modes of production of our entire continent by a special case." We shall not do so; and we shall show that the Argentine case, far from being special or an exception, was and continues to be the rule. Sugar-growing in Brazil—as was previously the case in the Mediterranean and Atlantic islands and, later, in the Caribbean islands, such as Barbados, St. Dominique (Haiti and Santo Domingo), Cuba, and others—"arose as a function of sales to the market, to the foreign market in the first instance." Sergio Sepulveda notes in *El Trigo Chileno en el Mercado Mundial* that "the Chilean colonial economy [was] essentially characterized by export and not by mere subsistence, as has sometimes been alleged. This characteristic is generic to the colonial economy of various countries."

Mario Góngora confirms this in *El Origen de los "Inquilinos" de Chile Central:*

> In the eighteenth century [Chile] underwent an important transfor-mation—trade in wheat with Peru—which brought with it a more intense organization of the hacienda and an increase in the value of land in the export areas from Aconagua to Colchagua. The tend-ency took the form of tenancy, and the amount of payment for tenancy use of the land became considerable . . . it showed in the greater dependence of the tenants [*arrendatarios*] and the increase of their obligations [to the landowner] . . . The large hacienda in-creasingly made the tenants bear its need for labor; the term *arrenda-tario*, which is also used for middle- or high-class persons, fell into disuse and was replaced by *inquilino*. In sum, then, rural tenancy, from rental to peonage [*inquilinaje*], has nothing to do with the *encomienda* or with the institutions of the Conquest. They arise in the second period of colonial history, when the landlords are stratified upward, and poor Spaniards and various kinds of mestizos and castes are stratified downward. . . . Stratification increases in the eighteenth and nineteenth centuries, and the obligations of the *inquilinos* increase proportionately. . . . The *inquilino* becomes [in the eighteenth century] a more and more dependent worker . . . in accordance with a tendency toward the proletarianization of the *inquilino* that increased in the nineteenth century.

### The Market Called the Mexican Hacienda into Being

Thus an examination of the facts reveals that what Puiggrós considers to be an exception is in fact the rule. Is Mexico (or Peru?) an exception to this rule? Puiggrós would have us believe so. The answer to this question is provided by the most outstand-ing observer of the colonial epoch, the German geographer Humboldt, in his celebrated *Political Essay on the Kingdom of New Spain:*

> Trips through the Andes highlands or the mountainous part of Mexico offer the most obvious examples of the beneficent influence of the mines on agriculture. Without the establishments formed for

the working of the mines, how many places would have remained unpopulated, how much land uncultivated, in the four districts of
Guanajuato, Zacatecas, San Luis Potosí, and Durango . . . ! The
foundation of a city follows immediately after the discovery of a
large mine. . . . Haciendas are established nearby; the scarcity of
foodstuffs and the high prices caused by consumer competition favors
agricultural products, compensates the grower for the deprivations
of life in the mountains. In this way, arising only out of the desire
for profit . . . a mine . . . is very quickly linked up with lands
long under cultivation . . .

and the latifundio is created.

Thus in Mexico, as in the Argentina of Puiggrós or the Chile of
Góngora, in the words of the latter: "Rural tenancy [of the
hacienda] has nothing to do with the *encomienda* or with the
institutions of the Conquest. It arises out of the second period
of colonial history." In fact, the well-known Mexican historians
Silvio Zavala and José Miranda long ago abandoned the old and
erroneous thesis that the *encomienda* or even the *encomendero*
gave rise to the hacienda.

The hacienda arose and grew, as Humboldt says, "out of the
desire for profit." "Hacienda," in the Spanish of Cervantes, meant
*"capital,"* and even today this meaning is essentially preserved
in the Ministry of Hacienda (Treasury). Only when capital began to be invested in rural properties and enterprises did the
word "hacienda" acquire the meaning of "latifundio." In New
Spain, this allocation of capital began, as Humboldt points out,
and as François Chevalier confirms in his already classic book
*La formación de los grandes latifundios en México* (*Land and
Society in Colonial Mexico: The Great Hacienda*),[1] in the sixteenth century when mines were opened and cities built which
required wheat, cattle, sugar, wood, and other products. As
Chevalier's research proved, "The exploitation of the silver mines
was closely linked with the birth and development of the big
rural haciendas of the north." Mining production reached its
apogee between 1591 and 1600, declined slowly until 1630, then
rapidly until 1660, before it began, during the last decade of the
seventeenth century, to recover to its level a century earlier. "It
was undoubtedly during this epoch of mining decadence," says

Chevalier, "that the hacienda turned in upon itself." This was the period Woodrow Borah called the "century of depression." In spite of these judgments, the facts discovered by both historians prove that this was also the epoch in which the Mexican latifundist haciendia was "consolidated," and became the object of growing capital investment coming from businessmen and miners. "Many businessmen became landowners, since land represented a safe investment," says Chevalier. At the same time, he asks "to what extent mining capital, from places like Pachuca and Taxco, was invested in rural enterprises in the Central zone." Commercial investment in land and the formation of large "feudal" latifundios in Mexico was not only safe during this period, but highly remunerative; and the shift, whatever the amount, of "capitalist" mining capital to "feudal" haciendas, which were baptized with the synonym of "capital," was highly logical. Chevalier points to one reason: "The main goal of many people was to monopolize all sources of income, mines, and land, which others might utilize for the purpose of remaining independent or for becoming competitors." But we believe that, behind this same process of monopolization and of investment in "feudal" haciendas, there was another more fundamental cause: it was good business. While the profitability of mining decreased both absolutely and relatively— because of increases in the cost of production and taxes, and because inflation meant a decrease in the value of silver (or money) —the profitability of agriculture increased absolutely and relatively, with respect to mining. The cause was a growth in population and urban demand—in spite of the accelerated decline in Indian population and production—which was accompanied by a disturbing scarcity of foodstuffs and alarming price inflation. All government efforts to check this trend—price ceilings, control of market trade and warehousing, and other anti-speculation measures—met with failure. Thus the "feudal" hacienda in Mexico and the modes of production and relations of work that developed on them—like the Chilean wheat latifundio; the sugar and cacao latifundios of Brazil, the Caribbean, Venezuela, etc.; and the "special" case of the Argentine cattle latifundio—grew and were consolidated when farming flourished due to an increase in prices and in demand, a decline in a competing business, road or technical improvements, or a combination of these, as long as there was sufficient cheap labor for business to be "good business" and as long as capital accumulation was possible, even though it be by monopolist merchants and "internal" to the overseas metropolitan economy. We believe that historical research will show that the incorrectly named feudal latifundios which were relatively isolated and possessed an alleged self-subsistence economy at some times and places were usually not originally organized as such, but were the result of an earlier commercial development which declined and left such ultra-underdeveloped regions as northeastern Brazil, highland Peru, and central Mexico.

If it was this way from the Conquest, which established Ibero-American agrarian "feudalism," to the second half of the last century, in spite of the first liberal efforts, would this pattern have disappeared in the course of the last century? As far as his period (before the Mexican Revolution of 1910) is concerned, Lauro Viadas, the Director-General of the Ministry of Agriculture, who was a well-known Porfirian *científico*, answers us:

Agriculture is, before and above all else, a business, and in every business the amount and safety of the profits are what determine the character of the enterprise. . . . If the large rural properties continue to exist it is because they are the logical consequence of the state of evolution of agriculture in our country, and they will have to continue to exist for the same reason, in spite of the firmest and best-intentioned plans, as long as those obstacles which hamper our agrarian progress are not removed. Large-scale agriculture asserts itself and excludes small-scale family agriculture; it takes possession of the land, attracted, and I would say strongly attracted, by economic advantages that spring from the two following causes: (1) The high price of the means of livelihood. . . . The high price of these goods leads first to a high profit for the growers and subsequently, a high price for arable land, which places it within the reach only of capitalist entrepreneurs. (2) The cheapness of labor, which reduces, relatively if not absolutely, the cost of production and produces, thereby, the above-mentioned effect of raising agricultural profits . . .

This report on Porfirian "feudal" agriculture and economy, at a time when North Americans had come to own one-seventh of the Mexican national territory—not to mention mining, industry, and trade—was presented in 1911 to the Madero government so that it and future generations of Mexicans would know how "to remove the obstacles that hamper our agrarian progress," and would remember that "they will, for the same reasons, have to subsist, in spite of the firmest and best-intentioned plans," as long as this is not done. Let us leave for the reader's meditation and judgment how much the "anti-feudal and anti-imperialist" Mexican Revolution and the "bourgeois agrarian reform" to which it gave birth went beyond firm goals or good intentions to remove the above-mentioned real and already very longstanding obstacles. Who dares to call the northern "nylon" *neo-latifundismo*—artificial because owned by non-farmer businessmen—neo-feudalism?

### Underdeveloped Capitalism and Capitalist Underdevelopment

How then can we explain the feeble capitalist weakness and the contemporary underdevelopment of Latin America? Not as a feudal survival which continues to wait for its replacement by capitalist development, but as the historical and even the continuing product of capitalist development itself in a single world system which—as Roger Bartra tells us—"is a dialectically dual society with different parts: one part exploited by the other." So that capitalist development undeniably—to use the Porfirian *científico's* word—also engenders the development of underdevelopment. We see a system, first mecantilist and later capitalist, that incorporated the entire world and whose "colonialist" structure and unequal development formed, not reformed as Puiggrós would have it, the modes of production and of life in Ibero-America and other parts of the world that are today, though they were not formerly, underdeveloped.

The colonialist structure of this system was, is, and will be fundamentally and highly monopolist. Monopoly, in turn, leads to the development of the monopolizer and the underdevelopment of the monopolized, while it uselessly wastes a great part of the productive resources or economic surplus which could, "theoretically," aid the greater development of both.

The essence of this metropolis-satellite monopolist structure did not change with Independence and still exists today; since in the new Latin American states the *criollos* replaced the Peninsular Spaniards in the structure, and they were in turn rapidly satellized by England, which source of dependence was later replaced by the United States. The *científicos* became the representatives and minor partners of North American imperialism during the period of Porfirio Díaz, and the same thing happened in other Ibero-American countries. By this we do not mean to say that the system remained static throughout four centuries. On the contrary, the historical development of this world system generated the development of the monopolizing metropolis and the underdevelopment of the monopolized satellites. The development of the national Ibero-American metropolis obviously could not and cannot be the "classical" capitalist development of the world metropolis, given that the latter is no one's satellite, unlike the national metropolises of today's underdeveloped countries. Of course, this fact of being a satellite within the world capitalist system and development imposes limits on the development of the national bourgeoisies and economies of Latin America and condemns their metropolises to underdeveloped development and their domestic satellites to total underdevelopment.

In the face of this fact, many of those who want to lean on Marx for an explanation of capitalist weakness so as to show us the way toward a higher order, want to convince us that this feebleness is due to feudalism, and the road to take is the road to capitalism. Those who are no longer convinced by this feudal tale, now begin to exhume the old Marxist typology of the Asiatic mode of production. But as we shall see, the refurbished Asiatic idea, like the old feudal tale, serves only to obscure the capitalist reality and its inevitable political implications.

### Colonialism, Classes, and a Higher Order

Let us pass on to the second problem presented to us by Puiggrós, which, although he is speaking of the past, constitutes the real preoccupation of Roger Bartra and Ettore di Robbio in their essays on modes of pre-capitalist production, namely "the possibilities that exist for passing to a higher social order" in the Ibero-American future. Bartra correctly attributes to us the "colonialist" focus utilized above and quotes us in this respect. But, unlike some, our use of this approach is not so much to point to internal or external colonialism, as it is to study, through its monopolist colonial structure, the nature and development of the world capitalist system in its totality so as better to understand and to change the nature and development of underdevelopment in Latin America. For this same reason, we also try to proceed dialectically. Our metropolis-satellite or "colonialist" approach is not simply "dual," not unless those of Marx and Bartra are also to be so considered merely because they speak of two classes. No less than an adequate approach and the real class structure, the approach and colonial structure is dialectical because it refers to the relation between the parts that define and determine it.

Therefore, we shall not try, as Bartra maintains, to replace the structure and study of classes by the colonial ones. We are aware that to follow the example of Pablo González Casanova, who claims that internal colonialism "has an explicative function that is much broader than that of social classes," can only lead to disguised bourgeois theses which, at bottom, defend and ultimately preserve the present structure; this happened to the above-mentioned author in his conclusions in *La Democracia en México* and to Rodolfo Stavenhagen in the seventh of his "mistaken theses on Latin America," in which he denies the possibility of a worker-peasant alliance. These conclusions are totally unacceptable to us because they lack the scientific exactitude that the "colonist" focus pretends to give them. Nor can we permit Bartra to link our name, work, and quotations therefrom with these procedures and conclusions, since on the occasion of a round table on González Casanova's book we stated (see Chapter 20):

> The theory of internal and foreign colonialism of the capitalist system cannot provide—as Pablo González Casanova attempts to convince us—an alternative to the theory of classes. On the contrary, the examination of the one and only metropolis-satellite structure, both international and national, throws into sharp relief the class structure in which the bourgeois is formed, develops fully or not, according to whether it is dominant or satellized, maintains it-

self economically on the basis of its exploitation of the people, both urban and rural, and therefore necessarily maintains itself and makes an effort politically to preserve this same exploitative and underdevelopment-generating structure.

## Words Have Miserably Been Taken for Facts

Let us accept provisionally the dubious thesis of the Pre-Colombian Asiatic mode of production and its conservation, during the first moments of the Conquest, by the Spaniards who replaced the Inca and Aztec power with their own. But the question arises: how long did the Asiatic mode of production last in Mexico and Peru? We shall find the answer by tracing the contradictions, and above all the second one, that this typology presents. How long did this despotic-communal entity last within the Mexican or Peruvian framework? No time. The *comuneros* were immediately integrated into a system whose despot and place of appropriation were found not in Tenochtitlán, Mexico City, Cuzco, or Lima, but in Spain. New Spain was not the despotic-communal unit of possible Asiatic production, nor was Spain, nor was the Spanish Empire; it was the entire mercantilist system which, a few years after the Conquest, included the Far East, where part of the American silver was put to rest, and most important, it included Italy, Holland, and England, where the surplus produced by the *comuneros* and brought by the Spaniards was invested without profit to the producers whose natural, human, and created resources—such as irrigation systems—were rapidly and effectively destroyed. To be sure, the Aztecs and Incas had also invaded and despotically subjected other peoples—as many invaders of the Hindu sub-continent had done—but they had taken good care not to kill the goose that laid the golden eggs. This is a very important difference through which the Asiatic mode of production was rapidly converted into the capitalist mode of production.

The rapid replacement of the old mode of production by the new system appears with even greater clarity if we follow a second tack and ask who appropriated the economic surplus. If it is true, as has sometimes been suggested, that Aztec state appropriation was in the process of developing toward private appropriation, within the state institutions, this process was suddenly accelerated by the arrival of the Spaniards. Even if the king and his Spanish "state" appropriated part of the surplus by means of the *quinto real* (Royal Fifth), etc., there is not the slightest doubt that since the Conquest the dominant appropriation was expropriation by private individuals and partnerships. It was they who financed the entire enterprise and it was they who received the profits, including a good part of the royal share, which went to the Genoese, Dutch, and German bankers who were financing the Spanish king (who was also the German emperor). Thus it only remains to say whether or not the new private appropriation was feudal. We think not.

We hope that the reader will forgive us if we conclude with the observations of a Mexican who undoubtedly knew his country very much better than we could hope to know it:

> Let us now see how the distribution of property has divided the population into the various classes that make up the state, the relations established among them, and the consequences of these relations. And this study, indispensable to anyone who wishes to know how a country is constituted, is all the more necessary in our case because we have committed grave errors by not recognizing that our society had its own physiognomy, and that it did not in any way resemble European societies, with which we are always comparing it, if only because we have borrowed the names of its social organization, without possessing any of its constitutive parts. When we have been told in all seriousness that we had an aristocracy, when we were exhorted to bring it up to date, and when we were told about European nobility and the feudal clergy, no one knew what was being said; unfortunately, words were taken for things, and a mistake in language has brought a mistake in politics; but, by a simple comparison of those classes with ours the spell is broken.

For Mariano Otero the spell had already been broken in June 1842, when he wrote these lines in his *Ensayo sobre el verdadero estado de la cuestión social y política que se agita en la República Mexicana*, and he transcended the political error when, at the same time, he added: "We need, then, a general change, and this should begin with the material relations of society."

## A Modest Reply *(to a Rejoinder by Puiggrós)*

In a debate on socialism between Paul Sweezy, the North American Marxist, and Milton Friedman, who was Senator Goldwater's principal adviser in his 1964 Presidential campaign, Sweezy began thus: "Considering my adversary's experience and recognized brilliance in debates, I urge the public to judge the truth, not in terms of the presentation of the argument, where my adversary has an advantage over me, but in terms of the content of the argument." Experience, obviously, obliges me to urge the reader to do the same.

My limited journalistic and debating experiences have already obliged me to eliminate the following phrases, among others, from the galleys of my last intervention in these pages: "We shall try not to fall into the common error which," according to Puiggrós, "consists of confusing the mercantile economy with capitalism. But unlike Mr. Puiggrós, we shall not neglect the effects that both national and international trade had and continue to have in opening the way to and determining modes of production in the presently enfeebled and underdeveloped Ibero-America, and in the presently capitalist and developed metropolis."

That was how I proceeded. Although Mr. Puiggrós did not notice it, his "deaf" dialogue affirms that I had not dedicated a line to the modes of production; I undertook throughout the article to examine and show how modes of production were formed and determined. Even if Mr. Puiggrós did not take notice, we saw how and why modes of production "inside" the haciendas were formed and transformed according to the needs and vicissitudes of the market and its integrants, principally landowners and merchants. Mario Góngora, the historian, showed us the "how" when he indicated that the demand for the products of the Chilean soil converted its free producers into "feudal" peons. The "why" was explained with clarity and alarming foresight by the Porfirian Lauro Viadas, who correctly attributed the state of agriculture in his and other epochs to the high price of land or of its products, and to the low price of labor. It was lack of space that prevented me from also pointing out why and how the peasants of Zapata's Morelos rented or sold their own land, working it later as "feudal" peons of the landlord, in each boom in sugar production from the sixteenth to the nineteenth century, and again in our own time.

The fact that the market turns out to be geographically more extensive than the hacienda and its mode of production does not imply that the latter is "internal" and the former is "external," except in the most mechanical or metaphysical sense. The dialectic reality of history and of today is that modes, and especially forms, of production inside the hacienda, and the development and fluctuations inside the market are intimately linked together. Therefore any attempt to understand one in isolation from the other is bound to fail. Mr. Puiggrós, whose attempt is to take as given that which is the fundamental question, will surely avoid this fate. As is suggested by the study of both the modes of production and the solution of the problem of the nine points, the answer to this question resides precisely in knowing the external cause in order to change the internal determining dynamic of the relevant social entity.

Inasmuch as Mr. Puiggrós is apparently not interested in the above-mentioned facts, and inasmuch as I am not blessed with sophistication nor with Greek sophism, I shall turn for assistance to a compatriot of mine, whose authority Mr. Puiggrós appears to recognize when he lectures at the National Autonomous University of Mexico on the economic and social theory of Marxism. Mr. Puiggrós asks: "What was the 'world system' of the sixteenth century that generated our societies?" In Volume I of *Capital*, the German scholar answers: "The modern history of capitalism begins with the creation, in the sixteenth century, of world trade and a world market." Mr. Puiggrós is concerned with what "happened inside [colonies such as Brazil and those in the Caribbean]—that is, with where the mode of slave-holding production prevailed." In Volume II of *La Historia crítica de la plusvalía*, by the same theorist whose theory Mr. Puiggrós teaches, we read:

> In the second class of colonies—the plantations, which are from the moment of their inception, commercial speculations, centers of production for the world market—a regime of capitalist production exists, if only in a formal way, since slavery among the Negroes ex-

cludes free wage-labor, which is the base on which capitalist production rests. However, those who deal in slave-trading are capitalists. The system of production introduced by them does not originate in slavery but was introduced into it. In this case the capitalist and the landlord are one person.

With respect to serfdom, with which Mr. Puiggrós is concerned but which he does not explain, Engels, his teacher's collaborator, noted in *The Mark* that in the fifteenth century the lords converted the free peasants of Europe into serfs, that "the capitalist era in the countryside begins with a period of large-scale agriculture, based on serf labor," and that in Eastern Europe, where a relatively free peasantry had arisen, the second reduction to vassalage of the peasants was due to, and grew in proportion to, the development of an export market for agricultural products.

Furthermore, taking the forms for the mode and system of production, and associating payment in kind with feudalism and payment in money with capitalism as Mr. Puiggrós appears to do, he would have to say that mines with company stores were and are feudal, but that capitalism arose in Ibero-America (to disappear again) when in 1532 the Indian tax or tribute was commuted, because "Now it appears that in some towns of New Spain they prefer maize and blankets and more willingly give gold, because in their exchange they earn enough for the tribute and for their maintenance"; or when in 1784 Inspector Gálvez complained of the "abuse that was being introduced consisting of providing the hacienda's day laborers with money for their usual rations . . . and it was not fair that . . . a poor worker should be defrauded of a large part of the remuneration for his work, paying him with scarcely half or a little more in *reals* of what his pay would be if computed in grain, in order to indulge their greed by selling it [the grain] at the price set by scarcity"; or when and where the more inflation there is in Latin America, the more the *hacendados* pay their peons in devaluated, though "capitalist," money, rather than in non-devaluated "feudal" produce.

In Eric Hobsbawm's introduction to the English edition of *Pre-Capitalist Economic Formations* by Marx (an abbreviated version of which was published in *El Gallo Ilustrado* and which opened this entire debate) he recalls that "this distinction between modes of production characterised by certain relations, and the 'forms' of such relations which can exist in a variety of periods or socio-economic settings, is already implicit in earlier Marxian thought." [2] Thus it is not surprising that some Marxists or modest students of underdevelopment, such as the author of these lines, do not need magnifying glasses in order to recognize these realities when they appear in Ibero-America, even if other theorists of Marxism do not wish to see these realities, or perhaps have anything to do with changing them.

## NOTES

1. François Chevalier, *Land and Society in Colonial Mexico: The Great Hacienda* (Berkeley: University of California Press, 1965). The quotations have been translated from the Spanish edition.
2. Karl Marx, *Pre-Capitalist Economic Formations*, E. J. Hobsbawm, ed. (London: Lawrence & Wishart, 1964), p. 59.

# 16

## RURAL ECONOMIC STRUCTURE
## AND PEASANT POLITICAL POWER

The community development approach was aptly evaluated forty years ago by José Carlos Mariátegui, writing about Peru:

> All theses about the Indian problem which do not see it as an economic-social problem, or which avoid it as such, are nothing but further sterile theoretical . . . and sometimes merely verbal . . . exercises which are condemned to absolute discredit. They are in no way redeemed by their good intentions . . . The Indian question grows out of our economy. It has roots in the system of land ownership. Any attempt to solve it by administrative or police measures, through education or road building, is superficial and beside the point.[1]

These inherent limitations still characterize most rural community development programs today and suggest the need for a different approach to community development. Accordingly, this essay suggests an approach to community development and *participación popular* for Latin America which seeks to change not so much the communities' physical or cultural attributes, as their people's relations with each other.

Confirming Mariátegui's prediction, a United Nations survey of recent experience in Asia and the Far East reported that the contribution of community development programs to the expansion of agricultural production is "not a particularly large one," [2]

1964. This essay is a slightly revised version of a Report the author made to the Seminar on Community Development in South America, held by the United Nations Economic Commission for Latin America in Santiago, Chile, in June 1964. The report was released for publication with the understanding that it does not necessarily represent the views of the United Nations.

248

to village industry is "far from impressive," [3] to capital formation is "nearly everywhere fairly small in total extent," [4] and to using surplus labor is "not impressive." [5]

These community development programs exhibit three main policies and related assumptions that condemn them to failure. Their scope is almost without exception limited to the community or residential neighborhood. Their usual stated objective is to assimilate or integrate the community inhabitants into the national society and economy. Finally, their policy is attributional. They seek to assimilate the values and behavioral attributes of the community members to the "national" pattern. The need for and success of the community development programs is evaluated in terms of such cultural attributes as use of the official language, kinds of food consumed, types of clothing, use of shoes, literacy, religion, importance attached to kinship relations, etc. The economic policy and social attributes of these programs are to increase the attribution of roads, irrigation, machinery, seeds, credit, technology, education, medical services, etc. The assumptions which underlie these policies are that the small rural community is a viable social unit, that it is not yet fully integrated into the national society and economy, and most importantly that there exists a community of interest among the inhabitants of the rural community. But these assumptions are entirely contrary to fact and condemn community development programs based on them to failure.

With respect to the first assumption, the above-cited United Nations report suggests that "problems of water development and control, rural electrification, transport, and communications must generally be tackled at the regional or district level rather than in the single community." [6]

In his *Quiet Crisis in India,* John Lewis devotes an entire chapter to arguing that the community lacks the economic and institutional resources and viability to serve effectively as the nucleus of a participant development effort and that the provincial market town, especially if more industrialized, in combination with its rural hinterland offers a much more viable social unit within which to organize such participant and development efforts. [7]

The second assumption is false for Latin America because in the densely settled Western highland regions, which still contain significant proportions of indigenous populations, the Conquest had already effectively integrated all the inhabitants into the national and international economy. If they have not been used and exploited directly as workers in mining or agricultural enterprises, they have been integrated into the same structure indirectly by being—still today—increasingly deprived of their fertile lands and forced to retreat into "subsistence" economies and corporate "folk" communities, where they have sought to salvage a minimum of economic power and human dignity.[8] The populations of the lowland countries' primarily settled under the impetus of European expansion were, of course, fully integrated into the society from the very beginning. The fact that some people find themselves rendered "marginal" to the current center of economic activity because world, national, or regional economic shifts have reduced the supply of or demand for their previous sugar, cocoa, gold, silver, tin, or even industrial output in no way obviates the fact that they occupy social and economic roles that are fully integrated in the structure of the society that places them in this unenviable position. This only means that the "marginal" or "floating" population is not so much "marginal" to the society as it is integrated in a way that prejudices its most vital interests. The problem of development is not to "assimilate" some people and to "integrate" them into society, but to relate people to each other and integrate them into their society in a very different way from that at present.

Finally, the United Nations itself attests to the invalidity of the third assumption—that the rural community is blessed by a community of interest. Referring to Asia, the United Nations suggests that: "Differences in the interests of various segments of the village population—as seen by themselves—fundamentally affect their willingness to participate in particular construction projects," [9] that "in many countries with private proprietorship in land, only a rather minor part of the all-important work of soil improvement and agricultural capital formation generally seems likely to come within a community classification. Small scale irrigation, drainage, flood control, and reforestation, for example, will for the most part be of direct benefit to individual proprietors or groups of proprietors only";[10] and that "people will only do, willingly, what they consider advantageous to them." [11] A United Nations mission to evaluate community development in India observes the same,[12] and goes on to note that "evidently, it is not easy to establish a real community of interests between the lender and the debtor, or between the landowner and the tenant who receives only half the crop although he bears all the cost of its production." [13]

In other words, the rural community is entirely conflict-ridden because it is an integral part of the exploitative class structure of the capitalist system. The real causes of poverty and low productivity are not so much due to the environmental and physical attributes of the community as they are caused by the exploitative social relations within the community and between most of its members and the centers of national and international economic and political power. To have any hopes of success, therefore, a community development program must begin by more adequately mobilizing and aiding peasants and others to confront the landlords, merchants, and political-military authorities that exploit and oppress them. This involves *participación popular*, not so much in the productive as in the economic and political process. Ultimately, of course, community development can only proceed through a change in the class structure of the community and the society as a whole. But this change itself can only be effected through increased peasant *participación popular* and power, which can and must initially be mobilized through intervention in the immediate local relationships that most affect peasant welfare.

Accordingly, this essay attempts to identify some of the key social relations that determine peasant welfare and to propose some ways to strengthen the peasant's bargaining power in these relations. The proposals emphasize economic relations and means to redress economic bargaining power through *participacion popular* and public intervention, although it is of course recognized that in a class society these are inseparable from political relations and political—including armed—struggle.[14]

The peasant's bargaining power is immediately limited by his lack of land, water, storage and transport facilities, capital and

credit, commercial monopoly position, and many kinds of institutional privileges or sources of political power. The high bargaining power of his rivals in the local economy is based on
monopolistic access to these same assets. Thus in the bargaining
process the economic and political significance of monopoly concentration of land ownership in a few hands lies not so much in
the access to land that it provides to the few as it does to the
denial of land to the many who, in order to gain some access to
land and its fruits, are in consequence forced to contribute their
labor and its fruits to the owning few, and that on bad bargaining
terms for the many and good ones for the few. The institutional
forms of these terms vary, of course, through manifold types of
tenure arrangements and their variations over time. But the economic, structural, and bargaining power substance behind them
is always essentially the same. The peasant's bargaining power
relative to his rivals is further reduced, moreover, by the all-to-
common institutionalized coalition of his rivals as expressed by
their oligopolistic control of local economic and political life
and by the frequent joint ownership by a single person or family
of land, capital, commercial monopoly, and political power. Nonetheless, this economic, political, and social structure provides
room for *participación popular* in raising peasant income and
productivity in the short run, and in promoting social change in
the long run, by significantly increasing peasant bargaining power
in the labor market, in the product market, and through the
institutional setting.

## In the Rural Labor Market

The most obvious intervention to increase peasant bargaining
power in the labor market is the redistribution of land from large
to small owners. Such redistribution would increase some workers'
independence of the labor market and increase the bargaining
power of the remainder, while reducing the bargaining power of
the owning few. The redistribution would channel the use of
land and water into other productive uses, and would reduce the
present transfer of income from the poor to the rich in the short
run. Nonetheless, as the experience of Mexico and other countries

suggests, such land redistribution by itself—even with related credit and technological measures—only partially redresses the bargaining balance, and that in the short run. The structure of the bargaining process itself inevitably produces renewed concentration and inequality in the long run.

Insofar as such redistribution of privately owned land is presently politically unfeasible, *participación popular* and other measures can make this land reform more feasible in the future. Some legal provisions combined with *participación popular* in their enforcement can provide a step in that direction. Among these are progressive tax rates on land; better public regulation of water rights; stronger provisions for expropriation of land in the public interest in excess of certain limits, or of land not in specified productive use, or, as has been done in Venezuela to some extent, of land petitioned by organizations of neighboring peasants with little or no land. Enforcing compliance with such provisions on the part both of latifundistas and of local authorities or local representatives of national authorities can to some extent be based on *participación popular* of the interested peasants.

In some instances, it is possible to redress the rural balance of bargaining power to some extent through providing publicly owned lands to peasants and their organization for its productive use. To be economically effective and socially desirable and to change the balance of bargaining power directly, such distribution of public lands should preferably be in the most densely settled areas. Colonization schemes on new lands in far-off areas can accommodate only few peasants at high costs to themselves and the nation, and they can effect the inequality of bargaining power in densely settled rural areas only indirectly by syphoning off a small part of the labor supply. Where public agricultural lands are not available in settled areas, public distribution of grazing and/ or forested lands, if available, can make a significant immediate contribution to peasants who, participating in their use, cannot only raise their income, but can also free themselves to some extent from their dependence on latifundistas for access to grass for their animals and wood for themselves. Peasant unions and/ or cooperatives can help organize their use.

Apart from the obvious utility of public provision of agricultural credit, seeds, fertilizer, and other productive resources to small owners and tenants on favorable terms—and, as will be discussed below, through public cooperative organizations rather than independent and therefore necessarily weak peasant cooperatives—public participation in livestock production by minifundistas and tenants deserves special attention. The capital in and income from one or a few animals can afford peasants a significant measure of independence and security in their bargaining with landowners, especially if they are not in turn totally dependent on the latter for their animals' feed and water. Public participation in peasant livestock cooperatives for the provision of livestock marketing, transport and veterinary services, of credit, and of frost, drought, and disease insurance may be cheaper and more feasible than analogous measures in crop production as long as land concentration persists; and it could help ameliorate the large and growing protein deficiencey in most rural and urban diets.

A rural development program with *participación popular* can usefully include government/cooperative model farms. Of course, the provision of additional agricultural employment and produce directly helps the immediate participants and beneficiaries and through them the economy as a whole. The provision of additional and alternative employment can indirectly ameliorate the imbalance of bargaining power in the immediate area and therefore helps support peasant demands for a higher share of the agricultural income produced in the area.

To play a significant role in a *participación popular* development program, such farms should not be models of productivity to impress and be copied by owners or administrators of large haciendas, but should be models of *participación popular* to be seen by the peasants on these private latifundia. As such they should pay substantially *higher* than prevailing wages, have better than usual living conditions, and exhibit much stronger and more active union-organized *participación popular* among their peasant workers in the affairs of the farm as well as of the wider community or region of which they are a part. Such farms must, however, be part of a regional and national organization and program with outside economic and political support, rather than being set up

as independent local cooperatives whose economic and organizational weakness would render them easy prey for powerful, antagonistic, private neighbors. Only thus can such model farms, by
the force of their peasants and their example, contribute to rural
development and *participación popular* and help redress the imbalance of bargaining power in rural areas.

Public and communal works can serve some of the same
functions as model farms. But far from using unpaid voluntary
peasant labor—as community development programs have often
attempted with little success—it is suggested that these public/
communal works also pay wages substantially above those prevailing for agricultural labor in the area. The reasons are several.
Evidently, the higher the pay to peasants, the higher their earnings and the injection of resources into their economy. The higher
the earnings from public works, the lower the peasant community's dependence on the local landowners and the higher,
correspondingly, relative peasant bargaining power in the whole
complex of owner-worker relations.

The higher the public wages, moreover, the greater the demon-
strative pressure they can generate through *participación popular*
to elevate wages in the private rural economy. At the same time,
experience demonstrates, and innumerable observers testify, that
in a rural economy with high concentration of land ownership
there are precious few "communal" or "public" productivity-
increasing works which do not benefit the large owners of land
and capital and some inhabitants of the urban municipal center
to the virtual exclusion of the bulk of the peasants and especially
the landless or worst situated among them. This is notably true,
of course, for irrigation works; but it is substantially the case
for roads, hospitals, and even for schools to which many peasants
will have only limited use and access. Unpaid peasant labor on
such projects is not, therefore, likely to be forthcoming in large
quantities unless it is by forceful persuasion—which in turn does
not contribute to the development of *participación popular*. For
public communal works which differentially benefit the various
members of the community, the workers thus have to, and
should, be paid at a differential rate.

Provision of additional and alternative employment and production through village industries, though conceivably useful in the sense suggested above, generally has not shown favorable results in practice. The economic structure of the regional and national economy does not today make the village or the hacienda a viable economic, much less industrial, unit.

Public legal intervention and *participación popular* in law enforcement can supplement the aforementioned direct public intervention and *participación popular* to help redress the imbalance of bargaining power on the rural labor market in several respects. But the law can significantly intervene in the rural economy only in combination with organized or even institutionalized *participación popular* to provide for its compliance, as will be discussed in a later paragraph.

Forced labor should be made illegal. Institutional channels must be provided through which organized *participación popular* can denounce written and verbal contracts providing for essentially forced labor under semi-legal guises through which such contracts can then be effectively invalidated. The law should include provisions under which unpaid labor and labor obligations from one family member and generation to another can, in combination with *participación popular* denouncing them, be eliminated or at least combated.

The minimum wage legislation already common for urban employment should be extended to agricultural and other rural employment. Insofar as possible, some provisions should be made for the payment of higher wages for overtime employment in order partially to combat landowner attempts to evade higher wage payments by laying off workers and getting more work from the remainder. Similarly, the law should provide for minimum wage legislation in another form—that is, establishing maximum legal crop shares that owners can demand of their tenants. As long as the economy does not absorb surplus agricultural labor in other sectors, these provisions must probably be supplemented by others which impede the evasions of landlord substitution of capital in the form of machinery, and especially in the form of livestock, for agricultural labor that becomes more costly. Thus, such landowner attempts at reallocating resources in their private economy which do not so much reduce costs for the economy as

a whole as they shift these costs to other sectors of the economy
—such as the urban slums to which the peasants might migrate
—probably would have to be restrained by dissuading taxes. Such
tax proceeds can be used in other parts of a national development
and *participación popular* program. Again, enforcement of these
provisions would have to rest in large part on organized and
conscious *participación popular*.

Public legal intervention with the aid of *participación popular*
can provide for greater peasant security in the labor market. Legal
provision should be made for the greater employment security of
agricultural wage workers by setting a daily or other minimum
employment time and by providing for lay-off pay graduated by
length of employment. Similarly, the law should stipulate legal
minimum and appropriate seasonal periods of tenancy which especially seek to assure and protect the tenant's ability to plant and
harvest his crop in accordance with the local growing season. Related legal provisions should render it more difficult for landlords to deprive from their tenants the improvements in land,
buildings, or livestock that the peasants might make. Landlords
prohibiting their tenants from making such improvements or from
planting permanent crops or other crops that the tenant may
deem in his own interest should be held invalid under the law.

A minimum standard for providing workers and tenants with
housing, water, sanitation, and access to medical and educational
facilities, etc., should be provided for, as they already have been
in some countries.

These and other measures of legal and direct intervention in
the rural labor market should as far as possible be taken simultaneously in order to forestall some landowner attempts at evading
the law by shifting from a form of organization of their agricultural enterprise which is covered by the law to one which is not.

Most important of all, these legal measures must be coupled
with the organization of the conscious *participación popular* that
the peasant can stimulate and support and which, in turn, he
needs to enforce landowner compliance. This organization of
*participación popular* essentially involves the organization of
peasant labor unions and the provision of an institutional framework through which the peasant can effectively act to coordinate

his own with any public attempts to promote and protect the interests of increased peasant productivity and distributive justice. This matter is discussed under the heading institutional provisions below.

### In the Rural Product Market

The above discussion of the structure of the rural labor market suggests that the peasant finds himself in a very disadvantaged bargaining position in the market for goods and services—the product market. With little or no capital and only limited opportunity to acquaint himself with market conditions beyond his own immediate transactions, the peasant or other member of the rural population faces a highly monopolistic market structure in which relatively few people with ownership in, or other sources of access to, capital and credit outweigh him in bargaining power in the product market just as the big landowner does in the labor market. Though these market monopolists may for simplicity be called "merchants," they of course often include landowners as well. Indeed, landowner and merchant are all too often the same person or at least the same family.

It is sometimes suggested that the structure of the product market and his bargaining position in it is largely irrelevant to the poor and especially the indigenous peasant who buys and sells only very little in this market. But this is not so. The amount of each individual peasant's transaction in the market, though absolutely small, may play a relatively large and certainly plays a very considerable role in the commercial economy of the respective region or country. Furthermore, the fact that the peasant buys and sells little is not evidence—as is sometimes thought—of his absence from and unconcern for the market, but is evidence that this market affects him very directly and deeply, albeit adversely: if he were not so disadvantaged by his participation in this market, first as a seller and then as a buyer, the peasant would be able to buy and sell much more. Few peasants, anywhere, it is safe to suggest, would not sell and buy more in the market if they could do so with advantage to themselves; and many try to do so, even if generally unsuccessful.

It is also often noted that between the peasant producer and the final consumer, or indeed even between the peasant and the wholesaler and again between the latter and the consumer, there is a whole string or network of intermediaries. And it is observed that each of these intermediaries contributes to and shares in the producer-consumer price differential and that many peasants or their wives themselves participate in this network as intermediary merchants. This does not justify indiscriminate elimination of middlemen; for the most easily eliminated ones are the small peasant middlemen, while the lion's share of the merchandising profit is obtained by one or a very few large intermediary merchants, who in turn exploit the weaker intermediaries as well. It is this very same market structure and the consequent allocation of benefits from commerce which force every intermediary, including the peasants, to try and establish, increase, and secure a stronger monopoly position for his own self-protection. The residual claimant in this whole process is ultimately, of course, the peasant producer—be he minifundista, tenant, or wage worker —who lacks all land, capital, and other sources of monopoly position in the economic structure and whose residual is accordingly, precious little.

His weak bargaining position due to his lack of land, credit, capital, market knowledge, transport facilities, and institutionally provided privileges forces the peasant producer to sell his product in the market at a low price to buy other goods, and often to buy back his own product at a high price. It also forces him to accept rather than evade or weather artificially created permanent and seasonal or other temporary restrictions in demand for the products he sells and restrictions in supply of the goods he buys.

A public/cooperative marketing organization helps redress this imbalance in bargaining power by intervening in the local and regional market to buy peasant-produced products in competition with existing buyers. This marketing organization, to be effective, need not necessarily supplant private merchants. It need only provide the competition that they restrict. To be most useful, the marketing organization should concentrate on the purchase of industrial or export cash crops, food staple cash crops, and, where necessary, popular food staples which are not produced in sufficient quantity because, due to their high bulk and low commercial value, private merchants do not provide a large or extensive enough organized market for them. To intervene effectively in the unsatisfactory structure of bargaining in the rural commodity markets, the public/cooperative marketing organization should compete with mercantile monopolists by offering a higher price for the purchase of the same product and by buying a sufficient quantity to prevent a private monopoly of or corner on the market in any one place and time. This way the marketing organization can to some extent, and on the most important commodities, counteract excessively low purchase prices and speculative supply and demand or price manipulations, and ultimately can combat high consumer prices as well. The purchasing activities of the public/cooperative marketing organization should be supplemented by the provision of storage, transportation, and of course credit facilities which would similarly help to increase the market alternatives and bargaining power of the peasant majority.

To provide for and assure *participación popular*, the public/cooperative marketing organization must limit access to its services and participation in its benefits to those whose existing bargaining power is relatively low. Though it may appear administratively inexpedient, the marketing organization must set relatively low limits to the purchase of commodities from a single seller. It must similarly limit access to its storage and transport facilities to small producers and traders. These provisions, in addition to benefiting directly the large majority of the presently disadvantaged, may indirectly benefit some of them by inducing large producers or merchants to sell off or otherwise assign some of their commodities to smaller producers or traders in order to share with them the benefits of the marketing organization's higher prices and additional storage and transportation facilities. Possibly, on the other hand, such resale or assignment possibilities would lead to unacceptable abuses and should be prevented or impeded. In the absence of these limitations of access to and participation in the operations of the public/cooperative marketing organizations, the latter, far from helping the productive, income, and bargaining position of the large majority of peasants, would become still another publicly provided resource and instrument in the hands of the few large landowners and merchants, increasing their relative bargaining and monopoly power and therefore placing the peasant majority in a still more disadvantageous position.

The same public/cooperative marketing organization or another can also intervene on the side of the market in which the rural majority is a disadvantaged buyer. It can use the stocks of staples previously accumulated as a special buyer from small producers, as well as staples purchased for this purpose from large producers at market prices, to sell to the public at market or below-market prices. Above all, the marketing organization can and should counteract natural or artificial local and/or temporary scarcities of this and that staple by selling, and if necessary dumping, in the scarcity-produced high price market. Any activity along this line can produce immeasurable increases in the income, and through that the productive capacity, of the rural majority.

The same or another marketing organization can also provide a measure of competition for local merchants in the sale of industrial and other products for urban centers and other regions. The mere existence of these public stores and/or consumer cooperatives that sell even some items at prices significantly lower than private merchants can reduce the imbalance of bargaining power between the relatively few sellers and the potentially many buyers, without replacing the private merchants.

The marketing organizations can and must have substantial representation from local and regional peasant organizations, in addition to public officials appointed from the nation's capital, on their local or regional policy-making boards. These local public/popular boards, in conjunction with national needs and policy, can have substantial autonomy in deciding what staples to buy and sell, at what times and places, and at what prices. On the basis of reports from their constituents, popular representatives can keep the local and national marketing organization informed of shortages and, especially, of monopolistic and speculative attempts to create artificial scarcities so that the organization can then combat them itself.

Membership on the policy-making boards must, of course, be limited to authentic representatives of peasant and other popular organizations lest the marketing organization fall into the hands of those whose already excessive bargaining power it should combat. And for this reason the public/cooperative marketing organization must remain independent of the local government, which is usually controlled by the same landowners and/or merchants.

Legal intervention in the structure of the product market is probably more difficult to provide for and enforce—because of the nature and variety of transactions—than it is in the labor market. Nonetheless, there is some scope for legal intervention in the rural product market in three principal areas.

First, foreign corporations and their domestic subsidiaries can and should be prohibited from operating in rural and provincial markets to purchase staples and industrial or export crops for foreign or domestic sale. Although these large foreign buyers sometimes eliminate local landlords and merchants from the marketing chain and offer higher prices to the producer, this only fortifies their already-too-great monopoly position in the national and often international market—especially insofar as these rural purchases, combined with the speculative supply-price manipulations that their dominant position in the market allows them, permit control of the national market. Moreover, the internationally derived financial strength of these foreign corporations generally involves them in national rural credit operations through which to their own, but not necessarily to the nation's, interest they can and do organize the selection, production, financing, and marketing of the major crop or crops of a whole region, country, or series of countries, and the promotion of industrial or export crops or livestock, to the prejudice of food crops needed for the provision of better diets for the rural and national population. Yet far from being only permitted, the monopolistic commercial activity of such foreign companies is often encouraged and even loan-financed by the national government. It should be prohibited and coupled with the substitution of public/cooperative marketing organizations that can through public and popular participation serve the popular and national interest.

Another area for legal intervention in the rural product market is that of landowner-peasant commercial relations. Many landowners are in effect much more merchant than agriculturalist.

The real economic meaning of their ownership of land is not access to the land, or even the aforementioned access to labor which may also produce little; it is the monopolistic access to an assured supply of agricultural produce with which to earn an income from essentially purely commercial operations. This monopoly position as buyer of peasant-produced commodities is, of course, often complemented by a monopoly position in the sale of the goods peasants purchase through a "company" store which works with private chips earned on the farm, and whose economic function and significance is not that of an "archaic feudal" institution but that of an all-too-modern monopoly capitalist one.

Combined with conscious organized *participación popular* to enforce compliance, there is room in this area of commercial landowner-peasant relations for legal intervention to prohibit or restrict forced sale and purchase which emanates from and reinforces monopoly positions based on large landownership. Written and verbal contracts providing for obligatory sale can be declared illegal and unbinding, and payment other than in kind and legal tender can be prohibited. Such legal provisions, difficult to enforce at best, would of course be ineffective without simultaneous provision of institutional means to prevent the prejudiced parties from denouncing them, as well as to prevent access to alternative buyers and sellers in order to evade them. In this respect, again, the aforementioned public/cooperative marketing and consumer organizations must play an important role.

Third, there is need for legal provisions which demand that all roads, especially those on private property, be freely open to public access. Failing such legal provision and its enforcement, *participación popular* in the pursuit of economic goals is obviously limited, and so is *participación popular* in general.

## Institutional Provisions for Participación Popular

Outside support and its institutionalization are necessary for such programs of community development and *participación popular*. It is for this reason that the aforementioned marketing organization(s) have always been referred to as public/cooperative ones. As has all too often been the case in practice, independent peasant cooperatives lack the necessary capital base to get an effective start and to weather the various storms created by natural and economic fluctuations and by the economic rivalry of the private monopolies they face. They must be public, it is suggested, to have the vertical integration and institutional affiliation and support that they need to counterbalance the bargaining power of the private monopolies. Experience suggests that, in the absence of public affiliation, such marketing cooperatives soon only convert themselves—or, rather, are converted or absorbed—into just another commercial monopoly in the hands of the same people who already have most of the bargaining power or in the hands of a few others who aspire to rival them and consequently must imitate them.

The marketing organization should be public/*cooperative* as well in order to elicit and permit the active *participación popular* necessary to provide for the peasant majority's real commercial interests and ultimately to alter the imbalance of bargaining power between them and owners of land and capital. Peasant and other popular representation on the policy-making boards of the marketing organization is necessary to supply information to and pressure on the organization to combat speculative and other restrictive monopolistic practices in the local product market.

Other forms and instruments of *participación popular* are appropriate for agricultural workers on haciendas and plantations. The existing institutional structure and administration within the hacienda is of course primarily at the service of its owner rather than the peasant worker. Short of eliminating the concentration of landownership, there seems to be little hope of reforming the administrative institutions of the hacienda or plantation to place them at the service of its workers or of the public interest generally. Even the above-proposed legal intervention in the market can only modify the internal structure of the latifundium in relatively minor degree. And even if the distribution of income within the hacienda can be improved, neither legal intervention nor *participación popular* can scarcely intervene effectively to improve the productive organization and decisions of the hacienda which, possibly to a greater extent than is sometimes thought, are largely determined, and from the point of view of the popular or public interest are largely misdirected, by the owner or his agent in accordance with incentives derived from a highly monopolized market for agricultural products.

The impossibility or difficulty of reforming the existing institutions of participation on the privately owned large hacienda suggests that, short of the latter's elimination, the only available alternative for increasing or improving *participación popular* in the hacienda is to provide for a second institution, administration, or organization within and through which such participation can take place. And, to serve any purpose at all, this institution and the *participación popular* it provides for must serve as a bargaining counterweight to the already existing administrative institutions of the hacienda. The provision and organization of such conscious *participación popular* involves, in a word, the unionization of hacienda workers.

To afford the bargaining power which the hacienda union needs to counterweigh the power which the hacienda derives from its ownership of land and capital and from its commercial and institutional connections beyond the hacienda, the hacienda union needs outside support and institutionalized connections as well. The union on one hacienda must be linked to similar unions on other haciendas. To serve as the effective counterweight to landowner, merchant, and other local bargaining power, the hacienda union must have authentic representation in the local, regional, and national governing boards of the aforementioned marketing organizations and it must have institutional access to regional, urban, and national centers of political power.

A common question for a prospective program of community development and *participación popular* is whether it should be administered through the existing institutions of national ministries and local governments or whether it should rely instead on an additional institution to be superimposed on the existing ones. The answer to this question cannot be sought or found primarily in terms of administrative convenience. Rather, the question must be cast in terms of the existing balance of bargaining power and its present institutionalization through local government and the local administrative and political arms of national government and even of international organizations which all serve to reinforce local landlord-merchant bargaining power. Forty years ago, José Carlos Mariátegui summarized the problem in terms that still hold true:

> *Gamonalismo* [local bossism] inevitably invalidates any law or ordinance for the protection of the Indians. Written law is impotent against the authority of the *hacendado* and *latifundista*, which is sustained by environment and habit. Unpaid labor is prohibited by law; nonetheless unpaid labor, and even forced labor, survive on the latifundio. The judge, the subprefecto, the commissar, the teacher, the tax collector, are all vassals of the latifundium. The law cannot win against the *gamonales*. Any functionary who might try to impose the law would be abandoned and sacrificed by the central authorities, over whom the influence of *gamonalismo* is always omnipotent, for it acts directly or through Parliament with equal efficiency.[15]

In 1963 the United Nations reported that national citizenship governed by impersonal rules "does not seem to have rejected relations of direct and personal dependence on the local power structure." [16]

Once the question is posed in these terms, it becomes clear that the development and survival of local *participación popular* also depends on direct access to one or more *foci* of political power elsewhere, often including the national center. Only thus will it in most cases be possible to take any steps toward redressing the imbalance of bargaining power at the local and regional levels. In addition to the developing nationwide mass movements and organizations, this involves providing means of evaluating institutional performance at the local level, which is relatively independent of the local institutions. At present, evaluation of the local services of national ministries and programs inevitably occurs in accordance with the criteria of evaluation selected by those in the existing positions of power on the local scene—that is, by the larger landowners and merchants themselves, as many an idealistic civil servant has found out to his sorrow and expense. It is therefore imperative to transfer the evaluation of community development and other local programs and offices out of the hands of the local elite and to develop alternative channels of evaluation through *participación popular*.[17]

## NOTES

1. José Carlos Mariátegui, *Siete ensayos de interpretación de la realidad peruana* (2nd. ed.; Lima: Editorial Librería Peruana, 1934), p. 27.

2. United Nations, *Community Development and Economic Development*, Part I, *A Study of the Contribution of Rural Community Development Programmes to National Economic Development in Asia and the Far East* (Bangkok, 1960), E/CN. 11/540, p. 33.

3. *Ibid.*, p. 37.

4. *Ibid.*, p. 51.

5. *Ibid.*, p. 166.

6. *Ibid.*, p. 59.

7. John Lewis, *Quiet Crisis in India* (Washington, D.C.: The Brookings Institution, 1962), Chapter 7.

8. For a description and analysis of this process see, for instance, Eric Wolf, *Sons of the Shaking Earth* (Chicago, 1960).

9. *Community Development and Economic Development*, p. 48.

10. *Ibid.*, p. 46.

11. *Ibid.*, p. 44.

12. Naciones Unidas, "Informe de una misión para evaluar el desarrollo de la comunidad en India" (Santiago), June 1964, TAO/IND/31, Documento de referencia No. 6, pp. 26–27.

13. *Ibid.*, p. 45.

14. This emphasis, or rather limitation, and the vocabulary employed was imposed by the United Nations, in whose confines those proposals were made. Though my own emphasis would be on political mobilization and self-reliance, I have left the proposals as originally made because at least they suggest what some of the problems and limitations to their solution in a class society are. Bargaining power is something of a euphemism for political power.

15. José Carlos Mariátegui, *Siete ensayos* . . . , pp. 29–30.

16. Naciones Unidas, CEPAL, *El Desarrollo Social de América Latina en la Postguerra*, E/CN. 12/660/, May 11, 1963, p. 36.

17. The original report went on to examine the class alignments that determine the political possibilities and limitations of public support for a community development program that incorporates

some of the above proposals. Since the limitations imposed by the United Nations made it especially difficult to discuss this problem in adequate terms, this section is omitted here. Even with all its limitations, this report and modest proposal was deemed to be "too explosive" and "too revolutionary" for publication or public distribution by the United Nations.

# 17

## VARIETIES OF LAND REFORM

Land reform projects are mushrooming all over the globe. But not all land reform programs are the same. In Latin America, especially under the impetus of the Alliance for Progress, several countries have passed or are discussing land reform laws. Concerned and progressive people everywhere scrutinize these proposals and laws, and often criticize them for being too mild or otherwise misdirected. It is important to distinguish between the varieties of land reform proposals and counter-proposals and to learn which deserve support and which opposition.

Fundamental to any analysis of the problem of land reform is the fact that it is not so much an administrative, or even an economic, as it is an essentially political process. Beginning, then, with this notion of a political process, we can conveniently distinguish three types of supposed land reform.

The first excludes any significant political change. It is the type of "land reform" proposed by conservatives. It is exemplified by the laws which the legislatures, often controlled by the landowners themselves, have recently found it convenient or necessary to pass in several Latin American countries today. In the same category should be included the voluntary donations of land by the Church or by the landowners themselves. This type of land reform is the last resort of the landowner and is really no reform at all.

The second attempts to incorporate all or part of the peasantry into the already existing national political community. This type of land reform finds much support among the critics of the first type and is proposed by several political groups, among them the

---

1962–63. This essay originally appeared in the April 1963 issue of *Monthly Review*. For an auto-critique, see Chapter 23.

Christian Democrats and, more often than not, the Communists, in Latin America. It has been exemplified in the Mexico of Cárdenas, the Guatemala of Arbenz, the Egypt of Nasser. My contention will be that, however persuasive the arguments in favor of it, land reform which aims merely to integrate the peasantry into the existing social order is likely to fail even to meet the announced ends of its proponents.

The third type of land reform attempts from the outset to effect a rapid and fundamental transformation of the existing order itself. It begins with a far-reaching change in the entire society, as exemplified in Cuba, and appears to be the only type which can meet minimum demands. It is therefore the only type of land reform worthy of the name.

A convenient index—although, as we shall see, it is also more than that—by which to distinguish the various types of land reform is the speed, or lack of speed, with which the reform is undertaken. At the rate at which land was distributed in Guatemala in the post-Arbenz years (1955 to 1961), it would take 148 years for all peasant families to receive some land—if there were no population growth in the meantime. The return of previously expropriated land to United Fruit and other owners, the government purchase of worn-out lands, and other related measures indicate that the Guatemala "reform" falls into the first type, in which there is no political change whatever. In Venezuela, the government is often cited as making a real effort at a land reform in depth—the Presidential propaganda figures speak of fifty thousand families receiving 3.5 million acres of land in the nearly four years of the Betancourt government.[1] However, in a report recently jointly published by the Venezuelan National Agrarian Institute, the Ministry of Agriculture, the Agrarian Bank, and the National Planning Office, it appears that in the last twenty-five years, all put together, no more than 1.4 million acres have been distributed to 35,622 families. It is not specified how much of this was distributed during the tenure of the present government. *On the other hand, it is true that 3.5 million acres were expropriated and paid for, often at exorbitant prices and in cash amounts in excess of the maximum prescribed by law.* This particular "land reform," in other words, has been big business for the landowners who have been able to sell no-longer-wanted land, and, no doubt, to invest the proceeds elsewhere (including abroad). The land reform laws recently enacted in Peru and Chile are even milder than the reforms already put into practice in Guatemala and Venezuela. Almost all imaginable protection is afforded to the landowner rather than to the peasant. The conclusion is inescapable: measures of this type are not land reforms at all. They are out-and-out frauds.

The second type of land reform merits more serious discussion. Its advocates propose to incorporate the peasants into the social and political life of the nation through a process which mobilizes all of the progressive forces against the conservatives but which leaves the foundations of power intact. The reformers would seek at the same time to redirect rural credit, technical assistance, etc., so that these measures would benefit the peasants and not just the medium and large landowners, as at present. The time period envisaged is usually of the order of five to fifteen years. Variations on this second type of land reform can be found in the experience of Mexico, of Guatemala before the counter-revolution of 1954, and of Egypt since 1952.

It seems to this writer that the viability of this second type of land reform is highly questionable, both on theoretical grounds and on the evidence of historical experience. Two particular daners arise which threaten its success: The first is that leaving the power of the conservatives intact ensures continued opposition to the reforms and puts roadblocks in the way of mobilizing the progressive forces. Though they may have been pushed out of government office, the conservatives nevertheless retain the ability to slow down and ultimately destroy the land reform. They can refuse to provide necessary investment funds, they can sabotage the operation of government agencies charged with implementing the reforms, organize hostile propaganda campaigns, enlist foreign support against their own government, and so on. At the same time, the political jockeying and maneuvering that progressives must engage in to counter this conservative opposition demands compromises which tend to undermine the reform and turn it into a series of half measures.

The second danger is that carrying out a land reform at

the slow rate of five to fifteen years and within the framework of the existing institutions creates groups which acquire a vested interest in maintaining their new advantages and which therefore readily ally themselves with conservatives in opposing the extension of the same benefits to still other groups.

The relevance and importance of these obstacles are demonstrated by the attempts, both successful and unsuccessful, to complete a land reform of the second type. The 1952 land reform of the Arbenz government in Guatemala was, of course, much swifter and more far-reaching than the so-called reforms of recent years in that country. Nonetheless, while the conservatives suffered losses, the sources of their power were hardly touched, with the result that they were able, with the help of the Dulles brothers, to organize a counter-revolution. Nor was it possible, because of the slowness of the reforms, to create beneficiary groups large and powerful enough to defend the reform movement against the counter-revolution. Thus history does not tell us whether continuation of the Arbenz reforms would in the long run have eliminated the second danger—the subsequent opposition of the early beneficiaries themselves.

This drag on reform emanating from the "new conservatives" appears very clearly in the Mexican Revolution. Only fifteen years after the administration of the revolutionary General Obregon and five years after the enactment of the agrarian measures of President Cárdenas, the reform process broke off halfway with the rise to power of the new bourgeoisie in the administration of Miguel Aleman. Today, despite the fact that in the 1950's Mexico had one of the world's highest industrial and agricultural growth rates, there is little doubt that the country is in a blind alley because of failure to solve its land problem. Mexico's agrarian reform was the most far reaching in Latin America before Cuba's and one which really did incorporate the peasants into national life. Nevertheless, the majority of Mexico's peasants in the *ejidos* are without resources, while the famed economic growth concentrated in the capital and the seven sparsely settled northern states encourages, here as elsewhere in Latin America, speculative monoculture for export and gains tremendous earnings for the children of the Revolution. For example, the son of the same General Obregón is now governor of one of the northern states and the owner of more than 7,500 acres of land irrigated at government expense. The gap between the capital and the seven northern states on the one hand and the rest of the country on the other keeps growing, while the class distribution of income becomes more and more unequal. Thus it appears that in Mexico, no less than in those countries of Latin America which have not even started their land reforms, the standard of living of the poor is going down. And that same social mobility which is both cause and effect of the integration of the peasants into national life often turns them into conservatives whose interests are opposed to the extension of the same benefits to others.

Other land reforms, such as those of Eastern Europe after World War I, of Bolivia, and of Egypt, confirm the dangers of the second type. In each case, reform governments proceeded more or less along the lines often proposed by progressives today. The reforms were introduced slowly within the existing structure of society, and the foundations of the power of the conservatives were left intact. I do not think it is an exaggeration to say that to date all of these attempts at land reform have failed, and it is to be expected that future attempts of the second type will likewise fail.

The experience of those countries which have had successful land reforms also attests to the faults of the second and the need for the third type of reform. The outstanding examples of relative success with land reform are to be found in the socialist countries. In China and Cuba, for example, the entire structure of society was, of course, changed at the very beginning, at the time land reform was initiated. This change was effected, significantly, by mobilizing the peasants themselves, and the ability of the conservatives to oppose the reforms was cut off at the root by the elimination of their sources of power. It is true that Japan and Taiwan have had a measure of success with land reform without at the same time radically altering the structure of their societies, but these are the kinds of exceptions which prove the rule. In both cases, the reforms were put through relatively quickly and under the authority of an occupying military power. In these circumstances, the strength of the conservative opposition was effectively neutralized.

It might seem that as far as Latin America is concerned, the change in social structure and the elimination of conservative power which are the distinguishing features of the third type of reform would result automatically from the liquidation of the latifundismo, often described as a feudal or semi-feudal institution. This seems to be the way matters are seen by the architects of the Alliance for Progress. But reality is different. Although it is true that there still exist landowning sectors in Latin America which might be called feudal or semi-feudal, and although there are landowners who still hold provincial political power, it is not the case that these groups are the politically decisive ones at the national level in any Latin American country. There, political and economic power is in the hands of others—of the domestic bourgeoisies of commerce, banking, and industry, and of the great foreign corporations.

These are the important conservers of the status quo; and they and the feudal-type landowners still mutually serve each other's interests in many Latin American countries. The capitalists who have ultimate power permit the "feudalists" to survive, thus sacrificing some rural markets. But in return the feudalists, by monopolizing the land and controlling the provinces, supply the capitalists with a cheap labor force, a conservative legislature and executive, and general political "stability" and quiet in the backyard. But, as the example of Mexico so clearly shows, elimination of the feudalists does not essentially change anything because it leaves intact the power of the capitalist bourgeoisie to oppose more far-reaching agricultural reforms. This power indeed is actually enhanced if, as is usually proposed, compensation for their lands permits the feudalists to convert themselves into capitalists.

The view that Latin America is, in the words of Carlos Fuentes, "a feudal castle with a capitalist façade" beclouds reality. The measures which the Alliance for Progress wishes to introduce, and which it hopes will substitute capitalism for feudalism, already have a century and a half of failure behind them in Latin America. It would be more accurate to say that Latin America is a capitalist castle with a feudal façade. Breaking the façade would not accomplish much, not even a land reform.

To summarize: land reform of the first type, for the benefit largely of the landowners themselves, is no reform at all. Land reform of the second type, undertaken largely by the bourgeoisie in its own interest, also holds little promise. Only land reform accompanied by a socialist transformation of society really works and is worthy of the name. Effective land reform cannot be made by conservatives or even against conservatives. It can be made only *without* conservatives.

## NOTE

1. See, for example, *Time* magazine, March 1, 1963, p. 22.

# 18

## INSTABILITY AND INTEGRATION
## IN URBAN LATIN AMERICA

Latin America already has a great and growing urban population[1] which in several of its countries exceeds 50 percent.[2] Nonetheless, the city has hardly been studied as an economic system; and as an economic unit or as part of the economy the city is only very inadequately understood.[3] Possibly this lacuna in our knowledge may be traced to economists' emphasis on the sectoral breakdown of the economy and on the distinctions among primary, secondary, and tertiary sectors. This last sector has become little more than a residual category for classifying the less stably structural and less well understood phases of economic activity.[4] Yet it is precisely this little understood sector which has been growing at such an alarming rate in Latin America and other underdeveloped countries.[5] Possibly the same gap in our knowledge of the socioeconomic structure of the city may also be traced to the sociologists' focus on the urban residential pattern and its socio-cultural manifestations which, possibly of necessity, relegate economic factors to relatively less well researched dependent variables.

The so-called floating population of urban areas presents a particular challenge. Like the indigenous population in rural areas, the floating population in urban areas is often thought to be

1964. This article forms part of a report and recommendations on rural and urban community development which the author prepared under contract to the United Nations Economic Commission for Latin America for their seminar on this topic in 1964. Nonetheless, this organization is not to be held responsible for anything said herein. It was first published in *Studies in Comparative International Development*, Vol. II, No. 5, 1966, as "Urban Poverty in Latin America."

"marginal" because of the way it is integrated into the society as a whole. Probably the most important study of this population has been of inhabitants of self-built and/or "irregular" [6] residential structures. It has often been thought that these settlements were of a temporary nature and that their inhabitants were merely recent rural migrants in transition to stable urban employment and residence. Recently it has become ever clearer that these settlements are for the foreseeable future not transitional and temporary but rather permanent and growing. Often many of their inhabitants are not migrants from rural areas at all but rather from other, usually smaller cities[7] and notably even from within the same city.[8] ECLA said these self-built settlements represent "the rejection by the city of native or other people who lived in it, who differ from the rest of the urban population more in the degree of their poverty than in their origins." [9] One student of the problem suggests, moreover, that they "must be considered as a permanent phenomenon which has its roots in the process of economic and social development." [10]

Nonetheless, it is possible to exaggerate the economic and socio-cultural importance of the urban-rural distinction. It may be useful, instead, to consider the distinction between what might be called the "stable" or well-structured and the "unstable" sectors of the economy; and the corresponding distinction between the "permanent" and the "floating" populations that are economically active or inactive in them. The stable sectors exist both in rural and urban environments and have been more exhaustively studied in their agricultural and their industrial forms. The unstable sector and floating population also exist in both the rural and the urban environments. One may venture to suggest that the rural and urban varieties of this "unstable" sector probably share a fairly similar economic structure and cause. Possibly more alike still are the rural and urban incumbents in these relatively "unstructured" and "unstable" roles. Certainly, they come from substantially the same socio-cultural group, especially if the society is a multi-racial or multi-ethnic one; and often they are the same individuals displaced from one environment to the other (and sometimes back again). Moreover, they often occupy a large variety of these roles simultaneously or in quick succession, shifting rapidly and easily among the "unstructured" roles, but not between these and the more "structured" ones.

Insofar as these people and their roles have been studied at all, primary emphasis has been placed on the social and cultural aspects of the problem. Nonetheless, the evidence from these studies does throw some light on and permit some limited insight into the allied economic undertones of the "unstable" sector. According to studies of internal migration, the economic sources of this problem lie in the failure of the "stable" primary goods production sector to expand and in the instability of its associated, often speculative, agricultural merchandising sector and in the consequent inability to provide employment and sustenance to the rural population. There is also the corresponding "stability" of the industrial sector and its associated unstable urban economy, which in turn cannot absorb the population thus expelled from the farms and small towns.[11] Much of this migration is rural to rural, rural to small town, small town to metropolitan, and not only rural to urban in the narrower sense of the word.[12] In the small towns the unstable sector is possibly still larger than in the metropolitan centers in which it has more forcefully pressed itself on the attention of the various students of the problem.[13]

Since the primary and secondary sectors are not expanding fast enough, much of the population in this "unstable" sector is attracted into, or rather forced into, the tertiary sector.[14] There, it does not of course go into the professions and others of the more traditionally "stable" and larger service institutions, but rather into small service establishments,[15] and it becomes individual self-employed "entrepreneurs," such as in street vending, odd jobs, and of course in domestic service.[16] Many of these people thus are literally "capitalists," but without financial, human, or educational capital. They might be called, as they have by Sol Tax, "Penny Capitalists" in an urban guise; but they lack even the small amount of capital and thus independence that their land affords the peasants in Panajachel, Guatemala.[17] The overlap between the unstable and the tertiary sector should not blind us to the great extent to which the secondary sector is similarly unstable. Thus, ECLA found in Santiago, Chile, that out of the 42 percent of the labor force in industry in the self-built *callampa* and out of the corresponding 32 percent industrial workers in the city as a whole, 19 percent and 6 percent respectively (or nearly half in the *callampa* and a fifth in the city) were in the notoriously occasional and unstable construction and not in the "stable" manufacturing part of the secondary sector.[18] But even in the manufacturing sector, "old," capital poor, and technologically inefficient small shops, with a probably uncertain lifespan and certainly unstable employment, are coming into being at a faster rate than modern, technologically advanced factories.[19] The former unstable ones absorb a larger number of workers than the latter stable ones;[20] but not unlike the relation between agricultural subsistence plots and haciendas or plantations, the small, inefficient, industrial producers have a satellite-metropolis relation with and live in the shadow of the larger "efficient" ones, often supplying the latter with part of their input, and always absorbing the brunt of much of the fluctuations in demand, supply, and price of the modern, "stable" manufacturing sector.

The existence and expansion of this large unstable—both urban and rural—sector in the structure of the national and international economy produces a correspondingly large unstable "floating" population with low educational and technological qualifications, highly unstable employment, and great insecurity. Thus, ECLA notes that "the worker of the *callampa* rarely has the security of a stable job; he faces the probability of a succession of badly paid jobs of uncertain duration." [21] A survey of Puerto Alegre, in Brazil, showed 40 percent of family heads to "work with irregularity" and another 55 percent to be entirely unemployed.[22] Many people shift frequently between irregular unskilled employment and often only partial self-employment,[23] and they must always look forward to having any particular source of income only for a short time. Perhaps paradoxically, multiple employment is closely associated with frequent and high unemployment. Thus a study of the *callampa* population in Santiago reports 41 percent of its employable people to have been unemployed between four and twelve months out of the year.[24] These conditions generate such low levels of income that, according to ECLA estimates, the adequate family "model diet" as established by the Department of Food and Nutrition of the

National Health Service of Chile would absorb 132 percent and 121 percent respectively of the incomes of Santiago's *callampa* dweller and worker.[25] And the instability of employment and insecurity of income is matched only by the 61 percent of respondents who, though living in Chile, which among Latin American countries is noted for having the best developed social insurance system, said that they are not covered by any social security system.[26]

As in the rural environment, the instability of the labor market, is, if not matched, at least approached by the instability of the product market. Possibly the urban dweller is less adversely affected than his rural counterpart by market monopoly, fluctuation, and speculation in the goods he buys (and partly sells), because geographical considerations in the larger cities probably reduce the possibility of monopolizing the local market. Nonetheless, the national and urban markets for many goods, including food and often housing, are notoriously monopolistic. Artificially created city-wide shortages, to permit price speculation in this or that consumer necessity, are an all-too-common occurrence in many parts of Latin America.[27] These inevitably absorb a share of the consumer's income which, though perhaps unknown, is very likely not insubstantial. It has been estimated, for instance, that 40 percent of the urban food price in Chile represents merchandising costs; and that these costs alone absorb 26 percent of the urban worker's entire family income.[28]

The degree and impact of this sort of monopolization, restriction of supply, and price speculation in consumer goods is probably greater in the "unstable" than the "stable" sector, especially insofar as it is physically and economically located in the self-built and low income suburban residential areas. These latter are far less well provided with urban services, including retail trade outlets, than the city as a whole.[29] Accordingly, retail monopoly and raised prices are that much more possible and likely in these urban areas.[30] The greater instability of family incomes in these areas, moreover, renders its population more exposed to usurious short-term credit practices than in other parts of the city. Since these people's incomes are low, they no doubt receive less credit than other urban dwellers, but they probably pay more for it and spend a higher share of their low incomes on high interest costs.

This economic structure of the city and the disadvantaged position in which it places many of its inhabitants of course has manifold social and cultural manifestations. In multi-racial and multi-ethnic countries this structure manifests itself in very unequal racial and ethnic residential distributions in the city.[31] Most notable, and most widely studied, is the resulting urban residential pattern. Large and usually growing parts of the urban population crowd into self-built,[32] antiquated, sub-standard,[33] and low-income suburban[34] residential structures and areas. Of these, the self-built residential settlements are probably those which have attracted the greatest attention of scientists and policy-makers alike. Though there are undoubtedly differences in occupational structure, income level, and various social-cultural indices between the self-built and the other two types of low-income urban settlements, ECLA has recently called the extent of such difference into serious question.[35] In Chile, which with Venezuela has had the most ambitious public housing program in Latin America, official estimates place 6 percent of the population of Santiago in *callampas*, 20 percent in *conventillos*, and more in the subdivisions and developments whose replacement of *callampas* has been able to reduce their growth in Santiago. In some of the other cities of Chile and Latin America in which the public building program is very much less extensive than in Santiago, the *callampa* population reaches much higher percentages, sometimes exceeding 50 percent. The *conventillo* population accounts for one-third of the families of urban workers and employees.[36] According to UNICEF, in Mexico City 30 percent of the population lives in self-built housing, 11 percent in antiquated sub-standard housing, 14 percent in "proletarian" housing, 26 percent in "antiquated housing," and only 19 percent live "in housing that may be classified as 'good'." [37] Commenting on the situation in Lima, the same organization notes:

> The majority of the "barriadas" are formed because the people want to have their own lot. They organize an "invasion" which then keeps growing into a continuous flow of people who leave the capital to settle in a place of their own and for which they usually do not have to pay. To this end they may look for vacant lots that

are state and even privately owned. A look at the average income of these people shows that almost none of them could live in any other way or pay the rents which the urban areas demand.[38]

The self-built settlements are almost by definition unplanned. As such, they usually are almost devoid of any urban services. They generally lack running water, forcing their usually female and/or minor inhabitants to fetch water in cans from nearby or even from outside communal sources. Sometimes the water is trucked in and sold at a considerable price. Electricity is either unavailable or clandestinely tapped from nearby wires. Sewage systems and often even cesspools are unknown. Garbage collection is non-existent—on the other hand, the settlement is often built on the garbage dump itself. Paving is non-existent; and, since these settlements perforce are often on hillsides or in riverbeds, recurrent flooding is all too common. Hospitals are distant, as are telephones with which to call for emergency medical assistance. Schools are far away and crowded or simply inaccessible. Many self-built settlements are far from the center of town, from employment opportunities, and transportation is inadequate and costly in time and money. Police and fire protection are rare. Retail trade, as was noted above, is scarce and costly. But, apart from the insecurity of employment, from the point of view of the inhabitant of self-built residential structures on land owned by others, far and away the worst of its features is the insecurity of his tenancy: "Because here we have no security, on a moment's notice they can kick us out," and "because here we live on charity and may have to move at any time by order of the City." [39]

The inhabitants of *conventillo*-type antiquated sub-standard housing do not suffer from these shortages of physical facilities to nearly so great an extent precisely because they are "urbanized" in the more traditional sense of the word. Their inhabitants also tend to be the members of the working and lower middle classes whose economic situation and length of residence more nearly afford them this less inadequate housing. The low-income suburban settlements, including those planned by public housing authorities, unfortunately appear all too often to suffer from many of the same deficiencies that are so characteristic of the self-built "irregular" settlements. Due to various economic and administrative impediments, many of these housing projects lack many of the same urban, educational, health, and retail facilities. And, of course, being often even more outlying than the self-built settlements, their inhabitants are seriously disadvantaged with respect to the employment opportunities which were not, and are not, located in these newer residential areas.[40]

Though the population of these settlements is very young—51 percent of Santiago's *callampa* population was found to be under fifteen years of age[41]—educational facilities and attainments are extremely deficient. The same study of *callampas* found 73 percent of the inhabitants above fifteen years of age to have 0–4 years of schooling.[42] More significant still, it appeared that earning capacity within this group was not influenced by educational attainment, suggesting that only *more than four years* of education— attained by only 27 percent of the people—equipped them with greater earning capacity than no education at all.[43] Failure to attend school was found in 38 percent[44] and 45 percent[45] of school-age children. As a consequence of the low income and sanitary conditions already referred to, health standards are also deplorably low. "The Preamble of the Constitution of the World Health Organization defines 'a state of complete physical, mental and social wellbeing, and not just the absence of illness or invalidity.' If we were to use this criterion to judge the health of the *callampa* population . . . we would have to conclude that the *callampa* population is a sick population."[46] The rate of days bedridden because of illness is considerably higher than the average despite the fact that the low incomes of these inhabitants probably militate against their sacrificing workdays.[47] The rate of infant mortality is very high and sometimes exceeds that of rural areas. And only 2 percent received medical attention covered by social security.[48]

The "unstable sector" of the economy on which the preceding pages have been focused results in widespread mobility and insecurity which call for special emphasis. It was noted above that the contemporary structure of the urban economy in Latin America brings with it a high degree of mobility, both in employment and residence, which tends to be particularly concentrated in the three types of "irregular" residential areas. The same may be said for insecurity, though with respect to this latter dimension it is important to distinguish between self-built settlements on the one hand and publicly built or sponsored suburban housing projects on the other. Economic insecurity is of course more in evidence in the former because the most economically insecure people perforce tend to settle there. Residential insecurity, on the other hand, is augmented by the very nature of the self-built settlements themselves and particularly by the fact that they are located on land belonging to others. If privately owned, this land is frequently held for speculative purposes and may be claimed by the owner for other uses at a moment's notice. But for various reasons of public policy, including "urban renewal" programs, even publicly owned urban land is often converted from this type of residential use to some other one. In Rio de Janeiro in 1964 a self-built *favela* was burnt to the ground by the city government to make room for a new luxury tourist hotel. One of the principal preoccupations of the self-built housing population is to get and keep even the most modest of roofs over their heads. For this reason among others, this population tends to concentrate its concern and attention on their own immediate day-to-day problems, to the virtual exclusion of any communal, let alone national or international, matters.[49] Their principal social contact tends to be with their own primary group and/or extended family. Neighborhood and other voluntary associations, including political parties, though they may exist in these settlements, enjoy scant participation.[50] This situation appears to be mitigated only in countries with Indian populations, such as Guatemala and Peru, in which neighborhood or city-wide "sons of the . . . (region)" clubs provide recent rural migrants with ties among each other and between them and "back home." Beyond that, the only significant spontaneous communal cooperation is stimulated by the sometimes cooperative efforts to "invade" a new area in order to build there and then to defend it against would-be interlopers or other sources of potential usurpation of their homes. Again, in more strongly ethnically and communally organized countries with large indigenous populations, such settlement and defense of new areas is sometimes organized on the basis of regional affiliation. But in countries like Venezuela and Chile and even in Brazil, such a pattern is hardly to be found. In no case, however, is there any noticeable familiarity with, or interest and participation in, anything that might be called "national affairs," or even in popular programs of national political parties.[51] An observer of the Santiago *callampa* scene suggests that "the plans that are made at the national level could not take account of the needs of the *callampas*, given that its population is highly unstable and is constantly on the move from one place to another, which practically leaves them out of any activity of national scope." [52] The same author observes, on the other hand, that

> these populations which we have called suburban or "semi-segregated" urban centers, as their name implies, really are semi-segregated for lack of urban services. But they are on a different and higher level than the *callampa* settlements in that they have been granted ownership of land, which offers their inhabitants a degree of security and confidence which they did not have before and permits them to engage in a series of efforts to improve the development of the settlement as far as possible. This new situation creates a new set of responsibilities for them, and to face these they unite into groups which have a clear idea of the goals that they pursue. This also reflects itself in an interest in participating in political activities in contrast to the apathy and disorganization found in the inhabitants of the *callampa* settlements.[53]

But taking the foreign circumstances into account, it cannot come as any surprise to find ECLA concluding that

> in these sectors the problems of urban life acquire an importance beyond those of work itself. Therefore, the collective organizations that are formed do not tend toward the defense of job interests, but toward the improvement of living conditions and, in general, toward obtaining the circumstances that are necessary to permit their members to survive in an urban environment which to them often appears hostile.[54]

The floating urban population is particularly sensitive to and immediately affected by the most common changes in government programs and monetary and fiscal policies. As was suggested above, the instability of the economic sector which forms the base of this population also transforms it into the urban shock absorber of the economic ups and downs of the "stable" sector

and the economy as a whole. To the extent, therefore, that government activity either dampens or amplifies these economic fluctuations, it impinges particularly heavily on the floating population.

This population is the last to be hired and the first to be fired
during fluctuations of the urban construction, manufacturing, and
service industries. Government monetary and fiscal policy therefore determines the economic situations very immediately via its
effects on the private sector. Employment opportunities are also
particularly sensitive to other government programs. In the past
in Latin America, the floating population has often seen its
sources of employment sharply increased by a surge of public
construction, associated usually with particular political circumstances, only to have them reduced again by similarly determined
cutbacks in public construction activity. Insofar as the prior
increase in jobs attracted still more people into the cities or
even into the country itself, its temporary nature contributes to
the floating urban population and its insecurity. Such recurrent
unemployment may force some people to abandon their homes
in the older *conventillo* slums and seek to establish them in newer
self-built ones. Insofar as benefits from social and employment
security programs are tied, as they largely are, to the economic
institutions in which the population occupies a relatively stable
place, the floating population which most needs such benefits
is left largely uncovered. In all respects, it suffers from the greatest
degree of insecurity, and of course, of poverty. Public policy
therefore cannot significantly alter, much less eliminate, the de-
plorable circumstances of this floating urban population in the
absence of basic changes in the structure of the society and economy which gives rise to it.

There is, however, one major area in which, it is suggested,
public policy can immediately intervene to improve the circumstances of the urban floating population and to lay the basis for
other development efforts. This is the area of residential housing
and the problems associated with self-built residential structures
in particular.

The above examination of the urban scene suggested that there
is a significant difference in the kind of social organization and

the sense of, and participation in, civic and political responsibility between the inhabitants of self-built residential structures and areas on the one hand and the remainder of the more or less floating urban population in older centrally located run-down and newer suburban project dwellings. Over and beyond economic and other circumstances that distinguish them, this difference between the inhabitants of self-built and those of other residential structures can be traced directly to the difference in security of residential tenure between the two groups. It is the insecurity in their claim to their house and home, coupled of course with job and other sources of insecurity, which appears to be one of the principal obstacles to cooperative and organized civic or political action in their neighborhood or elsewhere by this part of the floating urban populations. The insecurity of residential tenure, in turn, is due in large part to the lack of ownership or other legal claim to the land on which they live and to the relatively much greater power of the private and public owners or claimants who seek repeatedly to expel them from that land.

These considerations create an important task and opportunity for public policy and communal action in the amelioration of the economic and social circumstances of the urban population living in self-built residential structures and areas. It is vain to expect such communal action in these areas in the absence of any external, almost necessarily public, intervention. But with some appropriate, and not necessarily expensive, public intervention, communal action in this part of the population can significantly contribute to the future economic, social, and political development of the society as a whole. Beyond the obvious, but at this time possibly economically prohibitive, measure of building public housing for these populations, there may be other economically immediately feasible measures to stimulate and organize community organization and development among self-built residential areas and their inhabitants. Some of the possible measures for the amelioration of the problem of housing insecurity in self-built residential areas and for popular stimulation among their inhabitants are outlined below.[55]

It would be desirable for central urban municipalities to incorporate or amalgamate with their adjoining and even rural townships to form a larger urban or metropolitan area more susceptible to comprehensive urban planning. With a view to the housing problems of the floating urban population, it would then be desirable for the city to pursue a policy of land acquisition by the public authority well in excess of present construction needs.

Two major public policies are suggested with respect to such municipally owned land and the problem of self-built residential structures. First, existing self-built urban settlements on public land should receive public guarantees against eviction without very long-term notice and public provision for better alternative housing in other areas whose location and transportation facilities are not seriously prejudicial to the interests of the potential evictees. In fact, it would seem reasonable to abandon policies and programs of urban renewal which imply the destruction of homes and the eviction of their owners until the still-unforeseeable time when economic conditions permit this policy to be pursued without placing the cost on those members of the society who can least afford it. This applies not only to tourist hotels but also to other urban "improvements." Second, the municipality can subdivide publicly owned urban land and allot it to those in the floating population who have already built on it in settled areas and to those who wish to build on it in new self-built housing developments. These allotments should carry guarantees against evictions and could in return demand some minimal form of responsibility from the occupant. This possibility of transfer of allotments or lots should be provided for, but this must be coupled with measures to prevent acquisition and monopolization of multiple lots by private speculators.

It would be desirable to provide the maximum possible public protection to residents in self-built housing on privately owned tracts of land. The best protection against private expulsion from and speculation with such privately owned land is its acquisition under eminent domain and its subdivision by the municipality as described above. The purpose of public land acquisition in excess of residential construction needs is of course to forestall the development of such problems of private urban land speculation[56] (which is also desirable for reasons other than those connected with self-built housing) and of floating populations living on such land. However, it would be desirable to protect present inhabitants of self-built settlements on private lands against arbitrary expulsion as well by, in the public interest, limiting the terms under which such expulsion is legally possible.

More adequate, or less inadequate, self-built housing can be promoted by recourse to several measures of public policy and community action. To the extent that the foregoing measures to increase the security of residential tenure are adopted, it would be increasingly possible to include self-built residential structures and areas in the urban planning and zoning already applied to other parts of the city. Accordingly, it becomes administratively possible to provide a minimum of urban services, such as water sewage and electricity, to the floating population of self-built areas as well. Additionally, it would be possible to provide for their acquisition of building materials that can be at the same time of higher quality and of lower cost than those that are currently accessible to them through exclusively private channels, which are sometimes also monopolized.

Combining all or even some of these public measures to increase the security of tenure and decrease the cost of construction and maintenance for the urban population that must live in self-built housing would provide a substantially greater basis for communal participation of this population in matters of their own immediate interest as well as in those of wider social and political concern. At relatively low cost, these measures would permit the substantial duplication of the social, if not the physical, circumstances of such successful housing developments as "23 de Enero" in Caracas and "José María Caro" in Santiago, which latter incidentally includes a substantial proportion of self-built housing on municipally subdivided and allotted land. These measures, moreover, would permit the organization of residential building and maintenance cooperatives resting on communal participation in the process of planning, construction, and managing substantial settlements of self-built housing.

A further but more ambitious stimulus to such communal participation and organization would be for a public agency to organize the construction of self-built or semi-self-built housing.

The public agency would provide the financial resources it now devotes to public housing projects, but instead of channeling them through private contractors who hire construction labor in the usual fashion and retain part of the project funds for themselves—or instead, even, of having the public agency supplant the private contractors and assume the contracting and employment functions itself—the public agency would assume the responsibility of planning the project, supplying the materials, architectural and contracting services, and then employ members of the floating population in the construction of the project, recompensing them, instead of in wages, in rights to one of the completed dwellings after a certain number of hours of work has been contributed to its construction.

These self-built housing projects should not be confused, however, with such so-called self-built and aided mutual aid housing projects as are reviewed in South and especially in Central America by the Pan American Union in its *Self-Help Housing Guide*[57] and as are often financed by funds from the International Development Bank in Washington. A look at the cost breakdowns reported in this *Guide* shows that these projects are self-built only in name and not in fact. Thus, the attributed labor cost of the participant workers who are to be the subsequent owners is about 11 percent to 12 percent in most of the projects reviewed, and 4 percent in a Guatemalan one. That renders the term "self-built" a cruel joke. Cruel, because it turns out in the same cost breakdown that while contributed labor contributes little more than 10 percent of the cost of the house, the land the subsequent owners must purchase and have developed and the management and administration expenses they must pay for, contribute 50 percent of the cost of the house; and another 40 percent goes for building materials and professional labor. Having earlier taken note of high land costs, we may observe that administration and management costs accounted for 25 percent of the total in Guatemala and 50 percent and more of the total in Panama. If to these observations we add that the total cost of these houses is, more often than not, over $2,000 U.S. and sometimes passes $3,000 U.S., there can remain little doubt but that this *Guide* to so-called self-help mutual aid housing is little more than a grand scheme for the mutual aid of land speculators, land development contractors, building contractors, and bureaucrats.

To avoid repetition of this sort of thing and to provide for real self-built mutual aid housing projects, the following recommendations are made: Build much cheaper houses for much lower income receivers. Reduce the building time from the one and a half years common in the projects reviewed above to a maximum of one-half year and preferably less. To achieve these and other ends, build for and rely on the labor of people more largely in the tertiary and self-employed or unemployed sector who have more flexibility in the disposition of their time and residence than workers and employees. Insofar as possible, provide for the participants residing on the building site either in temporary shacks or by designing the houses so that they may be built and occupied in stages, room by room. To that end, in turn, introduce a maximum of standardization of building parts compatible with self rather than professionally built housing. Combine the building facets of these projects with the distribution of food, such as from the Food for Peace Program, and with some of the other urban community development programs, such as community centers, where the circumstances demand. It goes without saying, of course, that these recommendations and the publicly aided self-built projects themselves can come to no good whatever if it is not politically possible to eliminate the control of the projects by speculators, politicians, and others interested in the perpetuation and extension of the situation reviewed and even recommended as a *Guide* by the Organization of American States and its Pan American Union. Probably not surprisingly in view of the political differences between that country and some others in Latin America, Chile seems to be the country which has achieved the greatest measure of success in this direction; as the Pan American Union's own cost breakdowns show, it is in Chile that the proportionate costs of land and administration, though still high, are quite noticeably the lowest among the countries it reviews with so-called self-built aided mutual help housing projects.

Experience in Caracas suggests that any of these public approaches to the housing problem of the floating population can stimulate substantial social and political awareness and con-

scientious community action in otherwise very shiftless populations. Moreover, and significantly, it can do so without creating
a paternalistic and/or dependency relationship between the government or public agency and the participating population. On
the contrary, the Caracas, and to some extent the Santiago, experience suggests that permitting these populations access to
minimum security in residential tenure can lead to the development among them of a healthy sense of social responsibility and
political independence which manifests itself in very much
heightened communal participation in a variety of independent
voluntary organizations for the cooperative management and pursuit of housing, neighborhood, and other civic interests, and a
healthy if sometimes distant mutual respect between them and
the government and its public housing agency. Most symptomatic
of this sense of civic responsibility and political independence is
the extent of self-policing in Caracas' "23 de Enero" housing
project and the city police force's reluctance to interfere with that
urban community's internal affairs. More important perhaps than
its immediate implications for the problem of the housing and
neighborhood problems of the floating population are the stimulation by these measures of conscious and organized community
and political action which can become the basis of this population's more effective participation in other matters of concern to
national development and welfare. Thus, "the inhabitants of the
'*callampa* settlements' have often taken the initiative to organize
themselves to improve their living conditions and to handle their
local affairs, and sometimes getting to be veritable political organizations." [58]

## NOTES

1. For references see especially, Phillip M. Hauser, ed., *La Urbaniza-
ción en América Latina* (Paris: UNESCO, 1962), SS.61/V.9/S;
United Nations Economic Commission for Latin America
(ECLA), *The Social Development of Latin America in the Post-
war Period*, E/CN.12/660, May 11, 1963; United Nations
ECLA, *Urbanization in Latin America*, E/CN.12/662, March 13,

1963; Guillermo Rosenbluth L., *Problemas socioeconómicos de la marginalidad e integración urbana (El caso de "Las Poblaciones Callampas" en el Gran Santiago)* (Santiago: Universidad de Chile, 1963); Asociación Venezolana de Sociología, VI Congreso Latinoamericano de Sociología (Caracas: Imprenta Nacional, 1961), Vol. II.

2. Philip M. Hauser, ed., *La Urbanización en América Latina*, Chapter III.

3. Thus the recent ECLA study, *The Economic Development of Latin America in the Postwar Period*, E/CN.12/659, April 7, 1963, makes no reference to the urban economy; and its companion document, ECLA, *The Social Development of Latin America in the Postwar Period*, though concerned with the city as a socioeconomic unit, is unable to describe and analyze the situation as well as it would have done if economists had prepared the necessary studies of the contemporary urban economic structure.

4. For a criticism of this classification which indicates the varieties of the tertiary sector, see, Peter T. Bauer and Basil Yamey, "Further Notes on Economic Progress and Occupational Distribution," *Economic Journal* (March 1954). Also see Solomon Rottenberg, "Reflexiones sobre la industrialización y el desarrollo económico" (Santiago: Universidad Católica, 1957).

5. ECLA, *The Economic Development of Latin America* and *The Social Development of Latin America*.

6. This term is used in G. Rosenbluth L., *Problemas socioeconómicos*. For further discussion, see below.

7. For migration by stages see, for instance, Bertram Hutchinson, "The Migrant Population of Urban Brazil," *América Latina*, Año 6, No. 2 (April–June 1963), especially pp. 45–50.

8. ECLA, *Urbanization in Latin America*, pp. 15, 16, and 33.

9. *Ibid.*, p. 15.

10. Guillermo Rosenbluth L., *Problemas socioeconómicos*, p. 99.

11. Cf. ECLA, *The Economic Development of Latin America in the Postwar Period*, Chapter VII; and ECLA, *The Social Development of Latin America in the Postwar Period*, Chapters II and III.

12. See, for instance, Bertram Hutchinson, "The Migrant Population of Urban Brazil," p. 69, where he notes that 20–40 percent of this population in the metropolis comes from other cities.

13. ECLA, *Urbanization in Latin America*, p. 6.
14. ECLA, *The Social Development* . . . , pp. 63–65, and ECLA, *Urbanization in Latin America*, p. 28.
15. See ECLA, *The Social Development* . . . , p. 62.
16. See *ibid.*, p. 63, and ECLA, *Urbanization in Latin America*, p. 28, where 63 percent of employment in Greater Santiago and 45 percent in a *callampa* were found to be in the tertiary sector, and 17 percent and 33 percent respectively in the "self-employed" category.
17. See Sol Tax, *Penny Capitalism* (Chicago, 1953).
18. ECLA, *Urbanization in Latin America*, p. 28.
19. ECLA, *The Social Development of Latin America* . . . , pp. 59–61.
20. *Ibid.*, pp. 59–60.
21. ECLA, *Urbanization in Latin America*, p. 28.
22. Reported in G. Rosenbluth L., *Problemas socioeconómicos*, p. 32 (Table 14).
23. ECLA, *Urbanization in Latin America*, p. 28.
24. G. Rosenbluth L., *Problemas socioeconómicos*, p. 79.
25. Reported in *ibid.*, p. 65–66.
26. *Ibid.*, p. 64n.
27. A document issued by the Presidency of the Republic of Brazil, Conselho do Desenvolvimento, *Questão Agraria Brasileira* (by Ignacio Rangel), Brasilia, 1961, p. iii, speaks of monopoly which "methodically organizes scarcity" and thus "imposes extortionist prices on the consumer." The *Correo da Manha* (Rio de Janeiro), June 6, 1963, reports price mark-ups of 1,500 percent on food grown near Rio and sold in that city.
28. OCEPLAN, *Las Bases Técnicas del Plan de Acción del Gobierno Popular* (Santiago, 1964), p. 17.
29. *Urbanization in Latin America*, p. 10.
30. J. Chonchol, *La Reforma Agraria en América Latina* (Santiago: Editorial del Pacífico, 1964), p. 63, for instance, argues that the poorest areas and inhabitants of the city pay the highest per unit prices for their food.
31. See, for instance, "Aspectos Humanos da Favela Carioca," *O Estado de São Paulo*, April 15, 1960, for Rio de Janeiro; and Jose Matos Mar, "Migración y Urbanización—Las Barriadas Limeñas: Un Caso de Integración a la vida urbana," in P. M. Hauser, *La Urbanización en América Latina*, for Peru.

32. For distinctions in architectural, economic, social, and cultural terms among these three types of low-income urban dwellings, see, for instance, G. Rosenbluth L., *Problemas socioeconómicos*, Chapter III. The self-built settlements are usually either on the outskirts of the city or on undesirable centrally located hillsides and river embankments. They carry various names: *jacales* (Mexico), *ranchos* (Caracas), *barrios clandestinos* (Colombia), *barriadas* (Lima), *callampas* (Santiago), *villas miserias* (Buenos Aires), *villas malocas* (Puerto Alegre), *favelas* (Rio de Janeiro), *mocambos* (Recife), etc.

33. These structures and residential zones, like many slums in Europe and North America, are generally centrally located because they consist of old urban housing which is now in an advanced state of disrepair and which supports a very high concentration of occupancy. In Argentina and Chile they are called *conventillos* and in Mexico *tugurios*.

34. Several countries and cities, notably Caracas and Santiago, have undertaken extensive urban renewal programs which "eradicate" self-built and in some cases old housing and which resettle some of the displaced families in state-financed housing projects or publicly supervised subdivisions which provide assistance in self-construction of houses. These developments are, of course, usually on the outskirts of town and frequently quite distant from the center of town and/or centers of employment and retail trade.

35. ECLA, *Urbanization in Latin America*, pp. 11, 33.

36. *Ibid.*, p. 7.

37. UNICEF, *Boletín Trimestral del UNICEF*, No. 29, 1962, n.p.

38. *Ibid.*, n.p.

39. Quoted in ECLA, *Urbanization in Latin America*, p. 23.

40. *Ibid.*, pp. 9–10; Banco Obrero, *Proyecto de Evaluación de los Superbloques* (Caracas, 1961).

41. *Ibid.*, p. 18.

42. *Ibid.*, p. 19.

43. *Ibid.*, p. 20.

44. *Ibid.*, p. 21.

45. G. Rosenbluth L., *Problemas socioeconómicos*, p. 90.

46. *Ibid.*, p. 68.

47. *Ibid.*, pp. 58–69.

48. *Ibid.*, p. 70.

49. ECLA, *Urbanization in Latin America*, pp. 31–32. See also

296   *Andre Gunder Frank*

ECLA, *The Social Development* . . . , pp. 65–67.
50. ECLA, *Urbanization in Latin America*, pp. 30–31.
51. *Ibid.*, p. 32.
52. G. Rosenbluth L., *Problemas socioeconómicos*, p. 92.
53. *Ibid.*, p. 96. Similar observations have been made in the other Latin American city with large-scale public housing projects, Caracas. See, for instance, *Report of a Community Development Evaluation Mission to Venezuela*, prepared for the Government of Venezuela by Caroline F. Ware, Rubén Dario Utria, and Antoni Wojcicki (United Nations: Commissioner for Technical Assistance, Department of Economic and Social Affairs), TAO/VEN/15, December 1, 1963, particularly Annex I, and Annex E (unpublished). In Santiago, "José María Caro" housing project and in Caracas those of "23 de Enero" and "Simón Rodríguez" are outstanding in this respect. Each of these has upwards of 100,000 inhabitants. For a somewhat dimmer view, possibly because they compare the project reality with an ideal rather than with the reality of self-built communities, see also, Banco Obrero, *Proyecto de Evalución de Superbloques*.
54. ECLA, *The Social Development of Latin America in the Post-war Period*, p. 136.
55. In this connection also see Phillip M. Hauser, ed., *La urbanización en América Latina*, Chapter II, "Conclusiones del Seminario," and Chapter XIII, "Algunas Consecuencias Políticas de la Urbanización."
56. Thus, the *Self-Help Housing Guide* of the Inter-American Housing and Planning Center of the Pan American Union in Washington reports land costs that reach such amounts as 57 percent, 40 percent, and 35 percent of the total cost of even so-called self-built and aided mutual help project housing in Colombia, Nicaragua, and Costa Rica, including 33 percent for totally undeveloped land in Nicaragua (pp. 5, 29). Marshall Wolfe attributes such costs largely to speculation in his *Las clases medias en Centroamérica: características que presentan en la actualidad y requisitos para su desarrollo*, United Nations, E/CN.12/CCE/176/Rev. 2/1960, p. 1.
57. See *Self-Help Housing Guide*. The following data are all from this *Guide* and were culled out and combined by the present author into a single table covering the dozen or so projects reviewed there. This procedure, which the *Guide*'s authors did not choose to adopt, permits the above general picture which does

not emerge very clearly from the presentation, as in the *Guide*, of only the costs for each project taken singly and in isolation.

58. Philip M. Hauser, ed., *La Urbanización en América Latina*, pp. 57–58.

# 19

## MEXICO: THE JANUS FACES OF TWENTIETH-CENTURY BOURGEOIS REVOLUTION

Mexico's revolutionary break with her nineteenth-century legacy of feudalism and imperialism, carried out at the cost of a million lives, began in 1910. Many of the political, economic, and social fruits of the Mexican Revolution were slow in ripening, and many will be gathered only in the future. From the United States point of view, Mexico seemed to be setting the worst kind of example to the rest of Latin America. Accordingly, the U.S. first interfered economically and· diplomatically, then sent troops to capture Vera Cruz, and even as late as 1938 labeled the Mexican government "Bolshevik." At the same time, Latin America, still beset by the alliance between feudalism and imperialism, came to view the Mexican Revolution as a guiding star and shining example. By now, much has changed. Today, the United States is full of praise for Mexico's example of "economic progress with political stability"; and President Kennedy, indeed, is asking the Mexican government to become the pilot country in the Alliance for Progress. Latin America, in the meantime, has turned eyes toward Cuba and asks if the example of Mexico's fifty-year revolution is one to follow after all. Let us, therefore, turn to the lessons that Mexico's experience holds for Latin America and the world.

The Mexican Revolution resulted in a tremendous release of popular energy, which, after the fighting ended, went into the construction of a new society. The destruction of feudalism radi-

---

1962. This essay originally appeared in the November 1962 issue of *Monthly Review*. For an auto-critique, especially of the references to "feudalism," see the Preface and Chapter 23.

cally changed the social relations of man to man. The peasant's accession to human dignity, when compared with the conditions of servitude which still persist in, say, Guatemala and Peru, is perhaps the Revolution's most important accomplishment. That same energy was also released through improved health (the mortality rate has fallen by two-thirds since 1910) and transformed into large increases of work, education (illiteracy rate reduced by one-half), and skills, which in turn, particularly since 1940, have been transformed into Mexico's remarkable economic growth. Only a post- or non-feudal society could permit and produce such land reform (millions of small landholdings created), roads (sevenfold increase since 1940 so that now nearly half of all goods travel by truck and almost all passengers by bus), irrigation (an elevenfold increase since 1940 so that a third of all cropland is now irrigated), urbanization (to nearly 50 percent), industrialization (3.6-fold increase from 1940 to 1959), agricultural output (3.4-fold increase between 1940 and 1959); and, despite one of the world's highest rates of population growth, GNP per capita doubled from $150 to $300 a year. According to Rostow, Mexico has passed the threshold into self-sustained economic growth. Indeed, the annual rates of growth during the postwar years of both industrial and agricultural output rank Mexico among the first half-dozen countries in the world.

And yet Mexico's revolution has had another face as well. Its crude death rate of 12.5 remains higher than that of Bolivia or Peru, its infant mortality rate of 81 per 1000 higher than that of Argentina. Its ratio of doctors to people (1 to 2,200) is lower than Chile's and less than half of Argentina's. The 43 percent illiteracy that remained in 1950 hardly compares with 19 percent in Chile and 13 percent in Argentina. The ratio of working population engaged in manufacturing remains at 12 percent; and Mexico's per capita income of still less than $300 ranks it behind Chile, Argentina, Uruguay, and Cuba, to say nothing of oil-rich Venezuela. After the large-scale redistribution of land, over a million heads of rural families remained without land of their own; and, with population growth, the number may have risen to nearer two million (out of a total of maybe four million) since 1950. The average Mexican diet has a caloric deficit of −24.4 according to the United

Nations Food and Agriculture Organization; and the three million indigenous Indians out of today's population of over thirty million remain economically as badly or maybe worse off than the *poorest* of their forefathers of the time before the Conquest, four and a half centuries ago. However large the social change, the economic benefits of the Mexican Revolution have not reached, or have been withheld from, large parts of the population; about 50 percent receive today only 15 percent of the national income; and it has been estimated (although also challenged) that only 1 percent of the population disposes of 66 percent of the *money* income. Further, the inequality of income distribution is increasing, not decreasing.

The wealth and elegance of downtown Mexico City dazzle the visitor, and the heavy industry of Monterrey impresses as another Pittsburgh; but equally do the miles of Mexico City's shanty slums depress, as does the poverty of rural Tlaxcala and Chiapas dumfound. The question inevitably presents itself: have Mexico's fifty years of revolution really been a success or have they been a failure?

Compared to the experience of its closest neighbors, especially in Central America, Andean South America, and the Caribbean, Mexico's twentieth century has appeared as an obvious success, the more so as these countries are only in the present decade getting ready to break the bonds that shackle them. But has the Mexican Revolution also been a failure they should seek to avoid? Economic progress in Western Europe has been greater and its benefits more widely distributed within the society. Some of the countries, small and by nature ill-endowed ones among them, have eliminated poverty entirely. True, Western Europe has in general devoted longer to the task than has Mexico, but the recent adverse change in Mexico's distribution of income raises serious doubts about her prospects of following Europe in the foreseeable future. The comparison with socialism springs to mind as well. The Soviet Union, with its revolution coming after that of Mexico, has broken all previous records by its rate of economic growth, the more so if we allow for the ten-year period of World War II and reconstruction. It may be stretching comparisons too far to apply Russia's industrial experiences to Mexico, but the U.S.S.R. has eliminated illiteracy and gone on to challenge and in many ways surpass the United States in higher and technical education, providing the same opportunities to its indigenous and non-Russian-speaking peasant and nomadic peoples. And despite all agricultural difficulties, the U.S.S.R. displays a similar record in the fields of nutrition, health, and medicine. More recently, China's rate of industrial growth during the past decade, and its agricultural output growth rate in the 1950's, was still higher than that of Mexico. And now Cuba has eliminated its 30 percent illiteracy in a single year and nearly doubled its school enrollment in only two years since its revolution. These comparisons are no less inevitable.

Behind the two Janus faces of the Mexican Revolution there is a single head in a single and by now intricately balanced and developing organism. To learn Mexico's lesson for Latin America and the world, we must try to fathom the development, current operation, and future prospects of Mexico's revolutionary organism.

The history of Mexico seems to fall conveniently into the following periods: (1) the four centuries from the Conquest until 1910; (2) the nearly fifteen years of violent revolution, counter-revolution, and reconstruction, symbolized by Madera, Huerta, and Carranza; (3) the fifteen years of reform, carried through by Presidents Calles and Cárdenas; (4) the fifteen years after 1940 of the beginning of industrialization and the growth of bourgeois power, symbolized by President Alemán; and (5) the current consolidation of the "Mexican System" under bourgeois leadership and the Presidency of Lopez Mateos.

At the time of the Conquest, the Spaniards found an 150-year-old Aztec empire in Central Mexico, surviving Mayan culture in the South and Yucatan, and scattered semi-nomadic tribal Indians in the North, including today's Southwestern United States. The populous Center was soon colonized by Spaniards, the existing social system largely destroyed, the Indians' labor and land exploited, and their numbers reduced by half. The more arid, less populated, and tribal North, on the other hand, was settled only gradually and sparsely, as the extension of livestock ranching and mining in that area required. This difference between the North and the populous Center and South, as will emerge later, still dominates Mexico's social and economic experience in the last twenty years of our time.

In 1810, under the leadership of the priest Hidalgo, Mexico's peasants rebelled. Unmatched by peasant activity elsewhere in Spanish America, where peasants remained at best passive and often in support of the Spanish Crown, and unsupported by the Latin American-born Creole Spaniards, the rebellion came to nothing. Not until the landowning and particularly commercial Creoles took up the fight themselves did independence come to Mexico and the other Spanish colonies in America. In the 1850's, under the leadership of the Indian Benito Juárez, the Mexicans attempted reform in their feudal structure. But after the French intervention and under the thirty-year reign of Porfirio Díaz, peonage returned in full force and concentration of landownership became worse than ever. At the same time, foreign capital, increasingly American, entered the country on most favored terms until it reached over $400 million, concentrated in land, mines, and the transportation system required to ship produce abroad.

The Mexican Revolution was the product of alliance between the bourgeoisie, represented by Madera, and the peasants, led by Emiliano Zapata and Pancho Villa. They faced a common enemy, the feudal order and its supporting pillars of Church, army, and foreign capital. But their goals inevitably differed—freedom from domestic and foreign bonds and loosening of the economic structure for the bourgeoisie; land for the peasants. Although Zapata continued to press the interests of the peasants until his murder in 1919, the real leadership of the Revolution was never out of the hands of the bourgeoisie, except insofar as it was challenged by Huerta reaction and American intervention. (Even in the 1958 presidential election, only 23 percent of the population voted.) The elimination of feudal social relations was of course in the interest of the emerging bourgeoisie as well as of the peasants. Education became secularized, Church and state more widely separated. But accession to power by the peasantry was never really in the cards.

None of the early presidents were radicals in any sense of the word, nor could they have been and retained their positions. In the middle 1920's, during the administration of President Calles, there began the program of public works, and to a lesser extent irrigation, on the foundation of which much of Mexico's subsequent economic development rests. Then too were written the laws, pursuant to Article 27 of the relatively advanced Constitution of 1917, which were to guide the land reform until the 1940's. That article provided for expropriation of private lands in the public interest and for distribution of the land to neighboring villages, ranches, and communities whose supply of land is insufficient for their needs, "always respecting small property." Two important legal interpretations of this provision stand out: lands to be distributed to particular communities were to be taken from private properties exceeding certain sizes within a seven-kilometer radius of the communities; and a proportion of private land was to be expropriated corresponding to the increment in the land's value due to any irrigation or other improvements that may be undertaken by the state, thus preventing large landholders from becoming the favored beneficiaries of investments incurred at public expense.

Abroad, the Cárdenas administration (1934–40) may be best known for its expropriation of Mexico's privately owned petroleum, a step which was also provided for by the same Article 27 of the Constitution of 1917. But still more important domestically, the administration of President Cárdenas expropriated and redistributed more land than all other administrations, before and since, put together. Pursuant to the Constitution and the laws of the Calles administration, these lands were taken from the territories surrounding particular villages and were ceded to them communally as *ejidos*, to be worked in some cases collectively but in most cases individually. An *ejido* bank was established to provide the new owners with agricultural credit. Irrigation and other capital investment in agriculture was not, however, expanded at the same time. In fact, in retrospect it is clear that, although he undoubtedly had his heart in the right place, Cárdenas, as head of a bourgeois government, did not provide Mexican peasant agriculture with nearly enough resources to get it over the hump into self-sustained development.

From a careful study of the Bajio region of Central Mexico a decade after Cárdenas, the following findings, which are not unrepresentative for Mexico as a whole, emerge about the relative resource endowments of *ejido* and small private agriculture. (I shall turn to the discussion of large-scale agriculture when I come to the postwar period.) Relative to private farmers, *ejidatarios* have less land (3.8 as against 16.5 hectares per man); more third-quality and less first-quality land; less education (about one-tenth of their school-age children in primary school as against one-half for the private farmers); more reliance on family and female labor; female labor employed relatively more in cultivation and less in administration; less reliance on outside and permanently hired labor; more unemployment (85 percent of the total); less investment in irrigation (private farmers have 35 percent more irrigated surface and use 65 percent more water); less capital (40 percent of the amount that private owners have, although there are three times as many *ejidatarios*); more dependence on almost exclusively public credit and outside capital supplies, while private farmers have access to a much larger supply of private credit.

With such handicaps, it is perhaps no wonder that many *ejidatarios* have been unable to provide themselves with a decent living. Indeed, in several respects the situation is even worse than that described, and it appears that the political and economic structure that emerged from the Revolution was not really designed to, and does not, permit the large mass of peasants to share in its economic fruits. We should remember that more than a million, now approaching two million, rural family heads remain entirely landless.

Public agricultural credit accounts for no more than a third of all agricultural credit, and about half of that is supplied not by the Ejido Bank but by the Agricultural Bank, which lends to large private landholders. Oscar Lewis quotes the research director of the Ejido Bank: "We lend to about one-third of all *ejidatarios*, those that have the richest and best lands. We prefer risks that have fertile soil and preferably irrigation. We do not have enough money for loans to subsistence farmers, most of whom have the poorest lands." But private credit reaches the *ejidatario* still less; and much of it, like the 2.5 billion pesos annually lent to cotton growers by the American concern of Anderson and Clayton (compared to the 1.5 billion pesos lent by the Ejido Bank to all *ejidatarios* combined), is earmarked for special purposes.

For lack of working capital, many *ejidatarios* have found it necessary to lease their newly won land to private holders in command of capital and then to turn around and work for these capitalist farmers as hired laborers on their *own* land. Other *ejidatarios* and landless peasants, as is well known, find it necessary each year to migrate to the United States by the hundreds of thousands to work as migratory agricultural laborers there; or they emigrate to the growing city slums in search of work.

How then, we may well ask, has Mexico been able to show the increases of agricultural and industrial output that were cited previously, if it now appears that the economic condition of the bulk of her population has scarcely improved? Much of the answer emerges from the data collected by Paul L. Yates for his important study of regional economic development in Mexico. After the expiration of Cárdenas's term in the Presidency, and particularly with the accession of Miguel Alemán between 1946 and 1952, the bulk of investment went into the North and the Federal District. As we have already noted, the seven Northern states have traditionally had less of the total population, a lower population density, and a smaller percentage of the labor force engaged in agriculture than the heart of Mexico. While per capita investment remained well under 1,000 pesos for the period 1946–55 in the ten least favored states, it rose to well above 5,000 in the seven Northern states and the Federal District. The difference in funds devoted to irrigation between the North and the rest of the country is even more striking, with 60 percent of all irrigation investment between 1947 and 1958 going to the three states, Baja California del Norte, Sonora, and Tamaulipas alone. As a result, much of the increase in Mexico's sown area was concentrated in the relatively less populated North as well. The same area also absorbed the bulk of the increase of agricultural credit and virtually all mechanized farm equipment (an increase in the number of tractors from 4,620 in 1940 to 55,000 in 1955) that was not devoted to the production of sugar, another non-subsistence crop, in the South. Not one tractor was used on any of the million small holdings in 1950. Not surprisingly, agricultural output (though not income) rose in the North to state averages of 12,000, 20,000, and even 34,000 pesos per agricultural worker in 1960; while it remained at levels of 2,000 and 3,000 pesos in the older states.*

This growth in agricultural output, however, was concentrated in industrial crops, principally cotton, whose production rose 309 percent between 1939 and 1954, while that of food crops rose only 113 percent. Moreover, the bulk of these crops—cotton, vegetables, sugar (Center and Yucatan), coffee (Chiapas), and livestock—were destined for export to the North American market. The earnings from this agricultural export were used variously: some were ploughed back into the same export agriculture; some were invested in industry; some were consumed (we will turn later to the resulting distribution of income); and some, unfortunately for Mexico as for other countries exporting primary goods, were left in the importing country because of the decline, particularly after the Korean War, of raw material prices relative to those of industrial goods.

The exigencies of World War II had given impetus to domestic expansion of industry in Mexico as elsewhere in the underdeveloped world. Further industrialization was promoted by Alemán and his successors. Investment in industry and commerce had also been guided into the same eight favored states, with particular concentrations, of course, in the Federal District and Nuevo Leon, the sites of Mexico City and Monterrey. The older, more populated states were left largely unaffected and far behind. A significant portion of the investment funds, and particularly of the necessary foreign exchange, was undoubtedly contributed by the earnings from agricultural exports as well as from the rapid increase of tourism in Mexico and migrant *bracero* labor to the United States. But simultaneously, American direct investment, which had fallen to the Depression and post-petroleum-nationalization low of $267 million in 1939, began a rapid increase and now surpasses the $1 billion mark, or about one-tenth of U.S. investment in Latin America. This American investment has displayed a relative shift away from "social overhead" capital and into manufacturing and trade, so that in 1953, of the thirty-one com-

* One U.S. dollar equals 12.5 pesos.

panies with a gross annual income exceeding 100 million pesos, nineteen were U.S.-owned or controlled, five were in the hands of the Mexican government, and only seven were private domestic firms. Moreover, since the ownership certificates of Mexican enterprises are bearer and not name bonds and shares, and since after issuance these certificates typically tend to gravitate into the hands where capital is already concentrated, it is not always easy to determine where ownership, and particularly control, lies. Thus, U.S. control of Mexican industry today may well be close to 50 percent. Against this background, it is not surprising to hear the Mexican Chamber of Manufacturing Industries say that "the economic power of these large foreign enterprises constitutes a serious threat to the integrity of the nation and to the liberty of the country to plan its own economic development."

In Mexican agriculture as well, American capital plays a significant role. Although Americans no longer own large tracts of land, as they still do in Central America, the American cotton monopoly, Anderson and Clayton, as already noted, distributes about $200 million of credit for the production of cotton from sowing to shipping. Therewith it effectively determines the buyer and the price for the cotton and prevents Mexico from disposing of a large part of her cotton crop where and when it might wish. And worse, as we shall see below, this arrangement contributes to the maintenance of monoculture and a plantation economy using hired labor in large parts of the North. With good reason, "Mexicans are beginning to wonder whether they are returning to the days of Porfirio Díaz."

The relative effects of events since World War II on the Mexican South and North have already emerged from the foregoing discussion. They are perhaps best summarized by indexes of social welfare presented in the table below.

But much of the detail of the emerging allocation of resources and distribution of income remains hidden behind the regional averages to which the table is necessarily limited. To expose more, it is necessary to inquire into the organization of political and economic power and how it has developed since the days of Cárdenas. When Alemán launched his campaign of large-scale irrigation and industrialization, he also introduced some legal changes.

*Regional Differences in Economic Development in the Eight*

| | General Economic Indices | | | | Agriculture | | |
| | 51 | 85 | 83 | 104 | 71 | 54 | 104 |
| | *% labor force in agriculture, 1950* | *Total accum. invest. 1946–55, $/cap.* | *Invest. in infrastruct., 1946–55, $/cap.* | *GNP/cap, nat. av. = 100* | *Total invest. irrigat. $/cap. of 1950 labor force 1947–58* | *Agric. output per worker in ag., 1960, in pesos* | *Agric. productivity nat. average = 100* |
| | 1 | 2 | 3 | 4 | 5 | 6 | 7 |
|---|---|---|---|---|---|---|---|
| Baja Calif. Norte | 46 | 7900 | 3200 | 313 | 1300 | 34000 | 705 |
| Dist. Federal | 5 | 7000 | | 261 | | 19000 | 392 |
| Sonora | 54 | 5000 | 2800 | 167 | 8250 | 20000 | 408 |
| Nuevo León | 41 | 5900 | | 186 | | | 101 |
| Baja Calif. Sur | 52 | 4500 | 2500 | 124 | 1390 | 12000 | 252 |
| Tamaulipas | 53 | 5600 | 1400 | 154 | 5020 | 12000 | 259 |
| Coahuila | 49 | 3300 | | 134 | <u>93</u> | 8000 | 168 |
| Chihuahua | 55 | 4000 | 1000 | 110 | | 8000 | 163 |
| | | | | | | | |
| Chiapas | 79 | 500 | 300 | 38 | | | 89 |
| Oaxaca | 78 | 900 | | 27 | <u>1420</u> | 2000 | 41 |
| Tabasco | 76 | 900 | | 40 | | | 83 |
| Tlaxcala | 70 | 900 | 500 | 36 | 52 | 2000 | 40 |
| Guerrero | 81 | 500 | 200 | 37 | 136 | 2500 | 70 |
| Hidalgo | 71 | | | 33 | | | 52 |
| Querétaro | 70 | 900 | 400 | 43 | 129 | 2400 | 50 |
| Guanajuato | | | 400 | 49 | | 3000 | 62 |
| Zacatecas | 79 | | | 46 | | 2000 | 51 |
| Michoacán | 73 | 1000 | | 36 | | | 66 |

*Source:* Paul L. Yates, *El Desarrollo Regional de México.* Ciphers at top refer to Yates for each column.

*Notes:* The eight favored states are all at the northern boundary of Mexico, except for the Federal District which is the site of the capital. Least-favored

*Most-Favored (top) and Ten Least-Favored (bottom) States*

| Industry and Commerce | | | | | Social Welfare | | | |
|---|---|---|---|---|---|---|---|---|
| 79 | 41 | 81 | 58 | 104 | 105 | 105 | 105 | 105 |
| *Invest. in industry 1946–55, $/cap.* | *Indust. output per cap. 1955, in pesos* | *Invest. in commerce 1946–55, $/cap.* | *Employmt. in services 1950, % labor force* | *Productivity in indust. nat. av. = 100* | *Mortality (reciprocal) nat. av. = 100* | *Running water nat. av. = 100* | *Literacy nat. av. = 100* | *General welfare nat. av. = 100* |
| 8 | 9 | 10 | 11 | 12 | 13 | 14 | 15 | 16 |
| 2640 | 1030 | 3200 | 38 | 149 | 160 | 127 | 145 | 204 |
| 4260 | 3420 | 2200 | 62 | 175 | 124 | 215 | 145 | 188 |
| 1190 | 825 | 1080 | 30 | 89 | 106 | 97 | 128 | 157 |
| 3960 | 2890 | 1380 | 32 | 206 | 136 | 115 | 139 | 144 |
| 1210 | 960 | 821 | 29 | 82 | 123 | 92 | 138 | 148 |
| 3390 | 1149 | 775 | 32 | 135 | 134 | 123 | 132 | 136 |
| 1580 | 1162 | 707 | 30 | 95 | 108 | 132 | 130 | 136 |
| 2020 | 1200 | 553 | 27 | 119 | 103 | 104 | 128 | 147 |
| 41 | 45 | 117 | 14 | 10 | 91 | 80 | 61 | 52 |
| 164 | 98 | 88 | 11 | 14 | 75 | 65 | 64 | 43 |
| 167 | 81 | | 17 | 20 | 95 | 45 | 102 | 70 |
| | | 44 | 15 | 44 | 83 | 66 | 97 | 60 |
| 162 | 114 | 137 | 11 | 24 | <u>115</u> | 75 | 55 | 58 |
| | 201 | 53 | 17 | 26 | 74 | 84 | 71 | 65 |
| | 261 | | | 37 | 83 | 81 | 62 | 70 |
| | | | 17 | 51 | 82 | 76 | 77 | 65 |
| 269 | | 113 | 12 | 84 | 107 | 70 | 105 | 56 |
| 320 | 149 | 110 | 16 | 24 | 115 | 90 | 80 | 72 |

states are in the center and south. Blank spaces and underlining indicate that the particular state is not in the most- or least-favored group for that category, i.e., exceptions to pattern. Column 16 is Yates' composite of mortality, literacy, running water, sugar, gasoline, electric consumption, etc.

Recall the two provisions of Article 27 of the Constitution that have already been cited in discussing the administrations of Presidents Calles and Cárdenas. These provisions, referring to the distribution of land as *ejidos* contiguous to the communities that were to receive them and allowing expropriation only with due respect to small property, were to receive, under the guidance of Alemán, a significance quite contrary to what they had had before—and quite other, one might suspect, from what the framers of the Constitution had intended.

With respect to the first provision, it must be remembered that the Northern states are sparsely populated and contain vast areas in which there were no settled communities. When lands in such areas were opened to cultivation through irrigation, Article 27 was interpreted as excluding, or at least not requiring, their distribution as *ejidal* lands. At the same time, the Constitutional provision for due regard to "small property" now came, under a Law of Inaffectability, to be interpreted as excluding 100 hectares of irrigated, 150 hectares of ordinary, and more of grazing land from expropriation. Accordingly, existing private owners of larger tracts of relatively worthless land in the North, on learning of prospective state irrigation projects in their areas, rushed to "sell" their holdings in plots of the minimum inaffectable acreage to all available members of their families. The result was twofold: not only did they retain effective control of much of their lands—as an example, the son of a revolutionary general and president, himself now governor of a Northern state, is reputed to own 3,000 hectares of irrigated land in three estates—but they also reaped the benefit of the always large and often astronomical increase in its value due to the state-financed irrigation. Thus, they rendered inoperative the letter and intent of the earlier Calles law which was meant to channel the benefits of state-financed irrigation to the public at large. Instead, under the Alemán law, their lands had become inalienable! The legal assessments to the private owners to siphon off the increase in land values were and are more often than not essentially disregarded. In this manner, according to the 1950 Census, while *ejidal* holdings increased 21 percent, and small private holdings increased 20 percent, the larger private landholdings rose by 48 percent; and the share of landholdings larger than five hectares in the total of all cropland rose from 39 percent to 43 percent. The real amount of land which is effectively in large holdings is, however, undoubtedly greater and unknown because the census classification cannot adequately distinguish between actually and fictitiously separate landholdings. The matter appears to be further complicated by the holdings of livestock grazing lands, and it is placed entirely beyond inspection if we refer to *values*, and their spectacular increase, rather than to mere acreage.

The foregoing events of the postwar years have had their inevitable effect on the socio-political and economic structure of the society and on the lives of the people within it. They have meant the growth of a neo-latifundia agriculture, no longer organized under the feudal hacienda system which uses serfs to produce for home consumption, but organized instead as latter-day plantations, run as capitalist enterprises by city-dwelling owners, hiring agricultural wage laborers, and producing non-subsistence and often single crops for export.

The Northern states have thus become magnets of in-migration of *ejidal* or landless peasants who leave their villages in the Center and South. This movement contributes somewhat to redressing the balance of income distribution, for the agricultural workers of the North are economically somewhat better off than their *ejidal* and landless brother in the South. The tabular index of social welfare in terms of regions, however, probably results in a considerable overstatement of the Northern advantage if it is read not as a regional but as a personal difference between the farmer North and South, for the regional figure is probably heavily weighted also by the income differential between bourgeois and peasant. A trip through the North readily suggests that large masses of its inhabitants are not sharing its prosperity.

The new private landowners, large and small, and some of the old ones as well, are or are becoming bourgeois in every sense of the word. Even the smaller landowners among them, if they have any capital, have a position and income which affords them a middle-class style of life, and often urban life at that. Their agricultural business often affords them a handsome income, which they dispose of sometimes by real investment in Mexico, sometimes by investment abroad, sometimes by constructing and speculating in urban real estate, or luxury imports. And they have power, economic and political. They and their industrial, commercial, and sometimes professional brethren essentially own and run the state. Beginning particularly during the administration of Alemán, they have, as we have seen in part, been able to use that state to pull themselves up by their bootstraps. But it has not, so far, been their interest to pull the peasantry up behind them. Is it any wonder that, according to Mrs. Navarete's recent study of income distribution, the share of the total national income going to the richest 20 percent of families rose from 59.8 percent in 1950 to 61.4 percent in 1957, while that of the poorest 50 percent dropped from 18.1 percent to 15.6 percent?

It remains to ask how the "Mexican System" works today under the administration of President Lopez Mateos and what its prospects for the future are. Mexico is a social and economic pyramid, with a political pyramid inside. At the bottom are the indigenous Indians, remaining where they always were. In the next layer are the landless rural people and the unemployed or only occasionally employed urban ones. The latter, particularly, are a veritable lumpenproletariat, dispossessed by the rural and unabsorbed by the urban economy, living on the margin of society, isolated and alienated from it, from each other, and often from themselves. Next come the *ejidatarios* and such private small holders as are poor enough to work their land by themselves. Although economically more secure, they stand socially sometimes even below the marginal urban people, perhaps because the *chances* for social mobility are greater for the latter. Above them are the workers in the narrower sense of the word, particularly the unionized ones, who in Mexico as in many parts of Latin America, Asia, and Africa today comprise a sort of "aristocracy of the proletariat." The next layer may be termed the middle class or petty bourgeoisie. It comprises a large variety of economic walks of life—small landowner, professional, merchant, clergy, government and white collar worker, small politician—but it affords considerable lateral mobility within it, from one occupation to another. Their badge in Mexico is dark glasses as it is a briefcase in Eastern Europe, however dark it may be outside or however few papers there may be to carry. And that badge is a counterweight to the sometimes higher income of the workers below them. The bourgeois upper class, the principal manipulators and beneficiaries of the system, includes the large landholders, the effective directors of the financial, commercial, industrial, professional, governmental, and military apparatuses, and by *noblesse oblige* some intellectuals. The viable economic base of the more aristocratic upper class was destroyed by the Revolution. But many of its members and their wealth survived. Their money was invested in finance, commerce, industry, and later again agriculture; and the ex-aristocrats became the nucleus of the new bourgeoisie. Their ranks were soon supplemented by their erstwhile enemies, the individual beneficiaries of the same Revolution, many politicians and generals among them. As their economic position became consolidated, so did their political power—exercised through the PRI, the all-powerful Institutional Revolutionary Party through which they have managed Mexico's political, and thereby indirectly economic, life for the past generation. It is the PRI which allocates the presidency and other principal political offices (to its faithful), and not the electoral mechanism; and management and control of the PRI, in turn, by no means extends down to the bottom of the social and economic pyramid.

But Mexico's pyramid is not static; it is not a caste system, as for example that of Peru substantially remains; there is mobility. There are economic, political, and social paths which afford opportunities—or, maybe better, chances—for higher rank to those who play according to the rules of the game. There is the migration from Center and South to the North, involving not only geographical movement but also economic improvement coupled with some severance of communal ties and participation in a looser society. There is the very substantial rural-urban migration, especially to Mexico City which grew from 1.4 million and 7 percent of the population in 1940 to over 4 million and 13 percent today. Of course, such migration offers no guarantee of social or economic success, but it increases the statistical chances for the migrant. There is movement into white or off-white collar jobs and various kinds of speculation around the loose ends of a growing economy. And, of course, there is education and "suitable" marriage for those who can manage it. These two are perhaps the most important vehicles for the social and economic migrant himself, and virtually guarantee mobility to his children.

Social mobility, however, is individual-by-individual. Individuals, some of them, are permitted, indeed encouraged, to "better themselves," but within the system and according to its rules. In fact, the "System" and the Party co-opt people into their ranks to obviate their rocking the boat. Perhaps most symbolic of this process is the recent invitation by President Lopez Mateos to the seven living ex-Presidents, and their acceptance, to join his administration in semi-official, semi-honorary positions, a step that was taken to help stabilize the political situation in Mexico "after Cuba." In more pedestrian ways, labor leaders, popularly called *charros*, are co-opted into the business system and rewarded, to keep unions from rocking the boat. Even young Marxists can hope to attain positions of responsibility in later years and may therefore turn to defend the system. Indeed, the Mexican Communist Party is sometimes called Mexico's leading school for conservatives. Most important, the social structure and its mythology have given the lower-middle class, and even people in the lower class, the feeling that it is possible to rise up, partly in and partly with, the system.

While mobility individual-by-individual is permitted, mobility by group is not. If group pressure begins to build up anywhere in the politico-economic system, the first step, as suggested above, is to co-opt or recruit away the leadership. Additionally, small concessions may be used to abate the pressure and take the wind out of the movement's sails. Thus, for instance, the price of corn (*maiz*) and movies (!) is subsidized in the City of Mexico, some will say to help the poor and others to ward off popular unrest. Similarly, after substantial popular pressure had built up, President Lopez Mateos recently created some livestock *ejidos* in the North; however, he has yet to grant a single acre of irrigated land to an *ejido*. If these measures are not successful, the government finally resorts to repression. Strikes, particularly those with political overtones, such as those of the most militant among unions, the railroad workers' three years ago, and the teachers' last year, have been severely dealt with. Particularly since the increase of liveliness in political life and the full-scale introduction of the Cold War after the Cuban Revolution, left-wing labor leaders and others have increasingly found themselves sitting in jail. To prove that no one, no matter what his status, is immune from this fate, Mexico's most famous living painter, the sixty-five-year-old internationally known David Alfaro Siqueiros and his seventy-three-year-old friend, the noted journalist Filomena Mata, are in jail on eight-year (!) sentences for allegedly having caused the teachers' union, of which they are not even members, to go on strike. The official charge is threatening "social dissolution," whatever that may mean. On the other hand, rightist influence, even on the part of the Church, whose wings had been clipped 100 and again 50 years ago, has been steadily growing and consolidating itself.

Thus the System offers glory to some individuals, bread and circuses, often more circuses than bread, to the masses—supposedly ample rewards for repudiating militant leadership. Occasional economic, but no political concessions, are offered when necessary, and repression is resorted to if all else fails. On the whole, the System seems to work quite well: it is significant that Mexico devotes only 8 percent of her national budget to the army, compared to Colombia's 30 percent or Haiti's 45 percent; only relatively middle-class Costa Rica among the Latin American countries spends less. But it is also true that the System withholds real participation and benefits from the bulk of the Mexican people.

What are the prospects for the future? Industrialization, rapid as it has been, education, capitalization of agriculture, public works, and other "modernization" measures have not so far been sufficient really to absorb the population increase, let alone greatly to raise the economic level of the peasant base. Moreover, the present government has reduced Alemán's annual irrigation expenditures by nearly half; and the spectacular 8–10 percent rate of GNP increase of the mid-1950's has steadily declined to an alarming zero percent last year. With the existing economic organization and structure of bourgeois political and economic power, and the relative increase of private over public investment in recent years, there is enough reason to doubt that the Mexican economy will soon afford the bulk of its people a significantly better standard of life. It certainly does not promise the economic and cultural advances shown in this century, and particularly since World War II by the socialist countries. Yet, as we have seen, the System does lumber along, as those of Guatemala, Peru, yes, of Venezuela and Colombia, to say nothing of several other Latin American countries, no longer do. And it makes adjustments here and there. As the economy proceeds by co-optation, so does the political system and its political party, only more so. Nothing seems to be possible working from outside the PRI; and everything that is possible can be attained only by joining and working through the PRI. The office of the President is all-powerful no matter who fills it: it is more than a literary or journalistic quirk that Mexicans have transformed the names of their Presidents into nouns and adjectives for use in referring to their administrations, nay epochs. And an ex-President counts for no more than anyone else without political access to the current incumbent.

Thus, although Cárdenas, apparently spurred on by the Cuban Revolution, recently emerged from twenty-year political retirement to join younger men in founding the MLN (National Liberation Movement) which is designed to mobilize and unify Mexico's political Left, he nevertheless accepted the invitation to ex-Presidents to join the López Mateos administration along with his more conservative colleagues. It is no wonder the Left is disunited, nay fractionated; and the birth of the MLN is maybe more a sign of the need for unity on the Left than of its achievement. At the same time, the current wave of government repression against the Left need not mean a permanent move to the Right. As Latin America as a whole moves further to the Left in the coming years, the pressure on Mexico may become so great the Mexican Left will again have its day (helped along by U.S. repressive acts designed to prevent it)—but working within and through the PRI. Pablo González Casanova, dean of the always progressive School of Political and Social Sciences at the National University and prominent member of the MLN suggests: "We think that General Lázaro Cárdenas has indicated the right road: support the institution and organize the people."

It is easy to concur with this judgment. But organize the people for what? Only to wrest the control of their destinies away from the bourgeoisie and the PRI? While the Mexican people "organize," other Latin Americans will inevitably make revolutions far more radical than that of Mexico. As the Cuban Revolution has already done, these revolutions abroad will just as inevitably sharpen the antagonisms between the Left and Right in Mexico itself. Any short-run, moderate gains the Mexican Left can achieve within the present system by riding on the wave of social revolution among her neighbors, can only postpone the day when the Mexican Left must radically break the power of the bourgeoisie, and begin itself to direct Mexico's destiny.

## A Note on Sources

This essay was based in part on personal observation and inquiry and in part on published materials. In addition to Mexican newspapers and such U.S. press organs as the *New York Times* and *Time* magazine, the following were the chief sources relied upon:

Pablo González Casanova, "México: El Ciclo de una Revolución Agraria," *Cuadernos Americanos* (Jan.–Feb., 1962).

Carlos Manuel Castillo, "La Economía Agrícola e la Región del Bajío," *Problemas Agrícolas e Industriales*, Vol. VIII, Nos. 3–4, 1956.

Oscar Lewis, "Mexico Since Cárdenas," in Richard N. Adams et al., *Social Change in Latin America Today: Its Implications for United States Policy* (New York: Vintage Books, 1961).

Paul Lamartine Yates, *El Desarrollo Regional de México* (Banco de México, 1961).

# 20

## THE MEXICAN DEMOCRACY OF PABLO GONZÁLEZ CASANOVA

[On August 7, 1965, the National School of Political Science of the National University of Mexico held a round-table discussion (in Spanish) of La Democracia en México, by the school's former director, Dr. Pablo González Casanova. The participants were Antonio Pérez Elias, Dr. Edmundo Flores, Dr. Andre Gunder Frank, and Enrique Semo. The following is a corrected transcription of the remarks by A. G. Frank.]

I would like to thank the organizers of this round-table discussion on La Democracia en México for inviting me, a foreigner; and I wish to congratulate Dr. Pablo González Casanova for having written a book of such importance, not only for Mexicans but also for all who are interested in economic development in the underdeveloped countries. With his book Dr. González Casanova has joined outstanding authors like Celso Furtado and Helio Jaguaribe of Brazil, Aldo Ferrer and Gino Germani of Argentina, Aníbal Pinto and Alberto Baltra of Chile, and others in Latin America who have been concerned with what, to use Juscelino Kubitchek's felicitous expression, we may call "developmentism" (desenvolvimentismo). I hope that this round table will be able to do justice to Dr. González Casanova's topic and argument, which are of extreme importance for all scientific students of economic underdevelopment and development. It is strictly within this scientific context that I shall attempt to examine them. I shall leave the examination of the political aspects to

1965. This essay originally appeared in Historia y Sociedad, Autumn 1965, as a review of Pablo González Casanova's book La Democracia en México.

318

my colleagues at this table who are surely better qualified to deal with these matters.

The essential structure and development of the book's arguments are, as I understand them, the following: The author begins on page 5 with the statement that he will deal with the problem of economic development and its possible solution. In the second part, and especially in Chapter 5, he formulates the idea that will serve as the foundation for all his subsequent discussion; that is, the idea of a plural or dual society. On page 69 he refers to two Mexicos, one marginal to the other—especially culturally but also socially and politically and with regard to access to consumer goods, as he seeks to demonstrate with much statistical data. Since he believes that Mexico's marginalism is based, in the first place, on differences in ethnicity and on a predominantly subsistence economy, the most marginal people are the Indians. His second essential point, which he believes is based on and intimately tied to the first, is the fact of internal colonialism: there are two Mexicos and one colonizes the other.

The thesis culminates in Part IV. Here one finds the third essential point which also constitutes the key leading to all later conclusions. This point, affirmed on page 135, reiterated on page 138, and again on page 145, is that Mexico is not a capitalist country, but merely a pre- or semi-capitalist one. Besides attempting to base this affirmation on Marx, Engels, and Lenin, the author says that the characterization of Mexico as pre-capitalist is confirmed by two facts: (1) that internal colonialism exists here, and (2) that the bourgeoisie has not succeeded in imposing total domination and does not satisfactorily confront foreign domination. Therefore, Dr. González Casanova cannot find a fully developed capitalism in Mexico—as he says on page 136—as long as there is internal colonialism and as long as Mexico does not reach a level of relative equality with the United States. Hence, the author's conclusion that the two most opposing philosophies of our time, the Marxist and the liberal, point to —I quote—"one and the same path: the development of capitalism. Both have the same objective; the question is one of methods." The problem is, says the author on page 146, whether the bourgeoisie can triumph, whether the government can take

the route toward capitalism. Although on page 147 he mentions that in this regard there are some favorable and some
unfavorable conditions, the author ends the chapter on the
following page without telling us what these conditions might
be and, even less, if or why the conditions favorable to capitalist
development carry more weight than the unfavorable ones. In
his last chapter, he merely points out that some obstacles still
remain on the road to democracy, such as the plural society,
traditionalism, and political authoritarianism over the poor. All
in all, he assures us that, nonetheless, the probability of democracy
is increasing and that some North Americans have demonstrated
it statistically. And with this his analysis and argument ends.

After demonstrating that Mexico is not capitalist, he maintains that everybody, the proletarian and the consistent Marxist
specifically, becomes, along with the North American sociologist,
an ally of the bourgeoisie and that they are in agreement as to
the one and only road indicated by the author. This is: capitalist
economic development under the leadership of an as yet not
fully developed bourgeoisie. But the author does not indicate
whether this road is, or how it could be, feasible. Pablo González
Casanova leaves us the task of responding to this most important
question on the basis of a theoretical and empirical examination
of reality. I shall try to answer, to the extent that I am able,
by comparing the structure of historical and present-day reality
with the structure of the arguments in this book.

The second part of the book, which constitutes 40 percent
of the text, is devoted to those factors—dual society, internal
colonialism, and the strong links between the two—which provide
the foundation for the conclusion. Here we must first ask how
can this be. How can the 10–25 percent of the population of the
country live entirely on the margin in one Mexico—in a dual
society, as the author maintains—and at the same time be colonized by the other Mexico? How can there be a dual society
with internal colonialism? It is impossible. So, from the very
beginning, the basic thesis of this book involves a contradiction.
And if the reality were truly as described, it would present quite
a paradox. But when we examine true historical and current
reality, something which the book does not do despite its mass

of statistics, we see that the apparent paradox disappears and the contradiction is placed in even greater relief.

Reality resolves the paradox for two reasons: first, because in reality neither the dual society nor marginalism exist as the author affirms; second, because the internal colonialism which in reality exists is very different from that upon which the book bases its argument.

The sad truth is that with the arrival of Cortés a single and integral society was rapidly formed—totally integrated, furthermore, into the world system of mercantilist expansion and capitalist development; and this was nonetheless so because of the mere fact that some exploited others. Allow me to cite two statements that give the flavor of the beginnings of this history and contemporary reality. The first quote is from Hernán Cortés. As soon as he arrived here he declared that the Spaniards had a disease of the heart for which the specific remedy was gold. (To be sure, a little later they found another remedy: silver.)

The second quotation is from the contemporary historian José Miranda, analyzing the *encomienda* in New Spain:

The tribute given to the *encomenderos*, material and labor, constituted, in the early times of the colony, the fundamental basis of their enterprises. Both the capital and the labor that they utilized in order to strengthen the colonial economy were derived in large measure from tribute. . . . The *encomendero* invested his tribute in enterprises of all kinds: mining, agriculture, cattle, industry, and commerce. But the most concentrated investment, as is logical, was in mining and next, in cattle. . . . The *encomendero* is, above all, a man of his time, motivated by the hunger for riches . . . thus the *encomendero* gives place of pride to the capitalist grant element of the *encomienda*, which is the only one which can bring him what he pursues so earnestly: wealth. . . . In the complicated mechanisms of his enterprises the *encomendero* was frequently caught up in a complicated web of economic and legal relations: participation in various mining companies . . . ownership of a hog farm or of a flock of sheep, pastured on the lands of another *encomendero* . . . under the care of a young Spaniard . . . , and all this after having given general authority to a relative, friend, or servant who would administer his *encomienda* and after having conferred special authority on others to govern his hacienda or livestock ranch, his shop or sugar mill . . . or the management of his interests where necessary.

After gold came silver. This was no longer mined through the institution of the *encomienda* but rather by the *repartimiento* (using forced labor) and afterward by day laborers or the so-called free workers who were tied to the mine or hacienda by debt. The institutions changed but not the essential structure of the system. The production of silver was the driving force of the entire economy; it increased in the sixteenth century, declined in the seventeenth, and rose again in the eighteenth. It led to the establishment of large towns in the center of the country and made world-famous the names of Guanajuato, Zacatecas, San Luis Potosí, and Pachuca, the present capital of the state of Hidalgo.

Now, let us see where our book locates the marginal population of the alleged "dual" society. On page 154 the author refers to the South and Center. On page 92 he refers, textually, to Chiapas, Oaxaca, Guerrero, Tlaxcala, Hidalgo, Guanajuato, San Luis, and Zacatecas. He makes note of various characteristics of the greater part of these regions: on page 30, *caciquismo*; on page 109, the spoils system; on page 39, Catholicism and fanatic anti-communism; on page 92, poverty—all according to a pattern —and on page 154, the supposed reason for all this: "The market economy does not yet prevail." All true, except for the last point, which turns truth on its head, just as, according to Marx, Hegel had done. On the contrary, the center of the country, far from being outside the market, was, together with the capital, the most integrated and important part of the market economy: it was truly the heart and the blood supply, not only for the regional or national market, but for the world market. However, this came to an end and these ultradeveloped regions fell into decline, backwardness, and underdevelopment. It is an old story. It occurred and is occurring in Northeast Brazil and the Antilles, with their sugar; in Minas Gerais, the Peruvian Sierra, and Central Mexico, with their mines. All these areas are ultra-underdeveloped today, all are regions in which *caciquismo* flourishes—called *gamonalismo* in Peru and *coronelismo* in Brazil—

all are regions of the spoils system, of "Christianity yes, communism no," as they say in Minas Gerais where the *coup d'état* which brought the present military regime in Brazil to power originated. All this, not because the market-capitalism economy prevails, but because it had formerly prevailed, flourished, and fallen into decline in the normal, integral process of domestic and international capitalist development.

The task of scholar is not, as Pablo González Casanova claims, to take these facts as given or to attribute them to non-existent realities; the task is to look for their causes, to seek their explanations, just as Alexander Humboldt and Mariano Otero did in their time. Humboldt noted that "haciendas are being established near the mines . . . this influence from the mines on the growing decline of the country is more enduring than the haciendas themselves. When the veins are exhausted and mining is abandoned . . . the colonist remains sentimentally tied to the soil . . . both in early stages of civilization and in its decadence." Otero added that

> only the mines remain as an instrument of change. . . . Production has so diminished in this area of endeavor [mining] that today [1842] it amounts to scarcely half of what it was calculated to be by the scholar Baron Humboldt early in the century; the reduction in production, simultaneous with a tremendous increase in demand for luxury goods by the prosperous classes, has had truly terrible consequences. . . . Its principal cause is found in the ruinous and decadent state of trade or commerce in products, in a country where everything remains to be done. . . . This explains the lack of progress in agriculture; a stagnant commerce . . . the decline in agriculture, and the bankruptcy of most of its capital.

The miserable state of the country's central regions is not, of course, due to an alleged dualism and marginalism that supposedly means "the market economy [does] not yet prevail," as Dr. González Casanova maintains; but, as was pointed out by the scholar Humboldt and the progressive Otero, it is due to their integral incorporation in the unequal and contradictory development of the system of global and national capitalism.

Enough said concerning the center of the country; let us pass to the south.

Allow me to cite again: first, Dr. Stavenhagen of this School:

> The colonial system functioned, in effect, on two levels. The economic restrictions and prohibitions that Spain imposed on its colonies existed, but were many times worse, in the relations between the colonial world and the indigenous communities. The colony exercised over the indigenous communities the same commercial monopolies in production, the same political controls that Spain exercised over the colony. What Spain signified to the colony, the colony signified to indigenous communities: a colonial metropolis. It was then that mercantilism began penetrating the most isolated countries of New Spain.

The world metropolis converted the capital of this country and many others into satellites, and these, as national metropolises, in their turn converted the provinces into satellites. Thus, the national and international mercantilist system penetrated the most isolated and remote corner of the world and incorporated it fully into the system. As Humboldt observed:

> The more isolated the site of the hacienda, the more attraction it held for the mountain inhabitants. . . . Man appears to regret the subjection he has imposed on himself on entering society. . . . Long and sad experiences have disgusted him with social life. . . . The peoples of the Aztec race appear to live on the crests and slopes of the steepest mountains. This specific aspect of their customs contributes uniquely to the spread of the population in the most mountainous region of the kingdom of Mexico.

But, as we shall see, not even thus can they succeed in escaping. There is no such thing as a "dual" society.

If the Indians found themselves incorporated into the colonist system of the colony, were they "marginal" when mercantilism was converted into the current capitalist system? The National Indian Institute gives us the answer, not only for the post-Independence period, but also for the present period, after the Mexican Revolution of 1910:

> In reality the Indians rarely lived isolated from the mestizo or national population; among both population groups a symbiosis ex-

isted which must of necessity be taken into account. Among the mestizos, residents of the nuclear city of the region, and the Indian inhabitants of the peasant hinterland there is, in fact, a closer economic and social interdependence than that which might appear at first glance. . . . The mestizo population, in effect, always resides in a city, center of an intercultural region, which acts as a metropolis for an Indian region and maintains, together with the underdeveloped communities, an intimate connection which links the center with the satellite communities. The Indian or folk community [which was studied] was an interdependent part of a whole that functioned as a unit, in such a way that the actions taken in one part inevitably had repercussions on the others, and, consequently, on the whole. It was not possible to consider the community separately; one had to take into account the totality of the intercultural system of which it formed a part. . . . The perseverance of the great Indian mass in their situation of ancestral subordination, possessing a strongly stabilized folk culture, was not only desired by the city, but was even imposed by coercive methods. . . . In Ciudad de las Casas one sees even more clearly the control exercised by the *ladinos* over economic and political spheres and over property in general.

In a study the National Indian Institute made in the Tlaxiaco region, in the state of Oaxaca, the author, Alejandro Marroquín, points to some of the traits that characterize

the Indian or folk community [that] was an interdependent part of a whole that functioned as a unit: between the producer and the consumer seven pairs of hands were interposed which caused a rise in prices of eggs from .16 to .50—that is, more than 300 percent. Indian products reaching Tlaxiaco are then dispersed to the great urban centers of the country; but in their brief passage through Tlaxiaco they have contributed to the strengthening of the commercial sector of the town; the profit, extracted in parasite fashion from the hunger and poverty of the Indian, consolidates the power and concentric strength of Tlaxiaco, as the fundamental nucleus of the Mixteca region's economy: (1) the complete predominance of the mercantile capitalist system; (2) intense competitive struggle, as befits any capitalist economic system; (3) powerful influence of the distribution monopolies; (4) extensive network of intermediaries, which constitutes a heavy burden on the Indian economy; (5) parasitic aspect of the Tlaxiaco economy based on the exploitation of the Indian's underpaid labor. Conclusions: First, the economic concentration and centralization observed in Tlaxiaco has given rise to a notable contrast between the relatively opulent life of the city and the poor and wretched existence of the people of the district; that contrast manifests itself within the city itself, as well as between the scattered communities of the rural periphery and the urban nucleus of the center. Second, the city takes advantage of its privileged situation in respect to transportation facilities in order to exploit the Indian towns and communities. This engenders a profound contradiction between the urban nucleus and the rest of the district. Third, the agrarian reform of the Revolution broke the socioeconomic equilibrium of the peoples, after the disappearance of the hacienda, which had been the center of gravity of the former social system. . . . The store belonging to the large urban merchant became the new center of gravity of the region; the large merchant took on the patriarchal role that formerly belonged to the *hacendado*; the large merchant . . . then exploits and takes advantage of the production of the Indians. . . . Fifth, by its very economic structure Tlaxiaco is not a homogeneous whole; it is divided into social sectors and classes with relatively and increasingly antagonistic interests. Sixth, the new transport lines constructed during the past ten years have profoundly altered Tlaxiaco's economy. Its most important effects are: (1) ruin or decadence of most crafts and trades, such as the manufacture of candles and soap, mule driving, the textile industry, etc.; (2) a powerful stimulus to the making and consumption of alcohol; (3) the formation of an important new economic center: Chalcatongo; (4) the development of an artificial economy in Tlaxiaco, since this city, by not producing what it consumes, gave rise to the function of the intermediary, of distribution and concentration of products; (5) and lastly, the new transportation facilities made Tlaxiaco accessible to the representatives of the big monopolists of Mexico City, who pushed out the local monopolists, caused the cost of living to rise and, at the same time, indulging in large-scale speculative maneuvers, to the detriment of the Indian population.

What do we learn from this account? Many realities and truths that go unrecognized or are denied by the thesis presented in Pablo González Casanova's *La Democracia en México*. In the first place: the fact that there is no "dual" society. The Indians are not outside the market economy, nor were they ever, and they do not live in a subsistence economy. When they do not produce for the market, it is because it is not to their advantage to do so. When the price of coffee drops—due to the international price, monopolist manipulation, and local speculation—to the point where the Indian of Chiapas can buy only one kilo of maize for each kilo of coffee that he harvests, it is logical that he will cease to produce coffee and become a producer of maize; that is, he will become a *marginal*, so-called subsistence, peasant. Even so, he will not succeed in subsisting because he still lacks land and is obliged to produce straw hats and other commercial products, to work on the farms owned by others in Chiapas or far away in California, in order to buy the few goods he can, at high prices in the monopolized market. The other alternative for these "marginal ones" is to emigrate to Mexico City or to the northern states, where they can produce goods for the national or United States market, and where they will serve the local bourgeoisie as a source of cheap labor. Logically, the bulk of the emigration from the above-mentioned states (with the exception of Chiapas when the coffee crop is good), is considered by González Casanova to be marginal to the national economy and to be to places where "the market economy does not yet prevail." In spite of his broadness of outlook, Dr. González Casanova does not see the "whole that functions as a unit," which, as the National Indian Institute points out, "must be taken into account in its totality." Thus, the first lesson that this account offers us concerning "marginal communities," Indian or other, is that everything they are and the poverty in which they live are totally exclusively the product of their complete economic integration into the global and national system, under which they have lived since the Conquest. The ethnic traits and the low level of culture of these allegedly marginal people, which this book assumes as its point of departure, far from being a point of departure, or the real basis of their situation, is precisely the contrary—it is their "point of arrival," the product of domestic and foreign colonialism from which they suffer.

In the second place, facts reveal that internal colonialism really exists. But it is different from the "internal colonialism" that forms the basis of the book in question, in two highly important ways.

One is that this colonialism is essentially and primarily economic, and not cultural or social as the book claims. Although on pages 74–75 the author mentions the characteristics of decapitalization and exploitation, it is obvious that the essential skeleton of the argument and the dorsal column which leads from the base of the inter-ethnic dual society to its principal conclusion, is a so-called internal colonialism of cultural, social, political, and income differences, but not of *economic relations*. Reading the book demonstrates this, and the statistical appendix confirms it: not one of its sixty-five tables deals with these economic relationships, with decapitalization, exploitation, or real domestic colonialism.

The second point of difference between the so-called internal colonialism of this book and real internal colonialism, which exists here as it does in the other parts of the global capitalist system, is precisely that internal colonialism is part of and is intimately linked with external colonialism or imperialism. They are so closely linked that Mexico's "Fifty Years of Revolution" have not succeeded in breaking these links, which have existed since the Conquest and which have their roots in the structure and development of the global system itself, which was mercantilism and is now imperialism. The author is correct in saying that internal colonialism resembles foreign imperialism; but not because the foreign kind is· as inter-ethnic and cultural as he supposes the domestic kind to be, but because both colonialisms are essentially economic and still support each other mutually within the one and only world capitalist system.

This truth leads us to the third lesson of history and to an examination of the book's conclusion: We (in Mexico) live in a capitalist system, fully capitalist, with all the essential characteristics of the capitalist system, such as class structure, the colonialist metropolis-satellite structure, and contradictory and uneven development in which the metropolis develops at the expense of generating underdevelopment among its foreign and domestic satellites, and the bourgeoisie develops at the cost of exploiting the people. To call this system "pre-capitalist" as González Casanova wishes to do, so as to pave the way toward his conclusion and his political conceptions, is absolutely not scientifically acceptable, since it contravenes all empirical reality and theoretical procedure.

To maintain, as he does on page 136, that Mexico is pre-capitalist and will not be capitalist as long as there is domestic colonialism and as long as a relative degree of equality with the United States is not reached, is a theoretical absurdity and contradicts the sad empirical reality of a country, the United States, whose internal economic colonialism fills the world press with the demand, "Freedom Now," one hundred years after the emancipation of the black population that constitutes 10 percent of the population (just as 10 percent of the population of Mexico is Indian) and with President Johnson's promise of the "Great Society" for the 25 percent of the North Americans who, according to his statistics, live in the "other America" (and correspond to the 25 percent of "marginal Mexicans" mentioned by Pablo González Casanova).

The two primary facts on which the author bases his thesis that Mexico is not capitalist—its economic weakness and its internal colonialism—far from confirming his thesis, are precisely the two facts that have generated capitalist underdevelopment in Mexico. We saw that an entire series of chains of metropolises and satellites that begin in the world metropolis, now imperialist, cut across national, regional, and local capitals, and even incorporate the most isolated Indian of the so-called subsistence economy. Each metropolis colonized and continues to exploit its satellites monopolistically; these latter, in turn, exploit their own satellites. The world metropolis, which is nobody's satellite, underwent so-called classical capitalist development. In each national metropolis this type of "classical" development could not and still cannot manifest itself precisely because its development is limited by its condition as satellite to the world imperialist metropolis. It is a limited development or an underdeveloped development and the major part of its development is due, not to aid from the world metropolis, as is frequently claimed, but to the exploitation of its proletariat and its national satellites, whose development, consequently, is even more limited and underdeveloped. Thus, internal and external colonialism, the "marginalism" of the benefits of capitalist development, and underdevelopment itself, do not cease to be part of capitalist development but, on the contrary, were and continue to be both the source and the fruit of this capitalist development. Thus, there also are no empirical and theoretical—that is, scientific—bases for maintaining or expecting that these character-istics will disappear thanks to any bourgeois policy of replacing a so-called pre-capitalism by a "classical" capitalism, even though it be state capitalism.

Nor does internal colonialism have, as is claimed on page 76, "an explicative function much broader than social classes." The structure of internal colonialism—and also of external colonialism and the imperialist system—does not replace the class structure but, rather, complements it. Thus, the theory of internal and foreign colonialism of the capitalist system cannot provide—as Pablo González Casanova attempts to convince us—an alternative to the theory of classes. On the contrary, the examination of the one and only metropolis-satellite structure, both international and national, throws into sharp relief the class structure in which the bourgeoisie is formed, develops fully or not, according to whether it is dominant or satellized, maintains itself economically on the basis of its exploitation of the people, both urban and rural, and therefore necessarily maintains itself and makes an effort polit-ically to preserve this same exploitative and underdevelopment-generating structure.

Lastly, the author's empirically and theoretically unfounded analysis of Mexico's domestic relations is intimately linked with his examination of foreign relations. On page 7 the author says: "We do not refer to the problem as 'imperialism' because this term is a loaded one in terms of values and leads us to lose the perspective of *national power*. We refer to what Perroux calls 'the effect of domination' by the big nations and big companies." The truth, unfortunately, is exactly the reverse. Not to take into ac-count the existence, structure, and development of imperialism, leads to a loss of global and scientific perspective which is neces-sary for an evaluation of the limits of national power.

The contradictions of the imperialist system limit even the na-tional power of its center, the United States, as we see today in Vietnam, Europe, the Negro problem, the balance of payments situation, etc. Even the economic strength of the big powers of Western Europe is increasingly weakened, vis-à-vis the United States. The March 8, 1965, edition of *Newsweek* informs us of the opinion of an Olivetti manager: "We devoted ourselves to a very careful study of a European solution, but even if we had combined with Machines Bull in France or with Siemens in Germany [which later signed an agreement with R.C.A., *Newsweek* adds], we still would be midgets in comparison with U.S. giants, who would, in the long run, have closed us down, in spite of everything. There is no European solution for these problems. Research costs are too high. The technological gap is a fact of life." *Newsweek* summarizes by saying that the powerful industrialized and developed powers of Western Europe suffer increasing "colonization, satellization, and servitude." If this is a fact of trans-Atlantic life, what will be the fate of the weak, semi-industrialized, underdeveloped economies of Latin America and their respective national bourgeoisies? This is not a matter, as Pablo González Casanova affirms, of mere effect of domination which permits one to see the "national power" which imperialism supposedly conceals. It is a matter of a global system whose contradictory structure, and unequal development for some at the expense of others, inevitably benefits some at the expense of others; it is a system in which monopoly—to be based increasingly on technology in the future—exercises control over even the most powerful bourgeoisies. Argentina, the first Latin American country to attempt industrialization in this century had this experience more than a decade ago. Brazil had it last year (1964). Mexico is the third country to try.

First in Argentina and now in Brazil, the difficulties in which the bourgeoisie found itself, because of this and other events, did not lead to a democratization of the country; less yet did they lead to a limit on the exploitation of its people. On the contrary, as we witness the cruel and dramatic evidence in Brazil today, this process and the lowering of profits obliged the bourgeoisie to try to maintain its accustomed diet, reverting to an even greater degree of exploitation of the urban and salaried workers, to an increasingly acute domestic colonialism, and to "gorilla democracy." Where then is the national power that can make a poor pre-capitalist country independent, that can decolonize and democratize it?

In conclusion, I frankly do not know how to characterize Dr. González Casanova's attempt, on page 135, to call on the authority of Engels and Lenin in defense of the thesis of the existence of pre-capitalism and of the non-existence of imperialism here. But after an examination of the author's argument and of Mexico's reality, we know that the attempt to base one's arguments on the alleged existence of a "dual" society, on the so-called internal colonialism, and on the "effect of domination" itself, in order to maintain the claim that the historical development and the present underdevelopment of Mexico is "pre-capitalist" and not capitalist is empirically erroneous, theoretically illogical, and consequently, scientifically totally unacceptable.

This empirical, analytical, and theoretical basis for the affirmation on page 145 that, for the workers and peasants of Mexico who lack class consciousness because they live in a pre-capitalist country, "the integration of a genuine proletarian organization can only be achieved by utilizing the tactic of alliance and struggle together with the national bourgeoisie"; and the statement on page 162 that "this situation means that every *consistent* Marxist necessarily becomes an ally" of this same bourgeoisie, makes it indeed difficult for a worker, peasant, or consistent Marxist to share Dr. González Casanova's politics and still remain in touch with all of the reality in which he lives or remain faithful to any scientific standard. And to attribute "opportunism" or "verbal sectarianism and adventurism" to any reader who is not in accord with *La Democracia en México*, as Dr. González Casanova does on page 141, is not acceptable, nor is there any reason why it should be, to this reader.

[*These words were written, it may be remembered, three years before the "national bourgeoisie" and its "democratic" government—whom Dr. González Casanova claimed it was our duty to support in "pre-capitalist" Mexico—launched their ferocious pre-Olympic repression which in Tlatelolco alone murdered about 400 defenseless people in one evening, and which Dr. González Casanova now surely laments as much as the present author.*]

# 21

# THE BRAZILIAN PRE-REVOLUTION
# OF CELSO FURTADO

"Brazil: What Kind of Revolution?" is the question which Celso Furtado poses, both in an article which appeared in *Foreign Affairs* and elsewhere. In answering his own question, Furtado rejects a "Marxist-Leninist" revolution, proposing instead an "open society" and "gradualism" as the appropriate methods for the country's economic development. The thesis and the conclusion deserve special attention, nationally (in Brazil) as well as internationally, because they were incorporated in their author's work as director of SUDENE (a government agency for the promotion of economic development in northeastern Brazil) and subsequently as architect of the Goulart government's Three Year Plan. Furtado's affirmations, therefore, require critical examination and if they do not stand up under scrutiny—as we propose to show— Furtado's evolutionist conclusions and point of view must be rejected, or at least seriously questioned.

Furtado is apparently concerned with the problem of achieving humane economic development for Brazil. His study begins with an analysis of the country's poverty and the effects of an economic development whose fruits become increasingly concentrated in the hands of the few, leaving the immense majority of the Brazilian people in the most abject misery, with no increase at all in their incomes. He then asks how Brazil could attain greater economic development at lower human cost, and replies that the Marxist-Leninist solution, deeply rooted in the idealist youth of the country, not only provides a diagnosis of the problem but also a guide

1963. This essay was originally published in O *Semanario* (August 22–28, 1963).

for action. Furthermore, the Marxist road has to its credit the notable success of the growth of the U.S.S.R., although it "was achieved partly by the use of inhuman methods." Meanwhile, thousands of Brazilians die of hunger and disease every year. For this reason, says Furtado, the masses in underdeveloped countries do not generally value freedom in the same way as "we" do. In reality, Furtado goes on to say, the supposed inevitability of the conflict between individual liberty and a rapid economic development poses a false dilemma.

Furtado proceeds to the heart of his thesis. Marxism-Leninism showed its efficacy in the total subversion of rigid socio-political structures, as in Tsarist Russia, Japanese-occupied China, and Batista's Cuba. But the same methods proved inapplicable to "open societies," particularly those of Western Europe. Therefore, Furtado continues,

> the fundamental problem we face is to develop techniques which will make rapid social transformation possible, while retaining the pattern of an open society.
>
> Before turning to specifically Brazilian questions, I will indulge in one more observation on revolutionary methods. Since Marxism-Leninism is based on the substitution of the dictatorship of one class for that of another class, it would be politically retrogressive to apply it to societies which have attained more complex social forms—that is, to modern open societies.[1]

Referring specifically to Brazil, Furtado observes that its society is open for industrial workers but closed for peasants and rural workers. For the agricultural sector, Marxist-Leninist methods are still effective and a cataclysmic break is much more likely to occur than in the "open" sector, where change tends to assume the form of gradualism. Consequently, "in order to achieve a high rate of economic development, in accordance with truly social criteria, we shall have to bring about some important changes in our basic structures."

Three sentences later Furtado goes on to enlarge on the above ideas as follows: "If we are to avoid dictatorial régimes, whether of a social class or an ideological group or a rigid party machine, we must: (a) prevent all forms of retrogression in our social and political systems; and (b) create conditions for fast and efficient change in the country's archaic agrarian structure." [2] This conclusion, opening the rural sector to permit the gradual and evolutionary process (and preventing revolutionary change) provides the orientation for SUDENE and the Three Year Plans, directed by Furtado, and is the same program which provided the basis for the policy explicitly announced by Kennedy for the Alliance for Progress.

A more detailed examination of Furtado's argument reveals that he does not really reach his conclusions about "open gradualism" from a comparison of its efficacy with that of Marxism in achieving humane economic development. Moreover, even his argument about individual liberty is unacceptable and specious. We shall demonstrate that the argument is tautological in that the conclusion is already contained in the definition, just as the rabbit which a magician pulls out of a hat has been there all along.

Furtado begins by posing the problem of how to attain economic development at the least human cost and he sees only two possibilities, the Marxist road and that of the "open society." Despite this, and instead of going on to examine their relative efficacy in generating such development, Furtado interrupts his argument to consider two totally different matters: First, whether or not Marxism was successful in being introduced into Western Europe (not in bringing about its development), and second, which method provides more freedoms (thus contradicting his previous statement about the false dilemma between individual liberty and development). Arguing that since Marxism was not introduced into the "open societies" of Western Europe, and that where it was established it destroyed individual liberties, Furtado then arrives at the erroneous conclusion that Marxism should not be introduced into Brazil.

However, in order to make his argument with respect to these two new questions acceptable, Furtado would have to show (as he does not), that Brazil is today as developed, complex, and open as Europe was, for example, at the end of the War and that the alternative of gradualism does not destroy freedom as well. But these two propositions are completely contrary to fact. Moreover, as far as the Marxist alternative is concerned, Furtado should bear in mind that there is a difference between introducing socialism in a world in which there are already several socialist countries and introducing it in a world in which there is only one socialist country. Furthermore, it is possible—as the cases of China, Cuba, and Eastern Europe suggest—that humane economic development is presently easier to achieve through socialism than it was when the U.S.S.R. began its construction of socialism.

Thus, Furtado's argument does not sustain the conclusions which he derives from it. Even if he could nail down his theses with respect to these two questions, which were introduced as an afterthought, he would still leave the original and more important question completely unanswered and unconsidered. The important question is to know which is the most efficient way of achieving humane economic development. Furtado's claim to have attempted to extract his answer—"gradualism in an open society"—from an argument about how to achieve economic development, is thus, as we have noted, a trick similar to pulling a rabbit out of a hat.

If Celso Furtado were really to answer the basic question, as he claimed to do, of what the most efficient method for attaining economic development is, he would have to pose and answer as a minimum the following questions with respect to each of the two alternatives, Marxism and open gradualism, respectively:

(1) Do they offer a method for development? (2) Has the method been successful in practice? (3) Did it produce failures? (4) Is it possible to apply, introduce, and extend this method to Brazil? and lastly (5) Depending on the answers to the first four questions, can the method be successfully applied in Brazil? Furtado does not answer all of these questions; let us try to answer them for him.

(1) Furtado answers the first question: Marxism and open gradualism both promise methods of economic development, and each is widely accepted.

(2) As he emphasizes, the Marxist development method was successful, notably in the Soviet Union. The other method, although he does not mention it, has also been successful, if we disregard the fact that it was necessary to have bourgeois revolutions in order to put it into effect in England, France, and the United States (especially the Civil War between the industrialized North and the agrarian South).

(3) The Marxist method has not yet failed to produce economic development in the places where it has been applied. As we said before, Furtado's argument about the Marxist method is only that its failure lies in the inability to introduce it into Western Europe, and not in any failure to produce development in places where it has been possible to introduce it. On the other hand, in the present century the other method has failed to produce a developed economy in all the underdeveloped countries where it has been applied, with the possible partial exception of Japan. And if it had not failed in Brazil, Furtado would not have written this article and would not have invented SUDENE.

(4) Furtado himself believes that the introduction of Marxism into Brazil is possible and apparently that this would bring about economic development. In fact, he sees this as inevitable if the country does not follow the other road he prescribes. This brings us to what is probably the crucial question: can a gradualist society be introduced—or, to the extent to which it already exists, can it be extended—in such a way as to produce humane development, in Brazil? Furtado obviously believes that this can happen. But, as we saw above, in developing his argument he does not adduce a single reason to lead us to believe it. On the other hand, there are important facts accepted by both Marxists and non-Marxists, which he does not even consider, and which at the very least cast strong doubts on the possibility. First, contrary to what can be inferred from the article under discussion here, the structure of Brazilian society is obviously not the same as that of Western Europe. The fact of the existence of powerful industrialized countries, recognized by the ECLA and others—where Furtado himself was working when this idea was taking shape—lends the problem of development today quite a different form from that faced by the metropolitan countries one or two centuries ago. In fact, if some countries are presently underdeveloped, this is due precisely to the fact that others are developed. The countries which are presently developed might at one time have been *un*developed, but were never *under*developed in the present sense of the term. To apply many of the so-called lessons to underdeveloped countries outside the context of their own experience is confusing labels with reality.

Even if any illusions in this respect remained, an examination of the case of Mexico would suffice to destroy them. There we have an underdeveloped country which, despite the help of a revolution contemporaneous with the Soviet one (although a bourgeois and not a Marxist revolution), has been incapable, after fifty years, of adequately "opening" its society; and this society, by any definition of the term, continues to be underdeveloped even today. In the second place, the method of open gradualism has never ceased to bring about, both internally and externally (through slavery, colonialism, and imperialism), and of course especially in Brazil, precisely that expenditure of human suffering which both Furtado and the Marxist youth, each with their own method, want to prevent or eliminate.

(5) Furtado emphasizes that Marxism can successfully attain economic development for Brazil and there is nothing in his argument to suggest that he is wrong. Yet he also maintains that the other method can successfully be applied in Brazil. But as we saw, his argument is totally unacceptable. On the other hand, if we consider the obvious irrelevancy of the European example and the undeniable relevancy of the failure of the gradualist method when it was applied in all the underdeveloped world, Brazil included, and the cost in human suffering which the latter accentuates rather than eliminates, we must entertain serious doubts that the "open gradualist" method could be efficient in attaining a truly humane economic development in Brazil and elsewhere.

Finally, we can agree with Furtado when he says that the dilemma of economic development versus individual freedom is a false one. However, the reasons for this, which he does not mention, are twofold: First, the immense majority of Brazilians are, and have been for generations, not only hungry and disease-ridden, but also deprived of the most basic freedoms. In rural areas, this is because the landowner mobilizes all his power, vested in the economic, political, and police complex, against the peasant. In the cities, it is because the struggle to make a living does not permit him to enjoy freedom in the usual sense of the word. Second, in the countries that took the Marxist road there was an increase in freedom or a noticeable thaw after a relatively short period of time, and evident economic development as well. On the basis of these facts we must ask of the "open gradualist" system, sacrifice of liberty for what?

In conclusion, it is quite clear that for Furtado "pre-revolution" means "preventing revolution." But it is clear that the pre-dilection which Celso Furtado and others have for open evolution and their rejection of Marxist revolution is not, it seems, based on the relative efficacy of the first over the second in promoting economic development. Actually, Furtado himself recognizes that logically the second can be more efficient, and in fact it is. It is also clear that his decision in favor of evolution and against Marxism is not derived from a real interest in considering the possibilities of avoiding sacrifice of life and liberties of the people in the course of their historical and economic development. In fact, on this point as well as on the previous one, Furtado contradicts himself when he affirms that this alternative is a false dilemma, since Marxist revolutions have saved lives and liberties which capitalist evolution openly sacrifices. It is not, then, scientific interest and procedure that lead Furtado and others to arrive at their final conclusions. Therefore it is right and proper that we responsibly ask ourselves the following question: What exactly is the real *interest* behind the decision in favor of open evolution by Celso Furtado and his Three Year Plan and SUDENE in Brazil, and of the Alliance for Progress in Latin America?

[*These words were written and published in Brazil, it may be noted, in 1963 when Mr. Furtado was still Minister of Planning and before he was deprived of his civil rights and exiled by the military coup of April 1964.*]

## NOTES

1. Celso Furtado, "Brazil, What Kind of Revolution?", *Foreign Affairs* (April 1963), p. 532.
2. *Ibid.*, p. 534.

# 22

## THE NATIONAL BOURGEOISIE AND
## THE MILITARY COUP IN BRAZIL

There is some truth to the press reports that Brazil is witnessing "another of those familiar Latin American military coups." History is indeed repeating itself in a familiar pattern in Brazil. However, the press reporting of this pattern is not true and, thanks to consistent distortion, the reality behind it is not understood. For a perspective on the fate of President João Goulart, one must go back to the fate of his predecessor Janio Quadros in 1961, and further still to that of Goulart's political father, Getulio Vargas, in 1954.

Getulio Vargas killed himself in 1954. In his now famous "suicide note," he warned his fellow countrymen against the forces of foreign and domestic reaction that had driven him to his grave. The foreigners, he said, were sucking Brazil's scarce capital out of the country at an alarming rate; and their oligarchic domestic allies had effectively opposed his attempts to liberate Brazil from colonial status. Vargas had only just established the state petroleum company, called Petrobras, and was about to inaugurate its twin, Electrobras. Although Vargas had been recently elected, and although he had turned himself into a highly popular nationalist, the American wire services invariably referred to him as a "Fascist dictator." After the birth of Petrobras, American and Brazilian reaction mobilized all their forces and, charging him with political immorality, drove the septuagenarian Vargas into suicide. The loudest voice in this attack was that of Carlos Lacerda, a former Communist turned strident conservative (Lacerda

---

1964. This essay was written three days after the coup and originally appeared in *The Nation* of April 27, 1964, under the title "Brazil in Perspective: The Goulart Ouster."

340

is now Governor of Guanabara, which includes the city of Rio de Janeiro). The Electrobras proposal died with Vargas, and Petrobras, shorn of his protection and still opposed by foreign and domestic oil companies, was left with a most precarious lease on life. After eliminating popular leadership in labor, student, and other organizations, declaring the Communist Party illegal, and granting extensive privileges to foreign capital, reaction settled back into comfort under the leadership of Café Filho.

The next election brought Juscelino Kubitchek with his "developmentism" motto into the Presidency in 1956. He built Brasilia and brought the economic growth rate to 3.9 percent per capita for the years 1957–61. But he did so by increasing the external debt, granting still more privileges to American capital, and permitting foreign and domestic capital to flow into consumer goods and services which raise income in the short run, but cannot sustain growth. Corruption flourished; and the commercial, industrial, and agricultural interests were relatively satisfied.

The 1960 election swept Janio Quadros into the Presidency behind the moralistic broom he had used as his campaign symbol. João Goulart, political son and ex-labor minister of Getulio Vargas, and now head of the Vargas-founded Brazilian Labor Party (PTB), was elected Vice-President. Personally erratic, Quadros tried to rely directly on the people for his political base. He neglected his political relations with foreign and domestic interest groups, launched Brazil on a strongly nationalist and independent foreign policy, and unceremoniously threw those who came to object (including the American Presidential representative, A. A. Berle), out of his office. Pressure rose against him—again with Carlos Lacerda at its head—after Brazil's independent stand at Punta del Este and Quadros' decoration of Che Guevara, and he resigned in August 1961. It is thought that he hoped to be carried back to office by an aroused populace, which would give him enhanced strength to face reaction. But no organized popular support had been provided for and none appeared. Vice-President Goulart being out of the country, Rainieri Mazzilli, as president of the congress, became ad interim President of Brazil (he became so again earlier this month, with the difference that President Goulart has not resigned).

Having accomplished the suicide of the nationalist Vargas, whom they labeled Fascist, and the resignation of the nationalist Quadros, whom they called crazy, Carlos Lacerda and the foreign and domestic groups for whom he speaks tried to ignore the constitution and keep the Presidency out of the hands of Goulart. Conveniently forgetting that they had called his political mentor a Fascist, they now called Goulart a Communist. They were defeated in their objective only by the mobilization in Goulart's home state, Rio Grande do Sul, of popular forces led by Goulart's brother-in-law and then state Governor Leonel Brizola, and supported by the Third Army stationed in the state capital. Goulart returned to Brazil and assumed the Presidency. But against the urging of Brizola, who advised him to go all out while he had the nation behind him, Goulart accepted the opposition's proposal to amend the constitution by endorsing a European style parliamentary-ministerial system and diverting all power from the President to a prime minister. Retaining effective power anyway, Goulart governed weakly for eighteen months, during which the growth rate slipped to zero and inflation rose, until in a January 1963 plebiscite the voters turned the new parliamentary system down by a resounding 6-to-1 vote and restored Goulart to full Presidential powers.

Now, it was thought, Goulart would at last put into motion his much heralded reform program. With considerable fanfare, he launched a Three Year Plan for Social and Economic Reform to begin in 1963, its head to be the noted and progressive economist, Celso Furtado. The plan was to initiate agrarian and other reforms, as urged by the Alliance for Progress; it was to increase the annual economic growth rate to 7 percent gross and 4 percent per capita, and to reduce the rate of inflation to 30 percent in the first year and 10 percent in the third. Goulart's power and popularity raised anticipations of success, and the local currency rose with respect to the dollar. Yet during 1963, the economy actually declined, prices rose by 85 percent, and the reform proposals, instead of being implemented, never even reached congress.

History repeats itself. A year later Goulart was thrown out by the reaction, charged by the same Carlos Lacerda at home, and by the American wire services abroad, with being a dangerous extremist with totalitarian ambitions, bent on destroying democracy by means of a Communist-infiltrated government and ultra-radical reforms. This modernized version of the charges against Vargas and Quadros has, of course, become all too familiar through the press reports of the decline and fall of Frondizi in Argentina, Arosemena in Ecuador, Bosch in Santo Domingo, and others who, like Goulart, had made but not kept promises of reform and who had nonetheless soon been sent packing by military coups. If true, the charges against Goulart should arise out of a record of concrete progressive reforms and of political alliances made with left-wing forces capable of sustaining him in time of need. Yet Goulart's administrative record shows precisely the opposite: at home much talk about reforms, followed by consistent sellouts to the domestic and foreign forces that oppose any change at all; and abroad a vocally independent but still safe foreign policy, useful for appeasing the Brazilian Left. Goulart's domestic program turned out to be nothing more than a series of stop-gap measures serving the plutocratic interests and failing entirely to face up to the ever-deepening economic crisis which he and Brazil reaped from the "development" seeds earlier sown by Café Filho, Kubitchek, and their American allies. Far from espousing dangerously radical measures, it was Goulart's failure to press for any real reform that destroyed him.

Coming events were foreshadowed by the first cabinet he named after receiving full Presidential powers early in 1963. Faced with a crisis of industrial stagnation, inadequate agricultural production, increasing inflation, and a huge foreign debt, Goulart did not name the progressive cabinet expected in view of the political leeway given him by his overwhelming plebiscite victory. Instead, he named a conventional cabinet quite acceptable to the Right. His finance minister, San Thiago Dantas, quickly put into operation the first stage of the Three Year Plan, that bitter medicine prescribed by the United States and the International Monetary Fund as the initial price for loans. He eliminated the government subsidy to wheat, and, through petroleum, to transport, and slowed down still further the cost of living adjustments of public salaries already devalued by inflation. These measures were all at the expense of the lower- and middle-income groups; it was argued that they would combat inflation by reducing the need for government expenditures financed by paper money.

The plan was then abandoned as unworkable because the next step would have been to apply the main anti-inflationary remedy of slowing down the printing presses by which the government's Bank of Brazil feeds the private banks and through them the large private monopolies in Brazil, some of them American, which customarily work with loaned public capital. On the other hand, cutting out the expensive support of coffee prices for the benefit of the giant coffee exporters, again including Americans, did not have to be abandoned since it had never been contemplated. But before the plan was formally scrapped, Finance Minister Dantas made a pilgrimage to the United States to face up to Brazil's foreign debt and to collect loans for "anti-inflationary" services already rendered. While he was there, Congress released testimony from Lincoln Gordon, American Ambassador to Brazil, to the effect that Goulart's government was riddled with Communists. With this in the news, Dantas had to promise, before he could get his hands on the new loans, to use part of them to buy, at several times their value, some old and long since amortized American-owned public utilities which Brazil had been thinking of expropriating. And after all that, the foreign debt stands at $3 billion—half of it falling due this year and the next, thus obliging Brazil to keep making still further concessions in return for payment deferrals. The domestic Brazilian political repercussions of this renewed sellout to American interests and their reactionary Brazilian allies were so severe that Goulart had to sacrifice Dantas and Dantas' ministerial protégés.

At this point, many hoped, Goulart would form a cabinet less amenable to conservative demands for useless—except to them—stop-gap measures and be more determined to carry out the announced basic reforms. Instead, he named one that had the banker, Carvalho Pinto, in the all-important finance ministry. The American and Brazilian conservative press delightedly called the new minister "responsible." He had already served them well as Governor of São Paulo. The paper money presses speeded up and so did the inflation.

Goulart kept talking about the coming agrarian reform but took no political steps to bring it about. Even the weakest of several reform bills was never even brought to a congressional vote. Still, aroused by Goulart's many mass meetings and similar bravado, the landowners were busy buying machine guns, just in case. In one political crisis after another, Goulart talked loud and on the quiet gave in to right-wing pressure. This was especially the case when he had to decide whether or not to support labor union strikes over political issues, movements which could have been organized to support him later. When Goulart's war minister, General Kruel, actively sided with the Right in these and other issues, the President did dismiss him; but he refused to name in his place the First Army's commanding general Osvino Alves, who had the full support of the political Center and Left. Instead, Goulart called to the war post the Third Army's less political Jair Dantas. Again, when the Second Army's General Peri Belacuva joined São Paulo's ultra-reactionary Governor Ademar de Barros in repressing strikes and mass meetings called to support the reforms Goulart himself had announced, he removed Belacuva from that command, but made him chief of staff instead; and, to offend reaction still less, sent his old opponent, the equally reactionary Kruel, to São Paulo. So "dangerously left-wing extremist" were these most significant of Goulart's political moves that today the same Kruel uses his São Paulo command to lead the Second Army's rebellious attack on Goulart and Rio de Janeiro; the "non-political" Jair Dantas bows out of the war ministry post in mid-crisis "for reasons of health"; the now retired General Osvino Alves, newly installed as head of Petrobras, is tossed in jail; and Goulart is deserted even by the First and Third Armies of Rio and Puerto Alegre, whose earlier commanders had defended him and the constitution against industrial São Paulo's and the rural Northeast's Second and Fourth Armies (the latter commanded by General Costa Silva, later Minister of War and leader of the hard line), the traditional fomenters of reactionary coups.

These and similar moves by Goulart, which were formally neutral but actually conciliatory to the Right, insured that the reforms would never come to pass. Never being squarely faced by the government, the economic crisis inevitably deepened. In December 1963, Leonel Brizola observed that at one time it took the price level four years to double, then two, in the past months little more than one year, and that if in 1964 things kept going this way it would double in six months, then in three months, and before the elections scheduled for 1965 would finally be doubling every day. Thus, his brother-in-law Brizola, whose firm stand in August 1961 had saved the Presidency for Goulart, now argued publicly that if Goulart continued to evade a confrontation with the crisis, this same crisis would make it politically impossible to hold elections in 1965. Others, including this writer, argued that Goulart would never be able to complete his term of office. All through the end of 1963 and the beginning of 1964, a series of coups, preventive coups, and counter-coups were being planned, and several times were nearly launched, by groups representing various parts of the political and economic spectrum. It was almost certain that one of them would finally get under way. The only things in doubt were which pretext, moment, and instrument would be used and who finally would come out on top.

Following the classical Fascist pattern of Germany, Italy, France, and other countries, inflation, economic insecurity, and political instability attracted increasing middle-class and foreign and domestic financial support to Goulart's arch foes, "anti-Communist" Governors Carlos Lacerda and Ademar de Barros in Rio de Janeiro and São Paulo. A federal parliamentary inquiry disclosed that Lacerda, now liberally supplied with Alliance for Progress funds, had imported authentic storm troopers from Germany to help run his police force, set up a concentration camp, and torture political prisoners. Beyond that, he is the ultra-reaction's candidate for President and by his own proud admission has been chief plotter for the overthrow of President Goulart and his government.

The progressive forces, including Brazilian nationalist business interests, had offered Goulart an alternative: to let them take a real hand in governing. Banded together, though not organized, they formed an inter-party popular front that loosely united the progressive congressmen, peasant, and labor union federations, student associations, progressive officer and sergeant groups in the armed forces, as well as the national business groups that support them. This front urged Goulart to turn several ministries over to their representatives, with Leonel Brizola and General Osvino

Alves in the key finance and war ministries. Goulart vacillated—and refused. Naming instead still another banker representative of the Brazilian and American financial interests to the finance ministry, Goulart tried to continue doing political business as usual. The economic crisis continued: the cruzeiro, which had risen to 600 to the dollar after the plebiscite and had fallen to 1,000 at the end of the year, fell to beyond 1,700 shortly before the coup.

In March, Goulart again tried to put off demands of the progressive forces. In foreign matters he took a firm stand on the Cuba issue, a strong position in the Cyprus crisis and the Geneva disarmament debate, and above all in the Geneva World Trade Conference where Brazil and its national business interests took the leadership in the underdeveloped nations' challenge to American and European economic interests. And domestically he offered more political histrionics. After months of watering it down, Goulart finally signed an economically insignificant decree expropriating politically selected farms larger than 500 hectares that bordered on some federal transportation routes and waterways; he expropriated some small *Brazilian* petroleum companies (by which measure he strengthened their American rivals); and he introduced a bill into Congress which would again legalize a Communist Party—it already has two deputies—whose insignificantly small numbers supported him politically because they feared the personal persecution they and others will now suffer. (The Party has a long public record of being far more conservative than is the President's own brother-in-law, Brizola, and the business groups who back him.)

Now the American and domestic commercial agricultural interests and their·political and military representatives juggled various coup plans and alignments more feverishly than ever. Coincidence or not, it is worth noting that these finally crystallized into action —as happened after Vargas' Petrobras and Electrobras in 1954, and after Quadros' independent policy at the Punta del Este Conference in 1961—immediately following another Brazilian challenge to American interests, this time at the Geneva World Trade Conference. The only thing new is the speed and out-and-out callousness of American official support for the military coup. Within twenty-four hours, and long before it was known if President

Goulart would leave Brazil, Lyndon Johnson sent the old stand-in, · Rainieri Mazzilli, his "warmest good wishes for your inauguration as President of the United States of Brazil," and noted that "friendship and cooperation between our governments and people are . . . a precious good in the life of peace, prosperity, and liberty in this hemisphere and the whole world." Secretary of State Rusk and his assistant, Thomas Mann, swiftly promised more "aid" for this cooperation—in changing Brazil's policy on Cuba, trade, expropriations, etc.

It is apparent that, far from having ever launched or seriously threatened to launch a progressive, much less a radical, reform program, Goulart, like Frondizi and others before him, had consistently failed to attack any of the causes of the crisis whose victim he became. The lesson is clear. Goulart was felled by domestic and American conservatism, not because he moved to the Left, which he did not, but because he clung to the Right, and thus was utterly unable to confront the fundamental economic crisis. However far Right one moves in an atmosphere of economic and political chaos, reaction can only be temporarily appeased; it is never satisfied. Reaction in the end converts its reluctant servants into its sacrificial lambs.

[*Postscript (September 1964*)

"*I want to take this means to express my personal appreciation to each agent stationed in Brazil for the services rendered in the accomplishment of 'Overhaul'! . . . The CIA did their part well and accomplished a great deal; however, the efforts of our agents were especially valuable. I am particularly pleased that our participation in the affair was kept secret and that the Administration did not have to make any public denials. . . . Sincerely yours, J. E. Hoover.*" *So writes, confirming part of our analysis, the Chief of the United States Federal Bureau of Investigation (FBI) according to a photocopy of a letter on official stationery attributed to him and published by a Chilean newspaper.* "*Have you heard the story of how the Latin American bloc was used to break the solidarity of the '75' [underdeveloped countries] at the 1964 Trade and Development Conference at Geneva? A key role was played* by [*the new government in*] *Brazil in pulling the Latin Americans out, which gave the Western powers their way at last."* So reports, thereby confirming one of our predictions, an observer from Geneva. *"When Executives Turned Revolutionaries"*—this is how Fortune, *the United States Big Business magazine, titles an article which it subtitles: "A Story hitherto untold: how São Paulo busi- nessmen conspired to overthrow Brazil's Communist-infected gov- ernment."*]

# 23

## DESTROY CAPITALISM, NOT FEUDALISM

Carlos Fuentes' depiction of Latin America as a "decrepit feudal castle with a cardboard capitalist façade" is certainly poetic. But it is wrong. Latin America could better be called a decrepit capitalist castle with a feudal-seeming façade. Fuentes' error is symptomatic, if it does not go even straight to the heart of *Whither Latin America?* For the attribution by most of the book's authors of many past and present Latin American ills to feudalism rather than to capitalism betrays their misunderstanding of the continent's past development—and therewith of capitalism itself—and renders dubious and misleading, at best, their discussion of Latin America's future.

A composite picture of the twelve essays—excepting principally the concluding "Notes" by Sweezy and Huberman—may, I hope without violence or injustice to any of the nine authors, be sketched in the following propositions: (1) Latin America is only just entering the stream of world history as an integral and determinant part (Fuentes, page 23, Johnson, 25). (2) Its earlier (non) role is the result of European construction in Latin America of a feudal castle which, though it may have been glorious in its time, is now in a state of decay (Fuentes *passim*; Johnson, 33; Frank, 62, 72; O'Connor, 91; Juliao, 106; Agustin, 106). (3) In the meantime, the regions of advanced capitalism, developing more or less independently of the rest of the world, left Latin America behind stewing in its feudal juice (Fuentes, 10–11; Johnson, 27; Huberman, 50). (4) Because a similar process occurred

---

1963. This article originally appeared as a book review in the December 1963 issue of *Monthly Review*. The references to Frank refer to essays that are included as chapters 17 and 19 of the present book.

not only between but also within countries, Latin America now has dual—really two—societies, one agrarian, feudal or semi-feudal, archaic, backward, etc.; the other urban, capitalist, commercial, industrial, modern, etc.; each society being largely self-determining and independent of the other (Fuentes, 11–12; Frank, 62, 85). (5) Imperialism consists primarily of foreign exploitative economic activity; and it would help Latin America's economic development if this activity were stopped, curbed, or controlled (Fuentes, 14–15; Johnson, 33; Observer, 43; Huberman, 56; Frank, 80–81; Agustin, 120). (6) It is the foregoing features which, along with widespread and persistent poverty, characterize underdevelopment (Johnson, 28; Huberman, 48–49). (7) Economic development in Latin America—past, present, and future—is attributed largely to a sort of radiation from a domestic and/or foreign metropolitan center; and it is held that the periphery can, through cooperation, agreement, and alliance with the capitalist metropolis, benefit from such a flow relation (Fuentes, 23; Johnson, 28; Observer, 43, 45; Sweezy, 70). (8) This flow, and therefore economic development, has been too slow, thus resulting in two alternative or even simultaneous consequences: left-wing, bourgeois, parliamentary economic and political movements have sprung up, such as APRA in Peru, Acción Democrática in Venezuela, Goulartism in Brazil, which show or showed promise of really changing all the foregoing and thus rendering socialism meaningless for the country in question (Johnson, 28, 37); and/or (9) Latin America is now in such a revolutionary ferment that the people promise, by an act of will and decision, any day now to destroy this whole ramshackle structure and to substitute a liberating socialism in its place (Fuentes, 9; Observer, 46; Frank, 63, 89).

I submit that these interpretative descriptions are, taken individually, mostly wrong, and, taken as a whole, very seriously misleading.

Some of the authors' related errors of fact or interpretation are worthy of mention. The base of political power, contrary to Fuentes (13–14) is not the feudal landlords, and Latin American armies are not caste armies (18). Brazil's agricultural surpluses are not, as Johnson (27, 35) maintains, due to efficiency in agricultural production. Perón neither had a program of rapid industrialization in Argentina, nor did he cause the country's troubles (Johnson, 37). APRA and Acción Democrática are not left-wing parties (Johnson, 37). Venezuela's land reform is, except in maintaining the status quo, far from ambitious (Observer, 42). "Conservative Type I" land reform is not really just the last resort of the landowners (Frank, 57). Peasants are not really unincorporated in national society (Frank, 59). Mexico's failures are not due so exclusively to failure to solve the land problem (Frank, 66, 77). And the systems of Guatemala, Peru, Venezuela, Colombia, etc., still do lumber along and do not face imminent collapse (Frank, 88).

A factually more accurate and theoretically sounder picture might be sketched as follows: Latin American societies resulted from the worldwide expansion of "Western" mercantilism, capitalism, and imperialism. Characteristically, this expansion everywhere took the form of a simultaneous and interrelated dialectic development whose manifestations, each both the "result" and the "cause" of the other, are today known as economic development and economic underdevelopment. This capitalist development, with its associated exploitation of the "underdeveloped" sector by the "developed" counterpart through the latter's monopoly of force, capital, and commerce, manifests itself on many levels: internationally between the metropolitan and peripheral countries, and domestically between "advanced" and "backward" regions, between the city and the countryside, between commerce-industry and agriculture, between "modern" and "backward" agriculture. If this process is not viewed as a whole—as the dialectic development of a single capitalist system—the door is opened to misinterpreting the results as emanating from a dual system or from two systems—the world of the rich and the world of the poor—and to the associated misinterpretation of the former as "capitalist" and the latter as "feudal." Yet, as we shall see, this error runs with serious consequences through almost all of the essays under review.

As against the picture presented in *Whither Latin America?*, I offer the following: The continent has for nearly five centuries had an integral, contributory part in world development. Contrary to Carlos Fuentes and others, "backwardness," "underdevel-

opment," and feudal appearing relations, far from being the surviving remnants of some original feudal order in Latin America,
are the result of economic "development" under capitalism itself.
Indeed, it is hard to understand why or how, as is claimed, the expanding commercial and industrial capitalist system would have
had either the interest or the possibility to establish a feudal, that
is, closed system in Latin America. It did, of course, the opposite:
it incorporated Latin America (and Asia and Africa as well) into
its own structure. In this process, a sort of dual society did indeed
emerge in Latin America, but not in the above-cited sense of two
separate parts, with a "feudal" peasant sector "isolated" from
the capitalist national and international society. On the contrary,
it is a dialectically dual society with different, but not separate,
parts, one exploited by the other. If the Indians of the Andes
and the Sierra Madre are "isolated," it is because retreat has been
their only (and very partial) protection against capitalist exploitation of their land and labor. Power, like everything else in the
"provincial" rural sectors, is intimately related to urban and international capitalist society through the economic (above all
commercial), political (above all parliamentary backed by force),
and social relations that link them to each other. Surpluses,
agricultural or otherwise, are the result not of efficiency in production but on the contrary, along with the exploitation and
profits associated with them, are the product of the monopolization of the foregoing relations. Least of all is it true—or even
possible—that the base of national power in Latin America is
the "feudal" landlords. On the contrary, power and the determination of the country's fate has rested with the domestic and
foreign commercial and financial bourgeois oligarchy whose fortunes, in turn, are determined by their participation in the imperialist system.

Imperialism, thus, is not only this or that foreign company
exploiting Latin American economies; it is the structure of the
entire economic, political, social—yes, and cultural—system in
which Latin America and all its parts, however "isolated," find
themselves participating as exploited partners. The primacy of
this imperialist structure in the determination of all else renders it
quite impossible that the troubles of Argentina should be due

to Perón or even Peronism, and quite unlikely that the primary reason for the failure of the Mexican Revolution is to be found in its failure to solve the land problem—or that land reform is necessarily more significant than the nationalization of petroleum. Poverty and wealth are the symptoms of underdevelopment and development, which in turn are themselves imbedded in the exploitative structure of the colonialist-imperialist-capitalist system and determine the aluminum sky-scraper/tobacco road form it takes. Development cannot, therefore, radiate from the center out to the periphery. The periphery, instead, can develop only if it breaks out of the relation which has made and kept it underdeveloped, or if it can break up the system as a whole. Least of all is it true or even possible, therefore, that a relationship of cooperation or alliance between the two capitalist parts of the system can operate to the benefit of the underdeveloped one. On the contrary, this exploitative relationship is one of the primary contradictions of capitalism which, until resolved, will continue to produce even more underdevelopment.

If the foregoing picture of Latin America be accurate, even in its general outlines, then, as Sweezy and Huberman quite rightly observe in their "Notes," it cannot be that the bourgeois capitalist revolution (against feudalism) has still to be made in Latin America, or that bourgeois movements—through the electoral process, "land reform" such as Betancourt's, or any other process that remains within the present structure—can abolish underdevelopment and misery. The state in Latin America, even more so than the state discussed by Lenin in *The State and Revolution*, is an instrument of the bourgeoisie because it and its associated institutions are part not only of a national but of the international—that is imperialist—capitalist system. This exploitative entanglement must, accordingly, be broken; and this break, evidently, cannot be accomplished through exclusive reliance on the imperialist-capitalist institutions themselves. On the other hand, the foregoing picture gives us no reason to believe that the system can no longer lumber along—albeit at terrible costs—or that socialist revolution is imminent or will automatically occur if the Latin American masses decide that they have finally had enough and that the time has come to revolt. Instead, the revolution is the result of the deepening of these contradictions within capitalism and of the revolutionary organization which results from and must take advantage of these contradictions.

The second major weakness of the volume under review lies in the fact that the reporters almost unanimously fail to examine the relationship between the development of these contradictions and the organization of the revolutionary process and effort. Failing to link their discussion of the future to, or derive it from, their analysis of the past, they resort to *ad hoc* predictions, which therefore not surprisingly are also quite often wrong. The essays which least display this weakness—the concluding one of Sweezy and Huberman and that of Salazar Bondy—also turn out in their analysis of the past to be more consistent with the interpretation of capitalist development advanced in this review and less consistent with the composite picture painted in the remainder of the essays. As for the latter, their view of the future is subject to criticism (and rejection) on three principal grounds. First, their authors manage to derive quite inconsistent futures—imminent socialist revolution vs. bourgeois progress which renders socialism meaningless—from a common analysis of the past. Second, neither of these predictions gives any sign of being realized. And third, because there is no attempt made in these essays to indicate *how* these predictions and/or policies might be turned into reality.

It is naturally not possible within the space of a brief review to present anything like a rounded analysis of probable future developments in Latin America. Nevertheless, mere negative criticism is obviously not enough: an effort must be made at least to indicate some of the major factors that have to be taken into account.

The development of world capitalism since the Second World War has brought with it a deepening of the contradiction between development and underdevelopment in the non-socialist world. The gap has widened and the conflict deepened between the imperialist metropolis and its periphery; and underdevelopment has increased (not decreased) absolutely in the latter (as a symptom, food production and consumption per capita in non-socialist Asia, Africa, and Latin America have generally fallen since before the War). Similarly, the contradiction between development and underdevelopment has deepened between regions and sectors within the periphery itself. In Latin America, the depression and the war created relative isolation (protection!) which in turn resulted, in some countries, in a spurt of autonomous industrialization. A postwar honeymoon of war-built foreign exchange reserves and a wave of "liberalizing" regimes followed. But the honeymoon was soon over. Contemporary with capitalism's return to "normalcy" and its renewed offensive highlighted by the Korean War, Latin America's terms of trade began again to decline—and balance of payments deficits to increase—accompanied by a wave of "dictatorial" governments. With their countries already in trouble, these governments proceeded to intensify the problem—with results in evidence today—by providing "liberal" concessions to imperialism, now not only in mining and utilities but also in consumer goods and service industries catering mainly to the higher income recipients. Already in debt to and under the control of the metropolis, Latin America fell ever more deeply into imperialist subjugation. Despite the area's poverty and against all the rules of orthodox economics, capital exports to the metropolis, principally to the U.S., rose, thus opening the door to still greater dependence and subjugation.

The deepening domestic structural underdevelopment in Latin America was perhaps initially hidden from local eyes by being confused, as it is by metropolitan opinion to this day, with some outward appearances of economic development, especially in consumer goods manufacture and the provision of services, in the growth of the "middle classes" which produce and consume this output. Four social groups, one might say, grew to or in importance. The monopolization of agricultural production *and distribution*, the decline in the growth rate of primary goods exports, often the decline in export earnings, and, indeed, the increase in food imports from the U.S., forced peasants off the land in a massive rural exodus. Many of these former peasants remained "unincorporated" into the urban economy and became the ever increasing floating urban sub- or maybe lumpenproletariat of the ubiquitous slums. This is the first group referred to. Others thrown off the land and some from the slums came to be incorporated into the second group, the working class more narrowly defined, by getting manufacturing and service-industry jobs. A third group consisted for the most part of white-collar workers—employed in burgeoning government bureaucracies, commercial offices, banks, etc. In some countries this group has grown to 40–45 percent of the labor force. Finally, the profits from all these developments and above all from the inflation which accompanied them served both to swell and to modify the fourth group, the bourgeoisie properly speaking.

Contrary to expectations derived from theory based on the experience of the metropolis and of the earlier progressive role of the independent middle classes in the latter, these developments have contributed in Latin America not to development but instead to increasing underdevelopment. Furthermore, these groups are for the most part a conservative, not a progressive, force.

In Latin America the economy consists increasingly of a one-product primary-export economy depending on an unstable and ever more slowly growing foreign market which serves as the only base of an overblown service sector. What is lacking is basic producer-goods industries which, if they exist at all, are increasingly controlled by foreign interests that are infiltrating this sector at an alarming rate. In consequence, the economy inevitably has no long- or even medium-term self-sustaining growth possibilities, is subject to heavy inflationary pressures, is highly unstable, and is an easy prey for further imperialist penetration. All of these elements and forces aggravate each other and interact with the underlying conditions in a vicious spiral, best illustrated perhaps by the case of Argentina.

The political consequences are not immediately encouraging. The members of the first three social groups and the new members of the fourth typically regard their recent entrance into their group as constituting their "personal revolution." Not unlike C. Wright Mills' white-collar man, the members of the working and middle groups become dependent parts of a private or public bureaucracy which has a marked client relationship to the bourgeoisie: they get social position, welfarism, and apparent income from the bourgeoisie, which mark them off from the peasants and the lower urban proletariat; in return, especially through organized-labor and middle-group political support of right-wing and centrist political measures and figures, they support the status quo. The income is only apparent because, of course, inflation systematically wipes out their monetary gains and transfers income from all three of these groups, plus the peasants, to the bourgeoisie and the imperialists who benefit from the inflation-producing measures.

Still, these new arrivals are relatively privileged groups, often a veritable aristocracy of the proletariat, who can be a progressive force in a limited way as long as they hope to achieve further gains but who, when their past gains are threatened, especially the middle groups among them, turn out to provide the main source of popular support for far-right politicians and "solutions" which promise to "re-establish stability," i.e., to protect and conserve their newly won gains. Thus, when the bottom drops out of the export market and the higher incomes are menaced, these groups are the first to turn from clamoring for a better future to looking into the past and trying to conserve what they already have by supporting the (Fascist-type) Right. Paradoxically, they are joined in this political move by many who had a better past, often in the provinces, before the growing development-underdevelopment gap undermined their intermediary positions, and who now adopt a strictly ostrich-like attitude, burying their heads in the shifting sands of ultra-right-wing politics.

The bourgeoisie, both in Latin America and in the metropolis is, of course, the principal beneficiary of the system. Although there are conflicting interests and shifting alliances, the supposed fundamental contradictions between the "national bourgeoisie," the "feudal landlords," the "comprador bourgeoisie," and the "imperialists" are, as Sweezy and Huberman quite rightly point out and all talk to the contrary notwithstanding, very largely a myth. In the first place, as was pointed out above, the Latin American economies got to be what they are as part and parcel of the capitalist—first colonialist and now imperialist—system. Secondly, outside of Argentina, Mexico, and Brazil, there is no national bourgeoisie to speak of because the countries' role in the larger system left no room for national industry. Their bourgeoisies, far from being independent in the classical European sense, are the domestic groups which are the clients of foreign interests and the domestic beneficiaries of the whole capitalist system stretching from New York to the most "isolated" provincial farm or village. Far from being in fundamental conflict with any of these foreign imperialist or domestic "feudal" exploiters, the bourgeoisies intimately link them to each other, extracting their toll at the economic, political, and social crossroads of the system.

In the countries with some industry, the situation is not really fundamentally different. It is only more complicated in that the domestic industrial interests are also economically and politically intertwined with agrarian, mining, financial, domestic and international commercial, and speculative interests in general. Often several or all of these "sectors" are combined in a single financial group, company, or family. One group may be at odds with the others while they can afford it, but when the workings of the system and above all popular pressures threaten their common source of exploitative benefits, they quickly band together in a reactionary front, dragging with them as many of the other social groups as possible. The fundamental contradiction in the underdeveloped world being between all of them and those they exploit, how could it be otherwise?

Latin America—and indeed the world as a whole—is again in such a rightward wave. As the continent-wide stagnation in the growth rate and the mounting balance of payments crisis attest, the economy has again entered a phase of threatened disaster. At the same time, Cuba produced a certain panic among people with something to lose, and the United States launched an "anti-Communist" campaign in Latin America of unprecedented proportions. As a result of these factors, Latin America, far from "moving to the Left" as has been so widely proclaimed, is currently once again "moving to the Right," with the bourgeoisies engineering the move through "legal" parliamentary channels where it can and through the famous military coups where it must. How long this renewed, temporary rightward retrenchment will last is perhaps not yet to be foreseen.

The peasants and, in some cases some ex-peasant urban unemployed, are the ones who have nothing at all to lose from revolution and everything to gain. For many Latin American countries, such as Brazil, Venezuela, Argentina, and pre-revolutionary Cuba, it is in fact illegitimate and misleading to talk of "peasants" in the traditional sense of more or less independent and self-reliant cultivators. In fact, these "peasants" are the real proletariat—the dependent, insecure, often bureaucratized, residual-earning, exploited source of labor, whether they are still on the land or are now cast off into the city slums. It is on their shoulders that the entire "decrepit castle" rests. Paradoxically, however, most of the talk about revolution comes from the relatively more far-sighted and more privileged labor, middle, intellectual, and even army groups. These people, when the chips are down and often even before, tend to back out of the revolution and to be content with reforms. That is, the talk about revolution is, so far, mostly just talk. The rural and slum proletarians, in contrast, tend to be quite near-sighted and to see only the land and the jobs which they want but don't have. The "revolutionary" leadership, including most especially that of the trade unions and the Communist parties, has so far come only from the ranks of the talkers and has been, and as the facts demonstrate, quite reformist-revisionist. Furthermore, in all cases until Cuba and in most cases to this day, the leaders have only led each other around, leaving the rural and urban slum proletariat and, if that is what it really is, lumpenproletariat entirely to its own quite feeble devices. Even now that some efforts are beginning to be directed to the countryside, they are in effect mostly an extension to the land of the reformist revisionism of the city, long tried and found wanting.

Whence, then, the Revolution, and when? There can be no simple answer, and neither hope nor prophecy is enough. The development—underdevelopment contradiction will undoubtedly deepen internationally and domestically. The mechanism of dependent capitalism in the underdeveloped world has so far never permitted a way out of underdevelopment, and it shows no promise of doing so now. Underdevelopment will increase. The time-tested combination of successive (and sometimes simultaneous) "liberalizing" mystification with "dictatorial" retrenchment and intensified foreign infiltration, led by and for the bourgeoisie, will leave further marks on its victims. Right-wing "reforms" will, it seems probable, succeed less and less in their mystifying mission;

and their most offensive (from their point of view defensive) actions will here and there call forth popular left-wing reactions. These will have to be used to help create revolutionary conditions. The repeated failures of bourgeois reformism must be translated into popular clarification about the roots of the difficulties. Some of the popular near-sightedness must be corrected. This is the work of revolutionaries, since reformists only seek to induce the people to substitute one reform for another. The popular reactions to bourgeois attacks must be channeled into meaningful and cumulative revolutionary forms lest they dissipate popular energy and contribute to a popular feeling of helplessness and failure. That also is the work of revolutionaries, not of reformists. Both revolutionary tasks must be directed to winning over to the people's revolutionary movement some of the popular groups, including part of the military, whom the bourgeoisie has so far bribed into mystifying and repressing popular sentiment. All of this is in greater or lesser degree going on in Latin America today.

But the people and their leaders will also have to go on the offensive; they cannot simply wait for conditions to ripen. An advance guard of the revolution, such as the Armed Forces of National Liberation (FALN) in Venezuela, must take the offensive even while final victory is still out of sight, to hold out the goal domestically as the socialist world already does internationally; to force the hand of the bourgeoisie by, for instance, obliging it to take off its "democratic" mask, and to contribute to the accumulation of revolutionary experience. Most important, these steps must prepare the people and their leaders to act decisively when, generally with little or no forewarning, the opportunity is ripe. This is the work of revolutionaries. The revisionist reformists have, instead, in recent years led their people in Latin America to be less, not more, ready to take advantage of the revolutionary opportunity. It will not do only to wait to strike the iron when it is hot. The iron must, at least in part, also be struck to heat it—and to provide the experience necessary for striking when the time, indeed, has come. The recent opening of the "Third Great Debate" between Revolution and Reform will, perhaps, contribute to the training of revolutionaries in Latin America as the second debate in its time did in the Soviet Union.

# 24

# CLASS, POLITICS, AND DEBRAY

No honest and constructive criticism of Régis Debray's work can fail to pay due tribute to its importance and its merits. As a revolutionary document in the best tradition of political writing, Debray's series of essays squarely faces and has obliged all of us to deal with those most important political problems of our times that many have sought to evade. Debray has convincingly criticized pseudo-revolutionary tendencies and has affirmed an honest call to revolutionary arms. Furthermore, his personal conduct has been consistent with his appeal, which is more than most of us can say for ourselves. But all this, as he would doubtless be the first to agree, does not place Debray's work above criticism. If anything, it renders a critique of Debray's writings, where objectively warranted, all the more important.

Debray's theses, in our estimation, call for a critique on two fundamental grounds: first, they do not derive from a fundamental *analysis* of Latin American society, and still less of its *class* structure; and second, in consequence, they divorce *theory* from practice and, mistaking the nature of the Latin American revolution, they underestimate the *political* role of military activity and mass participation, and their interrelationships. The lack of analysis of society would not be serious in a political tract (as distinct from an analytic work) if it did not result in the perpetuation in a different form of the very political weakness of revolutionary policy in Latin America that Debray himself wants to overcome. In making these criticisms, we direct them at the well known central theses of Debray rather than at "quotable" isolated affirmations in his writings, which often contradict his own central theses.

---

1968. This essay originally appeared in the Summer 1968 issue of *Monthly Review*. It was co-authored with S. A. Shah.

(1) Debray's writings are, and should be appreciated as, political tracts and not political analyses of Latin American society. No economic and social analysis of Latin America is to be found in Debray's three essays, not even in "Problems of Revolutionary Strategy in Latin America," [1] which may be said to be the most analytic of them. Specifically, there is no analysis of the productive or the class structure of Latin America or any of its parts. Accordingly, Debray also makes no political analysis of Latin American society—as distinct from, and as a basis for, the analysis of Latin American political movements that he does make. Nor does Debray make any provision for such economic-social-political analysis anywhere in his political program for the Latin American revolution.

This lack of analysis—and failure to rely on analysis—of the social milieu and dynamic in which the Latin American revolutionary must work certainly distinguishes Debray, and the Cuban Revolution as well, from the Soviet, Chinese, and Vietnamese revolutions, in which not only Lenin, Mao Tse-tung, and Ho Chi Minh, but many other leaders distinguished themselves by the social analysis on which revolutionary theory and practice were both based. The leadership of these revolutions studied and understood the societies in which their successful political work was done. And, according to Debray's account at his "trial" in Bolivia, Che was himself writing a political economy of Latin America with one hand while fighting in Bolivia with the other.

Analysis, as contrasted to an empirical trial-and-error approach, does not mean importing the "national bourgeoisie vs. feudalism" schema from Moscow, or the "four group United Front" program from Peking, or the "uneven and combined development permanent revolution" formula of Trotsky. In Latin America it is necessary to analyze how the class structure was formed and is still being transformed through the colonial and neo-colonial structure that world capitalist development has imposed on all parts of the continent. This requires reliance on the Marxist *method* to study the reality, and the varieties of reality, in Latin America; and it does not permit the simple application of labels or schemas, used even by Debray, such as "feudal oligarchy."

(2) Debray divorces, or fails to marry, revolutionary theory and

revolutionary practice. In denying the validity of, and therewith refusing to answer, the question whether the Latin American revolution is bourgeois or socialist, Debray confuses the political nature of the revolution. This mistake is, we suggest, a direct consequence of his failure to make the necessary analysis of Latin American socioeconomic reality—however much, as has been claimed by many, Debray may or may not short-sell the relevance of European and Asian teachings. Furthermore, Debray's theory of the Cuban Revolution itself departs in important respects from Cuban revolutionary practice. For instance, the whole 26th of July Movement beyond the Sierra Maestra and its political significance for revolutionary practice and theory find no counterpart in Debray's model. The observation that this movement was of little use in supplying Fidel with weapons is not enough to dispose of its political significance and is only one òf many symptoms of Debray's underestimation of the politics of revolution, Cuban or otherwise. Again, the Cuban Revolution's success was not just achieved in the Sierra Maestra before January 1, 1959, as Debray implies, but also in its development throughout Cuba after that date, as Debray would probably agree. For, as Fidel noted in his speech of April 8, 1968,

> in all fairness, we cannot say that the first of January [1959] was the triumph of the Revolution. Traditionally we have identified the Revolution only with armed struggle, but really on the first of January the rebellion triumphed. . . . In those early times, could we say, in truth, that we knew what a revolution was? In those times we had a feeling, which was the feeling of the struggle, the feeling of rebellion. . . .

Thus, just as July 26, 1953, or December 2, 1956, need not have led to guerrilla warfare (after all, they were not intended to, and other planned or executed uprisings did not do so elsewhere), so the fighting in the Sierra Maestra need not necessarily have led to the socialist revolution. Had the Cuban Revolution been unable to go beyond 1959, it would of course have been derailed and defeated altogether. Fortunately, the Cuban Revolution's momentum and direction (derived in part from political mobilization beyond the Sierra Maestra) were able to get it over the bourgeois hump. Not all revolutionary movements, even guerrilla-led ones, have succeeded. Most of them, and notably the Algerian, failed; and from Prestes in Brazil to Machado in Venezuela armed struggle has not provided a political guarantee against reformism. By contrast, their political direction of military action has permitted the Chinese and Vietnamese to avoid derailment of the revolution. Furthermore, it must be noted that the Cuban class structure, the Cuban bourgeoisie's decision—and ability to decide—to throw in the towel and move to Miami, and the international correlation of forces made the hump to be overcome in Cuba significantly lower than it is in the rest of Latin America today. Thus, Debray's account is not quite accurate; and, especially if the Cuban Revolution is to be regarded as a vanguard and integral part of the Latin American revolution, his model cannot be a sure-fire guide.

If Debray had wedded a program for revolutionary action to an analysis of Latin American society, or perhaps even of Cuban society, instead of deriving it mainly from an analysis (adequate or not) of the Cuban and Latin American revolutionary movements, he could never have been led to counsel revolutionary practice without—or rather with—false revolutionary theory. Specifically, an analysis of the class and neocolonial structure of Latin America would lead Debray to see that the current development of socialist revolutionary theory in Latin America is certainly a necessary, if not a sufficient, condition for successful revolutionary practice. Specifically, correct revolutionary theory is necessary to insure that at the first obstacle supposedly revolutionary practice is not derailed into a *frente amplia* (broad front) such as that now joined by Prestes in Brazil, a *paz democrática* (democratic peace) such as that now advocated by Machado in Venezuela, or a NASAKOM (nationalism, Islam, and Communism) as practised in Indonesia under Sukarno—and to suffer their inevitable consequences.

An analysis of the Latin American class structure would reveal who is the enemy to be fought (the bourgeoisie as well as imperialism), what political weapons he has at his disposal (reformism and temptation), whom the revolution can count on, how it must politically mobilize these people—in a word, what the theory and practice of the Latin American revolution must be. It is not for nothing that in his call for "Two, Three, Many Vietnams" Che said that it "shall be in Our America, almost certainly, a Socialist Revolution."

Debray's failure to analyze Latin American society and to link revolutionary theory and practice adequately leads him to underestimate the importance of political mass participation in the revolution and to omit the political role of military activity in organizing this mass participation. Debray appeals for a guerrilla push to get the revolution started, and he hopes that by putting its leadership into rural guerrilla rather than urban party or even *kaffeeklatsch* hands, the revolution will proceed to victory through the formation of a people's army. But nowhere does Debray suggest how the guerrilla band is later to develop into the people's army and the popular political movement the revolution requires. Far from suggesting how the guerrilla *foco* might create the political, or even military, conditions for this further development, Debray's critique of self-defense and guerrilla political work in rural areas and his disregard of guerrilla ties to a "26th of July"-type movement in Cuba as well as elsewhere in Latin America would seem to argue against the organization of a wider political movement. Yet Fidel told the OLAS conference that the need for a guerrilla nucleus of the revolutionary movement "does not mean that the guerrilla movement can rise without any previous work; it does not mean that the guerrilla movement is something that can exist without political direction. No! We do not deny the role of political organizations. The guerrilla is organized by a political movement, by a political organization."

Thus, military actions require adequate political direction and support, lest like a house built on weak foundations the first storm destroy both foundation and superstructure. Clear class analysis is essential for carefully (tactically) selected and politically (strategically) guided armed actions to be militarily successful against the enemy, and politically successful in mobilizing the people as friends of the revolution. Not only is a *popular* base area necessary to assure the supply, communication, and propaganda requirements of military activity; but the latter must—and is essential to —assure further political mobilization and participation of the people. Thus, successful military action and correct political mobilization require adequate class analysis of Latin American society.

Such political analysis unquestionably also points to the necessity of rural guerrilla warfare, but it would eliminate some of the contradictions and enhance the political strategy of Debray's program for the Latin American revolution.

## NOTE

1. *New Left Review,* September–October, 1967.

# V

## WHO IS THE IMMEDIATE ENEMY?

# 25

## CAPITALIST UNDERDEVELOPMENT
## OR SOCIALIST REVOLUTION

This essay advances the following theses:

1. The immediate enemy of national liberation in Latin America tactically is the native bourgeoisie in Brazil, Bolivia, Mexico, etc., and the local bourgeoisie in the Latin American countryside. This is so—in Asia and Africa included—notwithstanding that strategically the principal enemy undoubtedly is imperialism.

2. The Latin American class structure was formed and transformed by the development of the colonial structure of international capitalism, from mercantilism to imperialism. Through this colonial structure, the consecutive metropolises of Spain, Britain, and North America have subjected Latin America to an economic exploitation and political domination which determined its present class and socio-cultural structure. The same colonial structure extends throughout Latin America, where national metropolises subject their provincial centers, and these the local centers, to a similar internal colonialism. Since the structures are completely interpenetrated, the determination of the Latin American class-structure by the colonial structure does not prevent the fundamental contradictions of Latin America from being "internal." The same is true for Asia and Africa.

3. Today the anti-imperialist struggle in Latin America must be carried out through class struggle. Popular mobilization against the immediate class enemy on the national and local levels produces a stronger confrontation with the principal imperialist enemy than does direct anti-imperialist mobilization. Nationalist mobilization through the political alliance of the broadest anti-imperialist forces

1967–68. This is an extended version of a paper presented at the Cultural Congress of Havana in January 1968.

does not adequately challenge the immediate class enemy, and generally it does not even result in a real and necessary confrontation with the imperialist enemy. This also applies to the neo-colonial countries of Asia and Africa and perhaps to some colonial countries, unless they are already militarily occupied by imperialism.

4. The strategic coincidence of class struggle and the anti-imperialist struggle, and the tactical precedence of class struggle in Latin America over the anti-imperialist struggle against the metropolitan bourgeoisie, is obviously valid for guerrilla warfare, which must begin against the national bourgeoisie of the country; and it is also valid for the ideological and political struggle that must be directed not only against the imperialist and colonial enemy but against the native class enemy.

The fundamental political question of who must make the revolution against whom may be reformulated: Who is the principal enemy and who is the immediate enemy? There is universal agreement among revolutionaries and even among many reformists that the principal enemy is imperialism. But who is the *immediate* enemy, the first enemy to be fought in the revolutionary struggle? Is the immediate enemy also imperialism and the metropolitan bourgeoisie; or is the immediate enemy the Latin American (or Brazilian, Peruvian, Guatemalan, Mexican) bourgeoisie and in fact the local bourgeoisie in the countryside? Is the maximum popular force mobilized against the weakest points of the imperialist capitalist system by the broadest possible political coalition against imperialism as the principal enemy, or by the strongest possible popular struggle against the Latin American bourgeoisie as the immediate enemy? Is the ideological counterpart of this revolutionary struggle to be limited to the colonial battleground of nationalism or must it be extended to the class struggle for socialism?

To answer these questions, it is useful to distinguish between the colonial (or neo-colonial) structure and the class structure of Latin America. The class structure may be identified by the people's relation to the means of production and by their participation in the productive process in one place or another. The colonial structure relates one place or sector or identifiable ethnic or racial group with another. The capitalist system has a colonial structure through which the imperialist metropolis exploits its Latin American and other colonies (and its Afro-American internal colonies at home) and through which—through "internal colonialism"—the national metropolises of Latin America exploit their provincial centers, and these in turn their respective hinterlands, in a colonial chain that extends without a break from the imperialist center out to the most isolated rural region of Latin American and other underdeveloped countries.

This distinction is not made to suggest that the colonial and class structures are separate, but on the contrary to inquire how they are mutually determined or related and to find where and how to combat them both. Historical and social scientific research along the lines proposed below is likely to show that throughout the history of Latin America the colonial and neo-colonial productive and distributive relations between the mercantile capitalist or imperialist metropolis and Latin America and also between the Latin American national metropolises and the internal colonies in their respective hinterlands have shaped the class structure of Latin America on both the national and local levels more than the other way around. As a result, it is suggested here that though it may seem paradoxical, popular mobilization against the immediate class enemy at the local and the national levels in Latin America generates a stronger challenge and produces a greater confrontation with the principal colonial or imperialist enemy than does mobilization against the imperialist enemy directly; and nationalist mobilization against imperialism as the principal enemy does not adequately confront the Latin American capitalist class enemy at the national or local level. Though imperialism is the principal enemy, it must be fought through immediate struggle against the class enemy at home.

This suggestion, which appears to contradict widely accepted tenets of revolutionary policy in Latin America, is by no means, as some might suspect, an attempt to dampen or deflect the necessary anti-imperialist struggle in Latin America. It is a suggestion for discussion and scientific inquiry into Latin American circumstances, such as that proposed below. And there is evidence from revolutionary experience to support this suggestion: the confrontation between the Cuban people and imperialism was produced by popular mobilization against the Cuban class enemy, both in the Sierra Maestra and in Havana, and not the other way around. The October Revolution, which produced contradiction and the confrontation between socialism and imperialism, was the result of a struggle against the domestic class enemy, with even the partial neutralization of imperialism after Brest-Litovsk. And several failures of socialist revolutions, it may be suggested, must be attributed to excessive emphasis on a foreign enemy to the exclusion of the domestic and local one. Even the confrontation of the constitutionalist forces in Santo Domingo with imperialism did not come until the former had challenged the local class enemy. But due to the colonial structure of the imperialist and domestic capitalist system and thanks to the mutual reinforcement of the colonial and class structures, popular overthrow of the bourgeois class, or even popular challenge to its hegemony, draws the imperialist forces into the struggle. Unless they are already in the country as an occupying military force—as they were in China, Yugoslavia, and Vietnam, or as they are in a colonial, as distinct from a neo-colonial, country—imperialist forces would seem to be more strongly challenged through struggle against the immediate class enemy at home than through nationalist class coalition attempts to mobilize the people against an imperialist and often enough all-too-abstract-appearing imperialist enemy abroad. In rural areas, particularly, people will wish to—and should be asked to—struggle against the immediate class enemy who oppresses them there, rather than against a foreign enemy they do not see and know. And guerrilla foco strategy certainly must be directed and must mobilize people against the immediate class enemy, not only in the national capital but in the local guerrilla zone itself. That, but only that, will produce the real confrontation with imperialism soon enough.

## History

What, then, is the class and colonial structure of Latin America; what are its characteristics in different parts of the continent; what is their relationship to the imperialist system as a whole; and how can or must Latin American class and colonial exploitation be converted into revolution?

Latin America and the other parts of the world which became underdeveloped were long ago incorporated into the expanding world mercantile capitalist and then imperialist system as political and/or economic colonies. Any adequate comprehension of the economic, social, political, and cultural characteristics of Latin America and other underdeveloped areas therefore requires the scientific examination not only of their societies in and of themselves, but also of the colonial and class structure of this world system as a whole. This study, both in its historical and contemporary aspects, must in part be undertaken by historians and social scientists from the underdeveloped countries themselves if they wish to understand their own societies. This is all the more necessary, inasmuch as the analysis of the productive capacity and relations of capitalism and imperialism, even by most Marxists, has so far been pursued from a metropolitan perspective in which the colonial countries are viewed more as supplementary annexes than as integral parts of the structure and development of this capitalist system. The resulting distorted picture and analysis of capitalism must be corrected, especially by social scientists from the capitalist system's underdeveloped part, through scientific examination from a worldwide perspective which corresponds to capitalism's worldwide reality.

Latin American reality and underdevelopment derives from its integration in this world mercantile capitalist and imperialist system. The understanding of this reality and the analysis of the causes of this underdevelopment must be derived from the scientific examination of Latin American participation in the historical and still on-going process of world capitalist development. This is most evidently the case for those parts of Latin America which comprise the majority of its population and land area—notably the Caribbean, Brazil, and the southern cone countries—where this historical process painted contemporary society on what was virtually a tabula rasa with either no population or an immediately replaced population when the Europeans arrived. Nonetheless, the contemporary society of Indoamerica, in which lived nearly fifty million descendants of the pre-hispanic population, was no less shaped by this same historical process: the Indians involuntarily gave their land and labor to the development of the national and overseas metropolises in the colonial, national, and still-contemporary period. To hold that these Indians have been left essentially untouched by this historical process, or that they are substantially isolated from Latin American and world capitalist society today, is contrary to all historical and contemporary fact.

The class structure of Latin America has throughout this process essentially been the product of the colonial structure which the Iberian, and later the British and North American, metropolis imposed and impressed on Latin America in the successful drive to make the latter's people into the producers and suppliers of raw materials *and capital* for the world productive process that led to metropolitan economic development. Thus, and this is true not only on the national level but also on the local one, Latin America came to have and still has the class structure of a colonial or neo-colonial export economy.

Ferrer notes:

> Mining, tropical agriculture, fishing, hunting, and lumbering (all of which are basically connected with export trade) were the developing industries in the colonial economies and, as such, attracted available capital and labor resources. . . . The groups with interests in exporting activities were merchants and property owners with high incomes and high Crown and Church officials. These sectors of the population . . . constituted both the internal colonial market and the source of capital accumulation. . . . The greater the concentration of wealth in the hands of a small group of property owners, merchants, and influential politicians, the greater the propensity to obtain durable and manufactured consumer goods from abroad . . . Thus, the export sector by its very nature would not allow the transformation of the system as a whole . . . [and was] the basic obstacle to the diversification of the internal productive structure and, therefore, to the consequent elevation of the technical and cultural levels of the population, the development of social groups connected with the evolution of internal markets, and the search for new lines of exportation free from the metropolitan authority.[1]

Of the remaining potentially investible capital, the structure of underdevelopment directed a large part into mining, agricultural, transport, and commercial enterprises for *export* to the metropolis, much of the rest to luxury *import* from the metropolis, and only very little into manufacturing and consumption related to the internal market. Thanks to foreign trade and finance, the economic and political interests of the mining, agricultural, and commercial bourgeoisie did not lie with internal development.[2]

The productive relations and class structure of the latifundium, the mine, and their economic and social hinterland grew up in response to the colonialist exploitative needs of the overseas and Latin American metropolises. They were not, as is so widely but falsely claimed, the result of the transfer of Iberian feudal institutions during the sixteenth century. The development of this class structure and its contemporary economic and political consequences still demand additional research.

Nonetheless, even on the basis of the facts that are already universally known today, it is possible to affirm with confidence that the class structure and productive relations associated with the nineteenth and twentieth century latifundium in Cuba, Argentina, coastal Peru, coffee-growing São Paulo, and contemporary post-agrarian reform northern Mexico can have absolutely nothing to do with the supposed importation of feudal institutions from the Iberian peninsula during colonial times (nor can, of course, the quite similar institutions in the British West Indies). As I have argued in the first essay in this book, the same thing, exactly, is shown by the historical evidence from eighteenth-century Chile, seventeenth-century Mexico, and elsewhere. In reality, though this requires further study, it is the productive and mercantile requirements of the colonial mercantile capitalist and imperialist system which have shaped the essentially capitalist class structure of the agricultural and mining export regions. The consequences of introducing modern industry into this colonial and class structure will be touched on below.

Until imperialism, the only exception to this pattern had been the weakening of the ties of foreign trade and finance during metropolitan wars or depressions, such as that of the seventeenth century, and the initial absence of such effective ties between the metropolis and isolated non-overseas export-oriented regions which permitted a temporary or incipient autonomous capital accumulation and industrial development for the internal market, such as that of the eighteenth century in São Paulo in Brazil, in Tucumán and other places in Argentina, Asunción in Paraguay, Quórétaro and Puebla in Mexico, and others.

In the colonial era of capitalist development, then, foreign finance was primarily a stimulatory adjunct to the pillage of resources, the exploitation of labor, and the colonial trade which initiated the development of the European metropolis and simultaneously the underdevelopment of the Latin American satellites.

The economic and political ascendancy of Great Britain and the political independence of Latin America after the Napoleonic Wars left three major interest groups to decide the future of Latin America through their tripartite struggle: (1) The Latin American agricultural, mining, and commercial interests which sought to maintain the underdevelopment-generating export economy structure—and only wanted to replace their Iberian rivals from their privileged positions in it; (2) the industrial and other interest groups from the aforementioned and other interior regions, which sought to defend their budding but still weak development-generating economies from more free trade and foreign finance, which was threatening to force them out of existence; and (3) the victorious and industrializing British whose Foreign Minister Lord Canning noted in 1824: "Spanish America is free; and if we do not mismanage our affairs, she is English." The battlelines were drawn with the traditional Latin American import-export and metropolitan industrial-merchant bourgeoisies in natural alliance against the weak Latin American provincial and industrial nationalists. The outcome was practically predetermined by the past historical process of capitalist development, which had stacked the cards this way.

During the period from the mid-twenties to the mid-forties or fifties, the nationalist interests from the interior were still able to force their governments to impose protective tariffs on many countries. Industry, national flag shipping, and other development-generating activities showed spurts of life. At the same time, Latin Americans rehabilitated old and opened new mines, and began to develop their agricultural and other primary goods export sectors. To permit and promote internal economic development as well as to respond to increasing external demand for raw materials, the liberals pressed for land and other reforms, as well as for immigration to increase the domestic labor force and expand the internal market.

The export-import metropolitan-oriented Latin American bourgeoisies and their national mining and agricultural allies opposed this autonomous capitalist development because, with tariff protection, it took place at the cost of their export-import interests; and they fought and defeated the provincial and industrial nationalists, who claimed the protection of federal states' rights, in the federalist-unitarist civil wars of the thirties and forties. The metropolitan powers aided their Latin American junior trade partners with arms, naval blockades, and where necessary with direct military intervention and instigation of new wars, such as that of the Triple Alliance against Paraguay, which cost 6/7 of its male population in the defense of its nationally financed railroad and genuinely independent autonomous development effort.

Trade and sword were readying Latin America for metropolitan free trade, and to do so the competition of Latin American industrial development had to be eliminated; and, with the victory of the outward-oriented economic interest groups over the inward-oriented ones, ever more of the Latin American economy and state as well had to be subordinated to the metropolis. Only then would trade become free and would foreign finance again come into its own. A contemporary Argentinian nationalist noted that

> after 1810 . . . the country's balance of trade had been consistently unfavorable, and at the same time native merchants had suffered irreparable losses. Both wholesale export trade and retail import commerce had passed into foreign hands. The conclusion seems inescapable, therefore, that the opening of the country to foreigners proved harmful on balance. Foreigners displaced natives not only in commerce but in industry and agriculture as well.

Another added:

> It is not possible that Buenos Aires should have sacrificed blood and wealth solely for the purpose of becoming a consumer of the products and manufacture of foreign countries, for such is degrading and does not correspond to the great potentialities which nature has

bestowed upon the country. . . . It is erroneous to assume that protection breeds monopoly. The fact is that Argentina, which has been under a regime of free trade for over twenty years, is now controlled by a handful of foreigners. If protection was going to dislodge foreign merchants from their positions of economic pre-eminence, the country would have occasion to congratulate itself on making the first step toward regaining its economic independ-ence. . . . The nation cannot continue without restricting foreign trade, since restriction alone would make industrial expansion pos-sible; it must no longer endure the weight of foreign monopoly which strangles every attempt at industrialization.[3]

But it did.

As Burgin correctly analyzes in his study of Argentine federal-ism,

the economic development of post-revolutionary Argentina was char-acterized by a shift of the economic center of gravity from the interior toward the seacoast, brought about by the rapid expansion of the latter and the simultaneous retrogression of the former. The uneven character of economic development resulted in what was to some extent a self-perpetuating inequality. The country became divided into poor and rich provinces. The interior provinces were forced to relinquish ever larger portions of the national income to Buenos Aires and other provinces of the East.[4]

In Brazil, Chile, Mexico, and throughout Latin America, indus-trialists, patriots, and foresighted economists similarly denounced this same inevitable process of capitalist underdevelopment. But in vain: World capitalist development and the sword had made free trade the order of the day. And with it came foreign capital.

Free trade, as the German nationalist Friedrich List aptly noted, became Great Britain's principal export. It was not for nothing that Manchester Liberalism was born in Cottonopolis. But it was embraced with enthusiasm, as Claudio Veliz has pointed out, by the three legs of the Latin American economic and political table, which had survived since colonial times, had defeated their na-tional developmentist domestic rivals and captured the Latin American state, and which were now naturally allied and subservi-ent to the foreign metropolitan interests because free foreign trade secured their and the foreigners' closed national monopoly.

Not surprisingly, but in terms both of historical reality and present-day political and ideological needs regrettably, we owe most existing interpretations of these and other events in Latin America to interested liberal contemporaries and historians who have shaped our image of the events in terms of their interests. Unfortunately, Marxists who have drawn primarily on metropolitan theory have also drawn primarily on liberal-researched fact for their analyses. In consequence, they have also all too often bottled a liberal admixture of wine and water under a Marxist label. Revolutionary political policy today could well benefit from a truly scientific Marxist re-interpretation of such historical figures as Rosas and Rivadavia in Argentina, Dr. Francia and Lopez (father and son) in Paraguay, Rengifo and Balmaceda in Chile, Mauá and Nabuco in Brazil, Mora or Lucas Alamán and Juarez in Mexico, and their respective economic and political policies or epochs. Even by the early nineteenth century, some of these appear to have attempted, and others to have opposed or co-opted, the bourgeois democratic revolution and nationalist industrialization program for which certain political interests are even now not trying to rally' popular support in Latin America.

The previous period paved the way for the emergence of imperialism and its new forms of foreign investment both in the metropolis and in Latin America, where free trade and liberal land and other reforms had concentrated land into fewer hands, had thus created a larger agricultural and unemployed labor force, and had brought forth governments dependent on the metropolis; these now opened the door not only to more metropolitan trade but to the new imperialist investment finance which was quick to take advantage of these developments.

The new metropolitan demand for and Latin American profitability of raw materials production and export attracted both private and public Latin American capital into expanding the infrastructure necessary for this export production. In Brazil, Argentina, Paraguay, Chile, Guatemala, and Mexico (to the author's knowledge, but probably in other countries as well), domestic or national capital built the first railroad. In Chile, it opened up the nitrate and copper mines that were to become the world's principal supplier of commercial fertilizer and red metal, in Brazil it opened the coffee plantations that supplied nearly all the world's tables, and similarly elsewhere. Only after this proved to be a booming business—as when Britain had had to find outlets for its steel—did foreign capital enter into these sectors and take over the ownership and management of these initially Latin American enterprises by buying out, often with Latin American capital, the native's concessions.

In Latin America, this same imperialist trade and finance did more than increase the amount of production, trade, and profit by accumulating about U.S. $10,000 million of investment capital there. The imperialist metropolis used its foreign trade and finance to penetrate the Latin American economy far more completely, and to use the latter's productive potential far more efficiently and exhaustively for metropolitan development, than the colonial metropolis had ever been able to do. As Rosa Luxemburg noted of a similar process elsewhere, "stripped of all obscuring connecting links, these relations consist in the simple fact the European capital has largely swallowed up the Egyptian peasant economy. Enormous tracts of land, labour, and labour products without number, accruing to the state as taxes, have ultimately been converted into European capital and have been accumulated." [5]

Indeed, in Latin America imperialism went further. It not only availed itself of the state to invade agriculture; it took over nearly all economic and political institutions to incorporate the entire economy into the imperialist system. The latifundia grew at a pace and to proportions unknown in all previous history, especially in Argentina, Uruguay, Brazil, Cuba, Mexico, and Central America. With the aid of the Latin American governments, foreigners came to own—usually for next to nothing—immense tracts of land. And where they did not get the land, they got its products anyway, because the metropolis also took over and monopolized the merchandising of agricultural and most other products. The metropolis took over Latin American mines and expanded their output, sometimes exhausting irreplaceable resources, such as the Chilean nitrates, in a few years. To get these raw materials out of Latin America and to get its equipment and goods in, the metropolis stimulated the construction of ports, of railroads, and, to service all this, of public utilities. The railroad network and elec-

tric grid, far from being net- or grid-like, was ray-like and connected the hinterland of each country and sometimes of several
countries with the port of entry and exit, which was in turn
connected to the metropolis. Today, four-score years later, much
of this export-import pattern still remains, in part because the
railroad right-of-way is still laid out that way, and more importantly because the metropolitan-oriented urban, economic, and
political development which nineteenth-century imperialism generated in Latin America gave rise to vested class interests which
tried, and with metropolitan support managed, to maintain and
expand this development of Latin American underdevelopment
during the twentieth century.

Implanted in colonial and deepened in the free trade eras, the
colonial and class structure of underdevelopment was consolidated
in Latin America by nineteenth-century imperialist trade and
finance. Latin America was converted into a primary monoproduct
export economy with its latifundium and expropriated rural proletariat or even lumpenproletariat exploited by a satellized bourgeoisie acting through the corrupt state of a non-country: "Barba-
rous Mexico" (Turner[6]); the "Banana Republics" of Central
America, which are not company stores but "company countries";
"The Inexorable Evolution of the Latifundium: Overproduction,
Economic Dependence, and Growing Poverty in Cuba" (Guerra
y Sanchez[7]); "British Argentina"; and the "Pathological Chile"
of which the historian Francisco Encina wrote in 1912, under the
title "Our Economic Inferiority: Its Causes and Consequences":

> Our economic development of recent years exhibits symptoms which
> characterize a real pathological state. Until the middle of the
> nineteenth century, Chile's foreign trade was almost exclusively in
> the hands of Chileans. In less than fifty years, foreign trade has
> choked off our nascent commercial initiative abroad; and in our
> own home it has eliminated us from international trade and re-
> placed us, in large part, in retail trade. . . . The merchant marine
> . . . has fallen into sad straits and continues to cede ground to
> foreign shipping even in the coastwide trade. The majority of the
> insurance companies that operate among us have their head office
> abroad. The national banks have ceded and keep ceding ground to
> the branches of foreign banks. An ever-growing share of the bonds

of the savings institutions is passing into the hands of foreigners who live abroad.[8]

With the development of nineteenth-century imperialism, foreign investment came to play an almost co-equal part with foreign trade in harnessing Latin America to capitalist development and in transforming its economy, society, and policy until the structure of Latin American underdevelopment was firmly consolidated.

## Bourgeois Nationalism

In Latin America, World War I had given the satellite economies a respite from foreign trade and finance as well as from other ties with the metropolis. Accordingly, as had happened before and would again, Latin Americans generated their own industrial development, mostly for the internal consumer goods market. But no sooner did the war end, than did metropolitan, now increasingly United States-based, industry expand into precisely those regions and sectors—especially consumer goods manufacture in Buenos Aires and São Paulo—which Latin Americans had just opened up industrially and shown to be profitable. Here then, supported by their financial, technological, and political power, the giant American and British corporations displaced and even replaced—that is de-patriated—Latin American industry. The balance of payments crises that naturally followed were met by foreign loans to cover the Latin American deficits and to extract government concessions for increased metropolitan penetration of the Latin American economies.

The 1929 crash, contrary to international trade theory but true to historical precedent, sharply reduced foreign finance along with foreign trade and prices, and therefore also reduced the transfer of satellite investible resources to the metropolis. This weakening of economic ties with, and reduction of metropolitan political interference in, Latin America was begun by the Depression of 1930, maintained by the recession of 1937, and continued by the Second World War and its reconstruction aftermath until the early 1950's. It created economic conditions and permitted political changes in Latin America which resulted in the beginning of

its strongest nationalist policy and biggest independent industrialization drive since the post-independence 1830's and 1840's.

It is essential to understand that the recent changes in the class
structure of Brazil, Argentina, Chile, Venezuela, Mexico, and
other parts of Latin America have occurred both within their
external and internal colonial structure and substantially in response to metropolitan-generated changes in their colonial relations. And it is important to interpret these changes of class structure in terms of the colonial structure that underlies them. This
must be done primarily by Latin American social scientists and
other intellectuals who have been able to free themselves from
the ideological and political commitment to the bourgeois order
created by these developments.

The economic shock of the drastic reduction of Latin America's
import capacity, the decline of metropolitan manufacturing exports and of foreign investment and loans, which was caused by
the Depression in the metropolis, had far-reaching economic and
political consequences in many parts of Latin America. It is essential to understand both the extent *and the limitations* of these
consequences before we can adequately comprehend the resulting economic and political problems of today. The onset of the
Depression changed national income and its distribution in Latin
America so much that the existing institutional framework was
unable to cope with the necessary adjustments: Revolutions occurred in 1930 or soon thereafter in Brazil, Argentina, Chile,
Cuba; and the Mexican Revolution of 1910, which had nearly
come to a halt, was given a new impetus. Revolutionary activity
agitated other parts of the continent. The metropolitan-allied export interests were obliged to form a coalition with the still weak
industrial interests and (at least in Brazil) with new regional interests which forced themselves into the government. Counter-
revolutions representing some of the traditional interests were
attempted within two or three years, and were partially successful
in Cuba and Chile, though not in the three major Latin American
countries. Throughout, the relaxation of the economic colonial
ties with the metropolis and the relative paralysis of imperialist
political intervention (though not in Cuba) which the metropolitan Depression produced in Latin America also laid the economic

and political basis for new class alignments and industrialization policies. So long as the national governments continued to protect the export interests (as the Brazilian government did through coffee price supports), these interests were now willing and in some cases anxious to permit the promotion of domestic manufacturing—at a time when the Depression had ruined the export business anyway.

Some Latin American countries began to produce the consumer goods they previously imported. But this process of "import substitution" had two major built-in limitations, both of which derived from the existing class structure. First, they had to begin with the existing income distribution and demand structure. This meant that they had to concentrate on consumer goods, particularly for the high income market. Without a major change in the class structure and in income distribution, the internal market could not expand fast enough to sustain the import substitution process indefinitely. For the same reason, they did not produce enough industrial equipment or producers goods (Sector I in Marxist terms), so that they were increasingly obliged to import these from abroad in order even to keep the import substitution process going. That is, they ended up only substituting some imports for others. This renewed their dependence on the metropolis and led to the renewal of foreign investment. To have avoided these two limitations, these Latin American countries would have had to follow the Soviet industrialization model in which the state, rather than consumer demand, determined the goods—capital goods—to be produced first. But for that they would have had to have had a Soviet state, that is, a socialist class structure. The domestic political arrangements of the thirties were able to survive the Depression for some time because the Second World War, though it improved the export picture, still did not permit the renewal of imports from the metropolis. But the end of the Korean War finally terminated this Latin American honeymoon in which the colonial export interests had maintained an uneasy marriage with national bourgeois industrial interests and a growing industrial proletariat, producing as offspring an ill-formed national industry, and all with imperialism's grudging blessings.

It is particularly important to understand not only the successes but the limitations of this period, because two principal political problems of our day arise out of the survival of its deformed off-spring and out of some people's attempts to breathe new life into it or to produce another such child today. This period saw the flowering of the political and ideological movements of Vargas, Perón, Cárdenas, Haya de la Torre, Aguirre Cerda, Betancourt, Figueres, Arevalo-Arbenz (and, one might note, of Ghandi and Nehru in another colonial part of the same worldwide system). And it was the time of economic nationalism, national, and in some cases industrial, development, growth of urban industrial workers and middle sectors (*capas*), democratic reformism, wel-farism, and populism, all associated with these names (except for Haya, who never got the reins of government, and Betancourt, of whom, notably, this holds only for his first presidential period). These developments require further study, particularly to account for the differences in their scope and timing. Why, for instance, were Peronism and Arevalo-Arbenzism so late in this period, compared to developments in Brazil, Chile, Mexico?

We may be tempted to call this the work of the national bour-geoisie in Latin America, which perhaps attempted a colonial ver-sion of the "bourgeois democratic revolution" or of a "marriage of rye and iron" on the German Bismarkian or Japanese Mejii Restoration model, all while the colonial ties were temporarily weakened by depression and war in the imperialist metropolis. But perhaps, if we must look for any at all, it may be historically more accurate to look for the bourgeois democratic revolution a hundred years earlier when the generations of Francia, Lopez, Rosas (before he, like Betancourt after him, changed colors), Juarez, and later Nabuco and Balmaceda, had symbolized essen-tially similar attempts at nationalist and national development.

Irrespective of our answer to this question, it is imperative to understand that this industrial development, this bourgeois na-tionalism, this alliance of the working class with national bourgeois elements against imperialism abroad and the export interests at home, and the whole ideological superstructure that goes with them, all were the product of particular historical circumstances. They definitely came to an end with the recovery of the metropolis after the Second World War and with the important changes that the metropolis and the remainder of the world have undergone since then, particularly the technological revolution, the militarization of the United States, and the socialist revolution and development in some of the metropolis's ex-colonies. These events, these changes in the colonial structure of the world capitalist system, render the continuation of such bourgeois nationalist development in Latin America impossible and make all dreams of its re-initiation in the future entirely utopian—that is, utopian for the bourgeoisie, but politically suicidal for the people. And this is so not only in Latin America, but as the evidence from the new neo-colonies of Africa, Asia, and particularly Indonesia shows, it is true for the colonial part of the imperialist system generally.

## Neo-Imperialism

Imperialism is certainly the principal enemy of mankind today. But how does this enmity express itself in the heart of contemporary Latin American society? What expression does this enemy take there, and how must we fight it? To find answers to these questions it is well to inquire further into the complex and still changing relationship between colonial and class structure in Latin America. We may begin with some questions posed by recent changes in the colonial structure.

The classical colonial relationship between the metropolis and Latin America, in which the former's exploitation of the latter was principally arranged through the productive division of labor and the monopolistic exchange of manufactured commodities and raw materials, is being replaced or at least supplemented by a new form of exploitation through foreign investment and so-called aid. As the metropolis increasingly achieves more capital-intensive, and particularly more technologically complex, forms of production at home, it increasingly replaces simple foreign trade with foreign investment in manufacturing subsidiary facilities abroad, which now produce locally the formerly imported consumer and some producer goods—but with equipment and technology imported from the home office (*matriz*) in the imperialist metropolis. The Latin American and other colonies' loss of capital because of the terms of trade (not only the *deterioration* of the terms of trade of which ECLA and UNCTAD complain, but also the monopoly exploitation that these terms of trade represent at their least unfavorable level, such as that of the Korean War period) is thus increasingly supplemented by an additional flow of capital from the colonies to the metropolis because of profit remittance, debt service, royalties, etc. Thus, in 1961–63 Latin America's payment for these "invisible" financial "services" amounted to 40 percent of Latin America's foreign exchange earnings; and payment for foreign-provided transportation and other services amounted to another 21.5 percent, for a total of 61.5 percent of foreign exchange earnings that Latin America was obliged to spend for services, without the importation of a single penny's-worth of goods. This meant an annual expenditure of U.S. $6,000 million, or 7 percent of Latin America's gross national product for these years.[9] By comparison, the deterioration of the terms of trade since the early 1950's, which is CEPAL'S principal complaint, represented a 3 percent (additional) loss of Latin American GNP;[10] and total Latin American expenditures for education, from kindergarten through university, public and private, were 2.6 percent of its GNP.[11] Since that time the debt service component of this capital drain has risen from 15 percent to 19 percent (in 1966) of foreign exchange earnings, probably raising the total of service payments to over 65 percent of foreign exchange earnings, or nearly 8 percent of the GNP—plus the 3 percent or more represented by the deterioration of the terms of trade and an incalculable amount of loss through the monopoly exploitation in these terms of trade. Yet even this calculable capital drain out of Latin America is three or four times as great as that mentioned in the Second Declaration of Havana and in recent estimates by Fidel. No wonder this colonial relationship turns Latin America's balance of trade surplus into a chronic and growing balance of payments deficit, which, in a vicious spiral, makes the Latin American bourgeoisie ever more dependent on imperialism. This growing problem is worthy of much more study than it has so far received.

Nonetheless, worse than the drain of capital is the structure of underdevelopment and the brake and mischanneling to which it subjects national development, and which imperialism deepens through increasing foreign investment. The institutional mechanisms through which this flow of capital from the poor to the rich is effected also pose a number of questions. What is the source of this capital in Latin America, and most particularly how is foreign, principally United States, investment in Latin America financed? The evidence suggests that an increasingly small share of "North American" investment capital is brought to Latin America from North America, and that an ever greater part of it is raised in Latin America itself.

Thus, according to the United States Department of Commerce, of the total capital obtained and employed from all sources by United States operations in Brazil in 1957, 26 percent came from the United States and the remainder was raised in Brazil, including 36 percent from Brazilian sources outside the American firms.[12] Of the American capital directly invested in Canada that same year, 26 percent came from the United States while the remainder was raised in Canada.[13] By 1964, however, the part of American investment in Canada that entered from the United States had declined to 5 percent, making the average American contribution to the total capital used by American firms in Canada during the period 1957–64 only 15 percent. The remainder of the "foreign investment" was raised in Canada through retained earnings (42 percent), depreciation charges (31 percent), and funds raised by American firms on the Canadian capital market (12 percent). According to a survey of American direct investment firms operating in Canada in the period 1950–59, 79 percent of the firms raised over 25 percent of the capital for their Canadian operations in Canada, 65 percent of the firms raised over 50 percent in Canada, and 47 percent of the American firms with investments in Canada raised all of the capital for their Canadian operations in Canada. There is reason to believe that this American reliance on foreign capital to finance American "foreign investment" is still greater in the poor underdeveloped countries, which are weaker and more defenseless than Canada. This, then, is the source of the flow of capital on investment account from the poor underdeveloped countries to the rich developed ones.

No wonder that between 1950 and 1965 the flow of capital on

private investment account registered by the U.S. Department of Commerce was $9,000 million from the United States to the world other than Europe and Canada and $25,600 million from these same countries in Asia, Africa, and Latin America to the United States—of which $3,800 million went from the U.S. to Latin America and $11,300 million went from Latin America to the U.S.[14] It is therefore necessary to inquire with greater care into the Latin American banking system (government banks, nationally owned private banks, and foreign-owned private banks), stock markets and other financial institutions, and foreign and nationally owned and especially mixed-ownership industrial and commercial enterprises, which make this capital flow possible.

Especially important, both on economic and political grounds, is the growing association of foreign and national capital in these mixed enterprises; and most important—and least studied—is the recent emergence of mixed enterprises which associate private foreign capital with Latin American national governments, as in the "Chilenization" of copper. Who provides the bulk of the capital (the Latin Americans, presumably); who has or achieves effective control of the enterprises, and therefore decides what goods to produce, what industrial equipment and processes to use, when to expand and contract, etc. (the Americans, presumably); and who reaps the bulk of the profits (the Americans, presumably); and who is left with the losses when business is unfavorable (the Latin Americans, presumably)? What are the *political* consequences of this association—no, incorporation—not only of Latin American export interests but now also of the Latin American industrial bourgeoisie, the erstwhile "national" bourgeoisie, with/by the imperialist monopoly? Some Latin American countries passed laws requiring either 49 percent or 51 percent "national" participation in certain enterprises, supposedly to "protect" the national interest. It is now clear that these measures only serve to submerge surviving elements of the "national" bourgeoisie in the imperialist one. Some Latin American bourgeois governments propose to "protect" or even "further" the "national" interest by themselves entering such mixed partnerships. The result can only be that these colonial governments lose even what little political bargaining power they have left in their already all too junior partnership with imperialism. This matter also demands greater scientific and political clarification.

The other arm of the contemporary economic and political offensive of American imperialism in Latin America is "foreign aid" and particularly its institutional expression in the "Alliance for Progress" and "economic integration." These have both been denounced by the Left in Latin America, though the latter hardly even that; but they have by no means been adequately analyzed. Exactly who is allied to whom, and who is aided by whom? There is evidence, which bears further investigation, that much of the aid does not even go to the Latin American bourgeoisie, and of course much less goes to the Latin American people, but rather that it goes to the U.S. firms operating in Latin America. If the Latin American bourgeoisie is to benefit from this part of the "aid," it must do so through its association with these imperialist monopolies. What then, precisely, is the relation of this aid to foreign investment? Most denounced are the monetary, fiscal, exchange, and wage policy strings attached to the foreign loans of U.S. and UN agencies, especially the International Monetary Fund. Yet these policies do not benefit only the imperialist bourgeoisie but also benefit most sectors of the Latin American grand bourgeoisie, and the latter accept and execute them—like devaluation—eagerly. Why? With what political implications?

The Alliance for Progress began with substantial propaganda about land, fiscal, and other reforms, which had earlier been promoted by the more progressive and nationalist sectors of the Latin American bourgeoisie, and which more recently had been recommended by their ideological mouthpiece, the United Nations Economic Commission for Latin America (ECLA). But these reform proposals were soon archived along with their associated economic "plans" (for reasons to be inquired into below); and their pride of place has since been taken, as was confirmed by the last "Inter"-American Presidents' meeting in Punta del Este in 1967, by proposals to accelerate the formation of a "Latin American" common market. This latter proposal enjoys very much more economic realism and political backing from the point of view of the United States, the grand bourgeoisie in the major

Latin American countries, and the governments, including that of the "nationalist" Frei, which serve them. Evidently, it is much more realistic to try to expand industry in these Latin American countries by realigning the colonial structure abroad than by re-forming the class structure at home—especially if in the process the degree of monopolization and the amount of monopoly profit can be increased at the expense of the already weak medium bourgeoisie and the popular classes at home, that is, through what will amount to a counter-reform of the class structure at home. It is worthy of note that this "economic integration" proposal also enjoys the blessings of that defender of supposedly "national" bourgeois interests, ECLA. Yet there are scarcely half-a-dozen articles and not a single serious study of the economic basis or consequences and the political implications of this move toward economic—and with it political and military—integration by the imperialist and Latin American bourgeoisie. Who is to make *la patria América*, and on what basis, imperialism or revolution?

*Class Structure*

What then is the class structure in Latin America and how is the anti-colonial and class struggle to proceed to socialism? We may inquire into the national, urban, and rural class structure in turn. The "national" governments are mostly even more colonial than the bourgeoisies they represent. It seems legitimate to ask—and in the case of contemporary Africa there can be little question—to what extent national states in the classical sense have existed in Latin America since Independence, and to what extent the state machinery has been at most times since then an instrument of a coalition between the metropolitan bourgeoisie and the major sectors of the Latin American bourgeoisies, who have always been the junior partners or even merely the executors of imperialism. Military governments have been installed to manage state affairs for these interests when civilian governments were unable to do so. (The new military governments of Brazil and Argentina, which represent an important new departure, will be discussed below.)

The agricultural and mining export bourgeoisie owes its existence and survival to the colonial structure, and it is loyal to its colonial patron. This is true both of its productive sector and its commercial one, in the countryside and in the city. The latifundia "oligarchy" has no independent existence and—as we shall below —we must in fact question the extent to which it is even iden- tifiably separate from the commercial and now also industrial bourgeoisie. This latter sector of the bourgeoisie, as appears from the examination of foreign investment, has now also been solidly integrated into the coalition between imperialism and its Latin American comprador and bureaucratic bourgeois partners and executors. The combination of imperialist penetration, the decline in the terms of trade, devaluation, the consequent reduction in ability to import industrial equipment, the decline in growth and profit rates, and in some cases the inflation, has since the mid-1950's all but forced the medium industrial "national" manu- facturer and his distributor out of business or into the business empire of a foreign "investor" who bought him out. The foreign enterprise then sometimes converts him, literally, into a bureau- cratic employee of the imperialist enterprise in which he is allowed to continue as "manager" or as "consultant," with a salary or some stock in the imperialist enterprise for himself. What part of the national bourgeoisie, which developed under particular conditions during the thirties and forties, has been able to survive this process in the fifties and sixties? What political power, if any, do those who survive retain for use in any anti- imperialist struggle, when as in Brazil the imperialist squeeze obliges them to react by squeezing their workers, thereby under- mining their erstwhile political alliance with the unionized in- dustrial proletariat, which used to provide the national bourgeoisie with one of its major sources of political power?

In some Latin American countries industrial development produced an industrial proletariat of consequence. So did the mining and petroleum industries, though the latter has never accounted for a large part of the labor force. This industrial proletariat, especially in large industry, has been unionized in part under the aegis of the national bourgeoisie, which wanted to guarantee itself both political support from and control over this labor movement, and by Communist parties, who have been by-

and-large allied to the national bourgeoisie. The unionized industrial workers, though exploited, were often rewarded by wage incomes that are high relative to the bulk of the population, and by social security coverage that is hardly available to most others.

Since the metropolis pre-empts an increasing share of the most profitable Latin American business and forces the remainder into growing economic difficulties, the Latin American bourgeoisie that lives off this less profitable business is left no choice but to fight for its survival—even if vainly—by increasing the degree of wage and price exploitation of its petty bourgeoisie, workers, and peasants, in order to squeeze some additional blood out of that stone; and at times the Latin American bourgeoisie must resort to direct military force. For this reason—no doubt more than for idealistic or even ideological reasons—almost the entire Latin American bourgeoisie is thus thrown into political alliance with—that is, into the arms of—the metropolitan bourgeoisie: They have more than a common long-term interest in defending the system of capitalist exploitation; even in the short run, the Latin American bourgeoisie cannot be national or defend nationalist interests by opposing foreign encroachment on the alliance with Latin American workers and peasants—as the Popular Front rule book would have them do—because the same neo-imperialist encroachment is increasingly forcing the Latin American bourgeoisie to exploit its supposed worker and peasant allies and is thus forcing the bourgeoisie to forego this remaining source of political support. While the Latin American bourgeoisie is pursuing wage, price, and political policies that exploit its workers and repress their legitimate demands for relief from growing exploitation, the Latin American bourgeoisie cannot rally its support against the metropolitan bourgeoisie; meanwhile, the economic inefficiency of this exploitation interferes with domestic saving for investment and obliges the bourgeoisie to turn abroad for immediate foreign finance.

The Brazilian bourgeoisie has been trying to find another way out, first through the "independent" foreign policy of Presidents Quadros and Goulart (who sought new markets in Africa, Latin America, and the socialist countries) and, after that proved impossible in an already imperialized world, through the "interdependent" sub-imperialist foreign policy begun by the present military government as a junior partner to the United States. Brazilian sub-imperialism also requires low wages in Brazil so that the Brazilian bourgeoisie can enter the Latin American market on a low cost basis, which with obsolete but still modern American equipment is the only one possible. In the sub-imperialized countries of Latin America, the Brazilian invasion also leads to depressing wages, since doing so is the local bourgeoisie's only possible defensive reaction. Thus, sub-imperialism also aggravates the contradictions between the bourgeoisie and labor in each of these countries.

Therefore, neo-imperialism and monopoly capitalist development·in Latin America are drawing and driving the entire Latin American bourgeois class—including its comprador, bureaucratic, and national segments—into ever-closer economic and political alliance with and dependence on the imperialist metropolis. The road of national or state capitalism to economic development is already foreclosed to them by neo-imperialist development today. The political task of reversing the development of Latin American underdevelopment therefore falls to the people themselves.

Under these circumstances, what is the economic and political future of this industrial proletariat and its political organizations? The recent economic stagnation of much of Latin America has been translated, among other things, into declining real wages for these workers. This and the declining fortunes of the national bourgeoisie seems to have seriously undermined this worker-bourgeois alliance. The 1964 and 1966 military coups in Brazil and Argentina, which were not simple palace revolts in the "traditional" Latin American style, have substantially undone the remainder of the uneasy marriage between the colonial and national bourgeois interests of the Vargas and Perón eras and have effectively cemented the imperialist-export-foreign-association industry and the commerce-bourgeois marriage. (Internationally these coups correspond to the worldwide imperialist counter-offensive that also includes the African and Indonesian coups.) Will this new bourgeois regime continue to repress the economic and democratic political demands of the industrial workers, as it did in Brazil, or will it try to co-opt the labor movement and succeed as did the national bourgeoisie, perhaps on the Mexican model? And how will labor and its movement fare in the other Latin American countries? Have the Communist parties, whose principal political power rests on this labor union base, been substantially and bureaucratically integrated into the bourgeois establishment? What part will the industrial workers and the Communist parties play in the present stage of the revolutionary process?

Two other urban "sectors" remain, the petty bourgeois middle "class(es)" and the "marginal" or "floating" population, some but by no means all of whom are recent migrants from rural areas who live in the *favelas, villas miserias, callampas, barriadas, ranchos*, etc., and in the *conventillos* of the inner city (though some of these house industrial workers or ex-workers). These comprise the vast and still growing bulk of the urban population. It is no accident that these population groups are generally defined by their placement in the middle of the other classes and/or by their residence. This is because their relation to the means of production or even to the productive process is uncertain at best, and their political behavior is extremely volatile at worst. That is, both are characterized by extremely complex and changing patterns of economic and social relations and political behavior, which require considerable scientific clarification. Are the middle sectors, or particular parts of them, politically progressive because, except for the upper middle class, their income is compressed and their economic and social horizon is restricted by the polarization of the economy and the stagnation of many of its sectors? Or does reduction of their income and the threat of proletarianization make them pursue reactionary political policies in alliance with the grand bourgeoisie and its military regime? Large sectors of the middle class enthusiastically supported the Brazilian and other military coups, only to become disillusioned with the new regime's economic policies. Why does this middle "class" generate the progressive petty bourgeois and especially the student movements, which so far, however, do not represent the majority of their social base? Is it really correct to dampen the class struggle in order to maintain or attract these social groups into an "anti-imperialist" electoral struggle, or must larger sectors of the petty bourgeoisie be led into political opposition against the Latin American grand bourgeoisie, and thereby against imperialism?

Is the "floating" or "marginal" population, which may well account for half of the Latin American urban population (which in turn approaches half the total population) a "lumpenproletariat"? Are these people really ideologically untouchable and politically irresponsive and unorganizable? Imperialism and the bourgeoisie do not think so and are, so far all too successfully, harnessing them to their political purposes, which are only partially manifested by the electoral support these groups gave to Odria, Frei, Adehmar de Barros, etc. Yet in Caracas the Left was able to mobilize part of this population, and in Santo Domingo they ended up mobilizing Colonel Caamaño.

Perhaps the first and most important question to ask about the rural class structure is to what extent, if at all, it is separate and different from the national and urban class structure in Latin America. The importance of this question derives from the near-universal answer by both bourgeois and Marxist scholars and political leaders that much of rural Latin America is in another "semi-feudal" world apart from the urban, national, and international capitalist system—and from the political policy associated with this view. Does Latin America really have a "dual" economy and society, in one part of which a pattern of feudal or semi-feudal productive relations and even a non-capitalist class structure "survives"? Does this "survival" really call for a bourgeois democratic revolution or even a national democratic revolution to extend capitalism into the countryside? Or is this one of the series of supposedly scientific and revolutionary "Marxist" model numbers, 12, 13, 14, which Fidel denounced as a reactionary catechism in his OLAS speech?

The historical record and contemporary reality, whose scientific examination was recommended above, suggest that it has been the world and national capitalist colonial structure which has for over four centuries shaped the productive relations and class structure of rural Latin America. This part of society has therefore never been separate from the capitalist world and the national metropolises; and if it has been different, this is because the bourgeois interests of the latter have required rural Latin America to become and remain so. Rural Latin America has been colonially exploited by the world capitalist metropolis both directly and indirectly, through the Latin American national metropolises, which subject their rural (and urban) hinterland to the same kind of "internal" colonial exploitation and capital drain as they suffer at the hands of imperialism. The bourgeoisie in the national metropolis collaborates with imperialism in the class and colonial exploitation of its own people. And the parts of the bourgeoisie which own the latifundia and which exercise monopoly control over internal trade form an integral part of this capitalist colonial and class system. Far from asking how isolated and "feudal" this rural "oligarchy" is, we must inquire how commercially the latifundista bourgeoisie (if it is rural at all) is tied to the major urban commercial and industrial monopolies; to what extent in fact landed monopoly is owned by the same persons, families, or corporations as commercial and industrial monopoly; to what extent latifundistas derive their income from agricultural production on their land and to what extent their monopoly ownership of the land simply renders possible the commercial, financial, and political exploitation of those who work the latifundium and neighboring land. But this again leads to the question of how colonial capitalist exploitation creates and maintains the productive relations on the latifundium and the class structure in rural Latin America, which may superficially appear "feudal" but which make this capitalist exploitation possible. Finally, we must ask who wants to change these productive relations—certainly not the Latin American grand bourgeoisie; and how—certainly not by an "anti-feudal" or "anti-imperialist" bourgeois democratic revolution.

What, then, is the essential relationship between the large landowner-merchants and those who work the land in Latin America? Do the latter constitute a peasantry, serf-like or free? It is suggested that more careful inquiry will show that, irrespective of the multitude of *forms* of payment between those who own and those who work the land, the essential relation between them— no less than in industry—is the exploitation of the latter, who lack the means of production to support themselves, by the former, who own them. Far too little is known about the variety of forms, and particularly about the vast areas of Brazil (such as the Northeast), Argentina, the Caribbean, and also of Indian populated countries like Peru and Guatemala, in which large parts of the rural population are essentially agricultural workers —a rural proletariat—who work for what is essentially a wage, though a low and unsteady one, as they migrate from farm to farm, from region to region, and even from country to country (as do Mexican braceros) when economic and climatic conditions demand. Nor do they work only for large landowners; they work wherever and however they can, in and out of agriculture. And they are also hired by medium-scale owners, small owners, and even by tenants, who sometimes use them to fulfill their labor quota obligation to their own landlords. What is this complex pattern of exploitation? To what extent is this rural proletariat interested in land, and to what extent in higher wages or greater employment security? And to what extent are small owners and tenants, who are themselves exploited but who hire wage labor, interested in keeping wages from rising, and minimum wage laws from being passed or enforced in rural areas, lest their competitive position be worsened in the face of the larger landed monopolies which can better afford such wage increases? To what extent are these small owners and tenants themselves wage workers—and interested in higher wages—and/or merchants—and interested in higher or lower prices—because the land they own or rent or share-crop is insufficient to support their families? To what extent are owners of medium-sized farms not farmers at all, but rural and urban petty bourgeois merchants, employees, or professional people who want to squeeze the maximum out of those who work their land? Some claim that small owners and tenants can be politically mobilized before the rural proletarians, and revolutionary experience seems to agree. But others maintain the opposite. Where then must political work be begun, with what slogans, and with what allies?

Latin American Indians are said to live in a world apart. It is true that wherever they can, they try to preserve their culture and where possible a corporate community which presents a common front against the outsider. This has been their best—and at best inadequate—protection against the exploitation they suffer as a result of having been forced to the very bottom of both the internal colonial and domestic class structures. Far from being outside the colonial and class structure, they are its most integrally exploited members. As such, they have just suspicions, based on 400 years of experience, of all proposals to eliminate their exploitation by reforms from above. Does this mean that they will not incorporate themselves into revolutionary struggle from below, if they once come to perceive it as that—and if it once becomes revolutionary enough to permit and justify such perception? Historical evidence shows that the Indian can be politically mobilized, as in Guatemala; in fact, that his mass movement at the base can mobilize the revolutionary leadership into greater militancy, as in Bolivia in 1952. The question is not so much whether the Indian will participate in the struggle as it is whether the revolutionary leadership will be capable of channeling this participation into revolution or back into reform and reaction.

This raises questions about revolutionary and reformist organization in the countryside as a whole—and its relation to political organization for revolution in the city, the nation, the continent, and the world.

The weakest links in the world capitalist chain have so far proved to be not in the metropolitan class structure but in the imperialist colonial structure. It is here that the Soviet, Chinese, Cuban, and other revolutions took place. Where then, in the colonial structure of the world and Latin America, are the weakest links now? What is the imperialist and Latin American bourgeoisie doing in attempts to cement these links through community development, health, education, "land reform," and other programs, which at the Alliance for Progress conference at Punta del Este Che called the "latrinization" of Latin America? How far can these programs be carried—the latest effort, for instance, is to have the Latin American military occupation forces improve their reputation in the countryside by undertaking Latin American versions of the imperialist "pacification" program in Vietnam —and what effect will they have, if not for the acceleration of economic development, in the de-celeration of political development in the countryside?

If we can find the weakest links in the colonial and class structure, how do we break them? Certainly not by exhortation to fight an invisible imperialist enemy by nationalization for the benefit of "all the people"; nor by abstruse attempts to make Wall Street or perhaps even the Presidential Palace visible in the peasant or agricultural worker's hut. These will make *themselves* all too visible if the Latin American rural masses, or even a small part of them, move to struggle against their immediately visible oppressors of long standing, who are the local economic and political agents of the imperialist and national capitalist colonial and class structure. What allies will these popular forces have— what alliances can they have previously formed and on what basis— with those elsewhere in the country, in Latin America, in the world, who are in a position to support them when the Latin American and then the imperialist bourgeoisie move in to try to save their local agents and therewith the whole exploitative colonial and class structure of capitalism?

Revolutionary political organization and mobilization could benefit from a Marxist analysis of the class and colonial structure of particular regions or local areas. This study cannot, of course, be undertaken abroad and in terms of general preconceived schema. It must be pursued on the spot by revolutionary Marxists who participate in the political movement the study is intended to serve. But the same principle also applies to theoretical work on broader political problems. Real Marxist theory can only be produced through revolutionary political practice. And for the intellectual from Latin America and other underdeveloped countries, this also means ideological struggle.

## Ideology and Marxism

The colonial and class structures generate ideological counterparts to justify themselves, and these are also reflected in the social "science" used to "study" them. For revolutionaries, therefore, the battleground includes the field of ideology, as Fidel suggests. For revolutionary social scientists, the ideological battle extends to the field of social science. The preponderant ideology, including its social "scientific" component, was developed by the bourgeoisie in the metropolis for use at home and for export to the colonies.

The latter, at least in Latin America, have always had some awareness of the colonialist elements of this ideology and science.
Particularly during and after times of nationalist upsurge, the
nationalist sectors in Latin America have attempted to resist these
colonialist elements and to develop nationalist ones in their stead.
The nationalist alternatives are presented as a direct challenge to
the colonial order, and as such are supposedly substantially different from the imperialist ideology and science. But since this
nationalist alternative comes from the national bourgeoisie in Latin
America, it reaffirms rather than challenges the class order at
home. Revolutionaries must inquire how different this Latin American ideology and science really is. Perhaps in the ideological part
of the battleground, as well as in the political and military one,
we must also—or first—combat the class enemy's ideology, in
order thereby to combat this principal enemy, imperialism.

During the last century the principal imperialist bourgeois
ideological exports have been liberalism, positivism, and now a sort
of technological pragmatism or pragmatic technologism. A part of
the Latin American bourgeoisie has eagerly accepted each of
these, sometimes becoming more catholic than the Pope, as the
Latin American export interests did in the matter of the free
trade doctrine. Some bourgeois and petty bourgeois sectors resisted
the most flagrantly colonialist aspects of these doctrines, but they
nonetheless accepted their essentials when to do so served their
class interests with respect to the popular classes.

The latest ideological invasion proposes that North American
"know-how" and technology can solve all the problems of the
people of the world, if they would only allow the North Americans
to apply this know-how without interference. In industry this
means foreign investment and a higher degree of monopolization
—and unemployment. In agriculture it means North American
farming methods, seeds, fertilizers, farm machinery, etc.—and
fertilizer and machinery production by Standard Oil and Ford.
For the population this means birth control pills and drugs—and
drug companies. For culture it means the "American Way of Life"
through and with "mass" media, "popular" education, computerized statistical "science," etc.—all without, or rather against, any
political and social revolution. The Latin American grand bour-

geoisie accepts all this on a junior partner basis. The "nationalist" elements of the bourgeoisie and part of the petty bourgeoisie reject the "North American" part but accept the technological part: they say they will do it themselves—and better!

The imperialist ideological offensive in the social sciences may in recent times be said to have taken two major forms, structuralism and then its degeneration into institutionalism, culturalism, or behaviorism. Structuralism long dominated the economics and sociology, which claimed to analyze the market structure and the social structure. But this was—and is—either the abstract study of idealized modes of a competitive market or of a consensual society, which may refer to any possible imaginary social system ranging from a family to the whole world, but which does not explain any particular real social system. Or structuralists deal with some particular social systems, which are always local, regional, or national units that are not the determinant social whole. This abstract or concrete, but limited, "structuralism" diverts the investigator's attention away from the real worldwide capitalist system, its class and colonial structure, and the history of its development, which have determined social reality in both the metropolitan and colonial parts of the imperialist system.

Recent developments in metropolitan social science, and their export to the underdeveloped countries, divert the investigator's attention still further from fundamental social and political problems and solutions. Institutionalism describes the supposed social and political institutions of bourgeois society and "democracy" as they superficially appear. Culturalism focuses on cultural manifestations of the underlying economic and social structure, and more recently even on psycho- (that is, individual) cultural characteristics. Behaviorism, now rampant in political "science" and increasingly in other social sciences, advances ever more computerized techniques of rigorous statistical analysis of all sorts of social variables, without ever coming to terms with the structure and development of the social system—lest we get the idea that it requires structural change. In addition to the limitations (advantages from the point of view of the bourgeoisie) of structuralism, these degenerations permit the differentiation of the same thing and the comparison of different things: the fact that the metropolis and its colonies are part of the same capitalist system is masked by discovering in them the supposedly independent existence of the very cultural and institutional differences that this colonial relationship creates. At the same time the discovery of superficial institutional and behavioristic similarities between capitalist and socialist countries permits the bourgeoisie statistically (that is, in apparent ideological "neutrality") to "prove" to the class it exploits that the class structure is really irrelevant—and need not be changed.

This ideology in the guise of science is today being propagated throughout the capitalist world—and even into the socialist camp—through countless channels. The enlightened elements of the Latin American colonial bourgeoisie eagerly cooperate in this process today as they did in the past, while some national bourgeois elements have been attempting an ideological social scientific offensive of their own. After the bourgeois nationalist upsurge of the thirties and forties, but apparently with a cultural lag of a decade or more, these Latin American bourgeois interests established several institutions whose express purpose is the development of a nationalist scientific ideology. First and foremost among these is the United Nations Economic Commission for Latin America (ECLA) and its more recent offspring, the Instituto Latinoamericano de Planificación Económica y Social (ILPES), both in Santiago, Chile. In Brazil it was the Instituto Superior de Estudios Brasileiros (ISEB), in Argentina the Instituto Torcuato di Tella, in Mexico the Escuela Nacional de Ciencias Políticas y Sociales of the National University (UNAM). The names of their founders, directors, and principal collaborators have become universally known in Latin American social science and even broader intellectual circles: Raúl Prebisch, Aníbal Pinto, Osvaldo Sunkel, Celso Furtado, Helio Jaguaribe, Gino Germani, Pablo González Casanova, etc.

Their major theses are well known: The metropolis exploits Latin America, but primarily through declining terms of trade. Thus they complain of a colonial relationship, but they do not go on to analyze the monopolistic colonial structure and the increasing role of foreign investment and foreign aid within it, which they generally welcome, subject only to certain "safe-guards." They attribute Latin American underdevelopment to the mistaken choice of "underdevelopment toward the outside" when Latin America was finally awoken from its feudal slumber in the mid-nineteenth century. Had Latin America then "chosen development toward the inside" it would not have suffered from declining terms of trade and would have been able to industrialize. Therefore, they argue, Latin America should choose national capitalist development toward the inside now.

The obstacle to this is a small internal market, they say. Do-mestically, then, they advance virtually the same interpretation of Latin America as that embodied in the Alliance for Progress and enlightened structuralism: Latin America is divided into a "dual" economy and society, part capitalist and progressive and part feudal and retrograde. Land reform, tax reform, etc., and economic "planning" initiated by the progressive industrialists and middle classes would remove "feudal" obstacles and integrate the vast rural population, and especially the Indians, into the national market and society. These "scientific" ideologists argue that the rural poor are poor because they are outside the market or money economy, and that is why industrial and economic development does not proceed. They call themselves "structuralists," and they employ what they find useful in Marxist analysis and terminology —to propose *reform* for the structure.

But these "structuralists," who complain of metropolitan ex-ploitation, do not observe or analyze the internal colonial struc-ture of Latin America, through which the national metropolis sucks out of the "feudal" countryside most of the capital for its own limited industrial investment and development. Nor do these ideologists for the national bourgeoisie analyze the domestic class structure of Latin America. Instead they import the latest North American techniques for the study of "elites" and "social strati-fication," and their students increasingly fall prey to the new metropolitan offer to substitute objective statistical for scientific political analysis and solution of Latin American problems.

In other words, in the first place the Latin American "progres-sive nationalist" version of this bourgeois social science is super-ficially not fundamentally different from the imperialist model.

In the second place, the nationalist ideological offensive in the social sciences did not really begin until the economic, social, and political movement from which it came had passed its peak and had already begun to recede into history. Finally, imperialism has in the 1960's begun a counter-offensive in this field as well, with the result that its behavioral "science" is increasingly neutralizing elements of the Latin American petty bourgeoisie which a few years ago were still politically progressive. In this connection it is noteworthy that imperialism is now using invitations to conferences, scholarships, "joint" U.S.-Latin American "research" projects, etc., both in the United States and in its Latin American affiliates, to court precisely the Left Latin American (and other) intellectuals whom it had previously shunned and persecuted.

What is the Latin American revolutionary Left's response to this ideological offensive in the field of social science?

Many thousands of Latin American students and workers—among them perhaps another Fidel, Che, Camilo—are searching for scientific and political guidance beyond that offered by the metropolitan bourgeoisie, by their Latin American followers or revisers, or by certain Marxist revisionists. Are they to be instructed and guided by the metropolitan-derived "Marxists" models 14, 13, or 12 (as Fidel derided them at OLAS) according to which all humanity necessarily passes successively through stages from communal communism, through slavery, feudalism, capitalism, socialism, to communism? Will these students, as well as industrial and agricultural workers, be united by theorists who tell them—no less than the national bourgeois ideologists—that Latin America is now divided in two parts, one still in the feudal stage and the other already in the capitalist stage; that a feudal oligarchy and imperialism, but not the bourgeoisie, are the obstacles to national development? Latin Americans will never be led to revolution by the principal political thesis derived from this "Marxist" pseudo-science, which at OLAS Fidel called "the famous thesis about the role of the national bourgeoisies, for example . . . how much paper, how many phrases, how much empty talk have been wasted waiting for a liberal, progressive, anti-imperialist bourgeoisie. . . . And many people are told this is Marxism . . . and in what way is this different from catechism, and in what way is it different from a litany, from a rosary?"

This means that political necessity confronts us with an ideological task to fulfill, both to assure the firmness of the revolutionary militants, and to recruit more and more Latin Americans, especially young ones, to their ranks. We also have important theoretical work to do to complement revolutionary practice with the necessary revolutionary theory. And we need to analyze Latin American society, especially its rural regions, in order to help the popular forces in their revolutionary struggle. For that, Marxists will have to create the leading and revolutionary ideas which, as Fidel says, the Latin American revolution needs. Ideological clarity about these problems becomes especially essential when the revolutionary movement is temporarily slowed down, because it is at that time that ideological firmness is necessary in order to resist the temptations—which the bourgeoisie always offers—to recede toward a reformist policy, suggesting for example the supposed possibility and necessity of a "democratic peace," as the PCV is doing at this time. To reach this ideological and theoretical clarity, Marxists will have to work intellectually, but not only intellectually, inspired by the example of Che, who was revolutionary first and then intellectual.

To pursue this ideological and revolutionary objective, which is the real responsibility of the Latin American intellectual, and of the Marxists especially, will mean—as Che also found—leaving the institutional bounds of the Latin American and imperialist to the bourgeoisie. The Latin American intellectual—and this is as true for the artist or writer as it is for the social scientist—will have to become conscious of the fact that he has been working for the bourgeoisie. He will have to realize that the more acute the contradictions become and the more the revolutionary process advances, the less will the bourgeoisie permit the Latin American intellectual to take advantage of its bourgeois institutions—universities, publishing houses, press, etc.—for the development of a really revolutionary Marxist theory and practice. In some parts of the continent, the hour at which the doors of the bourgeois institutions close to the Marxist has already come; in the remaining parts that time will come soon. The Latin American intellectual and Marxist will have to decide whether he will remain inside pursuing reformism, or outside with the people making the revolution.

## NOTES

1. Aldo Ferrer, *The Argentine Economy* (Berkeley: University of California Press, 1967), pp. 31–33. The quote is from the Spanish edition.
2. For a more detailed analysis, see *Capitalism and Underdevelopment in Latin America.*
3. Quoted in Miron Burgin, *The Economic Aspects of Argentine Federalism 1820–1852* (Cambridge: Harvard University Press, 1946), p. 234.
4. *Ibid.*, p. 81.
5. Rosa Luxemburg, *The Accumulation of Capital* (New York: Monthly Review Press, 1964), p. 438.
6. John Kenneth Turner, *México Bárbaro* (Mexico: Ediciones del Instituto Nacional de la Juventud Mexicana, 1964). Originally published in English in 1908.
7. Ramiro Guerra y Sánchez, *Sugar and Society in the Caribbean: An Economic History of Cuban Agriculture* (New Haven: Yale University Press, 1964).
8. Francisco Encina, *Nuestra Inferioridad Económica: Sus Causas y Consecuencias* (Santiago, 1912).
9. Andre Gunder Frank, "Services Rendered," *Monthly Review*, Vol. 17, No. 2 (June 1966). See also Chapter 11 of this volume.
10. Computed from data in ECLA, *El Financiamiento de América Latina* (New York: United Nations), E/CN.12/649/Rev.1, December 1964.
11. Raymond F. Lyons, ed., *Problems and Strategies of Educational Planning. Lessons from Latin America.* (Paris: International Institute for Educational Planning, 1964), p. 63.
12. Claude McMillan, *International Enterprise in a Developing Economy: A Study of U.S. Business in Brazil*, M.S.U. Business Studies (East Lansing: Michigan State University Press, 1964), p. 205.
13. For all data on Canada, see A. E. Safarian, *Foreign Ownership of Canadian Industry* (Toronto: McGraw-Hill Company of Canada, 1966), pp. 235, 241.
14. Harry Magdoff, *The Age of Imperialism* (New York: Monthly Review Press, 1969).

# MONTHLY REVIEW

an independent socialist magazine

edited by Paul M. Sweezy and Harry Magdoff

*Business Week:* ". . . a brand of socialism that is thorough-going and tough-minded, drastic enough to provide the sharp break with the past that many left-wingers in the underdeveloped countries see as essential. At the same time they maintain a sturdy independence of both Moscow and Peking that appeals to neutralists. And their skill in manipulating the abstruse concepts of modern economics impresses would-be intellectuals. . . . Their analysis of the troubles of capitalism is just plausible enough to be disturbing."

*Bertrand Russell:* "Your journal has been of the greatest interest to me over a period of time. I am not a Marxist by any means as I have sought to show in critiques published in several books, but I recognize the power of much of your own analysis and where I disagree I find your journal valuable and of stimulating importance. I want to thank you for your work and to tell you of my appreciation of it."

*The Wellesley Department of Economics:* " . . . the leading Marxist intellectual (not Communist) economic journal published anywhere in the world, and is on our subscription list at the College library for good reasons."

*Albert Einstein:* "Clarity about the aims and problems of socialism is of greatest significance in our age of transition. . . . I consider the founding of this magazine to be an important public service." (In his article, "Why Socialism" in Vol. I, No. 1.)

DOMESTIC: $11 for one year, $20 for two years, $9 for one-year student subscription.

FOREIGN: $13 for one year, $23 for two years, $10 for one-year student subscription. (Subscription rates subject to change.)

62 West 14th Street, New York, New York 10011

# Modern Reader Paperbacks

www.ingramcontent.com/pod-product-compliance
Lightning Source LLC
Chambersburg PA
CBHW020313290526
45785CB00007B/2779